12-73

D0758720

CORBAN
C O L L E G E

5000 Deer Park Drive S. E., Salem, Oregon 97301-9392

THE APOSTOLIC PREACHING OF THE CROSS

The
Apostolic Preaching
of the Cross

by

LEON MORRIS B.Sc. M.Th. Ph.D.

Principal, Ridley College, Melbourne

Wm. B. EERDMAN PUBLISHING CO.
Grand Rapids, Michigan

Third Edition © Tyndale Press

First Edition	September 1955
Second Edition	October 1960
Third Edition	September 1965

Printed in Great Britain
by Bookprint Limited
Kingswood, Surrey

81406

CONTENTS

6　CONTENTS

PREFACE TO THE FIRST EDITION

WHEN THE PRESENT WRITER first began to read seriously on the atonement he discovered that some of the great theological words such as 'redemption', 'propitiation', and 'justification' are often used in a way which seems to indicate that they mean different things to different people. If we may take redemption, the subject of our opening chapter, as an example, some writers, as we there point out, practically equate it with deliverance; others see in it a reference to a substitutionary transaction; while others use it as a comprehensive term for the whole Christian salvation. For some it has a backward reference, pointing to the satisfaction for sin made on the cross, while for others it is essentially forward-looking and gives expression to the liberation from sin's bondage which enables the believer to live the Christ-like life. There is similar uncertainty and ambiguity attaching to the use of some other terms.

Now it ought to be possible to discover what the characteristic Christian expressions mean. One line of inquiry starts from the fact that the New Testament writers were steeped in the language and ideas of the Old Testament. An examination of the relevant Old Testament passages will reveal to us one of the influences which moulded the thinking of our writers, and which must, therefore, help us as we seek to understand their language.

Again, since the New Testament was written in the ordinary speech of ordinary men (and not the classical language of the scholar or literary man), the flood of light which has been thrown on this type of speech by modern discoveries of papyri, ostraka and inscriptions must illuminate many New Testament expressions. This, then, is a further field for investigation.

A third source is ancient Jewish literature. While the Christians vigorously repudiated many Rabbinic conclusions they yet discussed many of the same problems, and made use of the same terminology. Therefore it will usually repay us to examine the way the Rabbis used any term we are investigating.

This book, then, is not a full-scale study of the atonement, but a necessary preliminary. It is an attempt to understand certain key words, words which are crucial to the New Testament picture of the atonement, by seeing them against the background of the Greek Old Testament, the papyri, and the Rabbinic writings. Armed with our discoveries, we then proceed to examine them in their New Testament setting, always bearing in mind the possibility that the early Christians may modify or enrich any terms they may borrow.

In this volume I have incorporated the substance, and sometimes the actual wording, of a number of articles written previously for various journals. These are as follows: 'The Use of ἱλάσκεσθαι etc. in Biblical Greek' (*The Expository Times*, LXII, No. 8); 'The Wrath of God' (*The Expository Times*, LXIII, No. 5); 'The Biblical Use of the term "Blood" ' (*The Journal of Theological Studies*, New Series, III, Pt. 2); 'Justification by Faith: The Old Testament and Rabbinic Anticipation' (*The Evangelical Quarterly*, XXIV, No. 1); 'The Idea of Redemption in the Old Testament' (*The Reformed Theological Review*, XI, No. 3); 'The Biblical Idea of Atonement' (*The Australian Biblical Review*, II, Nos. 3, 4).

To the editors of these journals I would express my indebtedness for their ready permission to republish.

Many friends have assisted me at various points, and it is difficult to acknowledge all my indebtedness. But especially would I mention the Rev. Dr. Newton Flew, who discussed many of these chapters with me, the late Rev. H. W. Oldham, who advised me constantly during the earlier part of my labours, and also my colleague, Mr. F. I. Andersen, who has very kindly compiled the Index. Finally, I would like to place on record my gratitude to the publishers for all the help they have given during the various stages of production.

PREFACE TO THE THIRD EDITION

THE DEMAND FOR A NEW EDITION has given me the opportunity
of revising the book throughout. Many of the alterations are
merely verbal, but there have been one or two substantial changes.
The arrangement of the material has been altered here and there,
notably in the opening chapter, where there has been a rather
radical rearrangement. I have also taken advantage of the opportunity to include a certain amount of new material, notably the
new chapter IV, 'The Lamb of God', and the section on ἱλαστήριον
in chapter VI on 'Propitiation'. This latter has previously appeared
in *New Testament Studies*, II, No. 1, and I am grateful to the
editors for permission to republish it here.

It remains only for me to express my gratitude to those who by
their reviews and comments have helped in this revision. I have
given careful consideration to such comments as have been brought
to my notice, and the result is the multitude of small alterations I
have mentioned. But I am still convinced that the main outline of
the argument was essentially correct and I am glad of the opportunity of putting it forth in this new form.

Leon Morris

ABBREVIATIONS

AG   W. F. Arndt and F. W. Gingrich, *A Greek-English Lexicon of the New Testament* (Cambridge, 1957)

AV   The Authorized Version

BDB   F. Brown, S. R. Driver and C. A. Briggs, *A Hebrew and English Lexicon of the Old Testament* (Oxford, 1907)

BNTC   Black's New Testament Commentaries

CGT   The Cambridge Greek Testament

ET   *The Expository Times*

Enc.Bib.   T. K. Cheyne and J. S. Black (eds.), *Encyclopedia Biblica* (London, 1914)

HDAC   J. Hastings (ed.), *A Dictionary of the Apostolic Church* (Edinburgh, 1915)

HDB   J. Hastings (ed.), *A Dictionary of the Bible* (Edinburgh, 1904)

HDCG   J. Hastings (ed.), *A Dictionary of Christ and the Gospels* (Edinburgh, 1906)

HR   E. Hatch and H. A. Redpath, *A Concordance to the Septuagint* (Graz, 1954)

ICC   The International Critical Commentary

LS   *A Greek-English Lexicon*, compiled by H. G. Liddell and R. Scott, new edn. revised by H. S. Jones and R. McKenzie (Oxford, 1940)

LXX   The Septuagint

JTS   *The Journal of Theological Studies*

MM   J. H. Moulton and G. Milligan, *The Vocabulary of the Greek Testament*, (London, 1929)

MNTC   The Moffatt New Testament Commentary

MT   The Massoretic Text

NTS   *New Testament Studies*

PTR   *The Princeton Theological Review*

RV   The Revised Version

SB   H. L. Strack und P. Billerbeck, *Kommentar zum Neuen Testament aus Talmud und Midrasch* (München, 1922–28)

SJT   *The Scottish Journal of Theology*

TWBB   A. Richardson (ed.), *A Theological Word Book of the Bible* (London, 1950)

TWNT   G. Kittel (ed.), *Theologisches Wörterbuch zum Neuen Testament* (Stuttgart, 1949–   )

WH   B. F. Westcott and F. J. A. Hort, *The New Testament in the Original Greek* (London, 1881)

Customary abbreviations are used for the books of the Bible, for the tractates of the Mishnah and the Talmud (the prefix b indicates that a Talmudic tractate is from the Babylonian Talmud), and for the books of authors such as Josephus and Philo. Quotations from Scripture are normally in the Revised Version; Josephus and Philo are cited from the Loeb edition, and the Mishnah from H. Danby's translation.

CHAPTER I

REDEMPTION

REDEMPTION IS A TERM which is employed very loosely in much modern theological writing. It is often used almost exactly like 'deliverance'. Or Christianity may be classed as 'a religion of redemption', *i.e.* one which promises man salvation from his predicament as a sinner, in contrast to 'religions of law', which look to man to bring about this desirable state of affairs by his own efforts. It would be going too far to say that there are as many meanings as there are users of the word. But there is certainly a bewildering variety of meanings for it in circulation.

This wide use of the term 'redemption' is a modern development. We find it neither in antiquity in general nor in the Bible in particular. Indeed, when we consider how widely the term is used in modern theology we may well be surprised at the comparative rarity of its occurrence in the New Testament. And just as it is used less often in antiquity than with us, so also it is used with a narrower and more precise connotation. As we shall see, it does not mean deliverance in general, but a particular kind of deliverance. Another difference is that we use such words as 'redeemer', 'redemption', *etc*, as religious terms. Whenever we hear them our thoughts turn to religion. But when the man of the first century heard them he immediately thought in non-religious terms. Indeed, that was the reason words came to be used by the early Christians. Men in general knew quite well what redemption was. Therefore Christians found it a convenient term to use. It is our task to try to recapture this meaning and not simply to assume that redemption meant to the ancients exactly what it means to us.

I. ETYMOLOGICAL CONSIDERATIONS

The basic word in the word-group is λύτρον, 'ransom'. This word is derived from λύω, a verb with the general meaning of 'to loose'. It was used of all kinds of loosing, for example, for the loosening of one's clothing, the loosening of armour, of tied animals, and so on.

And sometimes it was used of men to indicate that they had been loosed from captivity or the like. Particularly did this apply to the loosing of prisoners of war when a ransom price had been paid. In time a new word-group was developed to give precise expression to this form of loosing. To the stem λυ- there was added the suffix -τρον to give the noun λύτρον. The suffix -τρον denoted originally the means whereby an action is performed. A typical use is for implements, e.g. ἄροτρον, 'a plough'. Secondly it came to denote the place where the action could take place, as θέατρον, 'a place for seeing', 'a theatre'. In the third stage the -τρον suffix was used, often in the plural, for the payment which brought about the action, such as τὰ διδάκτρα, 'the teacher's fee', or τὰ θρέπτρα, 'the payment for rearing', 'the nurse's wages'.[1] λύτρον, a comparatively late word, is a word of this third class. Its meaning accordingly is 'payment for loosing', 'ransom price'. From λύτρον a complete new word-group developed. Thus we have the verb λυτρόω, 'to release on receipt of ransom' (in the middle voice, 'to secure release by payment of ransom', 'to redeem'). Then there is the noun λύτρωσις, 'the process of release by payment', and various compounds of each of these forms, especially those with ἀπό and ἐκ.

It is important to realize that it is this idea of payment as the basis of release which is the reason for the existence of the whole word-group. Other words were available to denote simple release. Men could (and often did) go on using λύω, or ῥύομαι, etc. When they chose to use λύτρον (or its cognates) it was because they wanted a term which expressed in itself, and not simply by inference from the context, the idea of release by payment. Etymological considerations are, of course, not final. Usage must be our final criterion. But it is worth noting at the beginning that the very existence of this word-group is due to the desire to give precise expression to the conception of release by payment.[2] There is thus a

---

[1] Cf. A. Debrunner, *Griechische Wortbildungslehre* (Heidelberg, 1917), pp. 176f.; J. H. Moulton and W. F. Howard, *A Grammar of New Testament Greek*, II (Edinburgh, 1919), pp. 368f.

[2] There were also, of course, other words for the price of release, as ἄλλαγμα, ἀντάλλαγμα, τιμή, ποινή, ἄποινα, ζωάγρια, ἀντίψυχον. On the reason for the choice of this rather than another root, cf. B. B. Warfield, 'Its formation must be traced to the natural influence of its primitive, λύειν, dominating the mind when the idea of ransoming occupied it, and leading to the framing from it of derived vocables expressive of that idea. It "came natural" to a Greek, in other words, when he

prima facie case for holding that the redemption terminology is concerned with the price-paying method of release.

This seems to be borne out by Greek usage in general. The words are used again and again to denote this form of release. Now and then metaphorical ways of using the word-group are found, but they depend for their force on the recognition of the price-paying idea. Apart from this there would be no point to the metaphor. And in the overwhelming preponderance of cases the thought of the actual payment is to be found.

The word-group was not confined to its use with respect to prisoners of war. This use remained frequent, but there were others. Thus a slave might buy his freedom. He would save his meagre earnings and what other small amounts of money came his way, probably over a long period of time, until he had the necessary sum. Then he could be freed. B. P. Grenfell and A. S. Hunt outline one method of procedure in these words: 'the terms of freedom having been agreed upon by master and slave, a notification of the details of the transaction was sent to the agoranomus by the banker through whom the purchase money was paid, accompanied perhaps by his receipt for the payment . . . The slave was then presumably declared by the agoranomus to be free.'[1]

They cite a typical document of this type, dated AD 86, and their translation is as follows: 'Chaeremon to the agoranomus, greeting. Grant freedom to Euphrosyne, a slave, aged about 35 years, born in her owner's house of the slave Demetrous. She is being set at liberty under . . . by ransom (ἐπὶ λύτροι[ς]) by her mistress Aloine, daughter of Komon, son of Dionysius, of Oxyrhyncus, under the wardship of Komon, the son of Aloine's deceased

---

wished to say ransom, to say λύτρον, because when he thought of ransoming he thought in terms of λύειν' (*PTR*, XV, 1917, p. 207; he goes on to say that λυτροῦν 'meant and could mean nothing but to release for or by a ransom'); *cf.* also, 'The only reason for the existence of this verb was to set by the side of the ambiguous λύειν (ἀπολύειν) an unambiguous term which would convey with surety, and without aid from the context or from the general understanding ruling its use, the express sense of ransoming. We are not surprised to observe therefore that throughout the whole history of profane Greek literature λυτροῦν, λυτροῦσθαι maintained this sense unbrokenly. Its one meaning is just "to ransom" ' (*op. cit.*, p. 208).

[1] *The Oxyrhyncus Papyri*, I (London, 1898), p. 105.

brother Dioscorus. The price paid is 10 drachmae of coined silver and 10 talents, 3,000 drachmae of copper. Farewell.'[1]

Or the slave might be freed by the process of sacral manumission. In this case he paid the money into the temple treasury of some god. Then his master went through the solemn rigmarole of selling him to the god. Quite often the document would include some such expression as 'for freedom', 'let no man henceforth enslave him' (cf. Gal. 5: 1). Technically he remained the slave of the god (and a few pious obligations might be laid on him to remind him of the fact), but as far as men were concerned he was a free man. A. Deissmann shows the importance of this process for an understanding of many New Testament passages. He gives an example of this form of manumission from an inscription on the polygonal wall at Delphi, dated 200–199 BC: 'Date. Apollo the Pythian, *bought* from Sosibius of Amphissa, *for freedom*, a female slave, whose name is Nicaea, by race a Roman, *with a price* of three minae of silver and a half-mina. Former seller according to the law: Eumnastus of Amphissa. The *price* he hath received. The purchase, however, Nicaea hath committed unto Apollo, *for freedom.*'[2]

From all this it is plain that the word was one in common use, and that its connection with the release from captivity was well known. Indeed, Deissmann could go so far as to say: 'when anybody heard the Greek word λύτρον, "ransom," in the first century, it was natural for him to think of the purchase-money for manumitting slaves.'[3]

Sometimes the word-group was employed to denote expiatory offerings.[4] This does not call for much comment, as it is a very

---

[1] *Op. cit.*, p. 106. The ransom is explicitly mentioned, and the same is the case elsewhere, *e.g.* documents 49, 722 in the same series.

[2] *Light from the Ancient East* (London, 1927), p. 323. C. K. Barrett cites the same inscription, but takes ὠνάν, rendered by Deissmann as 'purchase', to mean 'deed of sale', *i.e.* the inscription itself (*The New Testament Background: Selected Documents*, London, 1956, pp. 52f.). This is probably how Deissmann understands it for he rejects the translation 'purchase money'. LS give both meanings for ὠνή (they do not cite a form ὠνά).

[3] *Op. cit.*, p. 327. Similarly AG define λύτρον as '*price of release, ransom* (esp. also the ransom money for the manumission of slaves . . .)'. They proceed to cite eight examples of the latter use.

[4] See the evidence cited in LS (8th edn.); F. Steinleitner, *Die Beicht in Zusammenhange* (Leipzig, 1913), pp. 36f.; W. M. Ramsay, *The Journal of Hellenic Studies*, X, 1889, pp. 227f.

natural development. Worshippers find themselves in a serious plight on account of their sin. They buy themselves out of it with their redemptive offerings.

The importance of all this is that much of the New Testament was written to people living in a Gentile environment. While we cannot assume without further ado that this was the only association the word-group could have for them, yet we cannot overlook the extent and the significance of this usage. Good reason will need to be shown if it is claimed that they could use the redemption terminology without their words being understood in terms of this well-known and widely practised custom.[1]

Sometimes the word is used metaphorically, as when Philo speaks of the wise man as the 'ransom for the fool',[2] or of the 'aspirations of the reason to wisdom and knowledge' as " 'ransom" and "first-born" ' for the man's life.[3] But he brings out the force of ransom in the first passage by adding that the fool's existence 'could not endure for an hour, did not the wise provide for his preservation by compassion and forethought'. In the second, the force of 'ransom' is just as little destroyed by the metaphorical use as is that of 'first-born'. In other words, while Philo is an incurable allegorizer, he knows what 'ransom' really signifies.

The derivative verb λυτρόω usually means in the active 'to release on receipt of ransom', or possibly 'to hold to ransom'. In the middle the sense is rather 'to secure release by payment of ransom', i.e. 'to redeem'.[4] The meaning at bottom is the giving of a

[1] Büchsel rejects Deissmann's approach because it does not proceed from exegesis. The only way to understand the meaning Paul attaches to a word, he says, is to look at Paul's letters (*TWNT*, IV, p. 358, n.23). There is, of course, solid sense in this. Yet it is unreasonable to expect that Paul would use a word without a thought of its meaning in ordinary usage. Surely the right procedure is to find out what the word meant to his contemporaries, then to examine Paul's writing to see whether he used it in the same way, or whether he attached a new meaning to it. Moreover Büchsel pays no attention to Deissmann's showing that Paul makes use of quite a number of expressions common in the manumission documents, e.g. τῇ ἐλευθερίᾳ and ἐπ᾽ ἐλευθερίᾳ (Gal. 5: 1,13), the latter being a 'formula of the records'; bought 'with a price' τιμῆς (I Cor. 6: 20; 7: 23), etc.

[2] *De Sac.* 121.

[3] *Op. cit.*, 126.

[4] MM note that this 'verb and its kindred are well established in the vernacular', and they cite a catena of passages ranging from P.Eleph.19[8] (Ptol.) and P.Par.22[18] (c. 165 BC) to a Christian prayer of the late fourth century AD.

price in exchange, often for that which was one's own and which has somehow found its way into someone else's possession. There is also a derived noun λύτρωσις. This is a rare word, and the lexicons seem to cite but three occurrences in non-biblical Greek. It fits in with the usual sense of the word-group.

II. THE USE OF ἀπολύτρωσις

In view of the frequent use of ἀπολύτρωσις in the New Testament it is necessary to take notice of its use in non-biblical literature, despite the fact that it is a rare word. From its formation we might perhaps anticipate some emphasis on the freedom secured by ransom ('a ransoming away from – '). It is difficult, however, to detect such an emphasis in the usage. The word appears to be used in much the same sense as the uncompounded λύτρωσις. The following appear to be all the passages outside the New Testament in which the compound is cited.

1. Plutarch, 'Their flutes and stringed instruments and drinking bouts along every coast, their seizures of persons in high command, and their ransomings of captured cities, were a disgrace to the Roman supremacy.'[2] The term clearly denotes the release, upon receipt of a ransom price, of cities which had been captured.

2, 3. The Epistle of Aristeas, 'Thinking that the time had come to press the demand . . . for the emancipation of the Jews who had been transported from Judea by the king's father'; and again, 'the king ordered a letter to be written to Eleazar on the matter, giving also an account of the emancipation of the Jewish captives.'[2] In both passages the reference is to the release of prisoners of war, and the price is specifically mentioned, 'all who possess such captives are required to set them at liberty at once, receiving twenty drachmae per head as ransom money.'[3]

4, 5. Philo twice uses the term. He tells of a Laconian boy carried into captivity who 'judged that death was a happier lot than his present valueless life, and despairing of ransom, gladly put an end

[1] Pompey, 24. 5 (Loeb trans.).
[2] The Epistle of Aristeas 12.33 (cited from R. H. Charles, The Apocrypha and Pseudepigrapha of the Old Testament, II, Pseudepigrapha, Oxford, 1913).
[3] Ibid., 22.

to himself'.[1] This is the normal use of the term for release by ransom. Elsewhere he speaks of Abraham's plea for Sodom (Gn. 18: 23ff.), 'He begins indeed his supplication with fifty, the number of release, but ends with ten, which closes the possibility of redemption.'[2] Here the ten are regarded as the ransom. If the city produced them it was released from its doom. If it failed to produce them it was lost.

6. Josephus, 'the cost of redeeming them would be more than four hundred talents.'[3] The meaning of the word is plain.

7. Diodorus speaks of a manumission which was agreed upon by a slave and his masters. However, before it could be consummated, Scaevola intervened, and 'anticipating the ransoming . . . crucified him'.[4] There is not the slightest reason for thinking that this ἀπολύτρωσις is anything other than the normal release on payment.

8. An inscription from Cos refers to a process of sacral manumission.[5] A doubt has been thrown on the meaning of ἀπολύτρωσις here because the transaction is described also as an ἀπελευθέρωσις. Those who perform the ἀπελευθέρωσις are instructed 'not to make formal record of the ἀπολύτρωσις until the priests have reported that the necessary sacrifice has been made'. Too much, however, should not be read into this. The transaction might be looked at in more ways than one. It was an act of deliverance. The slave went free. Therefore it could rightly be called ἀπελευθέρωσις. But he was not simply set at liberty by a generous gesture of his owner. A price was paid. Therefore the transaction was also an ἀπολύτρωσις. It could be described loosely and generally, or exactly and specifically. But in view of the fact that there is no dispute about the payment of the price it is impossible to see ἀπολύτρωσις here as bearing anything other than its normal meaning.

9. The Scholiast on Lucian, in ridiculing the gods, refers to a story in which Zeus took the form of a ram to escape approaching

---

[1] *Quod Omnis Prober Liber Sit* 114.
[2] *De Congressu Quaerendae Eruditionis Gratia* 109.
[3] *Ant.* 12.27.
[4] *Fragments* 37.5.3 (cited from T. K. Abbott, *ICC* on Eph.1 : 7).
[5] W. R. Paton and E. L. Hicks, *The Inscriptions of Cos* (Oxford, 1891), p. 52 (no. 29).

disaster (τοῦ ἐπαναστάντος ὀλέθρου), and he goes on to speak of 'a fatted beast (βόσκημα) as ransom' for him.[1] Again the term is used in normal fashion.

10. There is one occurrence of the term in the LXX, when Nebuchadrezzar says, 'And at the completion of seven years the time of my redemption came' (Dn. 4: 30). Some understand ἀπολύτρωσις here to mean no more than deliverance.[2] But in the context it is difficult to maintain this. The king's words plainly echo those of Daniel in verse 24, 'pray to him concerning thy sins, and redeem all thy iniquities with almsgivings'. Granted that there is an element of metaphor, what gives it point is that alms are viewed as a kind of price by payment of which the king could redeem himself from the consequences of his sins.

No other examples of this noun appear to be cited. From these it is plain that the word has a clear and consistent meaning. In every passage, without exception, there is the payment of a ransom price to secure the desired release.[3]

III. THE JEWISH BACKGROUND

But it is time we left the Greeks and paid attention to the Jewish background of our word-group. It is a commonplace in much recent work on the New Testament that we must look to Hebraic rather than to Greek roots for the great ideas of the New Testament. I do not think that this can be pressed to such an extent that we ignore Greek usage; hence my examination of the way the Greeks use these terms. But the Old Testament usage is undoubtedly very important, and to that we now turn.

[1] *Scholia in Lucianum*, ed. H. Rake (Lipsiae, 1906), p. 220 (*Scholia in Luciani Peregrin.* 13).

[2] So, for example, Büchsel, *op. cit.*, p. 354.

[3] The corresponding verb, ἀπολυτρόω, does not occur in the New Testament, so there is no need to treat it fully. It is worth noting, however, that on almost every occasion on which it is found there is a mention of the ransom price. The passages are, Plato, *Laws* 919a; Demosthenes, 159.15 (Philip's Letter 3, Loeb edn., p. 336); Polybius, *The Histories* 2.6.6, 21.38.3; Plutarch, *Pompey* 24; Polyaenus, 5.40; Julian, *Sixth Oration, to the Uneducated Cynics, Works*, ed. Teubner, I, p. 253; Josephus, *Bell.* 2.14.1; Menander, *Misoumenos* 21; Philo, *Leg.Alleg.* 3.21; *Letter of Aristeas* 20; LXX, Ex.21: 8; Zp.3: 1 (but this seems an error). Warfield (*PTR*, XV, 1917, pp. 210f.) and T. K. Abbott (*ICC* on Eph.1: 7) both say that Lucian uses the verb of Achilles' ransoming Hector's body, but neither gives the reference.

The basic word, λύτρον, is used in the LXX in a perfectly straightforward fashion. It always denotes a ransom price.[1] It is used, for example, of the half shekel to be paid when the census was taken: 'When thou takest the sum of the children of Israel, according to those that are numbered of them, then shall they give every man a ransom for his soul unto the Lord, when thou numberest them; that there be no plague among them, when thou numberest them' (Ex. 30: 12). This is not the release of a prisoner of war or a slave. It is a death sentence that is in question. The man's life is forfeit. But his payment of the half shekel releases him from this sentence and enables him to walk out a free man. This is typical of the λύτρον passages. The usage is constant. Whenever men perform the act of redemption they do it by paying the price, and this price is denoted by λύτρον.

The most important word from this word-group in the LXX is the verb λυτρόω, which occurs 99 times. It is used in the characteristic sense on most occasions, but in addition, a new usage makes its appearance. Sometimes the word is used with God as subject and then there is no ransom price mentioned, nor, indeed, room for any ransom. God does not pay a ransom to men. This is an important group of passages. But it may be best if we approach them by way of the Hebrew words which underlie them. λυτρόω translates in the main two Hebrew verbs, g'l (45 times) and pdh (42 times). No other root is represented more than four or five times.[2] λύτρον introduces another Hebrew root, since it translates kōpher on six occasions. We examine these Hebrew words in order.

a. g'l[3]

The basic idea in this word-group has to do with family relation-

---

[1] *Cf.* MM, 'It may be noted that in the LXX the word is always used to denote an equivalent.'

[2] Other words from this word-group occur, namely λυτρωτός (Lv. 25: 31, 32), and ἐκλύτρωσις (Nu. 3: 49). But as these do not occur in the New Testament we have not given attention to them. In any case their use scarcely affects the main issue.

[3] *gā'al* and *gᵉ'ullāh* occur 118 times. They are translated by λύτρον etc. 59 times, ῥύομαι 12 times (11 in Isaiah), ἀγχιστεύω (='be next or near, be next of kin', LS) etc. 40 times, ἐξαιρέω twice, ἐκλαμβάνω once, while 4 times no one Greek word can be identified as the equivalent.

ship.[1] The word has about it a family air, and this is never quite lost in the various shades of meaning which it ultimately embraces.

We see the basic meaning of the root in passages where the participle is used simply to denote a kinsman, as when we read that Zimri 'smote all the house of Baasha: he left him not a single man child, neither of his kinsfolks (*gōʾalāyw*), nor of his friends' (1 Ki. 16:11; *cf.* also Nu. 5: 8; Ru. 2: 20; 3: 9,12). This is the meaning also in Job 3: 5, where the patriarch utters his desire that 'darkness and the shadow of death' should *gʾl, i.e.* 'claim as a kinsman', the day of his birth.

Discharging one's obligations as a kinsman involved a delightful variety of activities. It might mean marrying the widow of a deceased kinsman (Ru. 3:13), buying one of the family out of slavery (Lv. 25: 48f.), reclaiming a field which has been sold in time of financial distress (Lv. 25: 26), or slaying someone who has murdered a member of the family (Nu. 35: 19, *etc.*; here we have the 'avenger of blood', the kinsman *par excellence*). When the original owner wanted back again something he had sanctified to the Lord he was said to redeem it (Lv. 27: 13, 15, 19, 20, 27, 28, 31, 33; see also Lv. 27: 28, 33 for certain things which could not be redeemed in this way).

Thus in the Old Testament use of the word we find two distinct ideas. The primary thought is the general one of family obligation, and arising out of this is the narrower concept of the payment of price, of redemption. The transition is an easy one, and the Hebrew term continued to be used for either idea; but the LXX translators made a distinction, for they use only the λύτρον word-group as a rendering for *gʾl* when a ransom is involved. There is no place where a member of the λύτρον group translates *gʾl* with a human subject without a ransom being mentioned or implied. *gʾl* may justly be held to involve a family obligation, but it is not this so

---

[1] BDB give the meaning as, 'redeem, act as kinsman', and O. Procksch says, '*gʾl* is a concept in family-law' (*TWNT*, IV, p. 331). So also C. Ryder Smith says that, of the various translations of the verb, ' "to do the part of a kinsman" . . . is nearest to the Hebrew'. He adds, 'One could wish that there were some such English verb as "to kinsman" ' (*The Bible Doctrine of Salvation*, London, 1946, p. 19). S. R. Driver's view that the verb means 'properly *to resume a claim or right* which has lapsed, *to reclaim, re-vindicate*' (on Dt. 7: 8, *ICC*) does not go to the heart of the matter.

much as the paying of a redemption price as a consequence of this relationship which the LXX translators seek to express by λυτρόω.

There are some very important passages wherein Yahweh is the subject of the verb *g'l*. In these we are to think of God as the great Kinsman of His people, to whom they could look for succour in times of distress and, in particular, upon occasions when their liberty was lost or in jeopardy. Pre-eminently is this the case with the rescue of the people from their bondage in Egypt. 'I am Jehovah, and I will bring you out from under the burdens of the Egyptians, and I will rid you out of their bondage, and I will redeem you with a stretched out arm, and with great judgements: and I will take you to me for a people, and I will be to you a God' (Ex. 6: 6; see also Ex. 15: 13; Pss. 74: 2; 77: 16(15); 78: 35; 106: 10). This deliverance furnished the pattern for describing the later deliverance from Babylon as a redemption (Ps. 107: 2; Is. 43: 1; 44: 22, 23; 48: 20; 52: 3, 9; 63: 9; Je. 31: 11; Ho. 13: 14; Mi. 4: 10). It is in exactly similar vein that we have Yahweh spoken of as Redeemer (*gō'ēl*) thirteen times over in Isaiah 40–66, and the people referred to as 'the redeemed' (Ps. 107: 2; Is. 35: 9, *etc.*). Yahweh's redemptive activity is not confined to great national deliverances, for we find Jacob invoking 'the God which hath fed me all my life long unto this day, the angel which hath redeemed me from all evil' (Gn. 48: 15, 16). Similarly the psalmist thinks of a God who 'redeemeth thy life from destruction' (Ps. 103: 4; *cf.* also Pss. 69: 18; 72: 14; 119: 154).

It is sometimes argued from all this that the verb has lost its original significance and means simply 'to deliver'. But this does not seem quite to square up with the facts. Thus, if it were simply a term indicating deliverance, we should expect it to be used now and then of human deliverance without ransom. But such is not the case. Wherever the verb is used with a human subject the deliverance is always by payment of ransom. In other words, the word itself does not come to mean 'deliver' rather than 'redeem with a price', but it gets this meaning from the fact that Yahweh is its subject.

Examination of the passages in which Yahweh is the subject reveals the interesting fact that in many places the redemption He effects is not regarded as something He performs with effortless ease. Yet in other passages, sometimes not far from the redemption

ones, the idea is put forward that all the might of the nations is but a
puny thing, a thing of nought, in His sight. But, though they
accept this thought, when the Bible writers think of Yahweh as
Redeemer they prefer to think of Him as putting forward a strong
effort. Thus we read, 'I will redeem you with a stretched out arm'
(Ex. 6: 6); 'Thou art the God that doest wonders: Thou hast made
known thy strength among the peoples. Thou hast with thine arm
redeemed thy people' (Ps. 77: 14, 15); 'Enter not into the fields of
the fatherless: for their redeemer is strong' (Pr. 23: 10, 11); 'Their
redeemer is strong; the Lord of hosts is his name: he shall throughly
plead their cause' (Je. 50: 34). This stress on Yahweh's effort seems
to be the reason for applying the redemption terminology to His
dealings. The effort is regarded as the 'price' which gives point to
the metaphor. Yahweh's action is at cost to Himself. While He
could, so to speak, cope with the situation with a small expenditure
of effort, yet because He loves His people He 'hath made bare his
holy arm in the eyes of all the nations' (Is. 52: 10).[1]

b. pdh[2]

The ground meaning of this root is undoubtedly that of 'ransom by
the payment of a price', indicating something in the nature of a
commercial transaction without any obligation arising from kinship or the like which we have seen to be implied in *g'l*. A typical
use of the verb is found in the passage describing the procedure to
be adopted with regard to the first-born, 'Thou shalt set apart unto
the Lord all that openeth the womb, and every firstling which
thou hast that cometh of a beast; the males shall be the Lord's. And
every firstling of an ass thou shalt redeem with a lamb; and if thou
wilt not redeem it, then thou shalt break its neck: and all the first-

---

[1] *Cf.* B. F. Westcott: 'It cannot be said that God paid to the Egyptian oppressor
any price for the redemption of His people. On the other hand the idea of the
exertion of a mighty force, the idea that the "redemption" costs much, is everywhere present. The force may be represented by Divine might, or love, or self-
sacrifice, which become finally identical' (*op. cit.*, p. 296). So also F. J. Taylor: 'the
idea of payment is not wholly forgotten' (*TWBB*, p. 186).

[2] *pdh* is rendered in the LXX by λυτρόω 43 times, λύτρον twice, λύτρωσις once,
ἀπολυτρόω once, ἀλλάσσω 3 times, σώζω twice, ῥύομαι 4 times, ἀφορίζω once,
while προσηύξατο (1 Sa. 14: 45) looks like a paraphrase. It is not translated in
Nu. 18: 16. Cognate words are found 11 times, λύτρον *etc.* being represented 9
times, ῥύομαι once, διαστολή once.

born of man among thy sons shalt thou redeem' (Ex. 13: 12f.; *cf.* Nu. 18: 15–17). The first-born belong to the Lord; they should be sacrificed to Him upon the altar. But in certain cases it is permitted, or required, to offer a substitute in lieu of the forfeited life, and this idea of a substitute is basic to *pdh*. All the other uses may be seen to arise out of this one.

Arising out of Yahweh's claim to the first-born is the taking of the Levites in the stead of the first-born (Nu. 3: 40ff.). As there were more first-born Israelites than Levites, the excess, numbering 273, were redeemed by a payment of five shekels apiece (Nu. 3: 46.) There can be no doubt as to the substitutionary nature of the transaction, 'And thou shalt take the Levites for me (I am the Lord) instead of (*taḥath*; LXX ἀντί) all the firstborn among the children of Israel' (Nu. 3: 41).

It is quite in harmony with this usage that we find the word applied to the redemption of a slave-concubine (Ex. 21: 8; Lv. 19: 20). The Exodus passage says that, when a man is displeased with such a concubine, 'then shall he let her be redeemed'. The contention that this means he shall simply release her seems to be negatived by the alternative way in which she may become free mentioned in verse 11 where it is expressly said that it is 'for nothing, without money'.

In many of these cases it is open to the individual concerned to redeem or not as he sees fit. There is no element of obligation, as there would be in *gʼl* (which implies that there is a family duty to be performed). In line with this, anyone at all can perform the redemption indicated by *pdh* in almost every case, so that this verb may imply an element of grace.[1]

There are some passages where Yahweh is the subject of the verb. The deliverance from Egypt may be thus described, for example in the reference to 'thy people, which thou redeemedst to thee out of Egypt, from the nations and their gods' (2 Sa. 7: 23; see also Dt. 7: 8; 9: 26; 13: 5; 15: 15; 24: 18; 1 Ch. 17: 21; Ps. 78: 42, *etc.*). Redemption from the Exile is not often referred to by this verb (but see Is. 35: 10; 51: 11). There are passages where Yahweh's redemption is spoken of without any particular occasion being

---

[1] *Cf. TWNT*, IV, p. 333. Yet this element of grace ought not to be set in too sharp an antithesis to the obligation implied in *gʼl*. From Ru. 3: 13; 4: 4–6, it is clear that the *gōʼēl* might refuse to carry out the act of redemption.

specified, for example, 'Though I would redeem them, yet they have spoken lies against me' (Ho. 7: 13; see also Dt. 21: 8; Ne. 1: 10; Is. 1: 27; Je. 31: 11). Similar are passages referring to redemption from 'the power of the grave' (Ho. 13: 14), 'all his iniquities' (Ps. 130: 8), 'all his troubles' (Ps. 25: 22). There are also places where the verb is used of redemption of the individual (2 Sa. 4: 9; Jb. 5: 20; 33: 28; Pss. 31: 5; 69: 18; 119: 134, *etc.*).

A superficial reading of these passages might lead to the conclusion that redemption here means nothing more than deliverance. But, as we saw in the case of *g'l*, there is usually the underlying thought that Yahweh is bestirring Himself on His people's behalf; it is no ordinary activity that is in mind. Thus the psalmist complains, 'They remembered not his hand, nor the day when he redeemed them from the adversary. How he set his signs in Egypt, and his wonders in the field of Zoan' (Ps. 78: 42, 43); Nehemiah prays, 'Now these are thy servants and thy people, whom thou hast redeemed by thy great power, and by thy strong hand' (Ne. 1: 10); and David can say, 'What one nation in the earth is like thy people, even like Israel, whom God went to redeem unto himself for a people, and to make him a name, and to do great things for you, and terrible things for thy land. . . .?' (2 Sa. 7: 23). Even more impressive than specific quotation is the general implication of many passages that Yahweh was putting forth His mighty power on behalf of those He loved when He redeemed them.

In the face of this evidence it seems impossible to deduce that the word has become a mere synonym for 'deliver', though it may well be held that the thought of deliverance is prominent. We must feel that there was a real reason for the choice of this word to describe the divine activity. The Oxford Lexicon says that when Yahweh is the subject there is the 'underlying thought of payment', and this seems indeed to be the case. The word indicates deliverance at cost.

c. *kōpher*

The noun *kōpher* means a ransom price, and upon every occasion on which it is used it can be shown that there is the thought of a payment to be made. In its biblical usage it refers to the sum paid to redeem a forfeited life. The only places where this meaning is not compelled by the context are 1 Samuel 12: 3 and Amos 5: 12, both of which refer to bribes. Even here, however, J. Herrmann keeps open the possibility that not bribes in general are meant, but the wrongful reception of ransom from those whose lives were forfeit.[1]

The first occurrence of the noun is typical. It tells us of the man whose ox has gored another man, and whose life is forfeit in accordance with the ruling: 'the ox shall be stoned, and his owner also shall be put to death.' He is permitted to redeem his life by paying a *kōpher*, a sum of money 'laid on him' (Ex. 21:28ff.). We see the essential meaning also in the account of the institution of the half shekel tax at the census: 'When thou takest the sum of the children of Israel, according to those that are numbered of them, then shall they give every man a *kōpher* for his soul unto the Lord' (Ex. 30:12). Here the thought is that there would be plague among the people unless the command of Yahweh was complied with – the *kōpher* was accepted as substitute for the life that would otherwise perish in the plague. Similar examples are Job 33:24, where the imagery points us to a *kōpher* which delivers from 'going down to the pit' ('the price paid in lieu of forfeiting life'[2]); Job 36:18, with the difference that the sufferings of the patriarch are here thought of as the payment which delivers ('the severity of your sufferings, which form the ransom, or price (33²⁴), which God will accept in lieu of your life'[3]); Proverbs 13:8, where a man's riches are thought of as the ransom of his life; and Proverbs 21:18, where 'the wicked is a ransom for the righteous'.[4] There is one occasion where the word is used of Yahweh's deliverance of His people: 'I have given Egypt as thy ransom, Ethiopia and Seba for thee. Since thou hast been precious in my sight. . . . will I give men for thee

---

[1] His words are, 'When in 1 Sa.12:3 the aged Samuel can testify that he has taken no *kōpher* (LXX: ἐξίλασμα), it is not at all certain from the context whether there is meant here also "atonement money for a condemned life", but at the least it says nothing to the contrary. The same is true of Am. 5:12' (*TWNT*, III, p. 303).

[2] S. R. Driver and G. B. Gray (*ICC*), p. 291.

[3] *Ibid.*, p. 313; similarly E. C. S. Gibson quotes Delitzsch as referring to 'the ransom which is required of him as the price of restoration' (*in loc.*).

[4] C. H. Toy (*ICC*) says: 'The form of the couplet suggests the sense that the righteous would, in the ordinary course of justice, be punished, but that God takes the wicked as his substitute' (p. 406). He rejects that as 'too crude a conception', but he insists that the passage speaks of a 'substitution' thus bringing out the force of the *kōpher*.

and peoples for thy life' (Is. 43: 3f.). Here the ransom price is explicitly mentioned and the thought of substitution is plain. Herrmann brings out this latter point: 'In Is. 43: 3, 4 the thought of substitution is clearly bound up with *kōpher*; Egypt and the neighbouring kingdoms serve as substitutionary ransom price (*substitutives Lösegeld*) for Israel; that life for life is thereby meant is expressly said in verse 4.'[1]

For the sake of completeness we must notice that there are some circumstances wherein no *kōpher* can avail. Thus 'ye shall take no *kōpher* for the life of a manslayer, which is guilty of death: but he shall surely be put to death' (Nu. 35: 31). Again, when a man who has fled to a city of refuge after an accidental killing wants to return to his possession, 'ye shall take no *kōpher* for him' (Nu. 35: 32). That it is impossible for a man to find a ransom which will deliver from death is the thought behind the use of *kōpher* in Psalm 49: 8, while in a different sphere, an outraged husband will not accept a *kōpher* from the adulterer (Pr. 6: 35).

From these examples we see that this word necessarily involves thought of a ransom price, a substitute, this being demanded by every occurrence of the term. The force of this should not be overlooked in estimating the significance of λύτρον in the LXX, for, as Procksch remarks: 'As translation of *kōpher*, then, λύτρον (-α) always means a substitute-gift (Ersatzgabe), whose worth avails as covering for a debt, so that the debt is not simply struck out.'[2]

The investigation of the ideas conveyed by the three main word-groups which the λύτρον words translate in the LXX shows that redemption consistently signifies deliverance by payment of a price. There may be other ideas, like that of family obligation in *g'l*, or the element of grace in *pdh*, but as a stubborn substratum in every case there is the basic price-paying conception.

We saw that the idea of the price paid tends to fade when Yahweh is the subject of the verb, but that, nevertheless, it does not disappear. There is reference to price in the insistence that Yahweh's redemption is at the cost of the exertion of His mighty power. Moreover it should not be overlooked that, now and then, the thought of the ransom comes to the surface as in Isaiah 43 which we have just noticed. So in Psalm 73 (74): 2, 'Remember thy

[1] *Loc. cit.*
[2] *TWNT*, IV, p. 330.

synagogue which thou acquiredst (or perhaps, purchasedst, ἐκτήσω) in the beginning; thou redeemedst the rod of thine inheritance', and Isaiah 52: 3, 'For thus saith the Lord, you were sold for nothing, and you will not be redeemed with money.' In these last two passages it would seem that it is just as impossible to have redemption without a price as a sale. Both terms may be used metaphorically, but that should not blind us to their essential significance, which is what gives them their force in these metaphorical passages.

The general picture then is quite clear. The LXX usage is such as to leave us in no doubt but that λύτρον and its cognates are properly applied to redemption by payment of price, and though the idea of price may fade when God is the subject, it never disappears. Particularly clear is the connection of λύτρον itself with price, for there is no occurrence of the word in the LXX without a price being expressed or clearly implied. We can confidently say that, in as far as the New Testament writers were imbued with the LXX outlook, they must have had in their minds some idea of deliverance by payment of price when they used the words of this word-group.

IV. REDEMPTION IN RABBINIC WRITINGS

All three Hebrew roots that we have seen employed in the Old Testament to express the idea of redemption are employed in much the same way in the Rabbinic literature. Thus *g'l* is in use for redemption of property (*Arak.* 9: 1, 2, 3, 4, *etc.*) and for things dedicated to the Lord (*Arak.* 7: 3, 4, 5, *etc.*). If anything, the use of the term with regard to the deliverances effected by the Lord increases, and we find mention not only of past deliverances such as that from Egypt (*e.g. Pes.* 10: 6), but also there is frequent mention of a future deliverance when Israel's troubles will be over. We might cite the seventh of the Eighteen Benedictions as a typical example of this. 'Look but upon our affliction and fight our fight and redeem us speedily for the sake of Thy name: for Thou art a strong redeemer. Blessed art Thou, O Lord, the Redeemer of Israel.'[1] Here we discern the same idea of cost in the exercise of mighty power that we have already noted in the Old Testament. But it must be admitted that the use of the term tended to become

[1] Cited from *The Jewish Encyclopedia*, XI (New York and London, 1905), p. 271.

conventionalized, so that it is not always possible to insist upon this. A feature of the usage which cannot fail to have influenced Christian terminology is its association with the Messiah, who is often seen as the great Redeemer of the glorious future.[1]

pdh is in regular use for redemption of various kinds. Thus it refers to redemption of produce (*Men.* 10: 4), spoil (*Sanh.* 10: 6), second tithe (*B.M.* 4: 8), dedicated goods generally (*Arak.* 6: 2), goods belonging to the Temple (*Meil.* 6: 2), animal offerings (*Hul.* 10: 2). It was also the regular word for ransoming persons, especially prisoners of war, a duty which the Jews rated highly (see *Kid.* 3: 8; *Git.* 4: 9; *A. Zar.* 3: 9; *Ket.* 1: 2, etc.).

kōpher features largely in certain parts of the Talmud as the technical term for the ransom price which a man must pay to redeem his life when it becomes forfeit after his ox has gored a man (Ex. 21: 30), and in other similar cases. The idea of providing a *kōpher* for the release of another may lie behind the recurring expression, 'May I be an atonement for you', wherein one expresses his readiness to suffer on behalf of another. That the idea of payment for release had penetrated deeply into the Jewish consciousness is shown in the interpretation of Deuteronomy 25: 11f. which, as H. Danby points out, was 'the basis of the imposition of damages for "indignity". The penalty "thou shalt cut off her hand" is interpreted to mean, "she shall pay a money-fine" '.[2]

It is true that in some Jewish writings the idea of redemption by payment seems to have receded somewhat. Thus Sirach uses the verb λυτρόω five times, and in no case can we say that a payment is necessary, although possibly there is still the idea of God redeeming by the expenditure of effort regarded as a cost (see Sir., 51: 2, 3). But that the words of this group still retained their essential significance is seen, for example, by the frequency with which such a writer as Josephus uses λύτρον for the ransom paid for the redemption of prisoners of war.[3] There is an interesting use of the ransom idea in Enoch 98: 10, 'wherefore do not hope to live, ye sinners, but ye shall depart and die; for you know no ransom', a passage reminiscent of Psalm 49: 7–9.

[1] *Cf.* G. F. Moore, *Judaism*, II (Harvard, 1958), p. 298, and *Jewish Encyclopedia*, Art. 'Go'el'.

[2] *The Mishnah* (Oxford, 1933), p. 342, n. 8.

[3] See for example the passages listed in *TWNT*, IV, p. 341.

To sum up: Judaism, subsequent to the Old Testament, continued to use the three redemption word-groups we found in the Old Testament in much the same manner as the canonical books, while the writers in Greek recall the usage of the LXX, although there is a tendency sometimes to use the words with more emphasis on deliverance than on payment of price. Development there was, and extension of usage in both Greek and Hebrew terms, but the basic thought in most writings continues to be that of deliverance by payment of price.

We see then, that in Greek writings generally, in the Old Testament, and in Rabbinic writers, the basic idea in redemption is the paying of a ransom price to secure a liberation. Circumstances may vary, for the word applies to the freeing of a prisoner of war, or of a man under sentence of death because his ox has gored a man, or of articles in pawn, or of a slave seeking manumission. But always there is the idea of payment of a ransom to secure the desired effect.

When God is the subject of the verb we noticed a difference, for it is inconceivable that He should pay a ransom to men, and in those passages there tends to be a greater stress on the idea of deliverance than on the means by which it is brought about. Yet even here we saw that the Old Testament writers were not unmindful of the meaning of the words they were applying to God's dealings with His people, for they think of Him as delivering at some cost. Clearly the metaphor was one with point.

V. THE λύτρον WORD-GROUP IN THE NEW TESTAMENT

a. λύτρον

λύτρον is found in the New Testament in one saying only: 'For verily the Son of man came not to be ministered unto, but to minister, and to give his life a ransom for many (λύτρον ἀντὶ πολλῶν)' (Mk. 10: 45; Mt. 20: 28 is almost identical).

The genuineness of the saying has been denied by some, in the face of the fact of its occurrence in Mark, generally admitted to be the oldest of the Gospels, and of the absence of textual doubts. Hastings Rashdall vigorously assails the passage,[1] and offers four

---

[1] *The Idea of Atonement in Christian Theology* (London, 1919), pp. 29–37, 49–56.

main objections to its authenticity: (1) The critical words about ransom are absent from Luke 22: 26, 27. (2) The passage has every appearance of being an ecclesiastical or doctrinal gloss. (3) It is irrelevant to its context (this he regards as the strongest objection). (4) It is out of harmony with Christ's teaching as a whole. As other objectors do not seem to have anything of importance to add to this, we will take Rashdall's as the case against the passage.

The first point loses its force when we notice that Luke is not reporting the same incident as Mark. The Lucan narrative has to do with a dispute in the upper room as to which of the disciples was to be accounted the greatest; the Marcan refers to the request of the sons of Zebedee for the chief places for themselves. Unless we can be sure that Luke is basing his narrative on that of Mark's different incident, or on another report of that incident, his employment or omission of the ransom terminology is completely irrelevant to the genuineness of the Marcan passage. It must first be proved that Luke 22: 26, 27 and Mark 10: 45 go back ultimately to the same saying of Jesus, and this has not been done. That there are resemblances between the two is accounted for sufficiently by the likeness between the two occasions.[1]

R. Bultmann rejects the saying, speaking of it as a 'well-known dogmatic transformation . . . the original form of which may well be found in Lk. 22: 27'.[2] With respect to the passage, Mark 10: 42–45, he says, 'the section is made out of an older saying in v. 43f . . . a saying which originally referred generally to the greatness of service, was applied especially to the Christian Church in the Christian tradition. To that end it was provided with a foil in Mk. 10: 42 par. and at the end a reference to the example of Jesus was added. Indeed at the end Lk. 22: 27 is doubtless original over against Mk. 10: 45, which has formed its conception of Jesus from the redemption theories of Hellenistic Christianity.'[3] But this is not argument. It is dogmatic assertion. It can carry conviction only to those who are impressed by extreme subjectivity. C. E. B. Cranfield in rejecting the view that the verse is a 'dogmatic recast' of

[1] B. H. Branscomb remarks: 'this was one of Jesus' most constant themes judging from the number of times and slightly varying forms in which the teaching occurs in the Gospels' (*MNTC, Mark*, p. 190).

[2] *The History of the Synoptic Tradition* (Oxford, 1963), p. 93.

[3] *Op. cit.*, p. 144.

Luke 22: 27 'made under the influence of Pauline theology' points out that 'Lk xxii. 24–7 bears the marks of Gentile-Christian influence, while Mk x. 45 is strongly Palestinian in expression', and he cites Büchsel and Jeremias in support.[1]

The second objection is highly subjective, for what appears to be definitely a gloss to one mind may well bear the stamp of authenticity to another.[2] Branscomb gives some evidence for the idea of a gloss with his contention that the ransom idea is 'almost completely absent from the Gospels elsewhere', and 'so frequent in Paul's writings as to account adequately for its expression here'.[3] But that the idea is not common in the Gospels need mean only that it is not the central point in Jesus' teaching about His death; it certainly does not carry the implication that this saying cannot be authentic. The suggestion that the ransom idea is common in the Pauline writings can be received only with qualification. St. Paul never uses the word λύτρον in the extant Epistles, and, while he does make use of the redemption category, it is not as common as some would think, not nearly as common, for example, as is justification.[4] Another small point is that the language used is not what we should have expected in a doctrinal insertion, for the New Testament writers commonly use such expressions as 'the blood' or 'the death' of Christ, rather than referring to the offering of life.

But Rashdall regards the next point as the strongest objection, and we give it in his own words: 'Our Lord has been speaking of His death as a kind of service – a service which His disciples were to imitate. There is a sudden transition to a different order of ideas – which is then immediately dropped and in no way followed up or

[1] *CGT, in loc.* S. E. Johnson also rejects the idea that the saying reflects the theology of the Gentile church and maintains that 'one need not look further than Isa.lii.13–liii.12 for the background of this verse' (*BNTC, in loc.*).

[2] Thus J. Moffatt refers to the verse under discussion as 'a saying which is one of the most self-authenticating in the record' (*MNTC, 1 Corinthians*, p. 164).

[3] *Op. cit.*, pp. 190f.

[4] A. Richardson is scathing about this suggestion: 'It used to be held . . . that these words were not spoken by Jesus, but represent a Marcan insertion of Pauline theology into the teaching of Jesus: but all such contentions reflect the theological outlook of their exponents rather than that of the NT. It would indeed be remarkable that St Mark should have thus brilliantly summarized in a word the theology of St Paul, in order to attribute it to Jesus, especially when we note that that word (λύτρον) is never used in the extant writings of the Apostle' (*An Introduction to the Theology of the New Testament*, London, 1958, p. 220).

explained.'[1] But, in the first place, this is to demand in the words of
Jesus a sense of rigid logic which is foreign to the atmosphere of the
Gospels, and can be insisted upon only rarely if at all; and, in the
second, the statement in the form given by Rashdall cannot stand,
for our Lord has not been speaking of His death as a kind of service.
He has been speaking of the necessity for humble service on the
part of the disciples; 'whosoever would be first among you, shall
be servant of all'. This He drives home by an appeal to His own
purpose in coming to earth, namely that He might minister to
others and ransom them at the cost of His life. If Jesus thinks of His
death as service it does not seem illogical that He should explain, if
only briefly, in what the service consisted, *i.e.* in being a ransom
for many. The words about ransom may not be required by the
immediately preceding words, but they follow on quite naturally.

A variation on the argument from context is that since the
passage speaks of service any action here ascribed to Jesus must be
such as can be emulated by His followers. Thus E. P. Gould likens
the death of Jesus to that of the martyrs,[2] and Rashdall denies that
there is anything to suggest that the benefit procured by the death
of Christ 'was anything *sui generis* – different in kind from the
benefit which the sufferings of other righteous men might obtain
for them, or that the way in which it was to operate was by constituting an expiatory or substitutionary sacrifice'.[3] But such
interpretation seems to lean too heavily on the context. For, after
all, the context of a saying, while undoubtedly important, can
indicate only in a general way the drift of the saying; it cannot
finally determine its meaning in detail. Moreover in this case there

---

[1] *Op. cit.*, p. 51. He goes on to note that Loisy says: 'The idea of a life given in
ransom belongs to another course than that of service.'

[2] *ICC, in loc.* His words are, 'All that is required by the statement . . . is that his
life becomes the price by which men are freed from their bondage. The soldiers in
the American civil war gave their lives as a λύτρον for the slaves, and every martyr's
death is a λύτρον. There may be more than this involved in the death of the
Redeemer, but more than this is not involved in his words here.'

[3] *Op. cit.*, pp. 35f. Similarly W. Russell Maltby: 'He lived and died serving; and
the supreme service which He did for mankind was to die for them. In that context
then, it was fitting to speak of His dying as the supreme example for us all to follow.
But in all this there is no expiatory reference' (*Christ and His Cross*, London, 1935, p.
136). It may be freely admitted that Christ's death is 'the supreme service', but that
does not mean that there is no thought of substitutionary ransom.

seems to be a tendency to undue limitation. If the death of Jesus is *sui generis* that does not mean that there are no aspects in which it can be imitated. There seems no particular reason why our Lord should not have directed the attention of the disciples to the aspects of self-abnegation and of service to others which are seen in His death, and then have gone on to indicate also that the supreme service lay elsewhere.

The objection that the ransom saying is out of harmony with the teaching of Jesus as a whole does not seem tenable these days, if only because there is considerable agreement that Jesus saw in the prophecy of the suffering servant a picture of His vocation. If He thought of His mission as in any way comparable to that described in Isaiah 53,[1] then, clearly, it is congruous to refer to it as a process of ransom. There are other relevant considerations, such as the repeated predictions of His death by Jesus, and the whole attitude that finally led to Calvary, so that this objection cannot be said to have any great weight.

Thus none of the objections urged against the saying can be said to be decisive. It may be true, as W. Manson says, that 'It is not in our power to prove the authenticity of *any* word which tradition has ascribed to Jesus'.[2] Yet at the very least we can say, in the words of the same scholar, 'it will not do to pronounce it impossible or unlikely that Jesus, who saw his work and teaching to be fraught with critical significance for his nation, should think of his sacrifice in terms of an '*asham* for many, as completing and consummating the work – the conversion and redemption of the many – which he had sought by his life to effect.'[3] Most of us will feel that the authenticity of the ransom saying is as well established as the facts of the case make possible.

We now turn to the meaning of the terms used. We have seen that λύτρον in the LXX consistently denotes the payment of a ransom price substitutionary in character, and the same we saw to be true almost universally outside the Bible. While it is not impossible for

---

[1] The ransom saying itself is held by many scholars to echo Is. 53, *e.g.* W. F. Howard, *ET*, L (1938–39), pp. 109f.; A. Richardson, *loc. cit.*; R. H. Fuller, *The Mission and Achievement of Jesus* (London, 1954), p. 57.

[2] *Jesus the Messiah* (London, 1943), p. 132.

[3] *Op. cit.*, p. 133. Manson's examination of the evidence (pp. 131ff.) affords strong reason for accepting the genuineness of the ransom saying.

the word to be used in a metaphorical sense, it should nevertheless be recognized that this is rather unusual, and we are justified in demanding the strongest of evidence to remove a substitutionary meaning from a passage containing it.[1] In this case, so far from the context removing the substitutionary meaning, it actually reinforces it.

Scholars who have gone into the Semitic background of the ransom saying bring further evidence for the substitutionary conception, whether we regard the Semitic equivalent for λύτρον in this passage as *pidhyōn* with G. Dalman,[2] or as *kōpher* with O. Procksch.[3] For Dalman understands ransom as 'substitute for the forfeited life', and Procksch speaks of a substitution-idea (*Stellvertretungsgedanke*) 'which is always given with *kōpher*',[4] and again he says that by the equation *kōpher* = λύτρον there is always meant 'a substitutionary-offering for a human life'.[5]

The preposition ἀντί characteristically has the meaning 'in the place of', 'instead of', whether in the classics or in the κοινή.[6] This remains true for biblical Greek, and H. E. Dana and J. R. Mantey draw attention to LXX passages such as 'and offered him up for a burnt offering in the stead of (ἀντί) his son' (Gn. 22: 13), 'Let thy servant, I pray thee, abide instead of (ἀντί) the lad a bondman to my lord' (Gn. 44: 33), and 'I have taken the Levites from among the children of Israel instead of (ἀντί) all the first-born' (Nu. 3: 12). This usage they point out is continued in the New Testament; and they cite the statement that Archelaus reigned instead of (ἀντί) Herod (Mt. 2: 22), and the following phrases: 'and he for (ἀντί) a fish give

---

[1] Thus F. Steinleitner says that the sense of λύτρον in this passage is that of 'Loskaufgeld' (*Die Beicht in Zusammenhange*, Leipzig, 1913, p. 37). Similarly L. Pullan, 'The word "ransom" emphasises not only the idea of freedom gained for the believer and the great value of the price paid, but also the truth that His life is a substitute offered for our life in profound sympathy. Nothing short of this will satisfy the natural sense of the words employed' (*The Atonement*, London, 1907, p. 101).

[2] *Jesus-Jeshua* (London, 1929), p. 118.

[3] *TWNT*, IV, p. 331, So, too, Orr in *HDCG*, II, 468, and he adds, 'most admit the connexion'.

[4] *Op. cit.*, p. 330.

[5] *Ibid.*

[6] See Liddell and Scott for the classical use, and MM for the κοινή. *Cf.* MM: 'By far the commonest meaning of ἀντί is the simple "instead of."'

him a serpent' (Lk. 11: 11), 'for her hair is given her for (ἀντί) a covering' (1 Cor. 11: 15), 'Jesus . . . who for (ἀντί) the joy that was set before him endured the cross' (Heb. 12: 2).[1] There are other passages which Dana and Mantey do not mention where the translation 'instead of' is more difficult, as in the 'evil for evil' passages (Rom. 12: 17; 1 Pet. 3: 9; 1 Thes. 5: 15); though Büchsel would render the word even here by 'anstatt'[2] or where ἀνθ' ὧν or ἀντὶ τούτου are found. But when full allowance has been made for passages of this sort it still remains that the most common meaning of the preposition, both inside the New Testament and out, is 'instead of' or 'in exchange for'.

The force of this is occasionally denied.[3] It may be freely granted that now and then ἀντί is used in such a way as not to imply substitution. Matthew 17: 27 is such a case, and H. Wheeler Robinson appeals to this passage in support of his contention that 'The preposition *anti* means simply "for"'.[4] But it cannot be too strongly insisted that to determine the meaning of a word we must take it in its habitual sense and not fasten our attention on unusual cases (here on one case only). If the term is to be emptied of substitutionary force in the ransom saying this will be done, not by showing that in unusual circumstances ἀντί may occur without stress on substitution, but only by bringing forward reasons for thinking that this passage uses the term in an unusual way. But in point of fact its use is perfectly normal, and there seems no reason for disputing the conclusion reached by Dana and Mantey when they say that, in the ransom saying, ἀντί must mean either 'instead of' or 'in exchange for', and 'each implies substitution'. They add, '*The obscurity of this*

---

[1] *A Manual Grammar of the Greek New Testament* (New York, 1955), p. 100. *Cf.* also C. K. Barrett, 'In λύτρον the idea of equivalence is central'; 'this sense of equivalence or substitution is proper to λύτρον' (*New Testament Essays, Studies in Memory of Thomas Walter Manson*, ed. A. J. B. Higgins, Manchester, 1959, p. 6).

[2] *TWNT*, I, p. 373.

[3] *E.g.* by C. Ryder Smith, *op. cit.*, p. 157.

[4] *Redemption and Revelation* (London, 1942), p. 229. He may mean no more than that ἀντί means 'for' in this saying. If he means more, that this is its meaning generally, he has the lexicographers against him. In the overwhelming majority of places where it is found the word means 'in place of', 'in the stead of'. J. H. Moulton says that in the New Testament ἀντί 'retains its individuality'. He speaks of it as expressing 'the idea of equivalence or return or substitution' (*A Grammar of New Testament Greek*, I, *Prolegomena*, Edinburgh, 1930, p. 100).

passage is not the result of linguistic ambiguity, but of theological controversy.[1]

But in any case even if, with Wheeler Robinson, we take the substitutionary meaning out of the preposition, we have not taken it out of the passage, for the situation envisaged is one in which the many are condemned, their lives are forfeit. If Jesus gives His life 'a ransom for many' and thereby they are released from their condemnation, then a substitutionary transaction has taken place, understand the individual words as we will.[2]

The expression λύτρον ἀντί can be paralleled from Josephus who says, with reference to the visit of Crassus to the Temple, that a priest named Eleazar, seeing the Roman intent on plundering the sanctuary, gave him a bar of gold, λύτρον ἀντὶ πάντων.[3] There can be no doubt but that here a substitutionary meaning is to be attached to the expression – the bar of gold was to be a substitute for the treasures of the Temple. It is true that we are dealing in this situation with inanimate objects, but otherwise the saying is closely parallel to that in the Gospels, and it gives a presumption in favour of the substitutionary meaning.

Thus we have seen that there is no substantial reason for doubting the authenticity of the passage, and that the words, taken at their face value, contain a substitutionary meaning, indicating the offering of life for life quite in the style of Leviticus 27: 11.[4] H. B.

[1] *Ibid.* (my italics). Similarly F. J. Taylor says that the preposition 'suggests a substitutionary idea which is elsewhere expressed by reference to what Christ bore for men' (*TWBB*, p. 187).

[2] This is brought out by Büchsel's comment: 'In Mk.10.45: δοῦναι τὴν ψυχὴν αὐτοῦ λύτρον ἀντὶ πολλῶν the setting of ἀντὶ πολλῶν is dependent on λύτρον not on δοῦναι. Therefore ἀντί has the meaning *a* not *b* in the sense of Mt. 17. 27 (He has already given the meaning *a* as 'instead of' and *b* as 'for the benefit of'). The life of Jesus thus given is the sufficient price for the ransoming of the many. But if one were to connect ἀντὶ πολλῶν with δοῦναι and understand it in sense *b* the saying retains the actuality of a substitutionary conception. For that which the many are condemned to forfeit is not a cherished possession, but their life, their self; and what Jesus gives is His life, His self. For their advantage He does nothing other than stand in their place' (*TWNT*, I, p. 373).

[3] *Ant.* 14. 107.

[4] A. Lods' comment on Lv. 27: 11 reminds us of the ransom saying. 'It would seem from this passage that the life ("the soul") of the sinner is threatened by the holiness of God: he must give, as an equivalent, blood, that is a soul, a life. There is a ransom, a redemption, a death by proxy' (*The Prophets and the Rise of Judaism*, London, 1937, p. 294).

Swete comments, 'The Lord contemplates a λύτρον which is ψυχὴ ἀντὶ ψυχῆς (Lev. xxiv. 18), His own ψυχή (xiv. 34) given as a ransom for the ψυχαί of men.'[1]

The force of the passage is sometimes evaded even by those who feel the force of the language. Thus Büchsel correctly gives the sense of the ransom saying: 'The ransom saying in any case includes a substitutionary concept. For one might interpret ἀντί as "in place of" or "for the benefit of": when Jesus gives Himself in death there happens to Him what should happen to the many, He stands in their place. The saying clearly looks back to Mk. 8. 37, Mt. 16. 26.'[2] Yet later he denies any objective equivalence between the death of Jesus and that which the many owe, and proceeds: 'The equivalence for God is to be sought in this, that Jesus' giving of life is the proof of His complete obedience, and as such, as power in mankind, overcomes sin.'[3] It is not called in question that Jesus' death is the proof of His full obedience to the Father, nor that this is important for the understanding of the atonement. But the point is that the passage does not say this. It cannot be derived thence by exegesis. The point of the saying is not that Jesus was obedient, and that this obedience is what benefits sinners, but that the life of Jesus was given up to ransom them.

The language used rules out minimizing interpretations such as those of Gould and Rashdall, as C. G. Montefiore recognizes. Though he rejects the ransom saying he gives its meaning thus: 'It is true that to give your life for others is the highest possible service (McNeile), but the word "*lutron*" seems to imply something more. *Cp.* 4 Macc. vi. 29, xviii. 22, i. 11, 2 Macc. vii. 37. God somehow makes the death of Jesus help in the salvation of others. It is in this more special sense that Jesus gives his own life for the sake of many lives.'[4] While I am not satisfied that this fully explains the passage, it recognizes that the interpretations we have been discussing will not fit the words used. As with λύτρον so with ἀντί;[5] both imply

---

[1] *In loc.*

[2] *TWNT*, IV, p. 344. There are other strong statements about substitution in the same article, *e.g.* pp. 345, 346.

[3] *Op. cit.*, p. 348.

[4] *The Synoptic Gospels*, I (London, 1927), p. 253.

[5] *Cf.* A. M. Hunter: 'It would be rash to find here a doctrine of the Atonement; yet the preposition used (ἀντί, "instead of") clearly implies substitution. . . . At the

substitution, and we must interpret the passage in a highly unnatural manner if we are to overlook this. Again, the aorist tenses
'indicate that the allusion is not to a lifelong sacrifice but to one
definitive act of self-surrender',[1] and this may be of importance.
Finally, it is not seriously disputed that the critical words evoke
memories of Isaiah 53 and of the servant who suffered for many, and
in this Old Testament passage the thought of substitutionary
suffering is plain.[2]

To bring this discussion to a close: the natural meaning of the
ransom saying is that Jesus' death was in the stead of the many, He
was to give His life instead of their lives,[3] and we see no reason for
abandoning this interpretation. It may or may not be easy to
integrate this into some theory of the way the atonement works,
but either way we are not justified in evading the plain sense of the
Greek.[4]

b. λυτρόω

The first λυτρόω passage in the New Testament is the conversation
on the way to Emmaus, where the two disciples say, with reference
to Jesus, 'we hoped that it was he which should redeem Israel' (Lk.
24: 21). They are clearly using 'redeem' in the typically Jewish
manner of the long awaited intervention by Almighty God, when
His power would free His people from all their enemies and bring
in a period of blessing and prosperity. The passage is not of first
importance for our purposes. Obviously a redemption rendered

---

very least, then, we must say (it seems to me) that the death of Jesus takes the place
of "the many".' (*The Work and Words of Jesus*, London, 1950, p. 98).

[1] W. Manson, *op. cit.*, p. 131.

[2] 'The idea of substitution which is prominent in Isa. liii. 6, appears in the ransom
saying' (A. M. Hunter, *op. cit.*, p. 100). Similarly W. Manson: 'The Son of Man
here means Jesus on earth . . . and the claim is that he fulfils his vocation by accepting
the sacrificial function of the Servant of the Lord who gives his life "in compensation for the sins of the people, interposing for them as their substitute" ' (*op.
cit.*, p. 131). The quotation is from BDB, p. 80.

[3] *Cf.* J. Schniewind, 'Jesus Himself gives His own life as substitute for our lost
life' (*SJT*, V, 1952, p. 272).

[4] Vincent Taylor, dealing with certain objections to this saying, says, 'The idea
that no act of requital is due to a Holy God, or is needed by men, is a modern notion
which it would be a libel to attribute to the ancient world' (*Jesus and His Sacrifice*,
London, 1939, p. 105).

impossible by the cross can tell us little about the redemption effected by the cross.

In Titus 2: 14, however, we have a specifically Christian reference to redemption. Christ, we read, 'gave himself for us, that he might redeem us from all iniquity'. The fairly obvious reference to the ransom saying (Mk. 10: 45) points in the direction of substitution, and this is supported by the general usage of λυτρόω and by the specific mention of the ransom price ('gave himself').

Even clearer is the remaining passage where the price of our redemption is given as 'the precious blood, as of a lamb without blemish and without spot, even the blood of Christ' (1 Pet. 1: 18f.). The contrast with such prices as 'gold or silver' means that there is no possibility of missing the reference to a normal process of redemption.[1]

It seems clear that only special pleading can rid these two passages of the thought of a ransoming. In each case we find the price mentioned and an evil condition from which the ransoming has freed us. There is a substitutionary thought, for it is Christ, not the sinners, who has paid the price, so that He is acting in their stead in His redeeming death.

c. λύτρωσις

λύτρωσις like λυτρόω occurs three times in the New Testament (Lk. 1: 68; 2: 38 and Heb. 9: 12). In the two Lucan passages it is used in the Jewish sense, just as we have seen is the case with λυτρόω in Luke 24: 21. Neither of these passages is of great importance for our present purpose.

When we turn to Hebrews 9: 12 we find ourselves in a different sphere of thought altogether. Christ is pictured as a High Priest who, not 'through the blood of goats and calves, but through his own blood, entered in once for all into the holy place, having obtained eternal redemption', which brings us into the realm of sacrifice. But the sacrificial conception is blended with that of redemption, and 'his own blood' must be regarded as indicating

---

[1] It should also be noted here that the manner of introducing the ransom price, 'the precious blood of Christ as of a lamb without blemish and without spot', brings us into the sphere of sacrificial thought. Whether or not the writer thought of sacrifice in general as in the nature of a ransom, he certainly conceived that the death of Christ was both a ransom price and a sacrificial offering.

the price of redemption, as well as pointing to the sacrificial process (*cf.* 1 Pet. 1 : 18, 19 for this blending of the sacrificial with the redemptive concept).

It may be well to notice here that, although the writer to the Hebrews does not speak often of redemption, yet the thought of cost to Christ in the securing of our salvation is one which is frequently met with in the Epistle. Perhaps this is nowhere more forcefully put than in the reference to Him 'who in the days of his flesh, having offered up prayers and supplications with strong crying and tears unto him that was able to save him from death . . . learned obedience by the things which he suffered' (Heb. 5 : 7f.). This passage, referring primarily to the agony in Gethsemane,[1] brings out strongly the cost element in the process of salvation. Our redemption was not purchased cheaply. This thought is to be discerned in the statement that 'it became him . . . in bringing many sons unto glory, to make the author of their salvation perfect through sufferings' (Heb. 2 : 10). Again, there is the thought that Christ suffered through temptation (Heb. 2 : 18; and see 4 : 15), and it is said that He 'suffered without the gate' (Heb. 13 : 12). In similar vein are passages stressing the humiliation of the incarnation; He was made lower than the angels for the tasting of death (Heb. 2 : 9), He endured the cross despising its shame, and again, He endured the gainsaying of sinners (Heb. 12 : 2, 3). Thus from many directions we see a stress laid on the cost of our salvation, and this should be borne in mind in estimating the writer's thought on redemption. Even when he is not using that exact term, he has the idea of cost that it denotes.

d. ἀπολύτρωσις

ἀπολύτρωσις is a very rare word, there being, as far as I have been able to ascertain, only ten examples of its use outside the New Testament. Its structure could well give the thought of a 'ransoming away' with a corresponding emphasis on the result, the effective deliverance, rather than the mode whereby this is brought about, as Chrysostom notes.[2] But this cannot be pressed; for on the

---

[1] See, for example, Westcott, *in loc.*

[2] *Cf.* his often quoted remark on Rom. 3 : 24, καὶ οὐχ ἁπλῶς εἶπε λυτρώσεως, ἀλλ᾽ ἀπολυτρώσεως, ὡς μηκέτι ἡμᾶς ἐπανελθεῖν πάλιν ἐπὶ τὴν αὐτὴν δουλείαν: 'And he said not simply "ransoming", but "ransoming away", so that we no

one hand we have the well-known fondness for compounded forms which characterizes the κοινή writers, and on the other λύτρωσις may be used for the most effective deliverance. It is used, for example, of 'eternal redemption' (Heb. 9: 12), which is as final as is possible. Moreover the actual usage of ἀπολύτρωσις shows 'ransoming' rather than 'deliverance' to be the essential meaning of the word. In an earlier section we examined all the non-biblical passages in which the word occurs, and on each occasion we found that it signifies a process of obtaining release by payment of ransom (a process indicated also in almost every occurrence of the corresponding verb ἀπολυτρόω). This creates a presumption that in the New Testament it will continue to signify such a process.

The paucity of the occurrences of ἀπολύτρωσις in literature generally is somewhat in contrast with the New Testament where it appears as the typical term for redemption. There it occurs ten times as against nine times for all the other words from the same root put together. This is in contrast, too, with the usage of the LXX where ἀπολύτρωσις occurs but once, and that in a passage where there is no corresponding Hebrew word in the Massoretic Text. At the same time λυτρόομαι, which is the characteristic representative of this family in the LXX with its ninety-nine occurrences, is found but three times in the New Testament, and one of these is not in the specifically Christian sense. This difference in terminology is not always noticed, and it is difficult to account for. We have noted in the section on the LXX that the usage there is a little away from the general run of Greek literature, in that we have a number of passages (with God as the subject) where λυτρόομαι, etc., are used without a ransom being expressly implied. Accordingly it is just possible that the New Testament writers felt that the LXX usage was not quite what they wanted when they wished to express the redemption idea. Whether that is the explanation or not, it is beyond dispute that the terminology is different, and, therefore, to assume that the New Testament follows the LXX, as some writers do, is not justified. The New Testament must be allowed to speak for itself.

When we turn to the ten occurrences of the term ἀπολύτρωσις

---

more come again into the same slavery.' Chrysostom is not concerned here so much with the process as the result, and thus he stresses the preposition.

in the New Testament we find that the price is expressed three times and implied twice, on three occasions a future redemption with a certain eschatological significance is referred to, on one occasion the reference is perfectly general and there is one passage referring to a non-Christian redemption. Some writers (*e.g.* Büchsel, Abbott) make their point of departure one or other of the exceptional cases, but since we have seen a perfectly uniform usage outside the New Testament it would seem preferable to deal first of all with passages which conform to this general scheme.

The three clearest passages are Romans 3: 24, Ephesians 1: 7 and Hebrews 9: 15. There has been discussion about each of these, of course, and it would be an overstatement to say that there is a generally accepted conclusion in any one of them. Nevertheless it is a fact that there is a redemption price mentioned in each case, and accordingly, unless the strongest of reasons can be put forward, we must conclude that here again we have the typical usage of the word-group.

In Ephesians 1: 7 we read of Christ, 'in whom we have the redemption through his blood, the remission of sins, according to the riches of his grace . . .' One would have thought that 're-demption through his blood' is a plain enough indication of the payment of a ransom price, but we find, for example, T. K. Abbott disputing this. He says, rightly, that the verb ἀπολυτρόω 'signifies properly, not "to redeem" (λυτροῦσθαι), but to release on receiving a ransom' (though he should have noted that ἀπολυτροῦσθαι, as well as λυτροῦσθαι, means 'to redeem'). But when he goes on to consider the derived noun ἀπολύτρωσις, he cites a number of instances apparently to show that it is used to take up the sense of the active[1] and not of the middle, and says: 'As far as usage goes, then, it would seem that if we are to attach to ἀπολύτρωσις the idea of ransom, the word will mean "holding to ransom" or "release on receipt of ransom," not "payment of ransom." '

But this is in error. To begin with, the derived noun can just as well take up the sense of the middle as the active,[2] and there is no

---

[1] The passages he notes are Plutarch, *Pomp.* 24. 2; Josephus, *Ant.* 12. 2. 3; Philo, *Quod Omn. Prob. lib.* 17; Diod. *Frag.* lib. 37. 5. 3; Dn. 4: 30.

[2] Thus T. Zahn says: 'It is not to be overlooked that according to circumstances the regular meaning of the act. λυτροῦν, ἀπολυτροῦν (*dimittere*) or that of the mid. λυτροῦσθαι, ἀπολυτροῦσθαι (*redimere*) lies at the basis, also the derived substantive

particular reason for thinking that the active will be favoured. Then, incredibly, Abbott has not subjected his examples to a sufficiently close scrutiny, for the passage he cites from Philo is clearly a case of the middle sense. When Philo says ἀπογνοὺς ἀπολύτρωσιν ἀσμενος ἑαυτὸν διεχρήσατο the meaning plainly is 'despairing of ransoming he cheerfully slew himself'. It cannot possibly mean 'despairing of holding to ransom', because it is himself that is to be ransomed, not someone in his power. A similar criticism must be made of Abbott's failure to notice that ὁ χρόνος μου τῆς ἀπολυτρώσεως ἦλθε (Dn. 4: 30) also bears witness to the release by payment of ransom[1] rather than by receiving ransom. Nebuchadrezzar was not holding anyone to ransom, but was referring to his own release from trouble when he used the words, and thus the sense is definitely that of the middle. Abbott also cites Diodorus Siculus, who says that, after a certain slave had agreed with his owners for his manumission, Scaevola intervened, φθάσας τὴν ἀπολύτρωσιν . . . ἀνεσταύρωσεν.[2] The meaning of ἀπολύτρωσιν here is doubtful. It makes quite good sense, as Abbott suggests, to understand 'anticipating release on receipt of ransom', i.e. interpreting ἀπολύτρωσιν from the point of view of the owners. But it can also be understood quite well in this context from the point of view of the slave, 'anticipating release by paying ransom'. The most that can be said is that this passage is congruous with the former meaning; it certainly does not establish it. The difficulty in determining which meaning is the correct one is illustrated by the fact that Abbott seems to take a passage in Josephus[3] in the sense of the active, while Warfield[4] takes the same passage in the sense of the middle. Occurrences not treated in Abbott include the two

---

denotes either the action of him who discharges, releases the imprisoned man from the hold, or the action of him who through the payment of a ransom price or even without this accomplishes the freeing of another who is in custody whether person or thing' (*Der Brief des Paulus an die Römer*, Leipzig, 1910, pp. 179f.). Although he speaks of freeing without payment of a ransom it is noteworthy that he cites no examples of this, and it may be doubted whether there are such. Procksch also points out the dual meaning of ἀπολύτρωσις and gives it as his verdict that, in the Bible, it is used following the sense of the middle (*TWNT*, IV, p. 336).

[1] The ransom, namely almsgiving, is referred to in verse 24. See also above, p. 18.
[2] *Frag. lib.* 37.5.3.
[3] *Ant.* 12.27.
[4] *PTR*, XV (1917), p. 213, n.40.

references in the Letter of Aristeas, both of which are probably in the middle sense, and the inscription from Cos dealing with a slave's manumission where, again, the middle gives good sense.[1]

It does not seem possible, then, to maintain Abbott's position. The undisputed instances of ἀπολύτρωσις in the sense of 'holding to ransom, release on receipt of ransom' are reduced to the passage he cites from Plutarch, while all the other examples can bear the sense of 'release by payment of ransom', and some positively demand it. This being so, there remains no obstacle to interpreting Ephesians 1 : 7 in the natural way. The passage refers to Christ's redemption of believers through the price of His blood. Perhaps we may find a clue to the right interpretation in the passage from *Romeo and Juliet* which Abbott adduces, 'Before the time that Romeo come to redeem me'. Here unquestionably the word means 'deliver' and there is no thought of payment of price. Equally unquestionably it is not the normal English usage. The passage can be understood, but it is not a reliable guide to the understanding of the English verb. So is it with the idea of redemption in Greek. The basic meaning of the root is concerned with release by payment of a price, and while a metaphorical usage may appear it cannot be regarded as the standard. The price-paying conception is still in the background and it is this that gives force to the metaphor.

The occurrence of ἄφεσιν in apposition with ἀπολύτρωσιν does not really alter this seriously, for it indicates no more than that there were many ways of looking at the work of Christ and that no one way was by itself satisfactory. We have already had occasion to notice that in some passages there is a conjunction of references to redemption and sacrifice (*e.g.* Heb. 9 : 12; 1 Pet. 1 : 18, 19) and here we have a similar conjunction of redemption and forgiveness.[2]

Another attempt to evade the force of the passage is by referring τὴν ἀπολύτρωσιν here to the final eschatological deliverance. But even if this were the right interpretation of the passage it would

---

[1] See above, pp. 16ff.

[2] *Cf.* the comment of C. H. Dodd on Rom. 3 : 21-26: 'We find that he is combining three metaphors: the first taken from the law-court – the metaphor of justification; the second taken from the institution of slavery – that of emancipation; the third taken from the sacrificial ritual of ancient religion – that of expiation by blood. Under all three metaphors he describes an act of God for men' (*MNTC*, p. 56).

not empty ἀπολύτρωσιν of its force. Rather it would emphasize that redemption, even the final eschatological redemption, is dependent on the price paid on Calvary. The time when the redemption takes full effect does not seem to have any real bearing on the presence or otherwise of the implication of a ransom price.

But is there any real reason for understanding this passage in an eschatological sense? It would seem not. The writer uses the present tense (ἔχομεν) and appears to be thinking of a redemption already brought about so that it is the present possession of the believer. There is no more reason for thinking that redemption here signifies something in the far future than there is for understanding remission of sins (to which it is joined) in the same way. It is, of course, true that redemption has a final aspect, and that we cannot regard our redemption as fully consummated here and now. Its final perfection must await the advent of the Lord. But it is just as true that the New Testament does not regard redemption as something that is only in the future (cf. 'ye were redeemed', 1 Pet. 1: 18), and it is redemption as the present possession of the believer which occupies the attention of the writer here.

Romans 3: 24 comes in a context which presents difficult problems, but as far as ἀπολύτρωσις is concerned the meaning seems to be clear. Paul is here making use of the redemption metaphor again, and once more we have the price mentioned in the context, though in this case it is not formally joined to ἀπολύτρωσις. 'Being justified freely by his grace,' says the apostle, 'through the redemption that is in Christ Jesus: whom God set forth to be a propitiation, through faith, by his blood . . .' It is true that 'his blood' is more directly connected here with propitiation than with redemption, but there can be no doubt that there is also an indirect glance at the price paid, so that Moffatt is justified when he translates ἀπολυτρώσεως by 'ransom'. W. Sanday and A. C. Headlam come to a similar conclusion when on the idea of ἀπολυτρώσεως they say, 'we can hardly resist the conclusion that the idea of the λύτρον retains its full force, that it is identical with the τιμή, and that both are ways of describing the Death of Christ. The emphasis is on the *cost* of man's redemption.'[1]

---

[1] *ICC, in loc.* F. J. Leenhardt thinks that the term suggests 'the deliverance from Egypt on the one hand, and on the other the emancipation of a slave by the payment of his *peculium* to the liberating gods' (*in loc.*). C. K. Barrett maintains that the

The third passage where the thought of price is clear is Hebrews 9: 15, where we read of a death taking place 'for the redemption of the transgressions that were under the first covenant'. The expression 'redemption of the transgressions' is unusual, but it does not modify the central thought, namely that the redemption spoken of is the result of the death which has taken place; indeed, the death took place for the very purpose of effecting this redemption. Thus the idea that Christ has paid the price of our freedom in His death is present in this passage also.[1]

Of the other passages where the word occurs Ephesians 1: 14 must be taken in conjunction with Ephesians 1: 7. It is hardly conceivable that our author should use the one word in two completely different ways in the same context. (Actually, since the style is somewhat involved, the two occurrences of ἀπολύτρωσις are in successive sentences.) Since ἀπολύτρωσις bears its usual meaning in verse 7 it would be captious to urge that it has a different meaning in verse 14 unless some cogent reason can be found. But such does not appear.

The case is not otherwise with Colossians 1: 14, for this verse, as far as the reference to redemption is concerned, merely repeats Ephesians 1: 7, with the omission of the words referring to the price paid. If there is some compelling reason, we can of course say that the omission is significant and that ἀπολύτρωσις bears a different meaning here, but such a reason is not apparent. Indeed, the

---

noun can mean simply 'deliverance', but that here 'the connexion with blood and death suggests that it has not completely lost its original sense of "ransoming", emancipation by the payment of a price' (*in loc.*).

[1] The expression 'redemption of the transgressions' calls for some comment, and strange conclusions have sometimes been drawn from it as, for example, by Hofmann: 'It is the transgressions (παραβάσεις) themselves which are regarded as having fallen under the wrath of God, and so liable to punishment, and as delivered from this fall and liability by the work of the Redeemer' (quoted by F. Delitzsch, *Commentary on the Epistle to the Hebrews*, II, Edinburgh, 1887, p. 104). But in Greek the genitive can express various relationships. Thus it has often been noted that τὴν μετοικεσίαν Βαβυλῶνος in Mt. 1: 12 merely signifies 'a Babylon-removal', whether of, to or from Babylon the form does not and cannot say. But the context and our general knowledge of the position clears up any indefiniteness and the expression is seen to mean 'to Babylon'. So is it here. What is spoken of is a 'transgressions-redemption', and our knowledge of the general Christian context enables us to say that this means a redemption *from* transgressions. It is the transgressors, not the transgressions which are redeemed. Delitzsch has a helpful note *in loc.*

context favours a strict application of the ransom idea, for the metaphor of deliverance from captivity at the hand of a powerful enemy is being followed out. In verse 13 this takes place by the intervention of a stronger power defeating and overcoming the foe, but in verse 14 the metaphor changes from 'the victor who rescues the captive by force of arms (ver. 13 ἐρύσατο) to the philanthropist who releases him by the payment of a ransom'.[1] There can be no reasonable doubt in view of Ephesians 1 : 7 and the context here that we are to think of the payment of a ransom.

There are three passages wherein the thought is eschatological, namely: 'But when these things begin to come to pass, look up, and lift up your heads; because your redemption draweth nigh' (Lk. 21 : 28); 'but ourselves also, which have the firstfruits of the Spirit, even we ourselves groan within ourselves, waiting for our adoption, to wit, the redemption of our body' (Rom. 8 : 23); 'And grieve not the holy Spirit of God, in whom ye were sealed unto the day of redemption' (Eph. 4 : 30). There can be no doubt that in each of these cases redemption means something more than that which believers have already experienced. Just as the Jews of that day (and of all succeeding ages right down to our own) looked forward to a 'redemption', so did the Christians. One day their Messiah would return to the earth and thus there would be a great 'redemption' which would be of the greatest concern to them all. The resemblances to the Jewish conception are striking. The wording, the assurance of deliverance, the association of the deliverance with the Messiah, the earnest looking forward to it, in all these points we have resemblance to the Jewish idea.

But before we conclude that this is just another example of the Jewish usage and equate ἀπολύτρωσις in these passages with deliverance, there are certain factors which must be considered. The first of these reminds us of the difference in terminology. The Jewish conception is expressed usually by λυτρόομαι, which, in two of its three New Testament occurrences, indicates clearly a ransoming with the price explicitly mentioned. The noun λύτρωσις would accord better with the Jewish idea, but the word used of this eschatological redemption is not λύτρωσις but ἀπολύτρωσις. This difference in terminology may or may not amount to much, but it is there, and as far as it goes it signifies a different idea.

[1] J. B. Lightfoot, *in loc.*

But the great obstacle to believing that these passages refer simply to a final deliverance along purely Jewish lines lies in the fact that between the Old and the New Testaments stands the cross. The older writers spoke of a coming redemption, but without any precise idea of how God's Messiah would bring it about. The New Testament writers had in view a redemption purchased at the price of the precious blood. The words we have quoted must be interpreted in the light of the whole Christian experience of God's mighty intervention for man's salvation and not in isolation from it. As we read, for example, the glowing words of St. Paul it is impossible not to be struck by the fact that he sees everything in the light of the cross which for him has made all things new. It is difficult to think of a reason why redemption in two passages should form an exception to this. On the contrary, in the light of Paul's statements elsewhere about the cross, and about redemption, we must surely hold that here, too, he sees redemption only in the light of the cross.

It is, moreover, a definite strand in Christian teaching that salvation, although it is a present reality and not something which may, if all goes well, eventually be given to the believer, is nevertheless not capable of being realized in all its fullness here and now. Now we enjoy 'the earnest' of the Spirit, but only in the hereafter will the complete experience be possible. 'Beloved, now are we children of God, and it is not yet made manifest what we shall be' (1 Jn. 3: 2) is typical New Testament teaching, and it has its application to the concept of redemption. To speak of a future redemption is not to imply that there awaits us a redemption which has no relationship to that accomplished at Calvary, being simply a deliverance from some outward enemy in the typical Jewish style. On the contrary, the future redemption is the consummation, the outworking of the redemption which was accomplished once for all by the death of the Redeemer. While there is no reason to doubt that the three passages we have quoted point to some further tremendous action of divine power, it still remains that only by taking them out of their context in Christian life and thought can we separate them from the atonement wrought by Christ. The New Testament consistently bases our redemption on the payment of the price in the death on Calvary.[1]

[1] Orr well remarks: 'Alike in his (*i.e.* St. Paul's) thought and that of St. Peter

There remain for consideration only 1 Corinthians 1: 30 and Hebrews 11: 35. The former passage tells us that 'of him are ye in Christ Jesus, who was made unto us wisdom from God, and righteousness and sanctification, and redemption: that, according as it is written, He that glorieth, let him glory in the Lord'. There is nothing here which absolutely determines the sense of ἀπολύτρωσις, and we must take the meaning from general considerations, and from its meaning in other passages. If we are convinced from such other passages that ἀπολύτρωσις means nothing more than deliverance, then we shall naturally take the same meaning here.[1] But, if our study of its other occurrences leads us to feel that the word has a fuller meaning, we shall find nothing to forbid us applying that fuller meaning in this context. Indeed, in the concluding words, with their implication of man's total inability to do anything meritorious in the sight of God, we shall find positive encouragement for thinking of a full meaning in redemption.[2]

The final passage deals with times of persecution, and speaks of various tortures which were inflicted upon the sufferers. The fate of individuals varied, however, and the writer speaks of women receiving their dead by resurrection. But there were others who 'were tortured, not accepting the redemption', and this has been interpreted as meaning simply 'deliverance'. In the context this interpretation is not impossible, but it is certainly not demanded. There is no thought that the sufferers received an unconditional offer of freedom. On the contrary, their refusal of the redemption 'that they might obtain a better resurrection' certainly implies that there were conditions laid down, and such conditions as made it difficult or impossible to preserve their standing in the sight of God. In a word the context leads us to think that deliverance was offered to them only on condition of apostasy. They were asked to pay a

(cf. 1Pi[18.19]), the idea of a λύτρον is involved in the conception of ἀπολύτρωσις Redemption has the two aspects, which can never be separated – redemption by "ransom," i.e. from sin's guilt and condemnation; and redemption by power, from sin's bondage and other evil effects. The Apostolic gospel comprehended both' (HDCG, II, p. 469).

[1] As Johannes Weiss does, 'It is approximately = σωτηρία' (in loc.).

[2] A. Schlatter speaks of ἀπολύτρωσις here as 'the ransom (Loskauf)', and follows out the metaphor by saying 'through which the condemnation to death is taken from the congregation' (Paulus der Bote Jesu, Stuttgart, 1934, p. 97).

price, and for religious men a very heavy price, as the condition of deliverance.

The kind of situation that is meant is found in the stories of the death of Eleazar (2 Macc. 6: 18f.) and of the seven brothers (2 Macc. 7: 1f.). The case of the youngest of these is especially to the point, and may even have been in the mind of the writer to the Hebrews. After six of the brothers had died refusing to accept deliverance at the price of apostasy, the tyrant exhorted the lad's mother to urge him to save his life. She, instead, urged him to remain constant, and finished her exhortation with the words: 'Fear not this butcher, but, proving thyself worthy of thy brethren, accept thy death, that in the mercy of God I may receive thee again with thy brethren' (2 Macc. 7: 29).[1] If it was this kind of choice the writer to the Hebrews had in mind when he spoke of refusing the redemption in order to obtain a better resurrection, then his choice of the word ἀπολύτρωσις is peculiarly apt, for such a deliverance could be bought only at a considerable price. There is nothing in this passage to disturb the conclusions we have hitherto reached.

From our examination of the occurrences of ἀπολύτρωσις it would seem, then, that everything depends on the way we approach the question. If we forget the intrinsic meaning of the word, and begin with one of the more metaphorical examples, we may be able to build up quite a case for believing that in the New Testament the word has been emasculated.[2] But if we seek first to find out what the word means in Greek writers generally, and then approach the New Testament to see whether Christians used the term in the usual fashion or whether they whittled down its significance, it appears that the first Christians were no less colourful in their language than other men. In every case ἀπολύτρωσις may be allowed to have its natural meaning.

It is sometimes urged in support of the idea that redemption is a rather colourless conception for the early Christians that it has become a technical term for them, and that thereby it has taken to

---

[1] Cf. the last words of the second brother: 'Thou cursed miscreant! Thou dost despatch us from this life, but the King of the world shall raise us up, who have died for his laws, and revive us to life everlasting' (verse 9).

[2] Cf. Büchsel's comment that the etymological meaning of ἀπολύτρωσις is 'in Biblical usage "wiped out"' (TWNT, IV, p. 358). So too, C. Anderson Scott says, 'for the most part the meaning is weakened to simple "deliverance"' (Christianity According to St. Paul, Cambridge, 1932, p. 28).

itself a meaning which it holds nowhere else. Thus Büchsel says: 'The word ἀπολύτρωσις has become in early Christianity an expression with a religious content and has thus acquired a special meaning which is not found outside the same', and he goes on to speak of ἀπολύτρωσις as a 'terminus technicus'.[1] But it is difficult to see how this position can be made good. After all a technical term, to be understood, must be accepted by those to whom it is addressed as a technical term. It must be in use in the entire circle, or if used by one man only it must be explained by him, or, at the very least, used by him so frequently in the technical sense that there can be no doubt as to his meaning. What he cannot do is take a word with a known significance, give it a new meaning all his own, and use it occasionally in the new sense without explanation. But if Büchsel is right, it is precisely this of which we must accuse Paul! What sort of technical term is it about which it can be said (in Büchsel's own words) 'ἀπολύτρωσις does not belong to the leading ideas of the first Christian preaching and teaching. It is completely absent from Mk.–Mt., John, the Catholic epistles and the Apocalypse. Its occurrence in Lk. is rare. In Paul it cannot compare in importance with δικαιοσύνη or καταλλαγή'?[2] To take up such a position seems to be to avoid the issues raised by the redemption idea. There can be no doubt as to the significance of this word, and there can be no doubt that the normal significance fits the New Testament passages well.

e. ἀντιλύτρον

This word occurs but once in the New Testament (1 Tim. 2: 6) and its only known occurrences outside the Scripture are later. In meaning it does not seem to differ greatly from the simple λύτρον, but the preposition emphasizes the thought of substitution; it is a 'substitute-ransom' that is signified. Such a term well suits the Timothy passage which says of Christ, 'who gave himself a ransom for all'. The thought clearly resembles that of Mark 10: 45,[3] *i.e.* that Jesus has died in the stead of those who deserved death.[4] If the

---

[1] *TWNT*, IV, p. 358.
[2] *Loc. cit.*
[3] *Cf.* Büchsel, *op. cit.*, p. 351.
[4] *Cf.* Orr in *HDCG*, II, p. 469: ' "Ransom" has here its true and proper sense of "a price paid in exchange," and the ideas of "ransom" and expiatory sacrifice flow

thought of substitution is present in the Marcan passage there is even greater reason for holding it to be present here in view of the addition of the preposition which emphasizes substitution.

The position then appears to be that the words associated with λύτρον consistently express the ransom idea. They remind us of a conception that has disappeared, at least in large measure, from the modern scene, but which appealed to the early Christians as of value in illustrating one aspect of a vast and complex subject. Viewed from this aspect the atonement looked to them like a process of ransoming. Christians were men who had been under sentence of death (Rom. 6: 23), they had been enslaved to sin (Jn. 8: 34; Rom. 6: 17; 7: 14). Now they were ransomed from the death sentence (free 'from the law of death', Rom. 8: 2, and cf. 1 Cor. 15: 54f.; 1 Jn. 3: 14; 2 Tim. 1: 10; etc.),[1] they were free from sin (Jn. 10: 34–36; Rom. 6: 6f., 18, 22). Processes which were familiar to them from their ordinary daily life gave a vivid picture of what had happened in the spiritual realm when the Saviour gave His life for them.

G. A. Deissmann brings out the force of the redemption terminology for an ordinary man of the first century thus: 'A Christian slave of Corinth going up the path to the Acrocorinthus about Eastertide, when St. Paul's letter arrived, would see towards the north-west the snowy peak of Parnassus rising clearer and clearer before him, and everyone knew that within the circuit of that commanding summit lay the shrines at which Apollo or Serapis or Asclepius the Healer *bought slaves with a price, for freedom.* Then in the evening assembly was read the letter lately received from Ephesus, and straightway the new Healer was present in spirit with His worshippers, giving them freedom from another slavery, *redeeming with a price* the bondmen of sin and the law – and that price no pious fiction, first received by Him out of the hard-earned denarii of the slave, but paid by Himself with the re-

---

together in the unity of the thought of redemption through Christ's reconciling death.'

[1] In the Scripture men are spoken of as slaves with regard to sin (Rom. 6: 17), to men (1 Cor. 7: 23), corruption (Rom. 8: 20), the rudiments or elemental spirits of the world (Gal. 4: 3), while the Gentiles are said in addition to be slaves to their gods (Gal. 4: 8).

demption-money of His daily new self-sacrifice, rousing up *for freedom* those who languished in slavery.'[1]

There is no need to water down the language of the biblical writers, to reduce their colourful metaphors to a uniform drabness. They did not intend ransom to be taken as a full and sufficient statement of what the atonement was and did, but as far as it goes it gives a picture of one aspect of that great work. It is a metaphor which involves the payment of a price which is plainly stated in several places and understood in others to be the death of Christ. From the very nature of the imagery this involves a substitutionary idea; instead of our death there is His, instead of our slavery there is His blood. All our verbal juggling cannot remove this from the New Testament.

VI. THE USE OF ἀγοράζω

The word originally meant 'to frequent the forum' from which eventually the meaning 'to acquire, to buy in the forum' evolved, and this remains the standard meaning of the verb (though the connection with place, the forum, disappears). It is a usual word for 'to buy', and in this sense it is used in the New Testament twenty-four times with reference to such matters as a field (Mt. 13: 44) or food (Lk. 9: 13). But on six occasions Christians are said to be 'bought' and our concern is with these passages.

The LXX does not appear to help us greatly, as all the references there seem to be to simple commercial purchase of such items as food (Gn. 41: 57; 42: 5, 7, etc.), a threshing floor (1 Ch. 21: 24), etc. It translates the Hebrew roots *shbr* and *qnh* mainly, with one or two sporadic appearances of other roots which shed no light on our inquiry.

In Hellenistic Greek the usage for purchasing in general is quite common and a particular application which calls for comment is that in which the word refers to the buying of slaves,[2] a close parallel to the New Testament passages we are considering. The word does not occur as far as I know in connection with manumissions, but τιμῆς (price) which is used with this verb (1 Cor. 6:

---

[1] *Op. cit.*, p. 329.
[2] *E.g. P. Oxy.* 1149 (Grenfell and Hunt, *op. cit.*, VIII, p. 250).

20; 7: 23), occurs so frequently in this connection that Deissmann can call it 'quite a stereotyped expression'.[1]

If the conception that Christians have been bought fits in with the customs of the Greek-speaking world, it is no less at home in a Jewish setting, as the following parable from the Midrash Sifre on Numbers shows: 'It can be likened unto a king whose friend's son was taken prisoner. The king redeemed him, but expressly upon the understanding that he should become his slave, so that at any time, if he should disobey the king, the latter could say: "Thou art my slave!" As soon as they came into a country, the king said to him: "Put my sandals on for me! Take my clothes to the bath-house!" That son (of the king's friend) began to protest. And the king took out the bill of sale and said to him: "Thou art my slave!" '[2] The Midrash goes on to point out that in similar fashion Jehovah did not redeem the Israelites 'with the view that they should be (His) sons, but (His) slaves'.

When Paul then says, 'ye are not your own; for ye were bought with a price' (1 Cor. 6: 19, 20), or again, 'he that was called, being free, is Christ's slave. Ye were bought with a price; become not slaves of men' (1 Cor. 7: 22, 23), he is not drawing our attention to quite the same aspect of the Christian life as when he uses the redemption words we have considered hitherto. With them the emphasis is on the final freedom of the redeemed; here it is rather on the truth that the redeemed are paradoxically slaves, the slaves of God, for they were bought with a price. This thought is a necessary supplement to the former one. Believers are not brought by Christ into a liberty of selfish ease. Rather, since they have been bought by God at terrible cost, they have become God's slaves, to do His will.

This conception is used to bring out the heinousness of sin when the writer denounces false prophets 'who shall privily bring in destructive heresies, denying even the Master that bought them' (2 Pet. 2: 1). Having been bought by the Master, they were His and their lives should have been lived to His glory. It is only against this background that their sin can be seen in all its vileness. There is also probably a contrast between their faithlessness and the love of Christ who paid such a price in love for them.

---

[1] *Op. cit.*, p. 324, n. 2.
[2] *Midrash Sifre on Numbers*, 115 (trans. P. P. Levertoff, London, 1926), p. 110.

The divine ownership as a result of purchase comes out also in Revelation, 'thou wast slain, and didst purchase unto God with thy blood men of every tribe, and tongue, and people, and nation, and madest them to be unto our God a kingdom and priests' (Rev. 5: 9f.). Again, the one hundred and forty-four thousand are redeemed 'from the earth' and 'from among men', and are spoken of as 'the firstfruits unto God and unto the Lamb' (Rev. 14: 3, 4). In each case it is clear that those so purchased are in a special relationship to God, and it is this which determines their conduct.[1] In passing we might note that this thought is to be found in many passages which do not make explicit use of the redemption or purchase terminology, as for example when Christians are said to be 'slaves' of God or of Christ.

This way of regarding the atonement stresses the new life in Christ. It is because we are Christ's slaves that we are introduced into this way of living, and we are His slaves because we were bought by Him. There is no stress on substitution in this conception except to the extent that a price paid is an equivalent for the thing purchased. The main emphasis is on the fact that the redeemed are God's.

VII. THE USE OF ἐξαγοράζω

The preposition modifies the force of the uncompounded verb and we find ἐξαγοράζω used broadly in two senses, the one 'to redeem' (occurring for example in *Diod.* 36. 2 with reference to the redemption of a handmaid[2]) and the other 'to buy up', but this need not detain us as it is the former usage that we have in the two New Testament passages in which this verb is used of the atonement.

---

[1] The Hebrew *be*, denoting price, is probably behind the ascription in Rev. 1: 5, 'to him that loves us and loosed us from our sins ἐν τῷ αἵματι αὐτοῦ' in which case the sense of the passage is as J. Denney says, 'Christ's blood was the cost of our liberation, the ransom price which He paid' (*The Death of Christ*, London, 1951, p. 134). R. H. Charles supports this, and he quotes WH's explanation of the variant reading λούσαντι for λύσαντι as 'due to failure to understand the Hebraic use of ἐν to denote a price... and a certain misapplication of vii. 14' (*ICC, in loc.*).

[2] *Cf.* E. de W. Burton, who gives the meaning of the verb with which we are concerned as 'to redeem, to deliver at cost of some sort to the deliverer' (*ICC* on Gal. 3: 13).

The first of these reads: 'Christ redeemed us from the curse of the law, having become a curse for us' (Gal. 3: 13). Two questions in particular are raised here, namely, how the curse is considered to rest upon men, and how it is thought of as resting on Christ.

The first question is comparatively easy of solution, for κατάρας in verse 13 plainly refers back to Paul's earlier use of the same word in verse 10. There he says that those who are 'of works of law', *i.e.* those who base their hopes for eternity on living in conformity with law, are under a curse, and he proceeds to quote Deuteronomy 27: 26 (in LXX version with slight modifications which make his point a little clearer, but do not affect the sense of the LXX). The point of that passage is, as Paul says, 'Cursed is every one which continueth not in all things that are written in the book of the law to do them'. He is affirming that no man can be pleasing in the sight of God by his own efforts. Rather, the best that he can do will result only in disaster because the Scripture pronounces a curse on all who fail to keep the law in its entirety. Since no man does that, then all are under the curse.

How, then, does Paul conceive of Christ's removing the curse from men? Christ, he says, became a curse for us, and this is linked with a curse pronounced by the law on 'everyone that hangeth upon a tree'. A curse rests on everyone who does not fulfil the law; Christ died in such a way as to bear or be a curse; we who should have been accursed now go free.

The expression 'having become a curse for us' seems to rest on a Hebraic mode of thought, as in the similar expression in 2 Corinthians 5: 21 where God is said to have 'made' Christ 'sin' on our behalf. Lightfoot finds a parallel in the apocryphal passage wherein Anna says that she has become a curse, κατάρα ἐγενήθην ἐγὼ ἐνώπιον τῶν υἱῶν Ἰσραήλ (Protev. Jac. 3). This, he thinks, may be partly explained by the paucity of adjectives in Hebrew, 'but still more by the religious conception which it involves. The victim is regarded as bearing the sins of those for whom atonement is made. The curse is transferred from them to it. It becomes in a certain sense the impersonation of the sin and of the curse'.[1] He adduces

[1] *In loc. Cf.* his paraphrase: 'Christ ransomed us from this curse pronounced by the law, Himself taking our place and becoming a curse for our sakes.' V. F. Storr's comment is of importance, because although he does not accept such an idea himself he yet recognizes that Paul's language teaches it: 'Like a black thunder-

also the scapegoat, the use of ἁμαρτία (Lv. 4: 25) and ἁμάρτημα (Lv. 4: 29) to indicate the sin-offering as well as the sin, and the similar usage with the Heb. *ḥṭ'th*, as well as identical modes of thought among other nations. Identification seems to run through and through Hebrew religion and thought. Thus the prophetic action and the event which it foreshadows are in some way one (*e.g.* Je. 19; Ezk. 4), the name and the person are not separate, and so on. The identification of Christ and the curse then becomes a picturesque way of saying that He took our curse upon Himself, and we bear it no more.[1]

Much is sometimes made of Paul's omission of the words ὑπὸ θεοῦ in his citation of Deuteronomy 21: 23, and Sydney Cave, for example, can say: 'Whatever be the meaning of the words "He became a curse for us," it is clear from their context that the curse is not the curse of God but of the Law.'[2] But it is extremely doubtful

cloud the Law hung over men's heads, and they looked up to it in fear that at any minute the lightning of the divine judgment might flame out from its heart. What could be done? God took the initiative. Christ came and on the Cross bore for us the doom which sin involved ... Christ bore the penalty which in strict justice we ought to have borne ... Death was the curse of the Law, and that curse Christ took upon Himself' (*The Problem of the Cross*, London, 1924, p. 55).

[1] Similar interpretations are endorsed by many scholars of various periods, as Delitzsch: 'He so takes (the curse) upon Him, that He in person represents the executed curse' (*op. cit.*, p. 426). D. W. Simon describes the action of Christ in this verse as 'assuming the position or relationship of one who is under the curse' (*The Redemption of Man*, London, 1906, p. 267); while even H. Bushnell says: 'Probably the expression "being made a curse for us," does imply that He somehow comes under the retributive consequences of our sin' (*The Vicarious Sacrifice*, London, 1866, p. 121). J. Scott Lidgett comments: 'His being made a curse is His entering into the whole of those evil consequences which are the mark of the displeasure of the law' (*The Spiritual Principle of the Atonement*, London, 1914, p. 47). Similarly W. Manson can speak of Jesus 'taking the curse of their sin upon his spirit' (*Jesus the Messiah*, London, 1943, p. 165), and H. G. G. Herklots says: 'A curse indeed lay upon the one whom they hanged upon a tree; but it was the curse of man's sin borne freely by one in whom dwelt all the fulness of the Godhead bodily' (*A Fresh Approach to the New Testament*, London, 1950, p. 23).

[2] *The Doctrine of the Work of Christ* (London, 1937), p. 45, and *cf.* Burton: 'The curse of the law was, therefore, an actual curse in the sense that it expressed the verdict of legalism, but not in the sense that he on whom it fell was accursed of God' (*in loc.*); and again, commenting on Gal. 3: 10, 'The curse of which the verse speaks is not the curse of God, but as Paul expressly calls it in v. 13, the curse of the law.'

whether such a sharp antithesis can be justified in the case of such a writer as Paul. A study of the way he cites the Old Testament indicates plainly that he regarded its statements as of divine origin. While a modern writer might distinguish between a curse of God and a curse of the law, accepting the latter while rejecting the former, it is difficult, indeed, to imagine Paul taking such a course. Lightfoot says: 'He (*i.e.* Christ) had undergone that punishment, which under the law betokened the curse of God. So far He had become κατάρα. But He was in no literal sense κατάρατος ὑπὸ θεοῦ and St Paul instinctively omits those words which do not strictly apply, and which, if added, would have required some quali- fication.'[1] But this seems as far as we can go. Although Paul has some strong things to say about the law, they really boil down to this: the law can never bring salvation. If there is a curse of the law, then that ultimately, in Pauline thought, comes from God, and represents the divine judgment on sin.[2] It could not possibly to his way of thinking come from man, and to represent the law as a hypostatized entity is to misrepresent Paul. When, therefore, Paul speaks of Christ as having borne the curse of the law, he speaks of our removal from the legal plight into which we were fallen through our failure to keep the law of God. As Büchsel says: 'The essential meaning of this freeing from the curse of the Law is that He gives not only an actual, but a legally based freedom.'[3] The law of God has no more claim on us.

This involves a definitely substitutionary idea. If I should have been under a curse, but instead Christ was made a curse, so that now I am free, redeemed from the curse, then His action is of a substitutionary kind, as H. Wheeler Robinson recognizes when he finds in this passage 'one of the clearest indications that St. Paul conceived the death of Christ as both substitutionary and penal.'[4]

---

[1] *In loc.* H. L. Goudge does not shrink from speaking of 'the curse of God', saying, 'Thus, that Jesus had died upon the Cross had meant to St. Paul that He had died under the curse of God' (*Glorying in the Cross*, London, 1940, p. 97).

[2] *Cf.* G. S. Duncan: 'And if Paul does not say in so many words that the curse was imposed by God, he nevertheless believed, as his subsequent argument shows, that the Law which brought the curse in its train was introduced in order to further the divine purpose of redemption; and in so far as God was behind the giving of the Law, so far also was He a party to the curse' (*MNTC, Galatians*, p. 101).

[3] *TWNT*, I, pp. 126f.

[4] *Op. cit.*, p. 231. He also says, 'Christ *actually* bears a part of the universal curse

There may be more to it than substitution, but we cannot dismiss the substitutionary aspect without doing violence to the words.[1]

The second passage using this verb tells us that God sent forth His Son, 'born under the law, that he might redeem them which were under the law' (Gal. 4: 4). This indicates that the redemption spoken of was the whole purpose of the sending forth of the Son, and that the manner of the redemption included the Son coming Himself 'under the law'.

It is worthy of note, especially in view of the fact that the un-compounded verb ἀγοράζω seems to include the thought of the state into which the Christian is bought as an integral part of the conception of being bought by Christ, that on both occasions when ἐξαγοράζω is used there is added an expression indicative of the resultant state of the believer. From Galatians 3: 14 we learn that the redemption was 'that upon the Gentiles might come the blessing of Abraham in Christ Jesus; that we might receive the promise of the Spirit through faith', while Galatians 4: 5 tells us that we were redeemed 'that we might receive the adoption of sons (υἱοθεσίαν)'. It is wrong to separate the legal status, gained by the complete discharge of the claims the law had upon us, from the resultant life. The only redemption Paul knew was one in which the redeemed had received the gift of the Holy Spirit, and in which they lived as those who had been adopted into the family of God.

VIII. THE USE OF περιποιοῦμαι

There is one New Testament passage where this verb is used with reference to the atonement, namely Paul's speech to the elders at Miletus during the course of which he said to them: 'Take heed unto yourselves, and to all the flock, in the which the Holy Ghost hath made you bishops, to feed the church of God, which he

---

(in its consequences) and thus enables God graciously to remove it altogether' (*ibid.*). H. A. A. Kennedy with reference to this verse speaks of 'that redemption in which Christ became accursed . . . for our sakes' and goes on to refer to Christ as 'the Redeemer and Substitute of His people' (*The Expositor*, Eighth Series, X, p. 405). Similarly F. V. Filson puts Gal. 3: 13 at the head of a list of passages which show that 'From one aspect this death is thought of as a substitutionary suffering by Christ of the penalty due to men for their sins' (*St. Paul's Conception of Recompense*, Leipzig, 1931, p. 15).

[1] See additional note on this passage on pp. 62ff.

purchased with his own blood' (Acts 20: 28). The verb gives a thought allied to those of the passages we have considered in the earlier sections, but with an emphasis of its own.

περιποιέω really means, 'to make to remain over', hence 'to keep safe, to preserve'. In the middle it signifies, 'to keep or save for oneself', and thus, 'to acquire, gain possession of'. In the LXX it has the meaning 'to save, preserve alive, let live' more often than any other (cf. Lk. 17: 33), but there are a number of passages where 'to acquire' is clearly required (e.g. Gn. 31: 18; 36: 6; Je. 48: 36; etc.). K. Lake and H. J. Cadbury translate the verb in Paul's speech by 'rescued',[1] taking the former meaning, but this seems to be a mis-understanding of the passage. The thought that man needs only 'saving alive' is not a New Testament idea. On the contrary, Scripture consistently thinks of him as completely lost until he is brought out of his sinful condition by the action of Christ. Some such sense as 'purchased' (Moffatt) or 'obtained' (RSV) is demanded by the context. The sense then is that the Church was acquired by God at a price, namely διὰ τοῦ αἵματος τοῦ ἰδίου. Whether we adopt the suggestion of Lake and Cadbury and translate, 'by the blood of his Own', or retain with RV, 'with his own blood', the reference is clearly to the action of Christ in dying for man's redemption.

This verb seems to have about it a flavour of personal possession. Thus deacons may acquire a 'good standing' for themselves as their very own possession (1 Tim. 3: 13), while the corresponding noun περιποίησις seems to give much the same idea in 1 Peter 2: 9. This passage quotes Exodus 19: 5, and περιποίησις represents the Hebrew ṣegullâh, 'possession, property'. If it is legitimate to assume that this idea is present in Acts 20: 28, we get the thought of the Church as being acquired by God to be a possession peculiarly His own, His treasured possession.[2]

Whether we can say that this is to be deduced from the passage or not, it is yet clear that it bears witness to the thought of the Church being acquired at the price of the blood of Christ. Once again we have the thought of the price paid; the shedding of blood takes place instead of the loss of the sinners.

---

[1] *The Beginnings of Christianity*, ed. F. J. Foakes Jackson and K. Lake, IV (London, 1933), p. 261.

[2] *Cf.* the conjunction of the terms ἀπολύτρωσις and περιποίησις in Eph. 1: 14.

IX. CONCLUSION

From the foregoing examination then we see that where the redemption category is employed there are three aspects of the process of atonement especially in view.

a. The state of sin out of which man is to be redeemed

This is likened to a slavery, a captivity which man cannot himself break, so that redemption represents the intervention of an outside Person who pays the price which man cannot pay. The Bible sometimes speaks of this slavery in set terms (e.g. Jn. 8: 34; Rom. 7: 14), but more often assumes it. It is a basic tenet of biblical theology that man is completely unable to grapple with the position created by the fact of his sin, and the redemption passages must be interpreted in this context.

b. The price which is paid

This has been too much neglected by many exegetes who have tended to see in the redemption words no more than another way of saying 'deliverance'. But our study has shown that this is erroneous, for both inside and outside the New Testament the payment of price is a necessary component of the redemption idea. When the New Testament speaks of redemption, then, unless our linguistics are at fault, it means that Christ has paid the price of our redemption. To the extent that the price paid must be adequate for the purchase in question this indicates an equivalence, a substitution.

Sometimes, where redemption is conjoined with some other expression like 'redeemed from the curse', the thought goes further. In the case of this particular expression it does seem as though Paul is saying that Christ bore what we should have borne, that He is our Substitute. We have noted that many scholars subscribe to this interpretation, and their agreement is made the more impressive in that many who feel that this is a mistaken way of viewing the atonement yet recognize that this is the thought of the apostle. He found it necessary to bring in many categories to interpret what was done on Calvary, and it would seem impossible to escape the conclusion that substitution was one of them. The place and nature of the substitution may require careful definition, but that substitution is part of St. Paul's thought seems beyond reasonable doubt. And in view of such passages as the ransom saying of Mark 10: 45 we must hold that this substitutionary idea is not peculiar to St. Paul.

c. The resultant state of the believer

Holders of substitutionary ideas have sometimes been criticized as being indifferent to moral values, but this criticism cannot be urged against the biblical writers. In the Scripture we see the price paid, the curse borne, in order that those who are redeemed should be brought into the liberty of the sons of God, a liberty which may paradoxically be called slavery to God. The whole point of this redemption is that sin no longer has dominion; the redeemed are saved to do the will of their Master.

ADDITIONAL NOTE ON ὑπέρ IN GALATIANS 3:13

It seems likely that the preposition here conveys a substitutionary thought. It is true that the word usually signifies 'on behalf of', but this is not all the story. It can convey the idea of substitution. For example, in Euripides' *Alcestis*, where the plot centres on Alcestis' death as a substitute for her husband, the prepositions ἀντί, ὑπέρ and πρό are used practically interchangeably. ὑπέρ in such passages clearly means substitution. Again, the very existence of verbs like ὑπερθνήσκω and ὑπεραποθνήσκω shows that the preposition can denote substitution.

Just as this is true in the classics, so is it the case in the more popular language of the papyri. Thus E. Mayser says, 'Tolerably widespread is the use of ὑπέρ = instead of, in the place of, in substitution for someone, exclusively of persons, yet generally in such a way that it is not a simple, external, mechanical substitution, but there predominates the basic meaning, "in the name, in the interest, for the benefit of someone". Yet there also occur cases in which ὑπέρ stands completely in the sense of ἀντί.'[1] We see this, for

[1] *Grammatik der Griechischen Papyri aus der Ptolemäerzeit*, II, 2 (Berlin and Leipzig, 1934), p. 460.

example, in papyri wherein the scribe says that he is writing ὑπέρ someone else. However we choose to translate it, this cannot mean anything other than that he writes in the place of that other.

The New Testament use is such that Karl Barth can link ἀντί, ὑπέρ and περί as pointing to Christ's 'activity as our Representative and Substitute'. He says, 'They cannot be understood if – quite apart from the particular view of the atonement made in Him which dominates these passages – we do not see that in general these prepositions speak of a place which ought to be ours, that we ought to have taken this place, that we have been taken from it, that it is occupied by another, that this other acts in this place as only He can, in our cause and interest, that we cannot add to anything that He does there because the place where we might do so is occupied by Him, that anything further which might happen can result only from what is done by Him in our place and in our cause.'[1] This argument is apart from any one particular passage. Barth sees the force of the prepositions throughout the New Testament.

C. Hodge has a worth-while comment on 2 Corinthians 5: 14. He points out that ὑπέρ 'may have the general sense, *for the benefit of, in behalf of,* or the stricter sense, *in the place of*'. He further says, 'In all those passages in which one person is said to die for another . . . or in which the reference is to a sacrifice, the idea of substitution is clearly expressed. The argument does not rest on the force of the preposition, but on the nature of the case. The only way in which the death of the victim benefited the offerer, was by substitution. When, therefore, Christ is said to die as a sacrifice for us, the meaning is, he died in our stead. His death is taken in the place of ours so as to save us from death.'[2]

In the New Testament the substitutionary sense seems necessary in some passages. This is surely the case with the reference to those 'that are baptized ὑπέρ the dead' (1 Cor. 15: 29), however we translate the word. It is not otherwise with the reference to Onesimus' serving ὑπέρ σοῦ (Phm. 13; Goodspeed translates 'in your place'), or to the activity of the preachers who preach 'in Christ's stead' (2 Cor. 5: 20, AV). In view of the resemblance between 1

[1] *Church Dogmatics,* IV, *The Doctrine of Reconciliation,* Part One (Edinburgh, 1956), p. 230.
[2] *In loc.*

Timothy 2 : 6 and Mark 10 : 45 the ὑπέρ of the former must be very nearly identical in meaning with the ἀντί of the latter. Other passages where ὑπέρ is most naturally understood of substitution include John 10 : 11; 11 : 50; Romans 16 : 4.

From all this it seems plain enough that there is no reason why a substitutionary meaning may not be given to ὑπέρ in some at least of the passages where Christ is said to have died ὑπὲρ ἡμῶν. In the passage under discussion such an interpretation has strong claims.[1]

[1] A. T. Robertson includes this passage among those where 'ὑπέρ has the resultant notion of "instead", and only violence to the context can get rid of it' (*A Grammar of the Greek New Testament in the light of Historical Research*, New York, 1919, p. 631). He denies a rigid distinction between ἀντί and ὑπέρ. The idea of substitution, he thinks, 'depends on the nature of the action, not on ἀντί or ὑπέρ' (*op. cit.*, p. 630).

CHAPTER II

COVENANT

I. INTRODUCTION

COVENANT IS ONE of the leading conceptions of the Old Testament, and thus it is not surprising that the early Christians sought to interpret the new faith, in part at least, along the lines of this conception, all the more so since some of the prophets had envisaged a day when there would be a new covenant to replace the old. Of the thirty-three occurrences of the word διαθήκη in the New Testament sixteen refer to the new covenant and a seventeenth speaks of 'two covenants' contrasting the old with the new (Gal. 4: 24). Of the sixteen, six refer to 'the blood of the covenant' (or similar phrase) (Mt. 26: 28; Mk. 14: 24; Lk. 22: 20; 1 Cor. 11: 25; Heb. 9: 20; 10: 29), thus reminding us of the relevance of this subject to the discussion of the atonement, two refer to the new covenant as a 'better covenant' (Heb. 7: 22; 8: 6), four bring out the specific note of the fulfilment of prophecy in the new covenant (Rom. 11: 27; Heb. 8: 8, 10; 10: 16), one is a baffling reference to 'the ark of his covenant' in heaven (Rev. 11: 19), while the remaining three are more general (2 Cor. 3: 6; Heb. 9: 15; 12: 24).

It is of interest to notice that the covenant at Sinai seems to be alluded to eight times (including the 'two covenants' reference mentioned above) (2 Cor. 3: 14; Gal. 4: 24; Heb. 8: 9, 9; 9: 4, 4, 15, 20), and is probably included also in the plural 'covenants' in two other places (Rom. 9: 4; Eph. 2: 12); while the covenant with Abraham is spoken of four times (Lk. 1: 72; Acts 3: 25; 7: 8; Gal. 3: 17), and there are three allusions to 'covenants of men' (Gal. 3: 15; Heb. 9: 16, 17).

The writer to the Hebrews seems to have been specially interested in this aspect of things Christian, for he uses the term διαθήκη seventeen times as against sixteen for the whole of the rest of the New Testament (which sixteen include four references to the words of institution of the Lord's Supper), and he refers freely both to the Sinai covenant and to the new covenant although, interestingly enough, he does not mention the covenant with Abraham.

The verb διατίθεμαι is found half a dozen times in the New Testament, but as it occurs in connection with the noun διαθήκη in every case except Lk. 22:29 (where it means 'appoint' rather than 'make a covenant'), there seems to be no necessity for giving it separate consideration.[1]

At the outset we notice that a big difficulty is posed by the fact that in the LXX the word διαθήκη is used regularly to translate the Hebrew *berîth*, which is generally understood to signify 'covenant', whereas in non-biblical Greek διαθήκη almost invariably denotes a last will and testament. It is not easy to see which meaning should be understood as the New Testament meaning and there have not been wanting advocates of varying points of view. Thus G. A. Deissmann can say: 'no one in the Mediterranean world in the first century A.D. would have thought of finding in the word διαθήκη the idea of "covenant." St. Paul would not, and in fact did not.'[2] That this to him is a point of consequence appears from the statement which follows a little later: 'This one point concerns more than the merely superficial question whether we are to write "New Testament" or "New Covenant" on the title-page of the sacred volume; it becomes ultimately the great question of all religious history: a religion of grace, or a religion of works?'[3] On the other hand J. B. Lightfoot says: 'in the LXX it (*i.e.* διαθήκη) is as universally used of a covenant. . . . Nor in the New Testament is it ever found in any other sense, with one exception. Even in this exceptional case, Heb. ix. 15–17, the sacred writer starts from the sense of a "covenant," and glides into that of a "testament" .'[4] B. F. Westcott goes further, and argues that even this passage is to be understood of a covenant.[5] It thus appears that the most widely divergent views of the meaning of the word in the New Testament are held, and held strongly.

---

[1] It is, however, possible that the verb gives us a clue to the way in which the noun διαθήκη is to be understood in the Supper narrative. If this is so, the meaning of the verb here, 'appoint', would indicate a meaning like 'authoritative disposition' in the noun. For a discussion of this point see Candlish, *ET*, IV, p. 21.

[2] *Light from the Ancient East* (London, 1927), p. 337.

[3] *Op. cit.*, pp. 337f.

[4] *Saint Paul's Epistle to the Galatians* (London, 1902), p. 141.

[5] *The Epistle to the Hebrews* (London, 1892), pp. 300f.

II. THE IDEA OF COVENANT IN THE OLD TESTAMENT

a. The derivation of berîth

Our first task will be to examine the idea in the Hebrew term *berîth*. The derivation of the term is still rather obscure despite the optimistic statement of Henry S. Gehman: 'The etymology of the word in Hebrew is apparently quite clear: Akkadian *barū*, "to bind," "to fetter" and *birītu* "fettering," "fetters" suggest that Hebrew *berith* contains the sense of a binding or a bond.'[1] This is no doubt an attractive derivation, but it is not the only one in the field. Thus E. Kautsch says: 'After the thoroughgoing investigations of J. P. Valeton and R. Kraetzschmar, there can be no doubt that *bĕrîth* belongs primarily to the secular vocabulary, and means "cutting in pieces," namely, of one or more sacrificial victims ...'[2] Again, the form of the noun *berîth* is that of a feminine from the root *bry* which directs our attention to *bārâh*, a verb which actually occurs in the sense 'to eat', as does the noun *biryâh* 'food', and also the form *bārûth*. The derivation suggested by this root would make the sacred meal the important feature of covenant. There are other suggested derivations, but the whole subject is so obscure that not much can be made of it. Accordingly we must turn to the usage of the term for our information as to its significance.

b. The meaning of kārath berîth

The word occurs frequently in conjunction with the verb *kārath* in the expression 'to cut a covenant'. This would fit in with the derivation suggested by Kautsch, but it raises the question why a verb from another root is used, so not much weight can be laid on this. The thought of cutting is associated by H. Clay Trumbull with the rite of blood brotherhood among primitive men and he says, 'the primitive rite of blood-covenanting was by cutting into the flesh in order to the tasting of the blood'.[3] On this view to speak of 'cutting a covenant' was to use an archaic form of expression referring to a rite which had in earlier days been universally

[1] *Theology Today*, VII (1950), p. 27.
[2] *HDB*, V, p. 630b.
[3] *The Blood Covenant* (New York, 1885), p. 264.

practised at the making of a covenant, but which no longer was in use. This is possible; but on the whole it seems better to associate the expression with the cutting of sacrificial victims in pieces (Gn. 15: 9f.; Je. 34: 18). This seems to have been an integral part of the making of a covenant, even though it is not often mentioned in the Old Testament. As G. Quell puts it: 'To cut something with the result that a *berîth* appears, is concisely expressed by the formula "cut a *berîth*".'[1]

That the cutting of an animal in pieces was necessary to the making of a covenant seems clear enough (from Je. 34: 18 it would seem that also the passing of the partners between the pieces was required). Why this should be thought necessary is not so certain, for the ceremony is never explained. We are left to draw our conclusion from the fact that such an action did take place. Some writers talk of the action symbolizing the entrance of the partners into the mystical life of the victim.[2] But this is very difficult to accept. One wonders what meaning this would have to men like Laban or Abimelech (or for that matter to most men of today), and why this should solemnly seal the covenant. It is not sufficient to say that they thereby enter a common life, for the point is that, even if they do, it does not appear why being together in the life of an animal should consummate such a far-reaching compact as the *berîth* evidently was.

The cutting of the animals in pieces seems more intelligible as an invocation of the same fate upon the partners should they be guilty of breaking their compact. A. B. Davidson supports this point of view when he says that a necessary element in the making of the covenant was 'the imprecation or curse . . . invoked by each party on himself in case of failure, this curse being, at the same time, symbolically expressed by passing between the pieces of the slaughtered animal'.[3] E. Kautsch views the matter in a similar light,[4] and both men proceed to note that the Hebrew form of oath 'God do so to me and more also' probably connects with such ceremonies. This is probably supported also by the threat of Yahweh, 'And the men who transgressed my covenant . . . I will

---

[1] *TWNT*, II, p. 108.
[2] *Cf.* W. Robertson Smith quoted on p. 75 below.
[3] *HDB*, I, p. 510.
[4] *HDB*, V, p. 630.

make like the calf which they cut in two' (Je. 34: 18, RSV; the Hebrew is not completely clear).

This is explicit in the account of a Babylonian covenant, which mentions the sacrificing of a goat, and proceeds: ' "This head is not the head of the goat . . . it is the head of Mati'-ilu. . . . If Mati'-ilu (breaks) this oath, as the head of this goat is cut off . . . so shall the head of Mati'-ilu be cut off. . . . This loin is not the loin of the goat, it is the loin of Mati'-ilu," and so on.'[1] We could hardly have a more explicit statement as to the purpose of the cutting up of the animal, and this must be regarded as of importance, coming as it does from a land which had contact with the Hebrews at many points over centuries. Other rites could be cited from various lands to emphasize the same point, as is done for example by Trumbull.[2] The natural interpretation of the rite as described in the Bible, coupled with explicit interpretations of similar rites in non-Hebrew spheres, seems to show beyond reasonable doubt what the significance of the division of the animals is.

c. Actual covenants

Before beginning our discussion of actual covenants recorded in the Old Testament we should notice that in recent years light has been shed on the concept of covenant by the discovery that there was a widely used pattern in covenants in the ancient Near East.[3] The records that survive are mostly Hittite, but there seems no reasonable doubt but that the form was widespread. Especially valuable are the suzerainty treaties imposed by the great king on his vassals, for in these the terms are dictated by the superior authority. The inferior simply accepts them and agrees to perform the

[1] Cited from A. Jeremias, *The Old Testament in the Light of the Ancient East*, II (London, 1911), p. 49. The cutting of animals in pieces at the making of a covenant is widely attested.

[2] *Op. cit.*, pp. 44f., 53f.

[3] See the important article 'Covenant Forms in Israelite Tradition', by George E. Mendenhall, *The Biblical Archaeologist*, XVII (Sept. 1954), pp. 50–76. Mendenhall also has references to covenant in his article, 'Ancient Oriental and Biblical Law', *The Biblical Archaeologist*, XVII (May 1954), pp. 26–46. *Cf.* also R. de Vaux, *Ancient Israel Its Life and Institutions* (London, 1961), pp. 147–50; J. Bright, *A History of Israel* (London, 1960), pp. 134ff. There is a convenient summary of the evidence in J. A. Thompson's Tyndale Lecture, *The Ancient Near Eastern Treaties and the Old Testament* (London, 1964).

obligations imposed upon him. The resemblances to Yahweh's covenant with Israel are plain. The Hittite records show that the form was widespread and they also shed light on some aspects of the covenant. But there is an important difference in that, in the covenant in the Bible, Yahweh is not simply a witness and guarantor of the covenant as are the gods in the Hittite documents. He is a party to it. He actually enters into covenant relation with His people.

When we examine the references to covenant in the Old Testament then we are dealing with a widely used and well understood concept. It was used of agreements between men as well as of those between God and men. It will perhaps be more logical to begin with the former.

(i) *Covenants between men.* Most covenants of this kind are between representative persons, such as heads of clans, or rulers, there being, in the opinion of Quell,[1] only one covenant between purely private people in the whole Old Testament, namely that between David and Jonathan. This was a compact arising out of the mutual love of the pair, and its terms are not given, though David could say: 'Therefore deal kindly with thy servant; for thou hast brought thy servant into a covenant of the Lord with thee' (1 Sa. 20: 8). Evidently it gave each of them at least a general claim on the other. Of the manner of making this covenant we know little; the only information being that, when the covenant was made, Jonathan gave David presents of his apparel and weapons (1 Sa. 18: 4), a procedure which seems to have been widely observed in similar rites in other lands. That a religious element was involved, however, is evident from David's statement, quoted above, that it was 'a covenant of the Lord'.

This religious element is a prominent feature in other covenants, for example in that between Jacob and Laban (Gn. 31: 44f.). Jacob is explicitly said to have sworn an oath, 'by the Fear of his father Isaac'. There is also a sacrifice and a meal shared by the covenant brothers, evidently the sacrificial meal accompanying the peace offering. In this case the terms of the agreement are recorded, as is the fact that a heap of stones was set up as a witness

---

[1] *Op. cit.,* p. 112.

to the covenant. The witness in the covenant between Abraham and Abimelech is a group of seven ewe lambs (Gn. 21: 30, and *cf.* the reference to the tamarisk tree in verse 33). In the narrative of the making of this covenant the oath figures largely, though there is no mention of sacrifice or sacrificial meal. The omission, however, need not surprise us for, in fact, there are few if any places where we have the full ritual of covenant-making described. It is of interest in this connection that there is no mention of the dividing of the animals in pieces between the time of Abraham and that of Jeremiah, though we must hold that it continued throughout all those centuries. The men of antiquity knew quite well how a covenant was 'cut', and they did not write down unnecessary details.

Putting together the hints that we obtain from the various occasions on which human covenants are referred to we find that the following were important points in the making of a covenant: (1) The drawing up of terms of agreement. (2) The oath to keep the agreement. (3) The ritual slaughter of animals, including both the animal or animals to be divided and those to be offered up in sacrifice and consumed in the meal of fellowship. In addition there may have been other practices considered essential, such as the provision of witnesses in a heap of stones, a group of lambs, or a tree, each of which we have seen serving such a purpose.

(*ii*) *Covenants between God and men.* The use of the term 'covenant' to describe the relationship existing between God and men goes back to the story of the flood in which we read the word of the Lord to Noah: 'But I will establish my covenant with thee; and thou shalt come into the ark, thou, and thy sons, and thy wife, and thy sons' wives with thee' (Gn. 6: 18). Not only is the initiative with God, the whole 'covenant' is His. Noah is not represented as doing anything in the matter, either by way of seeking a covenant, or of performing covenant obligations. Nothing is said here, or in subsequent passages which refer to this covenant, of the method whereby the covenant was established. There is, therefore, little we can say about the procedure of covenant-making adopted. But we may notice that the covenant was made with Noah as a representative man rather than as an individual (Gn. 9: 9, 10), that the terms were stated in the form of a promise (Gn. 9: 11), and that there was a witness or sign that the covenant would be kept, namely the rainbow (Gn. 9: 12–16). An important point is that the covenant was one of grace. The Lord freely bestowed His blessing on His servant. He did not grant it as a return for services rendered.

The next covenant referred to is that with Abraham. In response to the patriarch's query as to how he should know that he would subsequently (in his seed) inherit the land of Canaan, Yahweh commanded him to take certain animals and divide them in two, after which, 'when the sun was going down, a deep sleep fell upon Abram; and, lo, an horror of great darkness fell upon him' (Gn. 15: 12). The divine promise was then renewed to him, and 'when the sun went down, and it was dark, behold a smoking furnace, and a flaming torch that passed between these pieces' (Gn. 15: 17). There are some interesting features of this process of covenant-making, the outstanding one being that again we see Yahweh as taking on Himself all the obligations. He alone symbolically passes through the pieces, probably because Abram was not taking upon himself any obligation. The patriarch was the recipient of a boon, or a promise, rather than a partner contracting to perform certain duties. Again, as in the case of the covenant with Noah, the covenant is with a representative man (Abraham's 'seed' are expressly mentioned), and the terms of the covenant are given in the form of the promise. On this occasion, however, there is nothing we can regard as a witness unless the smoking furnace and the flaming torch can be said to fulfil this requirement, which seems unlikely. Rather they symbolize the divine presence.

Later on we do find certain duties assigned to Abraham and linked to the covenant. 'This is my covenant, which ye shall keep, between me and you and thy seed after thee; every male among you shall be circumcised . . . and my covenant shall be in your flesh for an everlasting covenant. And the uncircumcised male who is not circumcised in the flesh of his foreskin, that soul shall be cut off from his people; he hath broken my covenant' (Gn. 17: 10–14). However, this hardly interferes with the principles of grace and of the divine initiative, for on the one hand circumcision is rather a sign, a seal, a badge of the covenant than a contractual obligation, and on the other it is a duty imposed by Yahweh and not assented to in free negotiation by Abraham. The absolute sovereignty of the divine will is apparent throughout the whole of this covenant.

From many such references in the Bible to covenants with Yahweh we must notice a third. In Exodus 24 we read of a covenant made, not with representative individuals, but with the whole people of Israel. Again the initiative is with Yahweh who called Moses and others to Him to the mount, Moses being assigned a position of privilege (see verse 2). Before they went, Moses told the people 'all the words of the Lord, and all the judgements', to which they responded: 'All the words which the Lord hath spoken will we do'. On a specially made altar burnt and peace offerings were offered up, and this not by priests, but by 'young men of the children of Israel'. The blood was collected and divided into two portions, one of which Moses proceeded to throw on the altar. Then he read from 'the book of the covenant', and again the people agreed to obey the Lord: 'All that the Lord hath spoken will we do, and be obedient'. After this undertaking Moses took the other half of the blood and threw it over the people, saying, 'Behold the blood of the covenant which the Lord hath made with you concerning all these words'. The ceremonies concluded with Moses and other representatives of the people going up into the mount where 'they beheld God, and did eat and drink', evidently an allusion to the sacrificial meal.

This ceremony was of the utmost importance for the later history of the people, for from this time the nation stood in a peculiar relationship to Yahweh, a relationship shared by no other.

Attention must be called to three features of this new arrangement, namely the participation of the people, the 'blood of the covenant', and the obligations resting upon the people. Concerning the first of these, it is important that this covenant was not made through some representative as had been the case with the earlier covenants, but with the principals themselves.[1] This point is emphasized when Moses says: 'The Lord our God made a covenant with us in Horeb. The Lord made not this covenant with our fathers, but with us, even us, who are all of us here alive this day' (Dt. 5: 2f.). On this verse H. H. Rowley comments: 'It is there implied that the Covenant with the patriarchs was not valid for the generation of the Exodus, but that only the Covenant into

---

[1] The narrative seems to stress the activity of the people, *e.g.* Ex. 24: 3, 7.

which they themselves entered could have validity and meaning for them. And by the same token their Covenant could not have automatic validity for the generations that followed.'[1] While we make no attempt to minimize the extent to which the fathers can claim the promise for their children, yet, in the last resort, there seems to be a principle of personal participation involved. No-one can live on the spiritual capital of his ancestors. As R. B. Y. Scott puts it, 'The religious group which only carries on the momentum in belief and practice of an age which has passed away, and has not made its own the covenant of the fathers, will find that the covenant is no longer valid, and the living God has passed on to seek a new people for Himself.'[2]

The blood is seen by some as the means of entering into blood brotherhood, a point of view which is well expressed by Trumbull: 'And now observe the celebration of the symbolic rite of the blood-covenant between the Lord and the Lord's people, with the substitute blood accepted on both sides, and with the covenant record agreed upon.'[3] Or again: 'When united Israel was to be inducted into the privileges of this covenant of blood-friendship at Mount Sinai, half of the blood came from the one party, and half of the blood came from the other party, to the sacred compact; both portions being supplied from a common and a mutually accepted symbolic substitute'.[4] According to this view the blood is essentially the same as that used in the making of blood brothers. But whereas, originally at any rate, in the establishment of this bond the brothers shared each other's blood, on Mt. Sinai a mutually acceptable substitute provided the blood for both parties (such a provision of a substitute is not unknown in other cases). This view stresses the closeness of the kinship between the two parties to the agreement, but it falls down at critical points. Thus there is nothing in the narrative to indicate that the blood was thought of by either party as a substitute for his or the other's blood; the idea has to be imported into the story. Again, it gives rise to the concept of an equality of the partners which does not appear to be justified. M. Buber's summary of the position is better

---

[1] *The Biblical Doctrine of Election* (London, 1950), p. 48.
[2] *The Relevance of the Prophets*, p. 210 (cited in Rowley, *op. cit.*, p. 139).
[3] *Op. cit.*, p. 239.
[4] *Op. cit.*, p. 240.

when he says: 'YHVH unites himself with Israel into a political, theo-political unity, "within which the two partners bear the relations towards each other of a primitive wandering community and its *melek*".'[1] Throughout the chapter there is no question but that Yahweh is directing all things. It is His will that the covenant should come about, and it is established on His terms. There is no idea that the people are acting independently.

W. Robertson Smith regards the use of the blood as essentially the same as the division of the animal into two parts: 'we see from Ex. xxiv. 8, "this is the blood of the covenant which Jehovah hath cut with you," that the dividing of the sacrifice and the application of the blood to both parties go together. The sacrifice presumably was divided into two parts (as in Ex. *l.c.* the blood is divided into two parts), when both parties joined in eating it; and when it ceased to be eaten, the parties stood between the pieces, as a symbol that they were taken within the mystical life of the victim.'[2] But this does not seem to fit into the picture very accurately. There is no reason to think that the sprinkling of the blood which we see here was characteristic of Hebrew covenants; in point of fact it is mentioned nowhere else in such a connection. Again, there appears no obvious reason for equating a sprinkling of blood with a division of corpses; the two actions seem distinct. And as we have already seen, the thought of being taken 'within the mystical life of the victim' is not one which we can readily credit to the typical Hebrew of antiquity. Moreover, in regarding this incident as a typical example of the blood covenant, Robertson Smith seems to miss the fact that this is a unique rite. To quote Buber again, this rite, 'though reminiscent of the Semitic custom of Blood Covenant, is nevertheless unique in character'.[3]

Others regard the rite as, in a measure at least, piacular. Thus Davidson cites Robertson Smith for the view that both parties have communion in the same blood, and comments: 'This may be; but in the main the sacrifice, being an offering to J", was piacular, atoning for and consecrating the people on their entering upon their new relation to J".'[4] This would be supported by the general

[1] *Moses* (Oxford, 1946), p. 115.
[2] *The Religion of the Semites* (London, 1927), p. 481.
[3] *Op. cit.*, p. 115.
[4] *HDB*, I, p. 512. See also L. Pullan, *The Atonement* (London, 1907), p. 110.

piacular character of the sacrifices.[1] It has Jewish support, for G. Dalman remarks: 'Onkelos and Targum Yer. I remark also that the second half of the blood was poured out towards the altar, "in order to propitiate the people". They think thus of a propitiation of the blood.'[2] There is inherent probability in the suggestion, too, for men in their sinful state would not be suitable candidates for membership in a covenant with God, and the removal of sin by an atoning offering seems a logical step. The difficulty in the way of a full acceptance of this point of view is the treatment of the blood. Part is sprinkled on the people, which is very difficult to explain in an atoning sacrifice.

The clue to this sprinkling seems to be given in the only two other incidents in the Old Testament wherein men are sprinkled with blood, namely, the consecration of Aaron and his sons to the priesthood, and the purification of a man healed of leprosy. In the former case we have an explicit statement of the effect of the sprinkling: 'And Moses took of the anointing oil, and of the blood which was upon the altar, and sprinkled it upon Aaron, upon his garments, and upon his sons, and upon his sons' garments with him; and sanctified (wayeqaddēsh) Aaron' (Lv. 8: 30). Here the blood is a part of a consecratory rite and the effect is to 'sanctify' those sprinkled. In the case of the healed leper we read that the priest is to take hyssop, etc., and he 'shall dip them . . . in the blood of the bird that was killed over the running water: and he shall sprinkle upon him that is to be cleansed from the leprosy seven times, and shall pronounce him clean' (Lv. 14: 6, 7). The sprinkling of the blood clearly had a purifying effect, for it was immediately followed by the priest's pronouncing the man clean. It is true that the cleansing here is from uncleanness rather than from sin, but in view of the close connection between the two in the Old Testament the use of the blood for such a purpose must be held to be significant.

From these two incidents, then, we get the principle that the sprinkling of blood is likely to signify the entry into a new state marked by cleansing from previous defilement and consecration to a holy purpose. Both these thoughts are probably present in Exodus 24. We should regard the blood as both piacular and

---

[1] Cf. J. Pedersen: 'Everything in any way connected with sacrifice acquired an expiatory power' (Israel, III–IV, London, 1947, p. 364).

[2] Jesus-Jeshua (London, 1929), p. 166.

consecratory. It cleanses the people from their sin and it sanctifies them for their part in the covenant. As F. J. A. Hort puts it: 'the primary purpose of the sprinkling was to consecrate the covenant between Jehovah and the people, the invisible bond between them being indicated by the community of origin of the blood on the altar, as representing Jehovah, and the blood on the persons of the people... the sprinkling of the people with this blood was regarded as a consecration and symbolic purification of themselves.'[1] W. Eichrodt notices these two passages concerning Aaron and the healed leper, but, strangely enough, dismisses them since there the blood sprinkling 'has quite another meaning, namely that of consecration and cleansing'.[2] It is curious that he does not notice that it is precisely these ideas of consecration and purification that make the passages relevant.

In passing we note that Psalm 50: 5 witnesses to the close connection between sacrifice and covenant with its 'Gather my saints together unto me; those that have made a covenant with me by sacrifice (*zābhaḥ*)', whether we are to understand this as referring to such an event as the establishing of the Sinai covenant,[3] or whether it signifies that every sacrifice could be regarded as confirming the covenant.[4] The 'blood of the covenant' is also referred to in Zechariah 9: 11, but the passage gives no indication as to the manner in which the blood was regarded and the significance that was attached to it.[5]

The people's promise of obedience next claims our attention, for, as we have seen, there is nothing like it in the earlier covenants.[6]

[1] *The First Epistle of St. Peter* (London, 1898), p. 23.

[2] *Theologie des Alten Testaments*, I (Leipzig, 1933), p. 73, n.8 (English translation, I, p. 157, n.2).

[3] Mishnah *San.* 10: 3 refers this verse to the wilderness generation on the authority of R. Eliezer.

[4] *Cf.* F. W. Dillistone: 'from now onwards (*i.e.* the making of the covenant in Ex. 24) in the life of Israel the covenant and the sacrifice are indissolubly bound together. Only through sacrifice could the covenant be renewed and deepened; every offering of sacrifice was, at least ideally, a witness to the original covenant' (*The Significance of the Cross*, London, 1946, p. 59).

[5] Among the Rabbis this verse was sometimes at least understood as referring to the Passover, and Dalman adopts this interpretation (*op. cit.*, pp. 166f.). But Midrash Rabbah Leviticus 6: 5 (Soncino trans., p. 85) understands it of the blood of the Sinai covenant.

[6] Bright stresses this: 'It will be noted that this form is markedly different from

The covenants made with Noah and with Abraham were covenants of sheer grace, with the promise of divine blessing upon the patriarchs and their seed but with no mention of corresponding obligations as resting upon them. At first sight it appears that in the Sinai covenant the principle of grace has been abandoned, and that it is now necessary for the people to earn the divine blessing. Merit, not grace, seems to be the criterion, all the more so since the passage speaks of the people's obedience to Yahweh, but says nothing of any promise on His part. This last point, however, cannot be held to be significant, for in other places we have made explicit what is implicit in Exodus 24, namely, that Yahweh will be Israel's God, and that He will give them His blessing (e.g. Ex. 19: 5, 6; Lv. 26: 9–12).

The place of the duties which devolved upon the people in the covenant should not be misunderstood. They do not represent concessions freely made, and which might have been withheld. It is clear that this whole process of covenant-making is regarded as taking place under divine direction. It is not a compact freely negotiated by independent parties with the people determining just how far they intend to go. Their part is unconditional surrender to whatever might be the will of God, their absolute Ruler.[1] As G. Vos puts it: 'Notwithstanding all the emphasis placed upon the two-sidedness of the Berith, Scripture always so represents it that the Berith in its origin and in the determination of its content is not two-sided but based on the sovereignty of God.'[2] There is nothing in Exodus 24 to indicate that the reason for God's choice of the people was their agreement to carry out His commands. Rather God in His free grace chose Israel to be His people, and having

─────────────────

that of the patriarchal covenant, however much features in the latter may have prepared the way for it. There covenant rests on unconditional promises for the future, in which the believer was obligated only to trust. Here, on the contrary, covenant is based on gracious acts already performed, and issues in heavy obligation' (op. cit., p. 135).

[1] Dt. 33: 5 might be translated, 'He became king in Jeshurun, when the heads of the people were gathered', in which case the covenant is being regarded as the people's acceptance of the kingship of Yahweh. Cf. S. R. Driver: 'Jehovah assumed, as it were, the sovereignty over Israel, when the tribes with their leaders (v. 21) were gathered about Him, on the "day of the assembly" (9[10] 10[4] 18[16]) at Sinai' (ICC, Deuteronomy, p. 394); see also the Rabbinic views in section III below.

[2] PTR, XI, 1913, p. 516.

chosen them, imposed upon them His commands. But the choice
is first and fundamental and in it we detect the element of grace.[1]

The difference between this process and the conclusion of a
bargain is readily seen if we compare a passage such as the one in
which Jacob says: 'If God will be with me, and will keep me in this
way that I go, and will give me bread to eat, and raiment to put on,
so that I come again to my father's house in peace, then shall the
Lord be my God . . . and of all that thou shalt give me I will surely
give the tenth unto thee' (Gn. 28: 20f.). Here we do find a process
involving bargaining as its essence. Jacob's attitude is, 'If Thou wilt
do these things for me, then will I do those things for Thee'. But
the thought of Exodus 24 is different. There Yahweh has already
been gracious to the people in delivering them from the power of
Egypt: 'ye have seen what I did unto the Egyptians, and how I
bare you on eagles' wings, and brought you unto myself' (Ex. 19:
4). The action of the nation is that of those who respond: 'Thou,
Lord, hast been gracious unto us. We acknowledge Thy goodness,
and we pledge ourselves to be Thine, and to do Thy will.'

A. M. Stibbs has an interesting passage in which he compares
the making of this covenant to a wedding: 'In the wilderness at
Sinai the Lord confronted Israel with His purpose for them and
with His demand for their co-operating response. He said, "I . .
brought you unto myself. Now therefore, if ye will obey my voice
indeed, and keep my covenant, then ye shall be a peculiar treasure
unto me above all people; . . . and ye shall be unto me a kingdom
of priests and an holy nation." And all the people answered
together and said, "All that the Lord hath spoken we will do".
This scene of covenant making was very similar to a wedding
ceremony, and the more so when later the covenant between God
and Israel was visibly sealed in sprinkled blood; just as in the
wedding ceremony the ring given and received is "a token and
pledge of the vow and covenant betwixt them made." Like the

---

[1] *Cf.* N. H. Snaith's comment on the covenant conception as we see it in Amos:
'Amos holds that God chose Israel in a special and unique way. "You only have I
known of all the families of the earth", iii. 2. With this choice there are certain
specific ethical demands . . . the choice comes first and the demand second. The
prophet speaks first of the Divine Election of Israel, and, secondly, says: "Therefore
I will visit upon you all your iniquities" ' (*The Distinctive Ideas of the Old Testament*,
London, 1944, p. 108).

bride answering, the Israelites solemnly said, "We will".[1] The covenant does not represent the people's endeavour to earn God's favour by performing meritorious works. Rather it is the people's acceptance of God's proffered grace, with all that that implies.

The implications are not unimportant. The Israelites were now the people of God, and they must henceforth live up to the obligations inherent in this proud title. The position is well summed up in the words: 'Keep silence, and hearken, O Israel; this day thou art become the people of the Lord thy God. Thou shalt therefore obey the voice of the Lord thy God, and do his commandments and his statutes' (Dt. 27: 9f.). They were not chosen merely in order that they might be the recipients of His blessings, but that they might do Him service. They were to be 'a kingdom of priests, and an holy nation' (Ex. 19: 6). Spiritual privilege and spiritual obligation are inextricably interwoven, so that those who refuse to obey the commandments of God place themselves outside the sphere of His blessing.

There is nothing automatic about the covenant, nothing which binds Yahweh to bless the nation henceforth irrespective of what they might do. It has often been pointed out that, among the other nations nearby, the concept of a physical kinship of the god with his people meant that the god rose or fell with his people, so that, in the last resort, he was bound to save them if he was to save himself, and that the concept of covenant delivered Israel from this error. If He chose them, He could also reject them; and the making of the keeping of His commandments integral to the covenant meant that He was insisting upon a certain way of life if the people were to receive His blessing. The keeping of the commandments of the Lord is thus not thought of as a peripheral thing (cf. Je. 11:

[1] *The Church Universal and Local* (London, 1948), pp. 18f. *Cf.* W. A. L. Elmslie: 'The Hebrew People's Pledge at Horeb declared *their* confession that this God had never ceased to be faithful to His covenant with their fathers, and to the forgetful children of those fathers had manifested His abiding mercy. The Pledge was *their* acknowledgement of God's continuing grace – to which *they* now responded, vowing themselves to be faithful, willing now to trust in His guidance and henceforth to walk in His ways' (*How Came Our Faith*, Cambridge, 1948, p. 210). So also H. H. Rowley: 'To effect that deliverance they (*i.e.* the Israelites) did not have to do anything, save trust their leader and follow him. After the deliverance was achieved they committed themselves to God in the obedience of the covenant' (*The Enduring Gospel*, ed. R. G. Smith, London, 1950, p. 28).

1ff.), but as of the very warp and woof of the whole covenant conception. Failure to walk in God's ways means the complete overthrow of the covenant, so that it may fittingly be described in terms of works, though this must not be understood in such a way as to overlook the element of grace which we have seen is so marked a feature.

Thus we reach something of a paradoxical conclusion. The covenant is of the free grace of God, but nevertheless, having chosen the people, God imposed upon them ethical demands, and these can be spoken of as the people's part in the covenant without thereby derogating from the freeness of God's grace. Over and over again we have the choice of the people explicitly said to be due to the love of God and not to anything in them, thus placing an emphasis on the unconditioned love of God. But without any apparent sense of contradiction we have passages in which it is said that the people have broken the convenant and thereby have drawn down upon them the wrath and the punishment of God. Both aspects are important for an understanding of Old Testament teaching.

It is not too much to say that the covenant conception came to dominate Israel's thought about her relationship to God. She was Yahweh's people; He was Israel's God. And through the centuries the people have clung almost fiercely to this central teaching. Not that in Old Testament times this gave grounds for appealing to Yahweh for assistance in time of need. Very occasionally the covenant relationship was pleaded, but this is exceptional, probably because of the very obvious fact that Israel had not kept her part of the covenant obligation. Accordingly she could not very well insist that the covenant gave her grounds for a claim. Rather the tendency is for her to plead the nature of God Himself, and thus we come upon pleas that He will help of His great mercy, for His Name's sake, etc.

But if Israel had no reason to feel that she had done her part in the covenant, she was sure, or at least her most spiritual minds were sure, that Yahweh had certainly kept His. 'If we are faithless, he abideth faithful; for he cannot deny himself' (2 Tim. 2: 13) is a New Testament saying; but it represents an Old Testament thought. Thus Snaith speaks of 'God's sure love for Israel', and goes on:

'Because of this sure, unswerving love, the Covenant can never be finally and completely broken. It takes two to make a covenant, and it also takes two to break it. Israel may have rejected God, but God has not rejected Israel.'[1] He is a covenant-keeping God, and His unwavering love to faithless Israel is one of the great Old Testament conceptions.

This thought of a God who is faithful to the covenant, even though the people are not, should not, however, be so interpreted as to give the impression that Yahweh is indifferent to Israel's moral state. It is characteristic of the Old Testament point of view that Yahweh never for one moment relaxes His high ethical demands. This for ever stamps the religion of Israel as something quite different from other religions of antiquity. It is not that Israel alone has the thought of covenant, for there is evidence that in other religions this conception found its place. We get a hint of this in the mention of Baal-berith (Jdg. 8: 33, *etc.*), and Quell cites a number of religions in antiquity where the covenant idea finds a place.[2] But what gave the religion of Israel its peculiar quality is the fact that the ethical demands which Yahweh made upon His people were both stringent and rigidly insisted upon. There is no hint of toning them down when it became apparent that the people would not be able to measure up to them.

It is true that the Old Testament envisages a replacement of the covenant by a new covenant, a thought which receives its classical expression in Jeremiah 31: 31ff. (and is also found in other parts of the Old Testament). It is here said that the new covenant will be 'not according to the covenant that I made with their fathers in the day that I took them by the hand to bring them out of the land of Egypt; which my covenant they brake, although I was an husband unto them, saith the Lord'. In its ethical demands, however, the new covenant was to be no less stringent than the old, for 'I will put my law in their inward parts, and in their heart will I write it'. As the sequel was to show, the new covenant would in some ways be radically new, but in its ethical content there is no whittling down of the divine requirements. Throughout the Old Testament the covenant idea is one which demands from the people a strenuous morality.

[1] *Op. cit.*, p. 112.
[2] *Op. cit.*, p. 121.

It remains to notice that there are some Scriptures which look forward to an association of a Person with the covenant, which must be the new covenant. Thus we read concerning the Servant, 'I the Lord . . . will . . . give thee for a covenant of the people, for a light of the Gentiles' (Is. 42: 6; the thought is repeated in 49: 8). T. K. Cheyne says: ' "A covenant of the people" means "the medium or mediator of a covenant between Jehovah and Israel." As the Servant is called "a light" in person, so he can be called "a covenant" in person.'[1] So also there is a reference to the 'messenger of the covenant' (Mal. 3: 1). There is also a passage in Zechariah where in place of 'As for thee also, because of the blood of thy covenant I have sent forth thy prisoners out of the pit', etc., the LXX reads, καὶ σὺ ἐν αἵματι διαθήκης σοῦ ἐξαπέστειλας δεσμίους σοῦ ἐκ λάκκου κτλ, 'and thou, in the blood of thy covenant, didst send forth thy prisoners out of the pit', etc. The thought thus vaguely intimated in the Old Testament was to have a very full place in the New Testament reinterpretation of the covenant idea.

III. THE IDEA OF COVENANT IN JUDAISM

The Rabbinic references to covenant are such as to shed light on the Old and New Testament conceptions at a number of points. We deal with the more important of these in order.

a. The blood of the covenant

The Rabbis sometimes take up the Old Testament thought that the blood of the covenant is piacular. Strack-Billerbeck bring this out by drawing attention to the Targums: 'In order to emphasize the atoning power of the blood Targ. Onk. does not translate "Moses sprinkled the blood on the people", but "Moses took the blood and sprinkled it on the altar to make atonement for the people, and he said: See, this is blood of the covenant which Jahve has concluded with you on the basis of all these words". Targ. Jerus. I is almost word for word the same.'[2] This is, of course, later than the Christian era, but it is interesting as showing the accepted line of Jewish interpretation. However, in other places this thought does not seem to be prominent, and, for example, it is not mentioned

---

[1] *The Prophecies of Isaiah*, I (London, 1884), p. 266.
[2] I, p. 991.

in a long section in Leviticus Rabbah dealing with the blood at Sinai. An interesting interpretation given in this passage suggests that the significance of the blood is a symbolical calling down of punishment if the covenant were broken: 'R. Isaac said: When a king administers an oath to his legions, he does so with a sword, the implication being: Whoever transgresses these conditions, let the sword pass over his neck. Similarly (at Sinai), *Moses took half of the blood*.'[1]

The blood of the covenant was sometimes interpreted in a quite different fashion, namely of the blood of circumcision whereby men were admitted into the covenant. Thus the Talmud reports a discussion between the rival schools of Shammai and Hillel: 'Beth Shammai maintain: One must cause a few drops of the covenant blood to flow from him (*i.e.* that is born circumcised), while Beth Hillel rule: It is unnecessary. R. Simeon b. Eleazar said: Beth Shammai and Beth Hillel did not differ concerning him who is born circumcised that you must cause a few drops of the covenant blood to flow from him.'[2] Of this manner of interpretation Strack-Billerbeck say: 'One commonly understands by "blood of the covenant" *dm bryth*, the circumcision blood.'[3] Not far removed in thought from this is the habit of referring to the 'covenant of circumcision'[4] and perhaps also of designating the Israelites as 'sons of the covenant',[5] although this latter usage may well be explained otherwise.

b. The new covenant

In the New Testament the new covenant prophesied by Jeremiah is enthusiastically applied to the new conditions brought about by the death of Christ, but there seems little interest in the conception

---

[1] *Lv. R.* 6: 5 (Soncino trans., p. 83).

[2] *Shab.* 135 a (Soncino trans., p. 679).

[3] I, p. 991. They quote only one passage, but indicate that it is repeated in a number of parallel passages.

[4] Although it should be noted that this designation is often referred directly to the covenant with Abraham, without mention being made of the Sinai covenant and its blood (see SB, II, p. 671). The expression is found once in the New Testament, namely Acts 7: 8.

[5] *Cf.* Acts 3: 25 on which SB say: ' "Sons of the covenant" (= υἱοὶ τῆς διαθήκης) means, when used absolutely, "sons of the covenant of circumcision" and designates Israelites in opposition to non-Israelites' (II, p. 627).

in the Rabbinic writings. One passage in the Midrash on the Song of Solomon says that the Israelites learnt from God and did not forget, then they learnt through Moses and forgot, so they came to Moses and said ' "Our master, Moses, would that God might be revealed to us a second time! Would that He would kiss us WITH THE KISSES OF HIS LIPS! Would that He would fix the knowledge of the Torah in our hearts as it was!" He replied to them: "This cannot be now, but it will be in the days to come," as it says, *I will put My law in their inward parts and in their heart will I write it*'.[1] This passage evidently refers the new covenant to the messianic days in the indefinite future, which seems to be the usual way in which the Rabbis understood the fulfilment of this prophecy. There is an interesting passage which affirms the permanency of the covenant with Abraham, and is evidently a polemic against the Christian view.[2] While this passage is late, it nevertheless indicates the typical Rabbinic interest in the first covenant, and unreadiness to pay much attention to the new covenant.

c. The covenant with Abraham

The passage just referred to stresses the permanence of the agreement between God and Abraham, and contains God's assurance that He will see to it that this covenant is not superseded. This continuance of the Abrahamic covenant is seen also in most of the passages referring to the 'sons of the covenant' referred to above, as also to the 'covenant of circumcision'. The unique place given to Abraham comes out in many places, for example: 'Five possessions did the Holy One, blessed is He, take to Himself in His world; and these are they: the Law is one possession, and the heaven and earth are one possession, Abraham is one possession, Israel is one possession, and the Temple is one possession.'[3] There can be no doubt that, just as the Christians thought of Abraham as showing the right method of approach to God, and of the covenant with Abraham as being of continuing force, so also did the Rabbis, although they interpreted both these points differently.

---

[1] *Cant. R.* i. 2, 4 (Soncino trans., p. 26).
[2] *Cant. R.* i. 14.
[3] *Ab.* vi. 10 and *cf. Ab.* v. 2, 3.

d. The concept of testament

In Old Testament times there does not seem to have been in existence among the Hebrews the practice of disposing of one's goods by means of a last will and testament, the matter being controlled by the laws of inheritance. But in later times the practice of testamentary disposition came into vogue, and the Greek word διαθήκη was transliterated into Hebrew to give the word for a will, diyyatēqê. Strack-Billerbeck have a long note explaining the Jewish law on the matter and referring to the Rabbinic sources for examples of its use, and it is sufficient simply to refer to their note.[1] It may be of significance in interpreting the difficult New Testament passages, in which there is doubt as to whether the sense of διαθήκη is 'covenant' or 'testament', that the Jews were at this time quite familiar with the concept of testament, and, indeed, had taken over the very Greek term used in the New Testament to describe it.

IV. διαθήκη IN THE SEPTUAGINT

When the LXX translators came to the Hebrew berîth they almost invariably rendered it by διαθήκη (277 times in all), and conversely berîth is the only word which διαθήκη translates with any frequency.[2] Clearly the LXX translators regarded διαθήκη as nearly equivalent in meaning to berîth.

An interesting point about this choice of rendering is that the translators passed over συνθήκη, the usual word for covenant in the sense of 'compact', or 'agreement'. The word they chose instead is one which indicates a unilateral arrangement, and thus is well adapted to indicating an arrangement where one partner is dominant and dictates the terms, as in all the cases where God is one of the partners. It is true that the word is used also in the LXX of covenants between men. The translators were perhaps influenced by the fact that the important covenants in the Old

[1] III, pp. 545ff.
[2] The other words represented are 'aḥawâh 'brotherhood', dābhār 'word', kāthûb 'that which is written', tôrâh 'law', each of which occurs once in this connection, and 'ēdhûth 'testimony', which is used four times. In addition διατίθεμαι διαθήκην once translates shlm (Hiph.).

Testament are all covenants which involve God. Having found a word which renders *berîth* in its typical Old Testament context, they were more or less bound to use it also for those other arrangements which were less typical.

Etymologically διαθήκη carries the notion of a laying-down, a disposition, the preposition with its indication of duality directing attention to a laying down with reference to another. Eventually it came to signify a disposition of property by testament, but before this stage was reached it is quite possible that it meant rather an authoritative disposition in general without regard to whether it took place in a testament or not. If this is so the usage of the LXX is explained, for as we have seen, this is the sort of idea which the Hebrew *berîth* conveys. In so far, then, as the underlying Hebrew gives us the meaning of διαθήκη, it indicates that the word signified a transaction between two parties in which one party held the decisive position, laid down the conditions of the agreement, and in general imposed his will, the sole function of the other party being to accept or reject what was determined by the dominant partner.

This sense is supported by the words in the LXX which occur in parallel with διαθήκη, such as νόμος, πρόσταγμα, ἐντολαί, δικαιώματα, κρίματα.[1] None of these terms accords with a compact or mutual agreement, but all rather indicate an ordering that is completely unilateral.

V. διαθήκη IN NON-BIBLICAL GREEK

Outside the LXX and the New Testament διαθήκη seems almost invariably to have meant a will or testament. Moulton and Milligan say, 'In papyri and inscrr. the word means *testament, will*, with absolute unanimity, and such frequency that illustration is superfluous.' By contrast συνθήκη 'is to the last the word for *compact*, just as διαθήκη is always and only the word for *will*'.[2]

W. D. Ferguson has examined legal terms in the Macedonian inscriptions, and of διαθήκη he concludes:

'1. That it is testamentary rather than contractual. It is not a

---

[1] See *TWNT*, II, p. 129.
[2] MM *sub* διαθήκη.

mutual compact to which both parties give assent, mutually contracting to do certain things, but the act of one person giving charges to another, or bestowing property on another, or both of these . . .

'2. The thing enjoined in the διαθήκη is apparently always to be executed after the decease of the testator . . .

'3. When property is bequeathed it may be accompanied by a charge to be fulfilled, and in such a way that the commission must be accepted in order to obtain the property . . .

'4. The usage of the term διαθήκη in the inscriptions is similar to its usage in the Old and the New Testaments in that the initiative is always taken by one person. . . . The one making the διαθήκη always assumes the right to command, and to withold his bequest if the conditions attached to it are not fulfilled'.[1]

F. O. Norton has conducted a thorough examination of the use of the word from the earliest times until well into the classical period and, in general, he supports the position reached by the writers cited above. But, while recognizing that διαθήκη generally signifies a testament, he recognizes that this is not its essential meaning. He understands it to refer 'to the arrangements or dispositions a person makes with reference to his property in view of death. This specific connotation is probably not necessary, but the context of the passages in which the word is found indicates that it has such reference in these instances. It is quite probable that, if we had more instances of its use, we should find it employed with reference to other things than distribution of property in view of death.'[2] This is in accordance with what we would expect from the etymology of the word, but Norton is able to cite only two passages in support of his contention that the word sometimes means a compact (*Isae.* 6: 27; Aristoph. *Av.* 440), and of these two, the former certainly refers to a testament, Norton's argument being that it is a compact as well as a will, and that the compact aspect is primary. However, this cannot be regarded as an impressive example, and we are left with but one use of διαθήκη in the classical writings to denote a compact, namely Aristophanes *Av.* 440. Certainly there can be no doubt about this one (despite W. M.

[1] *The Legal Terms Common to the Macedonian Inscriptions and the New Testament* (Chicago, 1913), p. 46.
[2] *A Lexicographical and Historical Study of* ΔΙΑΘΗΚΗ (Chicago, 1908), p. 30.

Ramsay's hesitation),[1] partly because such a sense is demanded by the immediate context, ('Not I, by Apollo, unless they make a covenant [διάθωνται διαθήκην] with me such as that monkey, the sword-maker, made [διέθετο] with his wife, not to bite me', etc.),[2] and partly because a little later the same agreement is referred to as τὰς σπονδάς.

However, when full allowance is made for the importance of this reference as an aid to the understanding of the history of διαθήκη, it must be admitted that it is well before New Testament times (*The Birds* is dated in the fifth century BC), and that this one clear example from such early days does little to invalidate the fact that, in the first century AD, and indeed for centuries before that, the uniform significance of διαθήκη (apart from the noteworthy exception of the LXX) was of a will, a testament.

We should point out, however, that the testament in mind was not exactly the same as a will in our sense of the term. In Greece in early days property seems to have descended automatically to the deceased's children, who performed certain duties in connection with the burial of the deceased, and afterwards indulged in a species of ancestor-cult. This came to be regarded as of very great importance and, accordingly, it was a serious matter for a man to die without male issue. Consequently, when a man had no heir, it was usual for him to adopt a son who would after his death receive his property and see that the appropriate rites were carried out. As Ramsay says: 'the Diatheke was primarily an arrangement for the devolution of religious duties and rights, and not merely a bequeathing of money and property.'[3]

The adoption of a son was a decisive step, and was, in fact, irrevocable. If, after an adoption, a natural son was born, the adopted son could not be disowned, but must share the inheritance with the natural son. In this particular matter the adopted son was on a better footing than the natural son, for the latter could be put away. Indeed Ramsay calls attention to a passage where a son who had been put away by his father, then restored to favour, and then

---

[1] He says: 'The only exception quoted . . . is not very clear. It contains a joke founded on some unknown popular story of the ape and the woman (or his wife)' (*The Expositor*, Fifth Series, VIII, p. 325n.).

[2] Cited from Norton, *op. cit.*, p. 37.

[3] *Op. cit.*, p. 324.

disowned again, makes his plea that this second putting away is illegal, for he now has the status of an adopted son.[1]

Ramsay makes this an argument for the irrevocability of the διαθήκη. But while this may have been the case in early days, the evidence adduced by Norton seems to show that, at later times, there was the necessary machinery to enable a testator who had changed his mind to give effect to his new desires.[2] (All early wills centred on an adoption, but in later times it was possible to bequeath one's property even where no adoption was in question.)

Thus the evidence from profane Greek indicates the possibility that διαθήκη at an early stage in its history denoted any authoritative disposition, but that, whether this were so or not, in later times the word became confined (as far as the extant sources show) to a last will and testament. The use in the LXX is exceptional, for there the postulated earlier use seems to be the usual, probably the only, one.

VI. διαθήκη IN THE NEW TESTAMENT

It is not easy to determine which of the two meanings of διαθήκη is to be understood in the New Testament. Some passages use the word with reference to Old Testament covenants and in such contexts it must be understood in the same sense as in the LXX. On the other hand, there are some passages where the meaning 'will' or 'testament' seems indicated, and the final determination of the word's significance in doubtful places is accordingly very difficult.

a. διαθήκαι of men

It will be convenient to begin our discussion with a consideration of the passages which appeal to the practice among men, and reason from this to the divine διαθήκη. We begin with some words of St. Paul: 'Brethren, I speak after the manner of men: Though it be but a man's διαθήκη, yet when it hath been confirmed, no one maketh it void, or addeth thereto . . . Now this I say: A διαθήκη confirmed beforehand by God, the law, which came four hundred and thirty years after, doth not disannul, so as to make the promise of none effect. For if the inheritance is of the law, it is no more of

[1] Op. cit., p. 302.
[2] Op. cit., pp. 63ff.

promise: but God hath granted it to Abraham by promise' (Gal. 3: 15f.). Here there are some considerations which point strongly in the direction of testament as the meaning of διαθήκη. The speaking 'after the manner of men' would naturally indicate that the term is to be understood in the normal way, and as we have seen, the extant literature is clear that that would be in the sense of a will. The unchangeability referred to might be understood (as by Ramsay) as a reference to a will involving an adoption, which would be an irrevocable provision. Further, the reference to 'inheritance' in verse 18 would accord well with a testamentary action.

While this looks a formidable body of evidence, it is not irrefutable. The speaking 'after the manner of men' may mean no more than that Paul, having derived his illustrations hitherto from Scripture, now proposes to use one from the affairs of men. Again, even a Greek will involving adoption could be modified later, as we have seen. Then, too, E. de W. Burton shows that the κληρονομία of verse 18 need not necessarily refer to inheritance in the strict sense of the word, the term being sometimes used to signify 'possession'.[1]

A strong argument that the word means 'covenant' is to be discerned in the fact that the reference to the transaction with Abraham in verse 17 is a reference to the Hebrew *berîth*. Thus διαθήκη here must be understood in the same sense as in the LXX. But the whole force of the argument demands that the διαθήκη of verse 15 be of the same type as that in verse 17. This seems a decisive consideration. Accordingly we adopt the view that διαθήκη here denotes 'covenant', rather than 'testament', while admitting the strength of the arguments for the opposite view. But we do so understanding the passage as does G. S. Duncan who says: 'it matters little which of the two renderings we adopt, for from a truly spiritual standpoint a "covenant" in which God takes part is as essentially a one-sided proposal as a "will" is.'[2] Further, it seems probable that, while covenant is the essential meaning of διαθήκη, here the apostle is making a play on the other meaning of the word. The death of Christ is not far from his thought.

The other passage which falls to be considered under this heading

[1] *ICC, Galatians*, pp. 185f., 503.
[2] *MNTC, Galatians*, p. 106.

reads: 'For where a διαθήκη is, there must of necessity be the death of him that made it. For a διαθήκη is of force where there hath been death: for doth it ever avail while he that made it liveth?' (Heb. 9: 16f.). Here, again, it would seem on a first reading as though the meaning is 'testament', and many commentators have adopted this rendering. To this it is objected that διαθήκη seems to be used in the sense 'covenant' both earlier and later than the verses cited. It should thus mean 'covenant' there also. Otherwise we should have to suppose that the writer began by thinking of the word as meaning 'covenant', changed over to 'testament', and then back again to 'covenant', which seems unlikely.

Again, Westcott draws attention to the use of the verb φέρεσθαι: 'It is not said that he who makes the covenant "must die," but that his death must be "brought forward," "presented," "introduced upon the scene," "set in evidence," so to speak.'[1] It is of consequence that we do not simply have it said that the maker of a διαθήκη must die, but Westcott does not seem to give sufficient heed to the value of the various alternatives which he notes. For example F. Delitzsch argues strongly that the verb conveys the thought that a will is valid only when the death has become 'a fact of common notoriety'. 'Before that is known and established, the testament has no legal force.'[2] The use of φέρεσθαι is curious, but it cannot be said to tell strongly against the meaning 'testament'. The same is true of the ἐπὶ νεκροῖς of verse 17. It is not what we would have expected, but in view of the second half of the verse with its reference to ὁ διαθέμενος, it cannot be held to be proof that anything other than the death of the testator is in the writer's mind. A. Carr remarks, 'it cannot be affirmed that a will is only of force on the death of the testator. A will properly drawn up and attested is valid or of force during the testator's lifetime.'[3] This, however, must be unhesitatingly dismissed, for it is surely obvious that a will remains completely inoperative until the testator's death. That is to say, a Roman will does, though we have already seen that a Greek will may become operative immediately. But there is agreement among the commentators that the *auctor ad Hebraeos* moves in the sphere of Roman law rather than Greek. It is the Roman will that

[1] *Op. cit.*, p. 265.
[2] *Commentary on the Epistle to the Hebrews*, II (Edinburgh, 1887), p. 107.
[3] *The Expositor*, Seventh Series, VII, p. 350.

is in view here if there is any reference to a will, and the Roman will was inoperative until the testator's death.

Carr's further suggestion that βεβαία and ἰσχύει point rather to a covenant than to a will[1] must similarly be dismissed. They apply quite well to a will, and the question must be decided on other grounds.

The crucial point seems to be the necessity for the death of the διαθέμενος if the διαθήκη is to become effectual. Westcott explains this as indicating the necessity of the death of the animal victim in covenant sacrifice, which symbolized the death of the party to the covenant so that he no longer had life or power in the matter. 'The unchangeableness of a covenant is seen in the fact that he who has made it has deprived himself of all further power of movement in this respect: while the ratification by death is still incomplete, while the victim, the representative of him who makes it, still lives, that is, while he who makes it still possesses the full power of action and freedom to change, the covenant is not of force.'[2] It may be noticed in passing that, to get this meaning out of the text, Westcott has had to abandon his idea that the meaning of blood is life rather than death, so that 'the blood of the covenant' would mean something different altogether from other sorts of blood. A stronger objection is that Westcott has put all the emphasis on the unchangeability of the covenant, the death being the indication that now the διαθέμενος has no further liberty in this matter. But the unalterable nature of the agreement is not what the writer to the Hebrews is emphasizing, but its coming into effect. Paul in Galatians was saying 'No-one annuls or adds to a διαθήκη', but that is not the thought of this passage, which is, rather, 'A διαθήκη is of force, is effectual, comes into operation, only when a man dies'. On the impossibility of fitting this naturally into the framework of covenant Westcott's interpretation breaks down, and we are left to conclude that the passage here must be held to have its natural meaning. The death of Jesus was a necessary thing, for it is only when a διαθέμενος dies that his διαθήκη comes into force.[3]

This discussion will have shown the extraordinary difficulty of

---

[1] *Ibid.*

[2] *Loc. cit.*

[3] James Moffatt speaks of the author as 'playing effectively upon the double sense of the term', and goes on to point out that this illustration of a will 'has its

giving a completely satisfying interpretation of διαθήκη in New Testament times. It may well be that the best interpretation is that which sees in διαθήκη essentially the thought of an authoritative disposition. This could naturally pass over into the thought of a testament, or to the sort of covenant we see in the Old Testament with all the emphasis on what God does, and not upon a two-sided compact, with God and man coming to some sort of agreement. The main point to be kept in mind is that the word denotes a divine action, with man the recipient of blessing; and we have no grounds for thinking that, in New Testament times, the word would have been understood of a compact with two partners agreeing that each should assume certain liabilities and obligations.[1]

b. The old διαθήκη

The passage which we have just considered (Heb. 9: 16f.) shows clearly that in at least one instance the New Testament uses διαθήκη in the sense of will or testament. Some think that this meaning is to be discerned also in the background of Galatians 3: 15f. The question may be asked, therefore, whether this use is not (as might be expected from secular usage) the dominant one in the New Testament. An examination, however, of the fourteen New Testament instances of the use of διαθήκη with reference to Old Testament covenants will show indisputably that the usage of the LXX is to be found in the New Testament also.

This use is undeniable in passages such as Hebrews 8: 9, where διαθήκη occurs twice in a quotation from Jeremiah 31. It is true that Jeremiah is speaking of the new covenant rather than the old, but the point is that διαθήκη is used at this point in Hebrews in exactly the LXX manner as the equivalent of the Hebrew berîth. The same must be said of the references to the ark of the covenant and to the tables of the covenant (Heb. 9: 4), which clearly point to the Old Testament and cannot be understood of a will.

The Sinai covenant seems to be in mind throughout Hebrews

defects, but only when it is pressed beyond what the writer means to imply' (ICC, Hebrews, p. 127).

[1] It denotes an action which in its main essentials is unilateral although that is not to deny that there is an aspect in which the people have to accept or reject the διαθήκη. But the word places the stress not so much on this acceptance or rejection as on the authoritative laying down of the provisions of the covenant.

9: 15ff., and this becomes obvious when we reach verse 19 with its reference to Moses sprinkling the people with blood. Then in verse 20 'the blood of the covenant which God commanded' is a clear allusion to Exodus 24: 8,[1] and it shows that the scene on Sinai was present to the minds of early Christians when they heard the words 'the blood of the covenant'. The change of verb from the covenant which God made (διέθετο) of Exodus 24: 8 to the covenant which God commanded (ἐνετείλατο) here should be noted, as it fits in with the general idea of διαθήκη as signifying an authoritative disposition. However we translate the word, and whatever we regard as the primary idea expressed by the Greek term, it is clear that what is denoted is an action in which the sovereignty of God has full sway.

A reference to the covenant at Sinai is to be found also in the phrases 'the first covenant' (Heb. 9: 15; cf. 8: 7) and 'the old covenant' (2 Cor. 3: 14). In the latter place Paul speaks of 'the reading of the old covenant', by which unusual turn of phrase he seems to be referring to the records of the old covenant. By this would be meant not only the account of the covenant making, whereby the nation was brought into covenant-relationship with God, but also all the documents which depend on this relationship and expound it. The adjective which he uses is παλαιός, a word which is often used 'of things not merely old, but worn by use'[2] and which gives the expression a flavour different from that which would result were ἀρχαῖος used. Both these phrases, it may be noted, have an implicit reference to the new covenant, and the same is true of Galatians 4: 24, where the Sinai covenant is contrasted with the new covenant.

In this last passage the plural διαθήκαι is used, and this is the case also in Romans 9: 4 and Ephesians 2: 12, where Old Testament covenants in general are indicated with no close definition, except that both passages regard them as peculiarly the possession of the Jew.[3] The Ephesians verse speaks of 'covenants of promise' (the

---

[1] This may be of importance in understanding other New Testament passages which speak of blood with reference to the new covenant.

[2] G. Abbott-Smith, *A Manual Greek Lexicon of the New Testament* (Edinburgh, 1944), *sub* παλαιός.

[3] The Rabbinic writings sometimes refer to covenants in the plural. See SB, III, p. 262.

verse in Romans also includes a reference to the promises) which directs attention to the characteristic emphasis on the divine side which is typical of the arrangements between God and men which the LXX calls διαθῆκαι.

Thus the references in the New Testament to the old covenant establish the use of διαθήκη to indicate 'covenant' rather than 'will', but only in such a manner as to indicate the sort of covenant which is dominated by one partner. This is supported by the reference to the covenant which God made with Abraham, which is explicitly mentioned four times in the New Testament (Lk. 1: 72; Acts 3: 25; 7: 8; Gal. 3: 17). On each occasion it is quite clear that the incident referred to is one which, in the Old Testament, is designated *berîth*. But again we notice that the emphasis is on what God has done, for the first passage mentioned equates the διαθήκη with 'the oath which he sware unto Abraham'; the second gives the essence of the διαθήκη as God's promise to Abraham, 'in thy seed shall all the families of the earth be blessed'; the third says God 'gave' the covenant; and the fourth is a critical part of Paul's argument that God's way with man is the way of promise, of free grace, and not a way of law-works of any sort.

Under all the circumstances it is, perhaps, unfortunate that διαθήκη is rendered in English by 'covenant', for this word carries with it associations of compact, of agreement, of conditions mutually determined, which are not to be found in the arrangements under consideration. But it is not easy to suggest a better translation, and in any case the rendering is so well established that it would be darkening counsel to suggest an alteration now. But it is important to bear in mind the limitations of this translation.

To sum up: the passages in the New Testament which refer to the old covenant make it clear that we cannot confine the meaning of διαθήκη in the New Testament to the signification 'will', but they do not shake the thought of almost unilateral action which this latter term connotes. The New Testament is just as firm as the Old in its insistence that any covenant with God is one in which God is supreme and man merely the consenting recipient of God's favours and directions.

c. The new διαθήκη

Underlying the early Christians' use of the term 'the new covenant' is that same presupposition which led later believers to speak of 'the Old Testament' and 'the New Testament', and which leads us to accept unhesitatingly this division of our Scriptures. It is the conception that in Jesus Christ God has done a new work bringing about a radical alteration in man's relationship to his Maker. Christ makes it possible for man to come to God in a way which is quite impossible apart from Him. Whereas hitherto men had tackled the problem of man's sin by the way of the law, they now found it dealt with in a different way, so that they were free from both the penalty and power of sin. As Paul put it: 'what the law could not do, in that it was weak through the flesh, God, sending his own Son in the likeness of sinful flesh and for sin, condemned sin in the flesh: that the ordinance of the law might be fulfilled in us, who walk not after the flesh, but after the Spirit' (Rom. 8: 3, 4). This conviction that in Jesus Christ God has acted decisively for man's salvation, thus bringing about an entirely new situation, is the master thought of the Christian faith. It underlies the entire New Testament.

When the writers speak of 'the new covenant', then, they are taking over a well-known concept (well-known, that is, to Jews and all those familiar with the Jewish Scriptures) to express an important aspect of this great new fact. The very fact that the expression 'the *new* covenant' is used indicates that the *berîth* of the old Scriptures is in mind and that the New Testament writers, when they use διαθήκη, are thinking primarily of a disposition of God along the lines of Old Testament models, and not the conception of a will. Nevertheless, in view of the universal use of the word outside the Scriptures and of the place they assigned to the death of Christ in the making of the new covenant, it seems probable that in most cases where διαθήκη occurs there is the secondary thought of a death to be discerned with a corresponding benefit to those who were heirs.

But it must be borne in mind that the New Testament writers conceived of the new covenant as in essential harmony with what was known of the nature of God in earlier days, particularly as He had revealed Himself to the patriarchs. There is an important difference in the ways in which they regard the Sinai covenant and that with Abraham, and we proceed to notice this difference.

(*i*) *The new covenant and the covenant with Abraham.* As we have already seen, the covenant with Abraham is referred to four times in the New Testament. In three of them it is regarded as of continuing force, the exception being Acts 7: 8, where 'the covenant of circumcision' is mentioned. Even here, however, it is possible to hold that what is emphasized is not circumcision, but the election of Abraham as shown in the covenant. Of the other passages Luke 1: 72f. tells us that the essence of the covenant is that 'we being delivered out of the hand of our enemies should serve him without fear, in holiness and righteousness before him all our days'. This overruling of God so that His people might serve Him is clearly thought of as continuing. The whole point of the passage is that, in the events which arouse Zachariah's song of praise, God is remembering His covenant and acting in accordance with it. The covenant with Abraham is not burdensome, but one characterized by God's 'visiting' and 'redeeming' His people, raising up 'a horn of salvation' for them, and 'showing mercy'.

Less poetic, but equally definite, is the reference in the speech of Peter in Acts 3. Moses, and then 'all the prophets from Samuel and them that followed after, as many as have spoken', are cited as witnessing to Christ. Then the speaker says: 'Ye are the sons of the prophets, and of the covenant which God made with your fathers, saying unto Abraham, And in thy seed shall all the families of the earth be blessed. Unto you first God, having raised up his Servant, sent him to bless you, in turning away every one of you from your iniquities' (Acts 3: 25, 26). Here again, the Abrahamic covenant is thought of as being of continuing force, and the coming of Christ is seen in the context of the promise made to the patriarch.

In the fourth passage the covenant with Abraham is contrasted with the giving of the law, and the conclusion is: 'A covenant confirmed beforehand by God, the law, which came four hundred and thirty years after, doth not disannul, so as to make the promise of none effect. For if the inheritance is of the law, it is no more of promise: but God hath granted it to Abraham by promise' (Gal. 3: 17f.). Plainly the Abrahamic covenant shows us God's permanent way of dealing with men, namely, by grace or promise, not by law. The Abrahamic covenant is of permanent validity, whereas the law is temporary. The law was 'added because of transgressions, till the seed should come to whom the promise hath been made'

(Gal. 3: 19).[1] Again, it was 'our tutor to bring us unto Christ, that we might be justified by faith. But now that faith is come, we are no longer under a tutor' (Gal. 3: 24f.). The whole passage stresses the subordinate place assigned to the law in the purposes of God (*cf.* also Rom. 3: 20; 5: 20; 8: 3; 10: 4; Gal. 2: 16, 21, *etc.*). The whole line of argument clearly assumes the permanency of the Abrahamic covenant. Because the covenant with Abraham has been confirmed of God, therefore nothing can be added to it nor can it be annulled, and the law can be interpreted only in the light of this fact.

Nor is this an isolated thought of the apostle. We find it again in Romans 4, where he is arguing that Abraham was saved by faith just as Christians are in later days. The continuity of the Christian revelation with the covenant with Abraham is assumed. The same basic assumption lies behind James 2: 21ff., although there the writer is concerned to establish the necessity for works rather than faith. But the point is that he assumes that the principles that determined Abraham's position in the sight of God are the same as those which determine the Christian's position. Again in Hebrews 11 the same thought is stressed, namely that Abraham was accepted with God in the same way as Christians are.

Thus it may fairly be claimed that the New Testament witnesses to a genuine continuity between the Abrahamic covenant and the Christian revelation, what was implicit in the former being revealed in the latter. God's dealings with the patriarch were on the principle of grace, and he received the blessings through faith. It is not otherwise with the Christian; only for him the principle of grace has reached its fulfilment in the life and work of Christ.

(ii) *The new covenant and the covenant on Sinai.* We saw when we were dealing with the Sinai covenant that it is possible to discern there the principle of grace, but that the law, which the people solemnly undertook to obey, is an integral part of this covenant. Further, there are many places in the Old Testament where the

---

[1] See the commentaries on this verse (*e.g.* Lightfoot, Duncan, Burton) for the thought that the law was essentially subordinate to the covenant, its function being only to convict men of sin. *Cf.* G. O. Griffith: 'The Law, properly understood, is in the service of grace; it is the means used by God to school man in the truth of his own insufficiency, and thus to lead him to righteousness where alone it can be found' (*St. Paul's Gospel to the Romans*, Oxford, 1949, p. 108).

prophets castigate the nation for failing to keep the covenant, which, in consequence, has become null and void. It is this legal aspect of the Sinai covenant on which the New Testament writers fasten their attention. It was just as natural for them to regard the Christian way as the antithesis of the Sinai covenant as it was for them to see in it the continuation and fulfilment of the Abrahamic covenant. In particular, they see in the Christian way a better way than that of Sinai, and a fulfilment of that which Sinai foreshadowed but could not perform, namely the remission of sin. We deal with these points in order.

1. The *auctor ad Hebraeos* explicitly speaks of the new as a 'better covenant' (Heb. 7: 22; 8: 6) and goes on to point out that 'if that first had been faultless, then would no place have been sought for a second' (Heb. 8: 7). He proceeds to quote Jeremiah's prophecy of the new covenant, significantly introducing it with the words, 'For finding fault with them, he saith' (Heb. 8: 8). He brings this section to a close by saying: 'In that he saith, A new covenant, he hath made the first old. But that which is becoming old and waxeth aged is nigh unto vanishing away' (Heb. 8: 13). There can be no question but what he conceived of the old covenant as having served its purpose[1] and of having now passed into disuse, being replaced by the new relationship made possible by the work of Jesus Christ. He enlarges upon this in chapter nine.

Although Paul does not use the category of covenant as fully as does the writer to the Hebrews, he can yet give expression to essentially the same thought, as when he speaks of 'ministers of a new covenant; not of the letter, but of the spirit', goes on to point out that 'the letter killeth, but the spirit giveth life', and contrasts 'the ministration of condemnation' with 'the ministration of righteousness' (2 Cor. 3: 6ff.). Here again we have the old way contrasted with the new, and the new is thought of as immeasurably superior to the old. It is one of Paul's leading ideas that before Christ men struggled to serve God by the way of the law, but that now it is the way of grace that has been revealed. Thus in Galatians

[1] *Cf.* F. C. N. Hicks: 'For the Old Testament – or, to speak more correctly, the whole pre-Christian experience of the chosen people – does not solve the problem of life. Its function is to discover it and to state it' (*The Fullness of Sacrifice*, London, 1946, p. 117).

3 he argues vehemently that the way of approach to God is the way of promise or grace; definitely it is not the way of law. It is true that in this chapter (and in others) he reasons that Abraham received the blessing, but he presses home his point that he did so because of his faith. This becomes another point in favour of his thesis that not law but grace is the way. His thought is that God has always accepted men by grace, and the way of approach by law was never valid. The law he regards as of divine origin, but as limited in scope. It was no more than a schoolmaster to bring men to Christ. The covenant associated with the giving of the law was thus immeasurably less than the new covenant which makes it abundantly plain that the way is by grace and through faith. There can be no doubt that he would have accepted the thought of Hebrews 9: 15 that the death of Christ availed for the transgressions committed under the first covenant, for he is positive that the one way of putting away sin is through the work of Jesus Christ. It is clear that for Paul, as for the writer to the Hebrews and, indeed, for all the New Testament writers, the new way transforms everything. It is infinitely better than the old way.

Wherein does the superiority of the new consist? Basically in that 'the letter killeth, but the spirit giveth life' (2 Cor. 3: 6). This saying recalls the words of the Lord, 'I came that they may have life, and may have it abundantly' (Jn. 10: 10). Indeed, it is characteristic of the New Testament writers that they stress the quality of the life that is possible for men now that Jesus has come and has wrought His great work of atonement. It is not that they despise the old covenant; on the contrary they regard it as of divine origin and appointment. But it was essentially preparatory and preliminary. The fulfilment of what it foreshadowed they find in the work of Christ. Thus the writer to the Hebrews assigns a subordinate place to the Jewish sacrifices: 'In those sacrifices there is a remembrance made of sins year by year. For it is impossible that the blood of bulls and goats should take away sins' (Heb. 10: 3f.). But it is of the very essence of his argument that what the blood of bulls and goats could not do, the blood of Christ both could and did do.

2. The new covenant is essentially concerned with the forgiveness of sin. This contrasts with the covenant of Exodus 24 where

the people readily acquiesce in the obligation to carry out the commandments of God. Through the years such obedience was seen to be impossible as generation after generation failed to live up to the standard set before them. It is significant that, when we come to Jeremiah's great prophecy of the new covenant, it includes the provision 'I will put my law in their inward parts, and in their heart will I write it . . . I will forgive their iniquity, and their sin will I remember no more' (Je. 31: 33f.). This aspect of the new covenant comes prominently before us in the New Testament passages. Thus when the writer to the Hebrews quotes the passage from Jeremiah and applies it to the Christian fulfilment (Heb. 8: 8f.), the words of the prophet are fully noted right down to the forgiveness of sin. It is at this point that the writer speaks of the new covenant as replacing the old which is 'nigh unto vanishing away'. This connection is even plainer a little later in the Epistle, when the writer again refers to the passage in Jeremiah. This time his quotation is much shorter and he picks out only the words important for his argument, thus: 'This is the covenant that I will make with them after those days, saith the Lord; I will put my laws on their heart, and upon their mind also will I write them; then saith he, And their sins and their iniquities will I remember no more' (Heb. 10: 16f.). Admittedly the 'then saith he' is an explanatory gloss of the translators, but it truly expressed the mind of the author, and it is significant that he couples the reference to forgiveness with that to the new covenant, though they are separated by several verses in the original. Obviously forgiveness was to him the essential part of the new covenant.[1] His Epistle shows plainly that our author found a large place for forgiveness in his total view of things Christian. The above citations show that, not only is this the case, but that this forgiveness was present to his mind *when he used the expression 'the new covenant'*. The element of grace, which, while present in the old covenant, was obscured by the necessity for keeping the law, he sees stressed in the new covenant. It is essentially a covenant based upon divine forgiveness of sin.

We see the same tendency towards associating the new covenant

[1] *Cf.* Moffatt, 'The real interest of the writer in this Jeremianic oracle is shown when he returns to it in 10[16-18]; what arrests him is the promise of a free, full pardon at the close' (*ICC*, on Heb. 8: 8).

with forgiveness of sin in St. Paul's only reference to the new covenant as having been foretold. Thus he quotes Isaiah as follows: 'There shall come out of Zion the Deliverer; he shall turn away ungodliness from Jacob: and this is my covenant unto them, when I shall take away their sins' (Rom. 11: 26f.). There is no particular difficulty about the first part of this quotation which is a rather free citation of Isaiah 59: 20 (LXX). But the words about forgiveness of sin are not to be found in this passage; they come from Isaiah 27: 9. Here we see at work, and in a more striking form, the same process we have already noted in Hebrews. Paul is writing about the covenant, and as he wishes to express its essence, he adds to his citation from Isaiah 59: 20 other words, separated in the original by many chapters, but which bring out the central truth expressed by the new covenant.

Thus, each time the New Testament refers to the new covenant as having been prophesied it links an explicit reference to forgiveness of sin with the new covenant. This happens also in a number of passages where prophecy is not in question. Thus in Hebrews 9: 15 we have the interesting expression, 'And for this cause he is the mediator of a new covenant, that a death having taken place for the redemption of the transgressions that were under the first covenant', where the death that inaugurates the new covenant is seen as providing the way of forgiveness, even for those transgressions committed under the first covenant. The obvious inference is that such sins could not really be forgiven under the first covenant, and that therefore the new covenant was an absolute necessity. Probably it is this truth that is in mind also when the same writer says that Jesus is 'the mediator of a better covenant, which hath been enacted upon better promises' (Heb. 8: 6). The better promises are those concerned with forgiveness and man's reconciliation with God, as is seen from the following section.

This thought is not so prominent, but nevertheless it seems to be in the background, in two Pauline references. When Paul speaks of the two covenants, contrasting the Jerusalem that now is with the Jerusalem that is above, the aspect that he stresses is that of the freedom that accrues to those in the new covenant. He says of the present Jerusalem that 'she is in bondage with her children' (Gal. 4: 25), whereas 'the Jerusalem that is above is free'. It seems clear that one aspect in this freedom is freedom from the power of sin, the freedom that comes to the believer because Christ has put away his sin. It is not otherwise with the passage in which Paul speaks of himself as a minister of a new covenant and proceeds to contrast 'the ministration of condemnation' with 'the ministration of righteousness'. For surely he means here that, whereas under the old covenant the outcome must be condemnation, under the new, man's sin is put away so that he is righteous.

This aspect of the new covenant seems also to be indicated by those passages which refer to the 'blood of the covenant', for it is by the shedding of Jesus' blood that sin is put away and the covenant established. There seems to be a linking of the two ideas, and this comes to the surface sometimes as in Matthew 26: 28: 'This is my blood of the covenant, which is shed for many unto remission of sins.' Most commentators regard 'unto remission of sins' as a gloss; if it is, the expression shows what covenant blood meant to a very early Christian.[1] The Marcan parallel lacks the reference to the forgiveness of sins, but it speaks of the blood as being shed for many. The corresponding Lucan passage runs: 'This cup is the new covenant in my blood, even that which is poured out for you',[2] so that it, too, stresses the place of the shedding of Christ's blood. While this does not demand for its interpretation that we understand the passage as referring to the remission of sins, at the very least it is quite consonant with such an understanding. The same may be said of the other passages where 'the blood of the covenant' is spoken of.

This is quite in accordance with what we saw in our treatment of the covenant of Exodus 24, and in particular of the significance of

[1] On this verse W. C. Allen comments: 'Mt., by adding εἰς ἄφεσιν ἁμαρτιῶν, shows that he understood the covenant to be a covenant between God and the many by which remission of sins was secured to them' (ICC, p. 276). More apposite for our present purpose is the comment of A. H. M'Neile who sees in 'This is my blood of the covenant' a reference to the peace-offering, and in 'unto remission of sins' a reference to the sin offering, and adds, 'But the latter is presupposed in the former, even if Jesus did not say "for the remission of sins"' (in loc.). That is, he sees the thought of remission in the very idea of the new covenant.

[2] There is a difficult textual problem here and most scholars reject the words. They are accepted as genuine, however, by G. Vos, HDCG, II, p. 375; A. J. B. Higgins, The Lord's Supper in the New Testament (London, 1952), pp. 37–40; J. Jeremias, The Eucharistic Words of Jesus (Oxford, 1955), pp. 87–106, and by an impressive list of writers cited by Jeremias, op. cit., p. 106, n. 1.

'the blood of the covenant' in that passage. There we saw reason for thinking that the expression symbolized both expiation and consecration, as the people were cleansed for their new relationship to God. So, in the new covenant, the blood shed was a means of purifying the people by providing for the remission of their sins, and of consecrating them to their new relationship to God. If, as seems probable, we are to see in the New Testament references to 'the blood of the covenant' allusions to Exodus 24: 8, then we must see in them also references to an expiatory and consecratory death, whereby men are brought into a new relationship with God.

It is, of course, just possible that the New Testament references to 'the blood of the covenant' point back to Zechariah 9: 11, rather than to Exodus 24: 8, and Vincent Taylor cites Joachim Jeremias as an exegete who adopts this interpretation.[1] Twice in the Rabbinic literature the blood of the Passover victim is spoken of as 'covenant-blood', Zechariah 9: 11 being interpreted of the deliverance of Israel from Egypt. Jeremias thinks that Jesus (who had this chapter of Zechariah in mind during His last days, as we see from Mt. 21: 5) was comparing His blood to that of the Passover lamb at the departure from Egypt. He maintains that Jesus is describing 'His death as an atoning death which establishes the new and eternal communion of a humanity cleansed from sin with its God – the communion of the Kingdom of God'. I agree with Dr. Taylor that this is not as probable as a reference to Exodus 24: 8, but, as the words last quoted show, even if Jeremias' view be accepted, the significance of the covenant-blood is much the same. It still remains true that it is the means of cleansing and that it brings men into communion with God.

3. The rite described in Exodus 24 had the effect of bringing the people into such a relationship with God that they could be called a holy people, and this can be paralleled in the new covenant. Thus we read of 'the blood of the covenant, wherewith he was sanctified' (Heb. 10: 29), and of coming to 'Jesus the mediator of a new covenant, and to the blood of sprinkling that speaketh better than that of Abel' (Heb. 12: 24). The reference to 'blood of sprinkling' seems to point to the sprinkling of the people recorded in Exodus

[1] *Jesus and His Sacrifice* (London, 1939), pp. 138f. R. Mackintosh (*Historic Theories of Atonement*, London, 1920, pp. 54f.) also accepts this point of view.

24 whereby they were consecrated to their new relationship to God and symbolically purified.[1] We have another reference to sprinkling in 1 Peter 1: 2, and here again we should see a reference to the covenant of Exodus 24 for, as Hort points out,[2] there are only three examples of people being sprinkled with blood in the Old Testament, and there is no reason to see in this passage an allusion to either of the others. The writer is thus directing the attention of his readers to the fact that Christians are brought into a new covenant with God, and that they have been sprinkled with blood as the means of admission thereto. The significance of this is, if we may again cite Hort, 'the sprinkling presupposed a shedding; the consecration of the New Covenant presupposed the antecedent sacrifice of the Cross'.[3] The fact that in this context the writer speaks of obedience gives another point of contact with the Old Testament passage, for there the people agreed to obey the commandments of Yahweh. Though the men of the new covenant rely for their acceptance on the work of Christ, and not on any deeds of their own, yet true faith brings forth in their lives the fruit of godly living. These passages indicating the sanctifying aspect of the new covenant bring this out.

But the passages cited teach more than that a high ethical standard is set before Christians. There is a power given them to enable them to live the sort of lives they should. The quotation from Jeremiah 31 in Hebrews 8: 8ff. includes the words: 'For this is the covenant that I will make with the house of Israel after those days, saith the Lord; I will put my laws into their mind, and on their heart also will I write them.' This activity within the people of the new covenant the early Christians found fulfilled in the activity of the Holy Spirit in their hearts. The empowering of the Holy Spirit of God is an integral feature of the new covenant, so that, while the standards are not relaxed one whit, the indwelling Spirit enables those in the new covenant to have a continual victory over the forces of evil.

4. A further aspect of New Testament teaching on the new

[1] Cf. Delitzsch: 'It is common to the blood-sprinkling under both Testaments that it is the medium whereby the apprehension of the promises proper to either covenant is realized' (op. cit., p. 354).

[2] Op. cit., p. 23.

[3] Op. cit., p. 24.

covenant is that which draws attention to the finality of the new arrangement. This might be held to be implied in the fact that the new covenant is based on forgiveness of sins, and of course its finality is directly prophesied with 'their sin will I remember *no more*' (Je. 31: 34). In the New Testament it comes to expression in such a passage as the benediction which speaks of 'the blood of the eternal covenant' (Heb. 13: 20), the adjective reminding us that this covenant passes not away. Probably we are to deduce the same from the reference to the ark of the covenant in heaven (Rev. 11: 19). The allusion is rather mysterious, but it seems to indicate that there is heavenly warrant for thinking that God's new covenant is permanent.

VII. CONCLUSION

There does not seem to be any necessary connection between covenant and substitution, unless the death of the victim, which formed a necessary part of the covenant-making process, is regarded as the symbolical death of the partners. This is possible, and, as we have seen, is adopted, for example, by Westcott. But we accept as more probable the idea that the death of the victim is a symbolic calling down of a curse on the one who breaks the covenant. Regarded in this way a covenant is a very solemn agreement between two partners which involves obligations and blessings, though in the case of any given covenant these may be one-sided. But there is no reason for associating substitution with such a covenant any more than with any other form of compact.

But though, in general, covenant may not be held to involve a process of substitution, it is quite possible that any given covenant may include a substitutionary aspect. Thus a number of commentators think there is a process of substitution involved in the incident related in Exodus 24, either from the point of view of the victim being thought of as a substitute for the partners in the blood-brotherhood, or as an atoning sacrifice substituting for the sinners.

In the New Testament there is a necessary connection between the death of Christ and the establishing of the covenant. Into his discussion of the new covenant the writer of the Epistle to the Hebrews inserts, 'for where a διαθήκη is, there must of necessity be

the death of him that made it', and this agrees with the general line
of New Testament teaching on the subject. Although it does not
often come to the surface, yet it seems to be understood by all that
there was a necessity in the death of Christ. Had He not died there
would have been, there could have been, no new covenant. This is
expressed at least in part by the use of διαθήκη to denote the new
covenant for, as we have seen, the word was in general use for a
will, and it would normally conjure up thoughts of death in men's
minds. Even when it is the thought of covenant rather than will
that is in mind the other meaning of the word must have been
present to give the expression an unusual flavour. 'A Hellenist like
the *auctor ad Hebraeos*, or even a Jew like Paul, with Greek language
in the very fibre of his thought, could never have used δ. for
covenant without the slightest consciousness of its ordinary and
invariable contemporary meaning.'[1]

This is implied, too, in the passages which associate forgiveness
with the covenant. As we have seen, this is a common New
Testament conception, and it is also common in the New Testament that the death of Christ is associated with our forgiveness. It
will not be seriously disputed that the New Testament writers
conceived of the death of Christ as necessary to the forgiveness of
sin, so that where they speak of this forgiveness as an essential
element in the new covenant they clearly make the death of the
Lord integral to the process, and not merely something incidental.

The same thing follows from the fact that the new covenant is
modelled on that of Exodus 24. Whatever may be said about
covenants in general it cannot be denied that the blood of the
victim was necessary in that rite. If the new covenant is derived
from the old, it may well be argued that the death of Christ is a
necessary part of the process accordingly. The same, too, would
follow from the repeated references to 'the blood of the covenant',
for, as we shall see in the next chapter, blood in the Scripture must
be understood of the infliction of death. The fact that the blood of
the covenant is met with on several occasions shows that it was not
regarded as a non-essential but as a very important part of the
process.

If we hold to the view that the essence of sacrifice was seen in

------

[1] MM, *sub* διαθήκη.

vicarious punishment in New Testament times,[1] then such considerations as these will impel us to believe that the establishment of the new covenant required the death of Him that established it as a substitute for the death of sinners. But this aspect is not stressed in the covenant terminology, for there the dominant idea is the new relationship between God and those who become the people of God.

Thus we may say that the use of the term covenant to describe the work of Christ reminds us that because of His death there has come into being the people of God, bound to Him by especially close ties. Looking backward this emphasizes forgiveness, for only those who are cleansed from sin may fittingly be termed God's people, and this explains the stress laid on forgiveness in connection with covenant. Looking forward it emphasizes newness of living, for God's people must be *God's* people.

ADDITIONAL NOTE: COVENANT AND MEDIATION

It will be convenient to add here a few words about the subject of mediation, since Jesus is said to have been 'the mediator' of a new or better covenant three times, and 'the surety' for it once.[2]

If we may begin with this latter term, the Greek word used is ἔγγυος, which seems to be derived from an old word for 'hand' and thus signifies 'in the hand'. It conveys the idea of guarantee, for what is in the hand is assured. The word according to MM is common in legal documents in the sense of surety, guarantor. When we read, then, that Jesus has become 'the surety of a better covenant' (Heb. 7: 22) the idea is that Jesus guarantees the new relationship. He has brought it about by His own action, and now nothing less than His Person assures us that the new relationship is valid.

The other term, μεσίτης, signifies etymologically 'one who

---

[1] So, for example, W. P. Paterson in *HDB*, Art. 'Sacrifice'; A. E. Garvie, *The Christian Certainty amid the Modern Perplexity* (London, 1910), p. 79; H. Maldwyn Hughes, *What is the Atonement?* (London, n.d.), p. 58.

[2] The idea of mediation is much more widespread than its mention in set terms. Ryder Smith says it 'pervades the New Testament' (*The Bible Doctrine of Salvation*, London, 1946, p. 183).

stands in the midst', and it is used of an arbitrator or of a peace-maker. A. Oepke distinguishes three senses: '1. The neutral, or trusted person (arbitrator or peace-negotiator), 2. The mediator in a general spatial sense, 3. The reconciler, negotiator in the sense of the restoration of a relationship which otherwise would not be in existence'.[1] He finds the first of these meanings in the Epistle to the Hebrews and the third in other parts of the New Testament, while the second is lacking in these writings. MM similarly find the word used often in the papyri for arbiter, also for intermediary and for surety.

Of the New Testament occurrences of the term, those in Galatians 3: 19f. are of importance, although they do not refer to the new covenant, because they show what was understood by the term. Paul says the law 'was ordained through angels by the hand of a mediator. Now a mediator is not of one; but God is one'. The first mediator is clearly Moses, and the sort of activity engaged in by this patriarch at the time of the establishing of the first covenant is mediatorship. Then comes the principle, 'a mediator is not of one', which is to say that the very presence of a mediator implies the existence of two parties; there could be no mediator if only one party were concerned. In Westcott's words: 'A covenant generally, and obviously a covenant between God and man, requires a mediator, one who standing between the contracting parties shall bring them duly into fellowship.'[2]

In the Epistle to the Hebrews there are three passages which fall to be considered: 'But now hath he obtained a ministry the more excellent, by how much also he is the mediator of a better covenant, which hath been enacted upon better promises' (Heb. 8: 6); 'And for this cause he is the mediator of a new covenant, that a death having taken place for the redemption of the transgressions that were under the first covenant, they that have been called may receive the promise of the eternal inheritance' (Heb. 9: 15); (ye are come) 'to Jesus the mediator of a new covenant, and to the blood of sprinkling that speaketh better than Abel' (Heb. 12: 24). All three passages speak of the blessings that accrue to those in the new covenant, and the latter two explicitly mention the death of the Lord, by which the covenant was brought about. The mediatorial

[1] *TWNT*, IV, pp. 603f.
[2] *Op. cit.*, p. 218.

activity seems to consist in that death which established the covenant and thus brought God and man together. Moffatt thinks that μεσίτης in these passages 'is practically . . . a synonym for ἔγγυος',[1] but this hardly seems warranted. It is better (with West-cott) to regard each word as retaining its own meaning, the establishing of the covenant being in mind in these passages and the guaranteeing of it in Hebrews 7: 22.

The idea of mediation, then, brings us the two thoughts that the new covenant is expressly guaranteed by Christ Himself, and that it is His activity which establishes the covenant. Both thoughts drive us back to the characteristic biblical position that our salvation is all of God, for it is all of Christ.

'For there is one God, one mediator also between God and men, himself man, Christ Jesus, who gave himself a ransom for all' (1 Tim. 2: 5f.).

---

[1] *ICC. Hebrews*, p. 107.

CHAPTER III

THE BLOOD

THE MEANING OF THE WORD 'blood' in Scripture, especially
with reference to the blood of the sacrifices in the Old Testament
and to the blood of Christ in the New, has been the subject of some
discussion, and the writings of W. Milligan, B. F. Westcott,
N. Hicks, and Vincent Taylor, to name but a few, have urged the
opinion that by 'the blood' life is meant rather than death, so that
the essential thing in sacrifice is the offering up of life. This view
has been opposed by such scholars as J. Denney, J. Moffatt, J.
Armitage Robinson, and more recently, J. Behm[1] and F. J. Taylor.[2]

I. 'BLOOD' IN THE OLD TESTAMENT

a. Classification of passages

The word *dām* is used in the Hebrew Bible 362 times with various
shades of meaning. The occurrences may be grouped as follows:

(i) *Death with violence of some kind*: 203 examples.

(1) Generally: 165 examples. Here I class passages like 'Whoso
sheddeth man's blood, by man shall his blood be shed' (Gn. 9: 6);
'the avenger of blood' (Nu. 35: 19, *etc.*); 'he that maketh in-
quisition for blood remembereth them' (Ps. 9: 12).

(2) In the phrase 'innocent blood': 21 examples. 'Thou shalt
put away the innocent blood from Israel' (Dt. 19: 13).

(3) One's blood being on oneself: 12 examples. 'For every one
that curseth his father or his mother shall surely be put to death
. . . his blood shall be upon him' (Lv. 20: 9).

(4) Death of animals: 5 examples. 'What man soever there be of
the house of Israel, that killeth an ox, or lamb, or goat . . . and
hath not brought it unto the door of the tent of meeting, to offer

---

[1] Art. αἷμα in *TWNT*.
[2] Art. 'Blood' in *TWBB*. See additional note on pp. 126ff. for some important
statements.

it as an oblation unto the Lord . . . blood shall be imputed unto that man; he hath shed blood' (Lv. 17: 3f.).

(ii) Connecting life with blood: 7 examples.

'For as to the life of all flesh, the blood thereof is all one with the life thereof' (Lv. 17: 14).

(iii) Eating meat with blood: 17 examples.

(1) The practice prohibited: 12 examples. 'Ye shall eat neither fat nor blood' (Lv. 3: 17).

(2) The practice occurring: 5 examples. 'The people did eat them with the blood' (1 Sa. 14: 32). This group is closely connected with the previous one as Leviticus 17: 11, 14 shows.

(iv) Sacrificial blood: 103 examples.[1]

(1) Generally: 94 examples. 'Thou shalt not offer the blood of my sacrifice with leavened bread' (Ex. 23: 18).

(2) The institution of the Passover: 6 examples.

(3) Heathen sacrifices: 3 examples.

(v) Other uses: 32 examples.

(1) Turning the Nile into blood: 8 examples.
(2) Processes of birth, *etc.*: 12 examples.
(3) Bleeding: 3 examples.
(4) Colour: 3 examples.
(5) Of grapes: 2 examples.
(6) 'A bridegroom of blood': 2 examples.
(7) Metaphorical: 2 examples. 'Shall I drink the blood of the men that went in jeopardy of their lives?' (2 Sa. 23: 17).

From these figures it is clear that the commonest use of *dām* is to denote death by violence, and, in particular, that this use is found about twice as often as that to denote the blood of sacrifice. There is a difference also in distribution, for the blood of the sacrifices is often mentioned in Leviticus and Exodus (the actual figures are fifty-nine for Leviticus and nineteen for Exodus), but rarely else-

---

[1] It may well be that after examination it will appear that the meaning of sacrificial blood is essentially that of one of the other groups, but for the present it seems best to leave it as a separate group.

where, there being no more than twenty-five references to sacrificial blood in all the rest of the Old Testament. By contrast the use of blood to denote violent death is not specially located in any part of the Old Testament, and is found almost throughout. As far as it goes, the statistical evidence indicates that the association most likely to be conjured up when the Hebrews heard the word 'blood' was that of violent death.

b. The connection between blood and life

Those who think that 'the blood' means essentially 'the life' pay a good deal of attention to Leviticus 17: 11, 'For the life of the flesh is in the blood: and I have given it to you upon the altar to make atonement for your souls: for it is the blood that maketh atonement by reason of the life'. Also important is the statement, 'the blood is the life' (Gn. 9: 4; Dt. 12: 23). They also draw attention to the prohibition of eating flesh with the blood yet in it (Lv. 3: 17; 7: 26f.; 17: 10, 12, 14, etc.), the refusal of David to 'drink the blood of the men that went in jeopardy of their lives' (2 Sa. 23: 17), the parallel statements that Yahweh will require 'your blood, the blood of your lives' and 'the life of man' (Gn. 9: 5), and the psalmist's parallel use of 'soul' and 'blood' (Ps. 72: 14). This represents a formidable body of evidence and indicates that among the Hebrews a close connection between life and blood was recognized.

But does it indicate more? Many think it does; for example, Vincent Taylor says: 'The victim is slain in order that its life, in the form of blood, may be released . . . the aim is to make it possible for life to be presented as an offering to the Deity. More and more students of comparative religion, and of Old Testament worship in particular, are insisting that the bestowal of life is the fundamental idea in sacrificial worship'.[1] On this view the slaughter of the animal is necessary, but only because there is no other way of obtaining the blood, the life. The death plays no real part in the sacrifice.

It is difficult to see how such a view can be substantiated. It goes

---

[1] *Jesus and His Sacrifice* (London, 1939), pp. 54f. *Cf.* also E. L. Mascall (summarizing Hicks), 'The slaying was merely an indispensable preliminary by which the life was set free to be offered' (*Corpus Christi*, London, 1955, p. 89).

beyond the words of the passages cited, for there is none which speaks of the blood as indicating life in distinction from death. Some of the passages adduced lend no real support to the idea when we look into them. Thus, while it is true that 'your blood, the blood of your lives' is used in the same fashion as 'the life of man' (Gn. 9: 5), yet its support of the theory is no more than superficial. 'Blood' here means death rather than life. When Yahweh says He will require the life or the blood of man, He is not asking men to produce life or hand it back to Him: He is saying that men will be held responsible for destroying life. It is not otherwise with the parallelism of 'soul' and 'blood' in Psalm 72: 14. What is meant by 'precious shall their blood be in his sight' is made clear by the very similar statement of Psalm 116: 15, 'Precious in the sight of the Lord is the death of his saints', so that redeeming the soul in the first half of the verse is an expression meaning 'to deliver from death' (cf. Ps. 116: 8).

Similarly David's refusal to 'drink the blood of the men that went in jeopardy of their lives' is a metaphorical statement and must be understood so. David certainly did not mean that he would literally be partaking of either the blood or the lives of the men, and the statement must not be tortured into giving an unreal meaning. It is a defect of the view we are considering that it insists on taking very literally certain statements about blood, when there is abundant evidence that the word was used continually in a variety of metaphorical senses. Thus we read of 'innocent blood', and there are many expressions like 'his blood be on his own head' which make nonsense if we try to take them in a literal sense. This is the case with 'Cursed be he that taketh reward to slay an innocent person (lit. the blood of the innocent)' (Dt. 27: 25), for it is manifestly impossible to limit the application of the words to murders where blood literally flows, whilst exempting those brought about without actual spilling of blood. Again, A. M. Stibbs draws attention to another figurative use of 'vivid word pictures involving "blood" . . . especially to indicate people's connection with someone's death',[1] and he cites Judah's saying concerning Joseph, 'What profit is it if we slay our brother, and conceal his blood?' (Gn. 37: 26), the description of Joab as one who 'shed the

---

[1] *The Meaning of the Word 'Blood' in Scripture* (London, 1954), p. 10.

blood of war in peace, and put the blood of war upon his girdle
. . . and in his shoes' (1 Ki. 2: 5), and the psalmist's idea of the
vengeance of the righteous when 'he shall wash his feet in the blood
of the wicked' (Ps. 58: 10). Such examples could be multiplied,
and in the face of them it is difficult to insist that passages like
Leviticus 17: 11 mean that life is literally in the blood.

Further, it may not be without significance that *nephesh*, which
is translated 'life' in Leviticus 17: 11, is not coterminous with the
English 'life'. It can mean something very like 'life yielded up in
death'. It occurs in passages which refer to 'taking away', 'losing',
'destroying', 'giving up' or 'devouring' life, to 'putting one's life
in one's hand' and to the life 'departing'. A not uncommon way of
referring to slaying is to speak of 'smiting the *nephesh*' (Gn. 37: 21;
Nu. 35: 11; Je. 40: 14, *etc.*), while those who desire to murder
someone are usually said to 'seek his *nephesh*', an expression which
occurs thirty times (*e.g.* Ex. 4: 19; Ps. 35: 4) and which is reinforced
by others which speak of 'lying in wait for the *nephesh*', 'laying a
snare for the *nephesh*', etc. (1 Sa. 28: 9; Pr. 1: 18). Some passages
speak of 'slaying the *nephesh*' or the *nephesh* 'dying' (Nu. 31: 19;
Ezk. 13: 19; 18: 4).

There is surely significance in the fact that the word is used in
such a variety of ways with regard to death. But even more important for our present purpose are certain passages where *nephesh*
plainly points to death. Thus the sailors, about to cast Jonah into
the sea, pray 'let us not perish for this man's *nephesh*' (Jon. 1: 14)
Clearly it is his death and not his life they have in mind. It is not
otherwise with a number of passages which speak of 'life for life'
as the punishment for murder, for example, 'Deliver him that
smote his brother, that we may kill him for the *nephesh* of his
brother whom he slew' (2 Sa. 14: 7).[1] Then there are passages
wherein *nephesh* is translated by 'dead' or a similar term, as 'Ye
shall not make any cuttings in your flesh for the dead (*lānephesh*)'
(Lv. 19: 28; *cf.* Lv. 21: 1; 22: 4; Nu. 5: 2; 6: 11; 9: 6, 7, 10; Hg. 2:
13, and, with the addition of *mēth*, Lv. 21: 11; Nu. 6: 6; 19: 11,
13). The expression 'blood of the life (lives)' is found twice (Pr. 28:
17; Je. 2: 34) and both times it signifies violent death.

---

[1] *Cf.* Ex. 21: 23; Lv. 24: 18; Dt. 19: 21, and passages where the letting go of a
prisoner is to be punished by the execution of the guard responsible, 1 Ki. 20: 39,
42; 2 Ki. 10: 24.

From all this it is clear that the association of *nephesh* with *dām* in Leviticus 17:11, etc., cannot be held to prove that life is thought of as still existent after the blood has been poured forth. This use of both *nephesh* and *dām* in other contexts makes it more probable that the meaning here is that of life given up in death.[1] This is supported by the fact that it is 'the life *of the flesh*' that is said to be in the blood, and it is precisely this life which ceases to exist when the blood is poured out. For the understanding of sacrifice there is an important use of *nephesh* in Isaiah 53:10ff., where the offering of the *nephesh* is spoken of in sacrificial terms (it is an *'asham*, a guilt offering). But in verse 12 we have this offering of *nephesh* described as 'he poured out his *nephesh* unto death'.

Again, to speak of the life as in some way existent in the blood subsequent to the slaughter of the animal is to ignore the Hebrew stress on the connection of life with the body. So far were the Hebrews from thinking of an immaterial principle of life that they associated life in the age to come not with the immortality of the soul, but with the resurrection of the body. If they found difficulty in thinking of human life as persisting after the death of the body, it is most unlikely that they would think of the life of an animal as persisting after slaughter. Indeed, in the case of most of the sacrifices there is explicit mention of the animal being killed before the blood is referred to. To take an example at random: it is very difficult to believe that the writer had life in mind when he said, with reference to the cleansing of a leprous house, the priest 'shall ... dip (certain things) in the blood of the slain bird' (Lv. 14:51), for the bird is expressly said to be 'slain'. We seem far from the extremely practical Hebrew turn of mind when we read of 'soul-substance' (with W. O. E. Oesterley and E. O. James), or of the term blood suggesting 'the thought of life, dedicated, offered, transformed, and open to our spiritual appropriation'.[2] It is much more likely that A. M. Stibbs is correct when he sums up as follows:

[1] *Cf.* Lods' explanation of the verse: 'There is a ransom, a redemption, a death by proxy' (*The Prophets and the Rise of Judaism*, London, 1937, p. 294).

[2] Vincent Taylor, *The Atonement in New Testament Teaching* (London, 1946), p. 198. It is largely his view of the meaning of blood which leads him to say 'those scholars are justified who insist that the most significant conception in sacrifice is that of life offered to God' (*Jesus and His Sacrifice*, London, 1939, p. 59). But he frankly admits 'It would be folly to pretend that this conception of sacrifice is taught in the Old Testament or was a theme of Rabbinical teaching' (*ibid.*).

'Blood shed stands, therefore, not for the release of life from the burden of the flesh, but for the bringing to an end of life in the flesh. It is a witness to physical death, not an evidence of spiritual survival.'[1]

c. The problem of atonement

Examination of the passages treating of atonement is relevant, for if they show that atonement is generally linked with life, then, in view of Leviticus 17: 11, they will support the idea that life and blood are much the same thing. This will strengthen the hands of those who feel that the essential thing in sacrifice is the offering of life. But if, on the other hand, we find that atonement is linked with death this will form evidence against both these conclusions.

Atonement seems to be connected with the blood in the manner of Leviticus 17: 11 eleven times outside that verse. Some of the passages are so specific as to leave us in no doubt as to the atoning efficacy of blood, as, for example, when we read of the bullock and goat 'whose blood was brought in to make atonement in the holy place' (Lv. 16: 27), or the direction that 'with the blood of the sin offering of atonement once in the year shall he make atonement for it' (Ex. 30: 10). But before we conclude that such passages mean that atonement is made by offering of life we must set beside them another verse in which blood is said to atone, namely, 'for blood, it polluteth the land: and no atonement can be made for the land for the blood that is shed therein, but by the blood of him that shed it' (Nu. 35: 33). Here we have explicit mention of atonement by blood, but it is certainly the execution of the murderer that is spoken of and not any presentation of his life before God. The importance of this verse as a commentary on Leviticus 17: 11 is not always realized. The Leviticus passage is ambiguous, for the reference to blood could be understood as signifying the presentation of life, or, equally, as indicating the infliction of death. This ambiguity is present in nearly all the other passages which connect blood and atonement. This enhances the importance of Numbers 35: 33, for in this verse there is no ambiguity – the blood which atones is that which flows when the death penalty is inflicted on the criminal. It is true that this is not a sacrifice in the

---

[1] Op. cit., p. 11.

strict meaning of the term, and therefore some will doubt the validity of its application to the sacrificial scene. But consider that in both cases it is expiation of sin that is in question, in both cases the means is blood, in both cases the action is directed towards God, and in both cases atonement is said to be secured. It is difficult to deny the relevance of the passage.

There are twenty-two other passages where atonement is effected by means other than the cultus, and these show that atonement and the offering of life were not inseparably connected in Hebrew thought. Four of them are particularly significant. In the first, Moses says he will try to make atonement for the sin of the people and makes his attempt by asking God to blot him out of the book which He has written (Ex. 32: 30–32). In the second, Phinehas is said to have made atonement by killing Zimri and Cozbi (Nu. 25: 13). The third is that in which David makes atonement by delivering up seven descendants of Saul to be hanged by the Gibeonites (2 Sa. 21: 3f.), while in the fourth the heifer is slain to avert punishment when murder has been committed by a person unknown (Dt. 21: 1–9). In each of these passages there is atonement made or contemplated, and in none of them can it fairly be argued that what is meant is the presentation of life to God. In each case it is the termination of life, the infliction of death that atones. So far from any symbol of life being presented to God, the descendants of Saul were hanged, and the heifer killed by having its neck broken. This last passage is remarkable in that in verses 7–9 blood is mentioned four times and the verb *kipper* occurs twice, yet atonement is not connected with blood at all.

Turning now to those passages where atonement is connected with the cultus, the usual way is to speak quite generally of the whole sacrifice, for example, 'he shall prepare the sin offering, and the meal offering, and the burnt offering, and the peace offerings, to make atonement for the house of Israel' (Ezk. 45: 17). Thirty-eight times in all atonement is referred to in this way, and the general impression from them all is that it is the whole offering, rather than the presentation of the blood, that is thought of as effecting atonement. This impression is strengthened by the fact that sometimes the mention of atonement is attached to a point in the ritual other than the manipulation of the blood. Thus it is mentioned in connection with the laying of hands on the head of the beast (Lv. 1: 4),[1] or with the burning of the fat (Lv. 4: 26).[2] These turns of expression are natural enough if it is the whole offering which atones, but they represent a strange way of speaking if the essence of it all is the offering of life contained in the blood.

Then there are passages in which atonement is mentioned in connection with rites prescribed by the cultus, but where the blood seems definitely to be excluded. Thus Aaron and his sons are instructed that 'they shall eat those things wherewith atonement was made' (Ex. 29: 33). Since the reference is to a carcass from which the blood has been drained, neither blood nor life can possibly be meant. Similar is the passage in which Moses rebukes the sons of Aaron, asking: 'Wherefore have ye not eaten the sin offering in the place of the sanctuary, seeing it is most holy, and he hath given it you to bear the iniquity of the congregation, to make atonement for them before the Lord?' (Lv. 10: 17). In neither of these examples does it seem possible to maintain that the essence of atonement is through offering of life. On the contrary, in both cases the death of the animal seems to be regarded as a necessity in the making of atonement.

Attention should be drawn also to certain passages in which the slaughter of nations is likened to sacrifice. Thus Jeremiah speaks of the destruction of the mighty men of Egypt and her allies and proceeds: 'And the sword shall devour and be satiate, and shall drink its fill of their blood: for the Lord, the Lord of hosts, hath a sacrifice in the north country' (Je. 46: 10). Similarly Zephaniah says, 'for the Lord hath prepared a sacrifice, he hath sanctified his guests' (Zp. 1: 7). If the essence of sacrifice is the presentation of life before God such passages are completely inexplicable. They

[1] Similarly in the Mishnah we find mention of atonement in the confession while hands are laid on the head of the animal (*Yom.* 3: 8; 4: 2; 6: 2).

[2] In view of this association of atonement with the fat it is worth noticing that a very important place is assigned to the fat throughout the sacrifices, so that this association with atonement is not surprising. Thus it is explicitly said that 'all the fat is the Lord's' (Lv. 3: 16), and there is a prohibition of eating the fat in exactly the same terms as that of partaking of the blood (Lv. 3: 17). Similarly the fat and the blood are closely associated with one another in Isaiah's denunciation (Is. 1: 11 and *cf.* Is. 34: 6). If the manipulation of blood and the final pouring of it at the base of the altar are essentials of sacrifice, no less so is the burning of the fat on the altar. Again, in David's lamentation over Saul and Jonathan (2 Sa. 1: 22) fat is clearly just as much a symbol of life (or death) as is blood.

receive adequate explanation only when we hold that sacrifice is inherently the destruction of the victims.

In other places atonement is connected with such ceremonies as the pouring of oil on the head of the cleansed leper (Lv. 14: 18, 29), the offering of incense (Nu. 16: 46), the scapegoat (Lv. 16: 10), and there are others. But these do not seem to forward our inquiry so we pass over them, merely noting that in each case the removal of the particular thing sacrificed from the possession of the offerer seems indicated.[1] In the case of the animal offerings this is almost invariably by death.

Attention should also be drawn to the Passover ritual. In the original Passover, although there is no mention of atonement, there is mention of the blood as a means of averting destruction. 'And the blood shall be to you for a token upon the houses where ye are: and when I see the blood, I will pass over you, and there shall no plague be upon you to destroy you, when I smite the land of Egypt' (Ex. 12: 13). It is impossible to understand from the splashing of blood on the lintel and doorposts that a life is being presented to anyone. The obvious symbolism is that a death has taken place, and this death substitutes for the death of the first-born.

We conclude, then, that the evidence afforded by the use of the term *dām* in the Old Testament indicates that it signifies life violently taken rather than the continued presence of life available for some new function, in short, death rather than life, and that this is supported by the references to atonement.

II. 'BLOOD' IN THE NEW TESTAMENT

The word αἷμα is found in all ninety-eight times in the New Testament, sometimes simply of blood without any implication of life or death or the like. Thus five times we meet the expression 'flesh and blood', there are four references to the woman with the issue of blood, and there is the unusual expression 'born not of bloods'

---

[1] H. Hubert and M. Mauss in their important examination of the concept of sacrifice concluded that the essential thing is the destruction of the victims, at least as regards possession by the worshipper (*L'Année Sociologique*, II, 1897–8, pp. 71, 75f., 133, *etc.*). Eugene Masure finds the essence of sacrifice in 'a religious transfer of property' (*The Christian Sacrifice*, London, 1944, p. 34).

(Jn. 1: 13). Altogether such passages account for twenty-four occurrences of the word.

Twenty-five times the word indicates violent death, this being the largest group, as we have already seen to be the case in the Old Testament. A good example is the statement of St. Paul, 'when the blood of Stephen thy witness was shed, I also was standing by' (Acts 22: 20). As that death was by stoning there is no emphasis on the literal outpouring of blood. The expression stands simply for violent death. So is it with the query of the martyrs in the Apocalypse, 'How long, O Master, the holy and true, dost thou not judge and avenge our blood on them that dwell on the earth?' (Rev. 6: 10). It makes nonsense of this passage to insist that there is any emphasis on a literal shedding of blood. The people in question are those 'that had been slain for the word of God, and for the testimony which they held' (Rev. 6: 9), quite irrespective of how they met their death. Very important in this group are the references to 'the blood of Abel' and the 'blood of Zachariah' (Lk. 11: 51), for they form parallels to 'the blood of Christ', and both of them plainly signify death and not any offering of life.

A usage which is probably derived from this is that in which 'blood' signifies spiritual, rather than physical, death, as when St. Paul says to the Jews opposing him: 'Your blood be upon your own heads; I am clean: from henceforth I will go unto the Gentiles' (Acts 18: 6; and see Acts 20: 26).

Twelve times we come across references to the blood of animal sacrifices, all of them in Hebrews; but with one exception they tell us little about the way sacrifice was regarded, being allusions to what was actually done without any attempt to explain why it was done. The only possible exception is Hebrews 9: 13 where 'the blood of goats and bulls' is linked with 'the ashes of a heifer', and since the latter undoubtedly points to death it may be held that the former does also, or at the very least that it is congruous with it.

The remaining passages all refer in one way or another to the blood of Christ, and on a number of occasions the reference seems plainly to His death, without any necessary implication of sacrifice. Thus in Romans 5: 9 we are said to be 'justified by his blood' and 'saved from the wrath through him'. This is parallel to 'reconciled ... through the death of his Son' and 'saved by his life' in the next verse, while it follows references to dying in each of the three preceding verses. It does not seem possible to resist the conclusion that 'his blood' here refers to the death of the Lord. It is not otherwise with 'the blood of his cross' (Col. 1: 20), for a cross has no place in the sacrificial system, and stands only for a particularly unpleasant death. There seems no reason for interpreting Ephesians 2: 13 in any other way, especially since here 'made nigh in the blood of Christ' seems to give much the same thought as 'might reconcile them both in one body unto God through the cross' (verse 16). Very clear is the word of the high priest to the apostles, 'ye have filled Jerusalem with your teaching, and intend to bring this man's blood upon us' (Acts 5: 28), where the reference is plainly to the death of Christ, this time with the added thought of responsibility for that death. The death is meant also in 1 John 5: 6, where Jesus is said to have come 'by water and blood'; of which passage even Westcott, who holds strongly to the thought that blood signifies release of life, can say: 'There can be no doubt that the Death upon the Cross satisfies the conception of "coming by blood."'[1] Probably we should include in this group also two passages in the Apocalypse, *viz.* those which refer to Him 'that loosed us from our sins by his blood' (Rev. 1: 5), and to His vesture, 'a garment sprinkled with (or dipped in) blood' (Rev. 19: 13), though perhaps some would prefer to include them among passages referring to sacrifice.

There is an interesting passage where the blood cannot be interpreted as a reference to sacrifice, namely that referring to the drinking of Christ's blood (Jn. 6: 53ff.), for there is no place in the Hebrew sacrificial system for drinking blood. To understand this passage as signifying a participation in the life of Christ is to assume the point at issue, for it certainly does not prove it. Indeed, the indications are the other way, for the mention of blood and flesh in separation points to death rather than life,[2] and, moreover, we cannot overlook the fact that drinking the blood is coupled with eating the flesh. There is no reason for thinking that the two expressions give essentially dissimilar ideas, and it is very difficult

[1] *In loc.*

[2] Bernard says that the use of the expression πίνειν τὸ αἷμα in Jn. 6: 53 'as distinct from φαγεῖν τὴν σάρκα, indicates that the Flesh and Blood have been separated, and thus it suggests death, even more definitely than φαγεῖν τὴν σάρκα does' (*ICC, in loc.*). Westcott also sees in the separation indication of violent death (*in loc.*).

to understand the latter expression of participation in the life. And if we do we have destroyed the case for thinking that the life is in the blood; it would then be also in the flesh. Plainly the passage points to the death of Christ.[1] Perhaps we should also notice 1 Corinthians 10: 16; 11: 27 here, for although neither of them speaks explicitly of drinking the blood, they are passages of the same type. All things considered, it would seem that the passages noticed in this paragraph are satisfactorily interpreted only if the blood of Christ be taken as pointing us to His death.

A further group refers to the blood of Christ as the price of our redemption (Acts 20: 28; Eph. 1: 7, *etc.*). This group seems to point to the blood as meaning death, but no stress is laid upon the passages which comprise it, because it would be possible to interpret them of the offering of life, if that could be substantiated from elsewhere.

The remaining passages seem to point to sacrificial blood. Six times there is reference to covenant blood, which calls for no comment to show the sacrificial reference: thus God is said to have set forth Christ as ἱλαστήριον . . . ἐν τῷ αὐτοῦ αἵματι (Rom. 3: 25), where the word ἱλαστήριον points us to the sacrifices.[2] In Hebrews 9 the whole context with its mention of the blood of sacrificial victims shows that verses 12, 14 carry a reference to the sacrificial system when they speak of the blood of Christ, and the same is true of 10: 19. The unusual phrase, 'blood of sprinkling' (Heb. 12: 24), points to a sacrificial action, and the context shows that in Hebrews 13: 12 the sin offering is in mind. The sprinkling of the blood in 1 Peter 1: 2 is a sacrificial action, while the blood 'as of a lamb without blemish and without spot' (1 Pet. 1: 19) is clearly sacrificial blood. The same is probably true of 'the blood of the Lamb' (Rev. 7: 14; 12: 11). Finally, the thought of cleansing associated with the blood in 1 John 1: 7 seems to be an allusion to sacrifice.

When we were dealing with sacrifice in the Old Testament we saw reason for thinking that the infliction of death rather than the release of life was the dominant thought, and these passages, which

---

[1] It may be noted that both expressions are found in a metaphorical sense in the Old Testament, namely Ps. 27: 2; 2 Sa. 23: 17.

[2] *Cf.* W. Sanday and A. C. Headlam: 'It is impossible to get rid from this passage of the double idea (1) of a sacrifice; (2) of a sacrifice which is propitiatory' (*ICC, Romans*, p. 91).

view the death of Christ as a sacrifice, do not disturb that conclusion. There is nothing in the context of any of them to show that
the writer was thinking of the offering of life when he spoke of
Christ's death in sacrificial terms. Contrariwise, each one of them
yields a natural interpretation when we think of the blood as
signifying death.

One or two of the sacrificial passages strengthen our impression
that the blood means death. Thus in Hebrews 9: 14f. we read:
'How much more shall the blood of Christ . . . cleanse your
conscience from dead works to serve the living God? And for this
cause he is the mediator of a new covenant, that a death having
taken place . . .' It is hard to envisage a reason for interpreting 'the
blood' here in a sense other than that given by the words which
follow: 'a death having taken place'.

If anything the connection between blood and death is even
plainer in Hebrews 12: 24 where we read of coming 'to Jesus the
mediator of a new covenant, and to the blood of sprinkling that
speaketh better than (that of) Abel'. Whether we include the words
in parentheses or not, the contrast is between the blood of Abel and
the blood of Jesus.[1] There can be no doubt that the blood of Abel is
a metaphorical way of referring to the death of that patriarch, and
it is unnatural accordingly to interpret the blood of Jesus as
signifying anything other than His death. Yet the reference to
sprinkling shows that the thought of sacrifice is in the writer's
mind, so that for him the blood of sacrifice seems to have pointed
to death.

Again, we read in Hebrews 13: 11f.: 'For the bodies of those
beasts, whose blood is brought into the holy place by the high
priest as an offering for sin, are burned without the camp. Wherefore Jesus also, that he might sanctify the people through his own
blood, suffered without the gate.' Here the comparison is made
between the sin offering and the blood of Jesus, but the point that is
singled out for notice in the Levitical sacrifice is not the presentation of the blood (though that, too, is important to this writer
as we see from his previous references to it), but the burning of the

---

[1] I regard the view that 'that of Abel' refers to the blood of Abel's sacrifice as
untenable, on the ground that the reference to the blood speaking marks the
passage as an allusion to Gn. 4: 10. There is no suggestion in Gn. 4 of the blood of
Abel's sacrifice speaking.

carcass outside the camp. This part of the sacrifice can point only to the death of the animal, and certainly not to any presentation of life. Once more we see that the sacrificial allusion indicates the death of Jesus.

Thus it seems tolerably certain that in both the Old and New Testaments the blood signifies essentially the death. It is freely admitted that there are some passages in which it is possible to interpret the blood as signifying life, but even these yield a better sense (and one which is consistent with the wider biblical usage) if understood to mean 'life given up in death'. In particular, there seems no reason for disputing the dictum of J. Behm: ' "Blood of Christ" is like "cross", only another, clearer expression for the death of Christ in its salvation meaning'.[1]

ADDITIONAL NOTE ON THE MEANING OF THE WORD 'BLOOD'

A. M. Stibbs, in his monograph *The Meaning of the Word 'Blood' in Scripture*,[2] gathers passages supporting the view that 'blood' means 'life released' rather than 'death inflicted' from the writings of Nathaniel Micklem, C. H. Dodd, O. C. Quick, F. C. N. Hicks, P. T. Forsyth, B. F. Westcott, and W. Sanday and A. C. Headlam. The list could easily be extended. The idea is specially prominent in H. Clay Trumbull's *The Blood Covenant*,[3] where statements abound like 'not merely that the blood is *essential* to life, but that, in a peculiar sense, it *is* life'.[4] Something very like this appears as early as H. Bushnell, who says: 'Not that the life thus offered, the life made sacred and mysterious by such associations gathered to it, carries effect by ceasing to live, that is, by death symbolized in the sprinkling of it. No, it gets its effect as being life, the sacred, mystic, new-creating touch of life.'[5] 'It is not death, but life, that is in it.'[6]

[1] *TWNT*, I, p. 173.
[2] 2nd edn. (London, 1954), pp. 4ff.
[3] New York, 1885.
[4] *Op. cit*, p. 38.
[5] *The Vicarious Sacrifice* (London, 1866), p. 401.
[6] *Op. cit*., p. 434.

He has similar statements in *Forgiveness and Law*,[1] but he does not make this view central to his understanding of the atonement.

Advocates of such views scarcely face the fact that, while the blood of Christ is said in the New Testament to bring about a variety of effects, none is specifically connected with life. As A. M. Farrer puts it: 'In the New Testament the Blood of Christ is a ransom-price, a means of purging, the element to ratify a solemn covenant; but the explanation offered for all these ideas – the communication of life – is never stated, but has to be read in.'[2] The point is important. The idea is never expressed in the New Testament. It must be read into the New Testament by those who have previously decided that this is what 'blood' must mean. When it is added that the sources exterior to the New Testament which are relied on do not yield all the support its advocates claim to the 'life' idea it will be seen that the whole idea is dubious to say the least.

Many reputable scholars strongly oppose the view. Thus James Moffatt can say: 'Semitic scholars warn us against finding in these words (Lv. 17[11]) either the popular idea of the substitution of the victim for the sinner, or even the theory that the essential thing in sacrifice is the offering of a life to God'.[3]

James Denney is very forthright in his opposition and speaks of 'the strange caprice which fascinated Westcott' in distinguishing in the blood of Christ '(i) His death, and (ii) His life; or (i) His blood shed, and (ii) His blood offered; or (i) His life laid down, and (ii) His life liberated and made available for men . . . I venture to say that a more groundless fancy never haunted and troubled the interpretation of any part of Scripture than that which is introduced by this distinction into the Epistle to the Hebrews and the First Epistle of John . . . there is no meaning in saying that by His death His life, as something other than His death, is "liberated" and "made available" for men. On the contrary, what makes His risen life significant and a saving power for sinners is neither more nor less than this that His death is in it.'[4]

J. Armitage Robinson's comment is, 'To the Jewish mind "blood" was not merely – nor even chiefly – the life-current flow-

[1] London, 1874.
[2] *The Parish Communion*, ed. A. G. Hebert (London, 1957), p. 89.
[3] *ICC, Hebrews*, p. xlii.
[4] *The Death of Christ* (London, 1951), pp. 149f.

ing in the veins of the living: it was especially the life poured out in death; and yet more particularly in its religious aspect it was the symbol of sacrificial death.'[1] Similarly Frederic Platt refuses to endorse Westcott's distinction between 'a life given' and 'a life liberated and made available for men',[2] while G. F. Moore deprecates the idea that 'the offering of a *life* to God is the essential thing in sacrifice', pointing out that 'No such theory appears in later Jewish thought'.[3] More recently F. J. Taylor has written: 'It is hardly likely that blood could signify life released . . . for early Hebrew thought had no adequate conception of a spiritual survival after death',[4] though C. R. North in the same volume accepts the view that the blood signifies the life.[5] J. Behm equates the death of Christ with 'the Blood'.[6] So C. Ryder Smith on Hebrews 10:19 says: 'As elsewhere in the New Testament, the Christian emphasis *under the great symbol* is not on life, but on death.'[7]

---

[1] *St. Paul's Epistle to the Ephesians* (London, 1904), p. 29.

[2] *HDAC*, I, p. 121.

[3] *Enc. Bib.*, col. 4221 and note.

[4] *TWBB*, p. 33.

[5] *TWBB*, Art. 'Sacrifice'.

[6] *TWNT*, II, p. 136. He reaches a similar conclusion in his treatment of αἷμα (*TWNT*, I, p. 173).

[7] *The Bible Doctrine of Salvation* (London, 1946), p. 233; and *cf.* J. S. Stewart, *A Man in Christ* (London, 1947), p. 237; F. W. Dillistone, *The Significance of the Cross* (London, 1946), p. 68; G. O. Griffith, *St. Paul's Gospel to the Romans* (Oxford, 1949), p. 17.

CHAPTER IV

THE LAMB OF GOD

TWICE JOHN THE BAPTIST is recorded as having spoken of
Jesus as 'the Lamb of God '(Jn. 1: 29, 36), and on the first occasion
he added, 'which taketh away the sin of the world!' 'The Lamb of
God' is a way of referring to Jesus which has made a powerful
appeal to Christian devotion through the centuries. The petition,
'O Lamb of God, that takest away the sins of the world, have mercy
upon us', occurs in many liturgies, while those who prefer ex-
tempore prayer often find the words 'Lamb of God' come easily
to their lips. Christian art has found the symbolism congenial, and
many are the pictures and the stained glass windows which show
forth the Lamb. There is something about the expression which
does not require explanation before it can appeal to the depths of
the heart. In the words themselves lurks a numinous quality.

We are so accustomed to using the expression that we rarely
stop to consider that it is a curious description of a man. Why
should Jesus be called 'God's lamb'? What precisely is meant when
He is so called? It is easier to ask the questions than to answer them.
John does not stop to explain and as the expression does not appear
to be used by anyone before him we cannot appeal to his pre-
decessors.

First, let us notice that the genitive, 'of God', is ambiguous. It
might mean 'belonging to God', or it might mean, 'provided by
God' (cf. Gn. 22: 8). The Lamb might be thought of as standing in
a special relationship to God. Or it might be understood in terms
of God's taking of the initiative in bringing men salvation. The
Lamb takes away the world's sin. In the Bible God is thought of as
the only one who can do this. Thus the Lamb may well be the
Lamb which God provides in order to bring about His will.

No sufficient reason has been given for deciding in favour of
either view. But it is a habit of the Fourth Evangelist to use
expressions which may be taken in more ways than one, evidently
with a view to including all the possible meanings. For example,
William Temple has pointed out that the opening words of this

Gospel, usually translated 'in the beginning', might also be understood as referring to the fundamental eternal reality. He says, 'So
the word really means both things; and here the expression used
means both "in the beginning of history" and "at the root of the
universe".'[1] A very well-known example of the same sort of thing
is found in the expression about being 'born ἄνωθεν' in chapter 3.
Does it mean 'born again' or 'born from above'? The Greek is
patient of either meaning. Most scholars agree that both are true
and that probably both are meant. John does this kind of thing
repeatedly. It is his habit to use words which may be understood in
more ways than one apparently with the deliberate intention that
the full meaning should be understood. The probability is that this
is what he is doing here. According to his habit he will want us to
think of both meanings.[2]

When we look for the antecedents of the term our search is very
barren. The exact expression 'the Lamb of God' (ὁ ἀμνὸς τοῦ θεοῦ)
is not found in any literature known to us before St. John's Gospel.
We are not in a position to say that John has taken the expression
from such-and-such a source. As far as we can see it originated with
him. We are driven accordingly to examine ideas and expressions
which are sufficiently akin to this one to be taken seriously as its
possible sources. For, of course, if we have the source we may
well find ourselves with the meaning. A number of suggestions
have been made.

1. *The Passover lamb.* Perhaps the commonest suggestion is that
the Passover is in mind. Support is found for this view in the fact
that there are indications throughout this Gospel that the Passover
imagery was often present to the mind of the evangelist. He
mentions the Passover more than any other feast. Most com-

---

[1] *Readings in St. John's Gospel* (London, 1947), p. 3.

[2] Perhaps another possibility should be noted, that the expression may reflect
the Hebraic construction whereby greatness is conveyed by referring to the deity
(as when Nineveh is described as 'a city great to God', *i.e.* 'a very great city', Jon. 3:
3). Thus J. C. Ryle suggests that 'the Lamb of God' may be a way of saying 'that
eminent, great, divine, and most excellent Lamb' and he instances 'thunderings of
God' (Ex. 9: 28) as an example of this construction (*Expository Thoughts on the
Gospels, St. John*, I, London, 1957, p. 60). He himself prefers the view that 'it
signifies the Lamb which God has provided from all eternity'.

mentators agree that he puts the death of Christ at the time the
Passover victims were being slain in the Temple, and in this way
identifies Christ's death with the Passover sacrifice, as does Paul in
1 Corinthians 5: 7 (Jn. 19: 36 is usually thought to be a citation of
Ex. 12: 46 or Nu. 9: 12, both of which refer to the Passover; some
see a reference to Ps. 33: 21, but this seems much less likely). The
suggestion is made accordingly that the inclusion of this saying of
the Baptist right at the beginning of his Gospel is John's way of
introducing this topic. Then he proceeds to develop it throughout
his Gospel.

The Passover imagery is highly appropriate as an illustration of
the work of Christ. It reminds us of the lambs and the kids that
were slain in Egypt those centuries before, and which were the
means of diverting destruction from the households where the
sacrifice was made and the blood placed on the doorposts. The
great deliverance lingered in the minds of the people, and throughout the Old Testament there are references to it. In some sense it
was the Exodus and the events associated with it which transformed
the slave rabble into the very people of God. All these things are
important for an understanding of Christ's work for us. His
sacrifice of Himself delivers men from the destruction that their
sins involved them in. And it transforms men from being slaves to
sin to being the people of God. The figure has force.

But objections are lodged against this interpretation. Some
scholars reject the identification on the grounds that the Passover
was not regarded as an expiatory sacrifice. The Lamb of God is here
expressly said to take away the sin of the world. The Passover, it is
objected, was not thought of as taking away sin. This objection,
however, even though it is sometimes made by reputable scholars,
will scarcely hold water. There is evidence that all sacrifice was held
to be expiatory,[1] and this will include the Passover. But in any case
there are Rabbinic passages which specifically include the Passover.
There is a Midrash which says, 'I will have pity on you, through
the blood of the Passover and the blood of circumcision, and I will

[1] Lv. 17: 11 connects atonement with 'the blood' (which was certainly shed in
the Passover sacrifice), and not with any particular sacrifice. *Cf.* J. Pedersen,
'Everything in any way connected with sacrifice acquired an expiatory power'
(*Israel*, III–IV, London, 1947, p. 364). So also, C. R. North: 'By the close of the OT
period, too, all sacrifices were believed to have atoning value' (*TWBB*, p. 206).

forgive you.'[1] The Midrash says that the Israelites were under God's condemnation on account of their idolatry. They were liable to the death penalty. But the Passover blood freed them. Plainly this sacrifice is regarded as expiatory. It dealt with their sins. This same idolatry in Egypt is mentioned in another connection and the Passover is equated with the sin offering. Numbers 7: 46 is cited and then the comment added, 'This was in allusion to the Paschal sacrifice'.[2] It is difficult to see how the Paschal sacrifice could be linked so closely with the sin offering were it not regarded as expiatory.

Another relevant passage is found in Josephus. He tells us that the Israelites in Egypt 'in readiness to start, sacrificed, purified the houses with the blood . . .'[3] This is a plain reference to the Passover and to the Passover as purging sin.

Such passages as these make it impossible to hold that the Passover was held not to be expiatory. Whatever be the case with the original institution, by the time of the New Testament it was certainly held in one of its aspects to be atoning. There seems no good reason then for maintaining that because 'the Lamb of God' takes away sin the reference cannot be to the Passover.

More important is the fact that there is no evidence at all that the Passover victim would have been recognized under the expression 'the Lamb of God'. We so often use the words, 'the Passover lamb', that we tend to overlook the fact that this is not a first-century expression. The victim offered at the Passover was in fact not necessarily a lamb at all. It might be, and often was, a kid of the goats.[4] There is no more reason for speaking of 'the Passover lamb'

---

[1] *Ex.R.* 15: 12 (Soncino edn., p. 176). Dalman translates the last expression as 'I propitiate your souls' (*Jesus-Jeshua*, London, 1929, p. 167); he cites another Midrash, 'I see the Paschal blood and propitiate you' (*ibid.*). J. Jeremias renders the same words 'and will atone for you (*mkpr 'l npshwtykm*)' (*The Eucharistic Words of Jesus*, Oxford, 1955, p. 147, n. 3). He cites several other Rabbinic passages which make it plain that the Passover was regarded as expiatory.

[2] *Nu.R.* 13: 20 (Soncino edn., p. 554). The passage goes on to cite the words, 'when I see the blood, I will pass over you' (Ex. 12: 13) as showing that they had been redeemed from their idol worship.

[3] *Ant.* ii. 312.

[4] The passage from *Numbers Rabbah* cited above explicitly speaks of a goat as the Passover victim: 'For a he-goat was offered as a sin-offering on account of the sin of idol-worship' (13: 20; Soncino edn., p. 554).

than of 'the Passover kid'. When the men of the first century wanted to refer to the Passover victim they called it neither a lamb nor a kid, but simply, 'the Passover', τὸ πασχα. A very well-known example is found in 1 Corinthians 5 : 7, where Paul speaks of Christ as 'our Passover' (τὸ πασχα ἡμῶν).

G. Buchanan Gray says forthrightly, 'the Paschal victim was . . . neither as a matter of fact necessarily a lamb, nor in the usage of the time was it called a lamb; the proper term for it was "Passover", and it is only reasonable to suppose that had the author of the Fourth Gospel intended this he would, like St. Paul, have used the correct and unambiguous designation.'[1]

For all its popularity I do not see how the interpretation which sees in the words a reference to the Passover can be substantiated. A modern habit of speech is no basis on which to erect the identification of an expression in use in the first century. 'God's lamb' is far too general a term to have aroused in the first century specific associations of the Passover. The connection is in modern minds, not in the Greek term.

2. *The 'lamb that is led to the slaughter'* (*Is.* 53: 7). This is certainly possible. Vincent Taylor, to name no other, sees in 'the Lamb of God' a reference to the Suffering Servant chapter, and specifically to Isaiah 53 :7,12.[2] But there is nothing in John which points to this identification .In John the lamb is 'the Lamb of God'.In Isaiah this designation is not used. The linguistics of the passages are against it.

The big point in favour of this view is that the lamb in Isaiah may be held to be linked with the taking away of sin, and the Lamb in John is certainly so linked. But even so, this is not convincing. The fact must be faced that, while in Isaiah 53 it is said that the Servant suffers for sin, it is not said that the lamb suffers in this way. The 'lamb that is led to the slaughter' is employed as an illustration of the humility and the submissiveness of the Servant, not of His function as sin-bearer.

It seems to me that the only way in which 'the Lamb of God' could be detected as an allusion to the lamb in Isaiah 53: 7 would be

---

[1] *Sacrifice in the Old Testament* (Oxford, 1925), p. 397.
[2] He says, 'the Evangelist is thinking of the Servant of Yahweh, for Isa. liii. 7 and 12 easily explain the references to a lamb and to sin-bearing' (*Jesus and His Sacrifice*, London, 1939, p. 227).

if 'the Lamb' were recognized as a messianic designation and if
Isaiah 53 were also widely recognized as messianic. Then the two
would come together naturally. The first point should probably
be conceded. The lamb symbolism in Revelation shows that some
early Christians referred to the Messiah in this way. But we
scarcely need that. The way John the Baptist uses the expression
in John 1 shows plainly enough that it was meant as a designation
of the Messiah. The difficulty is in the other point. If there was no
widely held idea that Isaiah 53 applies to the Messiah, then more
than this single expression will be needed to make plain a reference
to this prophecy. It seems to me that the evidence produced by
H. H. Rowley makes it more than difficult to hold that the Suffering
Servant was widely equated with the Messiah in pre-Christian
times.[1] So I do not think that this identification is at all probable.

3. *The Suffering Servant.* This view is rather like the one which
we have just been considering, but it does not rest so much on the
occurrence of the word 'lamb' in Isaiah 53. The thought is rather
that the term 'lamb' in John 1 is rightly understood only when it is
seen to mean 'servant'. 'The Lamb of God' then becomes almost
exactly equivalent to 'the Servant of the Lord'. J. Jeremias puts it
this way: 'the expression ὁ ἀμνὸς τοῦ θεοῦ conceals both a factual
and a linguistic difficulty. (1) The description of the Saviour as a
lamb is unknown to late Judaism. (2) The expression is an un-
paralleled genitive combination. Both difficulties are solved if we
refer to the Aramaic where *talyā'* means (*a*) the lamb, (*b*) the boy,
the servant. Probably behind the phrase ὁ ἀμνὸς τοῦ θεοῦ lies an
Aramaic *talyā dē'lāhā'* in the sense of '*ebhedh YHWH*.'[2]
Jeremias certainly succeeds in drawing our attention to the
difficulty. But it is not so certain that he has found the solution. He
has not shown, for example, that there are real grounds for holding
that the Greek ἀμνός, 'lamb', was regarded as an acceptable
translation of the Aramaic *talyā'*. Nor has he shown that this
Aramaic word was regarded as equivalent to the Hebrew '*ebhedh*,
'servant'.[3] Nor does he face the difficulties that it seems highly

---

[1] *Bulletin of the John Rylands Library*, Sept. 1950, p. 103, n. 4.

[2] W. Zimmerli and J. Jeremias, *The Servant of God* (London, 1957), p. 82.

[3] C. H. Dodd makes this criticism: 'ἀμνός in the LXX never translates *tāleh*. No
examples are adduced of *talyā'* as a rendering for '*ebhedh* ... Thus we lack evidence

unlikely that an expression as well known as 'the servant of the Lord' should not be recognized, and that it should be translated by such a difficult and unusual expression as 'the lamb of God'. Again I must insist that our familiarity with the expression should not lead us into the error of thinking it was either familiar or obvious to the men of the first century. Though it does not lack attractiveness the theory of Jeremias does not really seem as though it will explain the facts.

4. *The daily sacrifice.* Every morning and every evening a lamb was offered in sacrifice on the altar in the Temple. This would be the most familiar of offerings. Hoskyns may be named as one who sees in it the clue to John's meaning. 'Salvation', he writes, 'presupposes sacrifice. Salvation from sin depends upon that sacrifice of which the lambs, consecrated morning and evening in the Temple to be the possession of God, provide the proper analogy.'[1]

There seems no reason why this daily sacrifice should not have been referred to as 'God's lamb', and if it was, then it will certainly have been in John's mind. But we have no reason for thinking that it was so known. As far as our evidence goes it was never described in this way. This being so we can scarcely take this sacrifice as the origin of John's term.

5. *The 'gentle lamb'* (*Je.* 11: 19). On one occasion the prophet Jeremiah said, 'I was like a gentle lamb that is led to the slaughter' (Je. 11: 19), and it is possible that John had this passage in mind. The only attraction in this suggestion appears to be that the meekness of the lamb mentioned by the prophet may well point to the unresisting way in which Christ went to His death. There is an emphasis on innocency. But we have no reason for thinking that this particular piece of imagery was widely known so that 'the

in support of the view either that the Aramaic-speaking Church (or John the Baptist) could have spoken of the '*bd YHWH* as *ṭly' d'lh'*, or that a bilingual translator who took *ṭalyā'* in the sense of "lamb" would have chosen ἀμνός as its equivalent' (*The Interpretation of the Fourth Gospel*, Cambridge, 1953, pp. 235f.).

[1] E. C. Hoskyns, *The Fourth Gospel*, ed. F. N. Davey (London, 1950), p. 169. Again he speaks of 'the original and primary witness of John, who declares Jesus to be the property of God, by whose complete obedience the normal sacrifices in the Temple – a lamb without blemish was offered daily both morning and evening . . .– were fulfilled and superseded' (*op. cit.*, p. 176).

Lamb of God' would immediately recall it. Nor does Jeremiah associate his lamb with the taking away of sins, and that is the characteristic point about the lamb in John. Gentleness and innocency are not the same thing as expiation. There is ancient evidence for thinking of this passage in connection with the Johannine one. Origen mentioned it and linked it with Isaiah 53: 7.[1] But, despite this high authority, few have been persuaded.

6. *The scapegoat*. The fatal objection to the last suggestion was that the lamb of which Jeremiah speaks is not thought of as taking away sins. Perhaps in reaction to suggestions of this kind some have thought that the allusion may be to the scapegoat of Leviticus 16. The scapegoat certainly supplies what Jeremiah's lamb lacks, for if there is one thing that the scapegoat does it is to take away sin. It fits in very well with the words, 'which taketh away the sin of the world'.

But for all that it is more than a little difficult to see why the suggestion should be taken seriously. For after all the scapegoat was a goat and not a lamb. I see not the slightest reason for holding that the scapegoat could ever have been called 'God's lamb'. There is certainly no evidence that it ever bore this name or anything like it.

7. *The triumphant lamb of the apocalypses*. A most interesting suggestion arises from the frequent use of the lamb imagery in the apocalyptic imagery so popular in the first century. There the lamb was often used in a way which is, to us at least, quite unexpected. It was usual in the apocalypses to use beasts of various kinds as symbols for men. The lamb, and more especially the horned lamb, was used as the symbol of a leader, a triumphant conqueror. It may be that this animal was deliberately chosen by the apocalyptic writers because it was the last animal that would be suspected of pointing to military conquerors. It may be that there was the thought of the bell wether leading the flock and that this led on to the thought of the Messiah leading His people. Whatever the reasoning there can be no doubt as to the fact. The apocalypses did make use of the lamb in this way.

---

[1] See J. H. Bernard, *ICC, St. John*, I, p. 43.

Perhaps the outstanding illustration of this is in the Revelation. There Christ is seen as the mighty conqueror. This note runs through the book. And the writer's favourite way of referring to the victorious Lord is as 'the Lamb'. This title will carry an allusion to the Lord's death, for a lamb was a sacrificial animal, and Revelation not seldom brings out the thought that believers are saved only through the death of Christ. But coupled with this is the thought of Christ triumphant. The Lamb is supreme. 'Unto him that sitteth on the throne, and unto the Lamb, be the blessing, and the honour, and the glory, and the dominion, for ever and ever' (Rev. 5: 13).

Since Revelation so plainly shows that Christ can be spoken of as the Lamb who triumphs, some have thought that this gives us the clue to the imagery in John 1. They suggest that the Baptist with his deep interest in eschatology saw Jesus as God's triumphant Hero. This view has been powerfully argued by C. H. Dodd.[1] He thinks there are four possibilities, the sin offering, the paschal lamb, the suffering Servant and 'the young ram which is ἄρχων καὶ ἡγούμενος τῶν προβάτων, i.e. the Messiah as "King of Israel".'[2] He examines and rejects the first three and concludes that 'We are left with the idea of the lamb as a symbol of the Messiah as leader of the flock of God, i.e. as "King of Israel".'[3]

This is not the most convincing line of argument. It is note-worthy that Dodd cites little positive evidence. He is content with the weaknesses of the other positions and the general probability that a reference to a lamb in such a context will necessarily point us to the apocalyptic lamb with its associations of triumph.

There are objections. A minor one is that the triumphant lamb of the apocalypses is usually a horned lamb (cf. Rev. 5: 6). But no horn is mentioned in John 1. Again, the word for 'Lamb' in Revelation is ἀρνίον while that in John 1 is ἀμνός, but we should probably not make too much of this difference. A more weighty objection is that the specific function of the 'Lamb of God' in John is to take away sin, whereas this function is not associated with the triumphant lamb. He rather is the one who overthrows the enemies of God. While admittedly these two concepts are com-

[1] Op. cit., pp. 230–37.
[2] Op. cit., p. 233.
[3] Op. cit., p. 236.

patible yet the language of John 1 is not such as naturally to evoke memories of apocalyptic.

Dodd's answer to this point is that the Greek need mean no more than 'remove sin'. It does not necessarily point to atonement. He points out that 'To make an end of sin is a function of the Jewish Messiah, quite apart from any thought of a redemptive death'.[1] But this is to ignore the cross. A putting an end to sin which takes place quite apart from the cross can never give us the clue to the removal of sin in a system which makes the cross as central, as does Christianity in general, and the Fourth Gospel in particular. John's language is not the same as that of the writers Dodd cites, and it does seem to mean that the 'Lamb of God' will take away sin in a sense different from the conqueror of the apocalypses who brings in a new shape of affairs where sin finds no place.

C. K. Barrett agrees that Dodd does not do justice to the language used. He points out that the passages Dodd cites for the Messiah's making an end of sin do not contain the word αἴρειν. The expression αἴρειν ἁμαρτίαν he thinks suggests the Hebrew ns' ḥṭ', ns' 'wn, 'which occur not infrequently in cultic contexts, and often signify the removal not of evil simply but of guilt'.[2] This is the critical point. The Johannine language means more than Dodd is prepared to admit. It is different from the language of the apocalypses and full justice must be done to this difference.

A further objection arises from a consideration of the readers for whom the Fourth Gospel was written. To say that there are difficulties in deciding this question is a massive understatement. But, whoever were the precise first recipients of this Gospel, most scholars agree that in part, at any rate, it was meant to appeal to men whom Barrett calls 'adherents of the "higher religion of Hellenism"'. There is too much that would appeal to the Greek mind for us to think that it is accidental. Now it is difficult to see how such men could possibly discern the allusion to the horned lamb. To cite Barrett again, 'What, we may ask, would these men make of the horned lamb of Enoch? They could indeed speak of spiritual sacrifices, allegorizing the familiar cultus of the Hellenistic world, but anything less likely to appeal to them than the

---

[1] *Op. cit.*, p. 237.
[2] *NTS*, I, 1955, p. 210.

apocalyptic figure of the Lamb-Messiah would be difficult to imagine.'[1] These are strong words, but they appear to be justified. Unless we are prepared to maintain that this Gospel was written with no intention of appealing to the Hellenistic world, it is difficult to take Dodd's contention seriously. All the more is this the case in that we have no more than two references, neither of them with an explanation. In a book like Revelation references to 'the Lamb' are so frequent that any reader, Hellenist or Semitic, must begin to ask what they mean. But a couple of unexplained references are a different proposition. They are not prominent. They receive no particular emphasis. They do not form a leading idea of this Gospel. It seems to follow that they must have been recognizable by the Gospel's first readers at sight. It is more than difficult to envisage this with Hellenists if the apocalyptic conqueror is indeed in mind. And in any case it is to be borne in mind that there is less apocalyptic in the Fourth Gospel than in other parts of the New Testament.

There is also the fact that, while there are quite a number of references to the apocalyptic lamb, in none so far known to us is this lamb called 'the Lamb of God'. Once again it is necessary to insist that this is an unusual expression. If we are to claim that it applies to one particular lamb then we need convincing reason. And that has not been shown.

8. *The lamb that God provides* (Gn. 22: 8). When Abraham and Isaac were ascending Mount Moriah the boy was puzzled. 'Behold, the fire and the wood', he said to his father, 'but where is the lamb for a burnt offering?' Abraham replied, 'God will provide himself the lamb for a burnt offering my son' (Gn. 22: 7f.). John may have been thinking of this incident. The reference links God with the lamb. It is not unreasonable to hold that a lamb that God provides might be called 'God's lamb'. And the incident we know to have been very prominent in Jewish thought. The 'Binding of Isaac' was a well-known and well-loved Rabbinic theme. Isaac's willingness to be sacrificed profoundly impressed Jewish expositors and they often refer to the Binding (Akedah). The fact that it does not loom large in Christian thought ought not to blind us to its importance for first-century Jews.

[1] *Op. cit.,* p. 211.

So important was it that G. Vermes is of opinion that, when this is recognized, the passage in John should no longer be regarded as a difficulty. 'For the Palestinian Jew, all lamb sacrifice, and especially the Passover lamb and the Tamid offering, was a memorial of the Akedah with its effects of deliverance, forgiveness of sin and messianic salvation.'[1] Since all lamb sacrifice pointed back to the Akedah so must the reference to 'the Lamb of God'.

A. Richardson is another who supports the view, though perhaps not so forthrightly as Vermes. Richardson examines various suggested explanations of the expression 'the Lamb of God', but is most convinced by this one. He points out that 'Jewish thought increasingly came to hold that the covenant-relationship with God was founded upon Abraham's offering of Isaac: St John is asserting that the new relationship of God and man in Christ (the new covenant) is based upon the fulfilment of the promise contained in Gen. 22. 8, that God would provide the Lamb which would make atonement for universal sin . . . Christ is the Lamb of sacrifice promised by God to Abraham, the father of many nations, and thus he is the God-given universal Sin Bearer'.[2]

This is an interesting line of approach and Richardson has brought out very well the implications of this particular identification. But we would have more confidence in accepting it if we could be certain that the thought of John the Baptist and that of the Rabbis went along similar lines. At many points they certainly diverge, and to establish this identification it would need to be shown, or at least rendered probable, that they did not diverge in their view of the importance of the Akedah. It would also be a help if it could be shown that the victim provided in Isaac's stead (which incidentally proved to be a ram, not a lamb, Gn. 22: 13) was ever called by any name resembling 'God's lamb'. This expression is far from being self-explanatory and it carries no obvious or immediate reference to Genesis 22. For all the confidence of some of the supporters of this view it cannot be held to have been clearly established.

---

[1] *Scripture and Tradition in Judaism* (Leiden, 1961), p. 225. See also H. J. Schoeps, *Paul* (London, 1961), pp. 141–9.
[2] *An Introduction to the Theology of the New Testament* (London, 1958), p. 228. T. F. Glasson is another who inclines to the view that Gn. 22 is behind the expression (*Moses in the Fourth Gospel*, London, 1963, pp. 96–100).

9. *The guilt offering.* We are very much in the habit of thinking of the guilt offering as being a ram, and so it often was. But on certain occasions it was prescribed that a lamb should be sacrificed as a guilt offering (*e.g.* Lv. 14: 12ff., 21, 24f.; Nu. 6: 12). We even find the expression 'the lamb of the guilt offering' (Lv. 14: 24, *etc.*). There is thus some basis for the view that in John 1 the reference is to the guilt offering, the offering which took away sin. This seems very plain to James Morgenstern: 'Here, beyond all doubt, Jesus is conceived of, precisely as was the Servant, as an *'shm*, "a guilt-offering", sacrificing himself for the redemption of mankind from its iniquity and thus effecting its salvation.'[1]

No explanation is more satisfactory than this for the words which refer to the taking away of the world's sin. The guilt offering would fit admirably. But it is difficult to regard it as satisfactory for all that. After all, the guilt offering was so often another animal than a lamb. Characteristically it was a ram, and it might on occasion be a he-goat. 'A lamb' carries no necessary connection with this particular sacrifice. To put the objection the other way round, there seems no reason at all why the guilt offering should be spoken of as 'the Lamb of God'.

Thus there is no lack of suggestions as to the meaning of our expression. Widely divergent ideas are put forward and sometimes urged very confidently. We have seen that more than one of the suggestions has much to commend it, but that in every case it may fairly be urged that it is too specific. The fact is that 'God's Lamb' is too indefinite an expression for us to confine the meaning to any particular lamb, at least to any which has so far been suggested. It is a very general expression, and the suggestions made are all very specific. In each case that is a critical difficulty.

I find it difficult to escape the impression that the expression is sacrificial. The majority of the suggestions that have been made have this in common that in one way or another they understand the words to refer to the offering of Christ as a sacrifice availing to put away the world's sin. The conspicuous exception is that which sees the Lamb as an eschatological figure. Dodd sees it as an allusion to the victorious lamb of the apocalypses, and, while this Lamb is indeed sacrificial in the book of Revelation, it is not

[1] *Vetus Testamentum*, XI, p. 425.

sacrificial in the majority of the apocalypses. As we have seen, Barrett rejects Dodd's view. He cannot see a specific reference to the Lamb of the apocalypses. But the Lamb-imagery may well lead us, he thinks, to the idea that in part at least the Lamb is an eschatological conception. This he finds amply attested in Revelation, while it is also true that John the Baptist, who uses the expression 'the Lamb of God', was very interested in the last things. Indeed it would not be out of keeping to call him an eschatological figure. Out of all this Barrett lays down two propositions which, he feels, give us the key to the expression: '(1) It would be entirely consistent with John the Baptist's message in its original form that he should have described the Messiah as the Lamb of God in the apocalyptic sense. (2) It would be entirely consistent with the Church's handling of the Baptist tradition, and in particular with John the Evangelist's recasting of the earlier gospel tradition, if this "Lamb of God" became a less primitive and more profoundly theological conception. I venture to suggest that we have here the solution to the problem of the title, the "Lamb of God".'[1]

In view of the use of Revelation I imagine that it is not possible to deny outright that there is any eschatological content in the expression 'the Lamb of God'. But I am not persuaded by Barrett's arguments. His approach in this matter is highly speculative. It may be freely granted that more than one idea is fused together in the 'Lamb of God' concept. But I cannot feel that the case for eschatology has been made out. The Lamb in John 1 takes away sin. None of the eschatological references to the Lamb so far cited refers to such an activity.

And the fact ought to be faced that in the Old Testament the overwhelming majority of passages containing the term 'lamb' refer to sacrifice of one kind or another. There are a few references of a general character, but the great majority concern the offering of sacrifice. In the canonical Old Testament the LXX uses the noun ἀμνός a total of 96 times, and of these no less than 85 refer to the offering of a lamb or lambs in sacrifice (71 refer to the burnt offering). Add to this a reference to the taking away of sin and I do not see how a reference to sacrifice can possibly be excluded. None of the lambs mentioned in the Old Testament apart from those

[1] *Op. cit.*, pp. 213f.

used in sacrifice had anything to do with the putting away of sin.[1]
And no-one appears to have cited the use of the lamb imagery
outside the Old Testament for a lamb, other than a sacrificial lamb,
as being concerned in the taking away of sin.

We may fairly conclude that John has in mind the offering of
Christ as a sacrifice. No other lamb than a sacrificial lamb takes
away sin, and that is the critical point.

The difficulty comes when we try to define the reference with
greater precision. The sacrifice in the Old Testament above all
others where the LXX uses the term ἀμνός, 'lamb', is the burnt
offering, but there appears no particular reason for holding that
that sacrifice is expecially in mind in John 1. When we reviewed
the various suggestions put forward we noticed that several
suggestions have much to recommend them even though none is
completely satisfying. Add to this the fact which we noted earlier
that John has a habit of using expressions that may be understood
in more ways than one and the result is a composite picture.

'The Lamb of God' does appear to be definitely sacrificial, and it
awakes memories of more sacrifices than one. The conclusion to
which I am driven is that John intended by the expression to express
his conviction that in Jesus Christ there is fulfilled all that is foreshadowed in all the sacrifices. The term is sacrificial. But it refuses
to be bound to any one sacrifice. It is a most satisfying concept that
Jesus did accomplish the perfect sacrifice which completely removed the sin of the world. He is the complete embodiment of
all the truth to which the sacrificial system pointed.

That the Lamb is said to be 'of God' would seem, in accordance
with this view, to indicate that the perfect sacrifice is the one which
God Himself provides. Men might offer sacrifices which make this
or that aspect of truth plain. But it is only God who can produce
the sacrifice which completely deals with sin.

---

[1] It might perhaps be maintained that the 'lamb that is led to the slaughter' of
Is. 53: 7 is connected with the taking away of sin, since it refers to the Suffering
Servant and He is depicted as suffering for sin. But in the first place the suffering
for sin is not connected with the use of the term 'lamb', and in the second place the
Servant is spoken of as a guilt offering (Is. 53: 10, see RV mg.). There is no exception
here.

CHAPTER V

PROPITIATION (1)

I. INTRODUCTION

WE MEET THE VERB ἱλάσκομαι 'to propitiate' twice in the New Testament, namely in the prayer of the publican 'O God, be propitiated for me, the sinner' (Lk. 18: 13), and in the statement in Hebrews that Jesus was a High Priest 'to make propitiation for the sins of the people' (Heb. 2: 17). The noun ἱλασμός, 'propitiation', is found in the expression 'propitiation for our sins' which occurs twice in the First Epistle of St. John (1 Jn. 2: 2; 4: 10), while in Romans 3: 25 God is said to have set forth Christ as ἱλαστήριον through faith 'in his blood', and the same word occurs in Hebrews 9: 5 where it means 'the mercy-seat'. Then there is the adjective ἵλεως, which we find in the idiomatic expression 'Be it far from thee' (Mt. 16: 22), and also in the quotation 'I will be propitious with reference to their sins' (Heb. 8: 12, quoting from Je. 31: 34).

This is not a large number of passages, and some even of these (e.g. Mt. 16: 22 and Heb. 9: 5) do not refer to the atonement. Again, while Luke 18: 13 and Hebrews 8: 12 may teach us something about the way God and man are reconciled, they were not originally spoken with specific reference to Calvary. We are left, then, with but four undisputed references. But we should not, on that account, dismiss the concept as unimportant, for the idea is often present where this particular terminology is absent, for example in passages dealing with the wrath of God. So persuasive is this line of reasoning that S. R. Driver can regard propitiation as one of the three main categories used in the New Testament to interpret the death of Christ.[1]

ἵλεως is cognate with ἱλαρός, giving the original meaning of 'joyous', 'gay'. Thus Büchsel draws attention to the statement in Plato that wine ποιεῖ . . . ἵλεων, and to the frequent conjunction with εὐμενής.[2] From this is derived the verb ἱλάσκομαι with the sig-

[1] HDB, IV, p. 132.
[2] TWNT, III, p. 300.

nificance 'to make joyous or gracious', and hence, 'to appease, propitiate'. This became the characteristic meaning of the verb and governed the usage of the related words, so that the whole word-group came to refer to propitiation. The noun ἱλασμός then conveyed the idea 'that which makes propitiation', and the adjective ἱλαστήριος meant 'propitiatory'. Other words from this root occur, but apart from ἐξιλάσκομαι, which is found frequently in the LXX, none of them greatly concerns us.

II. THE ἱλάσκομαι WORD-GROUP IN NON-BIBLICAL GREEK

There is considerable agreement that this word-group denotes 'propitiation', 'appeasement', etc., in pagan usage. This point of view was put strongly by G. Smeaton when he said of ἱλασμός: 'The uniform acceptation of the word in classical Greek, when applied to the Deity, is the means of appeasing God, or of averting His anger; and not a single instance to the contrary occurs in the whole Greek literature.'[1] Since his day our knowledge, particularly of Hellenistic Greek, has increased immensely, but Moulton and Milligan assure us that in Hellenistic as in classical Greek the word group refers to placating. They comment that ἱλάσκομαι means '"render propitious to oneself" c. acc. of the person as in classical Greek',[2] and they go on to note 'A similar use of the compound ἐξιλάσκομαι, which extends to the LXX'.

Many similar citations could be made, but this would be superfluous, as the point is hardly disputed. Whatever may be the biblical usage there can be no doubts as to the prevailing use in all non-biblical writings. But the pagan use is said to be not quite unvarying. Thus C. H. Dodd says: 'In classical Greek and in the Koine ἱλάσκεσθαι, ἐξιλάσκεσθαι, have regularly the meaning "placate", "propitiate", with a personal object. As a secondary meaning ἐξιλάσκεσθαι also bears the sense "expiate", with an impersonal object'.[3] In similar vein is Büchsel's statement that 'It would be difficult to imagine that ἐξιλάσκομαι would be chosen as translation of *kipper* if it hitherto had only signified *make gracious*.

---

[1] *The Apostles' Doctrine of the Atonement* (Edinburgh, 1870), p. 455.
[2] MM *sub* ἱλάσκομαι.
[3] *JTS*, XXXII, 1930–31, p. 352. His article is reprinted without substantial alteration in *The Bible and the Greeks*.

Therefore it is easily conjectured that ἐξιλάσκομαι and ἱλάσκομαι acquired the meaning, *expiate, atone*'.[1]

It is noteworthy that Büchsel uses very guarded language. He gives it as his opinion only ('it is easily conjectured') that there was a trend away from crude ideas of propitiation. But he cites no specific passages. For the study of ἱλάσκομαι, *etc.* this is important. Even a man who thinks that men were moving away from early, crude ideas can find no instance wherein ἱλάσκομαι, *etc.*, reflect this trend. It is difficult to resist the conclusion that, while the general trend Büchsel speaks of may have been in evidence, yet the word-group under consideration was not used to express it. In other words, while men may have been modifying their ideas about the nature of the gods, when they used ἱλάσκομαι, *etc.*, it was to convey the older thought of propitiation rather than some later development. Failing specific examples of the newer meaning such must be held to be the usage.

Dodd urges two passages in favour of the meaning 'expiation', namely Plato, *Laws*, 862 c, and the Men Tyrannus inscription. The former passage reads τὸ ἀποίνοις ἐξιλασθὲν τοῖς δρῶσιν καὶ πάσχουσιν ἑκάστας τῶν βλάψεων ἐκ διαφορᾶς εἰς φιλίαν ἀεὶ πειρατέον καθιστάναι τοῖς νόμοις. The writer is saying that the legislator must endeavour to restore good relations by payment of indemnity for injuries, and the question at issue is whether τὸ ἀποίνοις ἐξιλασθέν refers to expiation of a crime or to appeasement of a person. The context seems to put it beyond doubt that a person is indicated.[2] The passage could, perhaps, be interpreted of an expiation; but the most natural exegesis sees in it the acceptance by the wronged party of a compensatory payment, by virtue of which his anger against the one who has injured him is soothed. Büchsel sums up the possibilities well when he comments '. . . one could understand ἐξιλασθέν as expiated in so far as the lawbreaker has become guiltless by means of the compensation which he has paid the wronged person; but it is better (understood) as: comprehended as appeased, in so far as the wronged person is brought by the compensation which settles the account to the abandonment of his wrath against the offender, so that the two can come to a state of

---

[1] *Op. cit.*, p. 316.

[2] *Cf.* Büchsel: 'It follows from the preceding parallel part that by the ἐξιλασθέν a person, not a thing, is meant' (*op. cit.*, p. 317, n. 75).

friendship with one another'.[1] It seems impossible, then, to maintain that ἐξιλασθέν here clearly means 'expiate'; the most that can
be said is that such an interpretation is not altogether excluded.

The Men Tyrannus inscription gives stronger support to the
upholders of the expiation theory inasmuch as sin is the object of
the verb, the relevant part of the inscription reading ἁμαρτίαν
ὀφειλέτω Μηνὶ Τυράννῳ ἣν οὐ μὴ δύνηται ἐξειλάσασθαι. This accusative of the sin is unique outside biblical writers, which leads us to the
conclusion that it is most probably an accusative of general
reference.[2] In view of the otherwise unvarying usage of pagan
writers it is probably best to take the passage as meaning that the
man who sins in the specified way commits a sin in respect of which
he will not be able to make propitiation. Such seems to be the way
in which MM understand it,[3] though Büchsel joins Dodd in giving
the verb here the meaning 'expiate'.[4] In any case the date of the
inscription (probably second-third century AD) makes it impossible to think that any usage reflected therein could have
affected the New Testament writers.

The most, then, that can be said in favour of the view that these
words may contain an expiatory meaning is that two passages (one
of them later than the Bible) could well be interpreted in this way.
But neither of them demands such an interpretation and, in view of
the otherwise consistent usage of the sources, we must draw the
conclusion that, when a first-century Greek heard the words of
this group, there would be aroused in his mind thoughts of
propitiation.

III. THE WRATH OF GOD IN THE OLD TESTAMENT

It has for long been recognized that the use of the word-group in
the LXX is not the same as that in profane sources. Westcott, for
example, has made much of this difference. In recent years none
has done more than C. H. Dodd to demonstrate both the fact and
the significance of this difference, and he roundly denies that we
should understand the word-group of 'propitiation' at all. 'Ex-

[1] *Ibid.*
[2] See below, pp. 203ff., for similar accusatives.
[3] *Loc. cit.*
[4] *Loc. cit.*

piation', he thinks, is the meaning. Thus he says of Romans 3 : 25: 'the meaning conveyed (in accordance with LXX usage, which is constantly determinative for Paul), is that of expiation, not that of propitiation. Most translators and commentators are wrong.'[1] Or again: 'The Johannine usage thus falls into line with biblical usage in general. The common rendering "propitiation" is illegitimate here as elsewhere.'[2]

These are important conclusions and they are being increasingly accepted, for it is a relief to know that we have solid grounds for our conviction that the God of the Bible is not a Being who can be propitiated after the fashion of a pagan deity. That this point has been conclusively demonstrated is certain. The Bible writers have nothing to do with pagan conceptions of a capricious and vin-dictive deity, inflicting arbitrary punishments on offending worshippers, who must then bribe him back to a good mood by the appropriate offerings. Dodd's important work makes this abundantly clear.

However, when we have rendered our full tribute to the work of this great scholar, we must ask to be forgiven for wondering whether the last word has yet been said. We readily agree that pagan ideas of wrath and propitiation are absent from the biblical view of God, but Dodd seems to say that all ideas of wrath and propitiation are absent from it. We have already noted his rejection of the idea of propitiation; but in his commentary on Romans he goes further and says that the wrath of God is 'an archaic phrase' suiting 'a thoroughly archaic idea'.[3] To many the wrath of God seems too well rooted in both Old and New Testaments to be rele-gated to the status of an archaism. Other questions suggest them-selves, such as, 'If the LXX translators and the New Testament writers did not mean propitiation, why did they choose to use words which signify propitiation and are saturated with pro-pitiatory associations?'[4] Such a procedure, one would think, is the

[1] *Op. cit.*, p. 360.
[2] *Ibid.*
[3] *MNTC, Romans*, pp. 20f.
[4] *Cf.* R. W. Dale on the Jewish use of the term: 'Not a solitary instance can be alleged in which to propitiate, or any of its derivatives, when used in relation to the restoration of kindly relations between man and man, denotes that by which a change is produced in the disposition of a person who has committed an offence; it always refers to that which changes the disposition of the person who has been

surest way of being misunderstood; and, if Dodd is right, their choice of words has, in fact, caused them to be misunderstood right up to our own day.

The wrath of God is often confused with that irrational passion we so frequently find in man and which was commonly ascribed to heathen deities. But this is not the only possibility. Thus Dr. Maldwyn Hughes says: 'Let it be granted that anger is not an ideal word for our purpose, and that we use it only, as Augustine would say, "in order that we may not keep silent." Our concern is with facts not with words. The fact which we have to face is that in the nature of things there must be an eternal recoil against the unholy on the part of the all-holy God'.[1] If we can understand the wrath of God in some such fashion as this there seems no insuperable objection to our thinking of that wrath as a reality to be reckoned with, and to seeing propitiation as the means of averting that wrath from the sinner, who, unless this can be done, finds himself in evil case.

To the men of the Old Testament the wrath of God is both very real and very serious. God is not thought of as capriciously angry (like the deities of the heathen), but, because He is a moral Being, His anger is directed towards wrongdoing in any shape or form. Once roused, this anger is not easily assuaged, and dire consequences may follow. But it is only fair to add that the Old Testament consistently regards God as a God of mercy. Though men sin and thus draw down upon themselves the consequences of His wrath, yet God does not delight in the death of the sinner. He provides ways in which the consequences of sin may be averted.

There are more than twenty words used to express 'wrath' as it applies to Yahweh (in addition to a number of other words which occur only with reference to human anger). These are used so frequently that there are over 580 occurrences to be taken into

---

offended; and when used in relation to offences against the Divine law, it always describes the means by which the sin was supposed to be covered in order that the Divine forgiveness might be secured' (*The Atonement*, London, 1902, pp. 162f.). James Denney has a remark which is worthy of note, 'The characteristic words of religion cannot be applied in new ways at will. Now the idea of ἱλασμός or propitiation is not an insulated idea. . . . It is part of a system of ideas' (*The Death of Christ*, London, 1951, p. 150).

[1] *What is the Atonement?* (London, n.d.), pp. 54f.

consideration. This constitutes such a formidable body of evidence that we cannot hope to deal with it fully, and can only indicate in general terms the result of detailed examination.

There is a consistency about the wrath of God in the Old Testament. It is no capricious passion, but the stern reaction of the divine nature towards evil. It is aroused only and inevitably by sin. This may be thought of in general terms (Jb. 21: 20; Je. 21: 12; Ezk. 24: 13), or it may be categorized more exactly as the shedding of blood (Ezk. 16: 38; 24: 8), adultery (Ezk. 23: 25), violence (Ezk. 8: 18), covetousness (Je. 6: 11), revenge (Ezk. 25: 17), afflicting widows and orphans (Ex. 22: 23f.), taking brethren captive (2 Ch. 28: 11–13), *etc.* Wrath comes upon Israel because of the evil of Jeroboam as repeated by Jehoahaz (2 Ki. 13: 3), and because of the evil of Manasseh (2 Ki. 23: 26), while Moses feared that the desire of the two and a half tribes not to pass over Jordan would have a similar effect (Nu. 32: 14). Profaning the sabbath arouses wrath (Ne. 13: 18), which comes also upon men who 'have not told the truth about' God (Jb. 42: 7, Moffatt), and Gideon feared that his repeated testing of the Lord would also cause God's anger (Jdg. 6: 39).

Perhaps we are able to see something of the root causes of the divine anger in such passages as 'anger also went up against Israel; because they believed not in God, and trusted not in his salvation' (Ps. 78: 21f.), or those linking rebellion with the divine wrath such as, 'We have transgressed and have rebelled; thou hast not pardoned. Thou hast covered with anger and pursued us' (La. 3: 42f.), or, 'It will be, seeing that ye rebel today against the Lord, that tomorrow he will be wroth with the whole congregation of Israel' (Jos. 22: 18). The sin above all sins which is said in the Old Testament to arouse God's wrath is the sin of idolatry. This may be asserted in general terms (Dt. 6: 14f.; Jos. 23: 16, *etc.*), or in connection with specific acts of idolatry such as the worship of the golden calf (Ex. 32: 10f.), or the iniquity of Baal-peor (Nu. 25: 3), or practices associated with idolatry (Is. 66: 15–17). Sometimes the accusation is accompanied by that of forsaking Jehovah (Dt. 29: 25ff.; 2 Ki. 22: 17), while, in Ezra 9: 14, breaking God's commandments and making affinity with the heathen are mentioned.

From these and many other examples it is clear that in the Old

Testament the anger of God may be expected to be visited upon the perpetrator of any sin. God made men for Himself, made them so that they should be His people, and live in accordance with His commandments. When they failed to do so they inevitably aroused His settled opposition, His wrath.

The effects of this wrath, the happenings which show that the Lord *is* angry, are such things as affliction in general (Ps. 88: 7), or specific evils such as pestilence (Ezk. 14: 19), 'the cup of staggering' (Is. 51: 22), slaughter (Ezk. 9: 8), destruction (Ezk. 5: 15), execration, reproach, *etc.* (Je. 42: 18), being delivered up to the enemy (2 Ch. 28: 9), the destruction of Jerusalem (La. 4: 11), desolation (Is. 13: 9; Je. 4: 26), drought (Dt. 11: 17), plague (2 Sa. 24: 1ff.), leprosy (Nu. 12: 9), and above all, the exile (2 Ki. 23: 26; Is. 42: 25; Ezk. 19: 12, *etc.*). There are other effects, and almost any disaster could be interpreted as a sign of the divine wrath.

Sometimes the linking of such disasters with the wrath of God is taken to indicate that this wrath denotes nothing more than an impersonal retribution. For example, C. H. Dodd says that the work of the prophets is such that ' "the Wrath of God" is taken out of the sphere of the purely mysterious, and brought into the sphere of cause and effect: sin is the cause, disaster the effect . . . in speaking of wrath and judgment the prophets and psalmists have their minds mainly on events, actual or expected, conceived as the inevitable results of sin; and when they speak of mercy they are thinking mainly of the personal relation between God and His people. Wrath is the effect of human sin: mercy is not the effect of human goodness, but is inherent in the character of God.'[1]

But this will not fit the facts. In the first place the prophets had a strongly developed view of the sovereignty of God. Nothing that men can do escapes Him, and nothing, it would seem, can be done without Him, for 'the most High ruleth in the kingdom of men' (Dn. 4: 17). The punishment consequent on sin is just as much due to God as is the forgiveness which remits such punishment, for God is in all of life. 'Shall evil befall a city, and the Lord hath not done it?' (Am. 3: 6) is the incredulous query of one of the prophets and he emphasizes also that it is the Lord who 'bringeth sudden destruction upon the strong' (Am. 5: 9). We read similarly in Isaiah 45: 6f.: 'I am the Lord, and there is none else. I form the light,

[1] *MNTC, Romans*, pp. 22f.

THE APOSTOLIC PREACHING OF THE CROSS

and create darkness; I make peace, and create evil; I am the Lord, that doeth all these things.' There is no point in continuing the list, for the Old Testament everywhere assumes that God is active throughout His creation, and that His hand is to be discerned in the chastisements which come upon men.

Then the prophets and the psalmists use the most strongly personal terms when they speak of the anger of the Lord. What else are we to make of passages like the following? 'Now will I shortly pour out my fury upon thee, and accomplish mine anger against thee . . . And mine eye shall not spare, neither will I have pity . . . and ye shall know that I the Lord do smite' (Ezk. 7: 8f.). Or 'The anger of the Lord shall not return, until he have executed, and till he have performed the intents of his heart' (Je. 23: 20). Or 'Behold, the name of the Lord cometh from far, burning with his anger, and in thick rising smoke: his lips are full of indignation, and his tongue is as a devouring fire: and his breath is as an overflowing stream, that reacheth even unto the neck, to sift the nations with the sieve of vanity . . . And the Lord shall cause his glorious voice to be heard, and shall shew the lighting down of his arm, with the indignation of his anger, and the flame of a devouring fire, with a blast, and tempest, and hailstones. For through the voice of the Lord shall the Assyrian be broken in pieces, 'etc. (Is. 30: 27–31). 'O God, thou hast cast us off, thou hast broken us down; thou hast been angry: . . . Thou hast made the land to tremble; thou hast rent it: . . . Thou hast shewed thy people hard things: thou hast made us to drink the wine of staggering' (Ps. 60: 1–3).

It is difficult to imagine how the prophets and psalmists could possibly have expressed more strongly the personal character of the wrath of God. While disaster is regarded as the inevitable result of man's sin, it is so in the view of the Old Testament, not by some inexorable law of an impersonal Nature, but because a holy God wills to pour out the vials of His wrath upon those who commit sin. Indeed, it is largely because wrath is so fully personal in the Old Testament that mercy becomes so fully personal, for mercy is the action of the same God who was angry, allowing His wrath to be turned away. It should be noted that many passages place the wrath and the mercy of God on the same plane as personal activities, for example, 'He retaineth not his anger for ever, because he delighteth in mercy' (Mi. 7: 18), or, 'Thou hast forgiven the iniquity of thy people, thou hast covered all their sin. Thou hast taken away all thy wrath: thou hast turned thyself from the fierceness of thine anger' (Ps. 85: 2f.).

It is true that some passages speak of wrath in more or less impersonal terms, or connect punishment directly with sin, but these always imply the continuing activity of Yahweh. For example Psalm 38: 3 says: 'There is no soundness in my flesh because of thine indignation; neither is there any health in my bones because of my sin.' This might well be cited in support of the contention that wrath is impersonal retribution were it not that the two preceding verses strongly emphasize the personal divine activity: 'O Lord, rebuke me not in thy wrath: neither chasten me in thy hot displeasure. For thine arrows stick fast in me, and thy hand presseth me sore.' This is typical Old Testament teaching. God is personally active in deeds of wrath as in deeds of mercy.

Let us now notice some of the ways in which the wrath of God is averted. One way is by purging out the sin, for example, by completely destroying an offending city (Dt. 13: 15–17), slaying those who had sinned at Baal-peor (Nu. 25: 4), releasing captives (2 Ch. 28: 11–13), or putting away heathen wives (Ezr. 10: 14). Sometimes the means is a right inward state, such as repentance (Jon. 3: 7, 10), or humbling oneself (2 Ch. 12: 7). Passages referring to judgment (Je. 21: 12) and circumcising the heart (Je. 4: 4) are not dissimilar. Both Moses and Jeremiah are said to have stood before God and turned away wrath from Israel, presumably by successful intercession (Ps. 106: 23; Je. 18: 20), while Job's prayer is similarly referred to (Jb. 42: 7f.).

Underlying the fact that these and other things are said to turn away the divine wrath is the basic truth that God is by nature merciful rather than wrathful. Indeed wrath may be thought of as His 'strange work', as in Isaiah 28: 21: 'For the Lord shall rise up as in mount Perazim, he shall be wroth as in the valley of Gibeon; that he may do his work, his strange work, and bring to pass his act, his strange act.' While wrath is a dreadful reality, it must not be taken as the last word about God. This is not contradicted by the statement that 'God will not withdraw his anger' (Jb. 9: 13), for this means not that He is implacable, but only that He is not to be diverted from His purposes by puny man. It is a denial of the heathen idea of a gift being accepted to appease anger. But it does not follow that He habitually punishes men to the fullest extent, as we see from Job 35: 15, 'he hath not visited in his anger', or from the incredulous questions of the psalmist, 'Hath God forgotten to be gracious? Hath he in anger shut up his tender mercies?' (Ps. 77: 9). A beautiful reminder that God's nature is merciful rather than wrathful comes from Micah: 'Who is a God like unto thee, that pardoneth iniquity, and passeth by the transgression of the remnant of his heritage? He retaineth not his anger for ever because he delighteth in mercy. He will turn again and have compassion upon us, he will tread our iniquities under foot: and thou wilt cast all their sins into the depths of the sea' (Mi. 7: 18f.).

Full of interest are ten passages in which God is said to be 'slow to anger' (Ex. 34: 6; Nu. 14: 18; Ne. 9: 17; Pss. 86: 15; 103: 8; 145: 8; Je. 15: 15; Joel 2: 13; Jon. 4: 2; Na. 1: 3). In reading them we are apt to fasten our attention on expressions like 'slow to anger and plenteous in mercy'. But we should not overlook the fact that the writers could, in the immediate context, say such things as, the Lord 'will by no means clear the guilty' (Nu. 14: 18), or 'turn ye unto me with all your heart, and with fasting, and with weeping, and with mourning' (Joel 2: 12). For those who wrote such words the idea that God is 'slow to anger' was not a truism. It was a surprising revelation, something to be received with awe and wonder.

This thinking reaches its climax in the passages where the removal of divine wrath is ascribed to God Himself. Thus Psalm 78: 38 tells us that 'many a time turned he his anger away, and did not stir up all his wrath', while in Isaiah 48: 9 God says, 'For my name's sake will I defer mine anger, and for my praise will I refrain for thee, that I cut thee not off' (cf. Ps. 85: 2f., where, incidentally, forgiveness and the turning away of wrath are nearly identical). Other passages could be quoted, but it seems hardly necessary. The general picture which the Old Testament gives us of God is of One who is by nature merciful, and who cannot be swayed by man's puny efforts. In the last resort forgiveness is always due to God's being what He is, and not to anything that man may do. Because God is God, He must react in the strongest manner to man's sin, and thus we reach the concept of the divine wrath. But because God is God, wrath cannot be the last word. 'The Lord is good; his mercy endureth for ever' (Ps. 100: 5).

IV. THE ἱλάσκομαι WORD-GROUP IN THE SEPTUAGINT

a. The work of C. H. Dodd

Dodd's valuable treatment of the word-group begins by showing that where the LXX does not use ἱλάσκομαι, etc., to translate kipper, it uses words with meanings like ' "to sanctify", "purify" persons or objects of ritual, or "to cancel", "purge away", "forgive" sins'; from which he concludes: 'We should therefore expect to find that they regard the ἱλάσκεσθαι class as conveying similar ideas.'[1] His next point is that, where ἱλάσκομαι, etc., are not the translation for kipper and its derivatives, 'they render words which fall into one or other of two classes: (i) with human subject, "to cleanse from sin or defilement", "to expiate"; (ii) with divine subject, "to be gracious", "to have mercy", "to forgive".'[2] His third main division is one in which he deals with those passages wherein ἱλάσκομαι, etc., render the kipper group, and here he concludes that 'the LXX translators did not regard kipper (when used as a religious term) as conveying the sense of propitiating the Deity, but the sense of performing an act whereby guilt or defilement is removed'.[3]

It might be urged in criticism of this method that it is capable of giving the meaning of the word-group in question only in a very general way. Thus Dodd has to group together in his first main section words whose meaning differs as greatly as 'to sanctify' and 'to cancel'. When there is such a vast gulf between different members of the same group obviously we cannot expect to get a very precise meaning for the ἱλάσκομαι group from them. And in fact Dodd has not indicated the full extent of the range. Roger R. Nicole, in an important article on 'C. H. Dodd and the Doctrine of Propitiation',[4] points out that Dodd has not taken into account a large group of words which translate kipper and its cognates (e.g. ἀφαιρεῖν, Is. 27: 9; ἀντάλλαγμα, Is. 43: 3; etc.). Nicole maintains that Dodd takes into account no more than 36 per cent of the evidence. He considers that when all the evidence is included Dodd's conclusion should be rewritten in this form: 'where the LXX trans-

---

[1] JTS, XXXII, 1931, p. 353.
[2] Op. cit., p. 356.
[3] Op. cit., p. 359.
[4] Westminster Theological Journal, XVII, 1955, pp. 117–157.

lators do not render *kipper* and its cognates by words of the ἱλάσκεσθαι class, they render it by words which give the meaning "to sanctify", "to forgive", "to remove", "to cover with pitch", "to ransom", "to contribute", "to give", "to veil", "to anoint", "the village", "the myrrh", or they have failed to render it altogether. We should therefore expect to find that they regard the ἱλάσκεσθαι class as conveying similar ideas.'[1] This, of course, makes the statement meaningless, which is Nicole's point.

The method is open to a further danger. To illustrate, the word κόσμος may on occasion be translated by 'adorning' (1 Pet. 3: 3, AV), though usually 'world' is used. But we cannot argue from this that 'adorning' and 'world' are words of similar meaning. The fact is that κόσμος in Greek covers a range of meaning for which we have no exact English equivalent, so that we must make use of various words, some of which differ considerably from one another in meaning. This is a commonplace of translation and it is difficult to see how Dodd has overlooked it. It may be true to say *kipper* and ἐξιλάσκομαι mean very nearly the same thing; but that does not carry with it the corollary that other Hebrew words which ἐξιλάσκομαι renders are akin in meaning to *kipper*, or that other Greek words which translate *kipper* are necessarily of similar significance to ἐξιλάσκομαι. The very reason for the choice of the different word may be that the second context demands a word differing in meaning from that appropriate in the first passage.[2]

The way to clear up such points is to pay close attention to the context in order to see, not so much what word, but what idea ἱλάσκομαι, *etc.*, translate. It may well be that, on occasion, the best word with which to render ἱλάσκομαι is 'forgive' or 'purge'; but if the particular forgiveness or purging of sin is one which involves, as a necessary feature, the putting away of the divine wrath, then it is idle to maintain that the word has been eviscerated of all idea

---

[1] *Op. cit.*, p. 129.

[2] J. Barr points out that even within one language we must be careful. Thus in English the word 'time' in some contexts does not differ greatly from 'occasion' and in others from 'period'. But 'occasion' and 'period' will 'in very many contexts, or in all, present great contrast with one another' (*Biblical Words for Time*, London, 1962, p. 108). This whole section of Barr's work forms a damaging criticism of the kind of method Dodd is employing, though he makes no explicit reference to it.

of propitiation. Dodd totally ignores the fact that in many passages there is explicit mention of the putting away of God's anger, and accordingly his conclusions cannot be accepted without serious modification.

b. ἱλάσκομαι

This verb occurs eleven times in all, always in the middle or passive, and always with the Lord as subject (sometimes in petition, 'Be thou, etc.').[1] The Hebrew verbs it translates convey thoughts like 'forgive', but we cannot glibly reason from this that therefore there is no thought of propitiation. Take, for example, Exodus 32: 14 (where the verb translates *nḥm*): 'And the Lord repented of the evil which he said he would do unto his people.' However we translate, we must notice that, in the context, it refers to a removal of wrath, for earlier Moses has asked the Lord, 'why doth thy wrath wax hot against thy people?' (verse 11), and has prayed, 'Turn from thy fierce wrath, and repent of this evil against thy people' (verse 12). The connection between wrath and the Lord's 'repenting' is plain.

Similarly in Lamentations 3: 42 ἱλάσκομαι translates *slḥ* and can be rendered 'forgive'. But the sort of forgiveness which is meant is one which includes a turning away of wrath, as we see as soon as we look at the expression in its context: 'We sinned, we behaved impiously and thou didst not forgive (or wast not propitiated). Thou didst visit in anger and pursue us.' So in Daniel 9: 19 (Th.) we read: 'O Lord, forgive', which is much the same as 'let thine anger and thy wrath, I pray thee, be turned away from thy city Jerusalem' (verse 16). In 2 Kings 24: 3f. the explicit mention of the Lord's anger, and the stress on the magnitude of Manasseh's sin, combine to show that the verb carries the meaning 'propitiate',[2] while in Psalm 77(78): 38 the idea of forgiveness conveyed by this verb is practically identical with the averting of the divine

---

[1] The verb is used absolutely four times, with dative of persons three times, with dative of sin three times, and with accusative of sin once. The underlying Hebrew is *slḥ* (six times), *kppr* (three times), *nḥm* (once), while there is no Hebrew corresponding to Est. 13: 17.

[2] Some would take θυμός here to mean something like 'purpose' since the Hebrew of the Massoretic text is עַל־פִּי יהוה. But even if this be accepted there is still the stress on the magnitude of the sin, and in any case that Manasseh had aroused the anger of the Lord is clear from other passages such as 2 Ki. 23: 26.

wrath, 'But he is compassionate and will forgive their sins, and he will not destroy (them); and he will many times turn away his anger, and will not kindle all his wrath'. We might make almost the same remark about the occurrence of the verb in Psalm 78(79): 9 (*cf.* verses 5ff.), and while wrath is not mentioned in Psalm 24(25): 11 the psalmist's sin is said to be 'great', and he is suffering what might well be understood as the wrath of God, for he is desolate and afflicted, in trouble, distress and travail, and his enemies are many (verses 16ff.).

Much is sometimes made of the fact that there is one passage where sin is the object of the verb and it is urged that 'expiate' rather than 'propitiate' must be the meaning (Ps. 64(65): 4). But even if we dismiss the fact that some MSS read the dative (Swete cites א c.a., T) the context tells us that 'Words of lawless men have overpowered us', and once more we see the kind of thing which would naturally be associated with divine wrath.[1]

So it is also with Esther 13: 17 (Addition C verse 10), for here the people are under sentence of death. In the only remaining passage, 2 Kings 5: 18 (where the verb occurs twice) Naaman asks pardon for bowing down in the house of Rimmon, an action prohibited in the Second Commandment on the grounds that Yahweh is a 'jealous God'. Moreover Naaman has just come out of heathendom, and might be expected to use the word in the typically heathen fashion.

To sum up: six times there is explicit mention of wrath in the immediate context, once the people are under sentence of death, twice the psalmist is greatly afflicted, and on the other occasion the action is that one above all others which the Old Testament regards as provoking God's wrath. We cannot say that the concept of the wrath of God is certainly absent from any of these passages, and in every one the rendering 'propitiate' is quite appropriate. In the face of all this it is manifestly impossible to maintain that the verb has been emptied of its force.[2]

---

[1] Nicole indicates the precariousness of relying on this accusative by drawing attention to the fact that, in the ἱλάσκομαι group as a whole, the accusative 'may be used to refer to the impurity removed, the object cleansed, the offering presented, the person reconciled!' (*op. cit.*, p. 131).

[2] The verb is also found in the Sixtine text of 2 Ch. 6: 30, but here again the context speaks of disasters which evidence the divine displeasure.

c. ἱλασμός

This noun occurs ten times in a variety of contexts. Sometimes it is connected with *kpr* as in 'day of atonement', *etc.* (We will deal with the idea of atonement when we come to ἐξιλάσκομαι.)

The word is used of forgiveness in Daniel 9: 8 (Th.), 'To the Lord our God belong mercies and forgivenesses'. Here again the situation involves the wrath of God, as we see from 'the curse has come upon us' (verse 11), He has brought 'great evils' upon His people (verse 12), and Daniel's prayer 'let thine anger and thy wrath, I pray thee, be turned away' (verse 16). The word occurs in Psalm 129 (130): 4, once more in a context of trouble: 'Out of the depths have I cried' (verse 1). Propitiation is clearly the meaning in 2 Maccabees 3: 33, where it is applied to the sacrifice offered by Onias to deliver Heliodorus from further chastisement, and where the whole tenor of the passage leaves no doubt that averting of wrath is being signified.

Thus the propitiatory idea which we have seen to be involved in ἱλάσκομαι is to be discerned also in ἱλασμός. Wherever it means 'forgiveness', the circumstances indicate the turning away of the divine wrath.[1]

d. ἱλαστήριον

This word is used of the mercy-seat over the ark of the covenant (twenty-two times) and of one of the ledges of Ezekiel's altar (five times). It means either 'place of atonement' (Manson) or 'means of atonement' (Büchsel, Deissmann, *etc.*), but in either case it is associated with the cultus, and we defer discussing the idea involved until we come to consider ἐξιλάσκομαι.

The term also occurs in 4 Maccabees 17: 22, though here it may be held to derive from the adjective rather than the substantive. The death of the seven brothers is spoken of: 'They having as it were become a ransom (ἀντίψυχον) for the nation's sin; and through the blood of these righteous men and their propitiatory death (or, the propitiation of their death) the divine providence delivered Israel.' Here the meaning 'propitiation' is plain, and this may be of significance for the interpretation of Romans 3: 25.

---

[1] ἱλασμός also occurs as the reading of A in Sir. 18: 20, and of ℵ* in Sir. 32: 5, but in both places ἐξιλασμός is the better attested reading.

e. ἵλεως

It hardly seems necessary to examine the 35 occurrences of this word in detail. In general we may say that its usage fits in with that of the other words of the word-group, in that the term usually denotes the attitude of the Lord in turning His anger away from the people. The adjective occurs several times in the prayer of Solomon at the dedication of the Temple (see 1 Ki. 8; 2 Ch. 6), a prayer of a cyclic character with the pattern, 'When the people commit sin and thou afflict them in such and such a way, if they repent and confess, then hear thou and forgive'. All the afflictions are such as might be caused by the divine wrath (and in one place or another of the Old Testament each is expressly said to be the result of the anger of the Lord), and it would be going contrary to the whole tenor of Old Testament thought to regard the afflictions mentioned as other than the outworking of the divine wrath. In view of the setting, then, 'forgive' here seems to have the implication of the removal of wrath. So is it when a man is found murdered and the elders of the nearest city are commanded to kill a heifer (Dt. 21: 8). It is difficult to interpret this other than as a propitiatory rite, after which 'Be propitiated for thy people Israel' is quite in place. In other passages where the word is found we usually find that the wrath of God is mentioned or implied, and we may well feel that this word, like the others we have considered, has reference, in the last resort, to the removal of wrath.

f. ἐξιλάσκομαι

Although the verb ἐξιλάσκομαι does not occur in the New Testament, yet because of its close kinship in meaning with ἱλάσκομαι, and because of its importance in the Old Testament, it is well to consider its usage. It is found 105 times, the number being accounted for in large measure because it is the usual verb for rendering the recurring expression 'to make atonement' (Heb. *kipper*) in connection with the sacrificial system. The fact that ἐξιλάσκομαι renders *kipper* eighty-three times and other Hebrew roots a total of eleven times only, shows that the two words ἐξιλάσκομαι and *kipper* are nearly synonymous in meaning, or at least that the LXX translators thought so.

The usage of *kipper* divides naturally into two sections, according as atonement is thought of as coming by a cultic action or by non-cultic means, the former being by far the larger section. But for our present purpose the latter is the more important group, enabling us, as it does, to see what the verb means in itself quite apart from the conventional use of the cultus. For it seems probable that, in the case of *kipper* (as no doubt of other words also), a word well understood from its use in connection with ordinary affairs was adopted and adapted by exponents of the cultus because it so well expressed one of the aspects of the cultic approach to God. It is likely that, in the process, a conventional meaning has become attached to the word, and not at all improbable that the cultic use differs somewhat from the secular use. That, however, will remain for examination, and does not affect our main contention that the non-cultic use is fundamental. This was noticed long ago by Dr. S. H. Langdon who said: 'Before examining the Hebrew cult term it will be much more logical to examine those passages in which the word is not employed in the rituals.'[1] But, unfortunately, he failed to notice more than a very few such passages. More recently J. Herrmann has also noticed the importance of the non-cultic passages.[2]

(i) *The non-cultic use of kipper.* The impressive thing about the passages in which *kipper* is used of atonement wrought without reference to the cultus, is the close kinship in meaning between it and the noun *kōpher* which we have already had occasion to consider,[3] and which we saw almost without exception (perhaps without any exception) to denote payment for the redemption of forfeited life.

Especially important is Exodus 30: 12–16 where *kipper* and *kōpher* occur together, and their connection is clear. The passage deals with the half shekel to be paid at the census as a *kōpher* in order that there be no plague. The thought of payment for a man's life is clear, and the money in question is referred to both as *kōpher naphshô* ('ransom for his soul', verse 12), and as *keseph hakkippūrim* ('atonement money', verse 16), while it is twice said 'to make atonement for your souls' (verses 15, 16). The verb *kipper* has here

[1] *ET*, XXII, p. 323.
[2] *TWNT*, III, p. 302.
[3] See above pp. 24ff.

the sense of atonement, and of atonement by the payment of a sum of money as ransom. A similar meaning is required when the men of war offer a part of the spoil which they term 'the Lord's oblation', and which is 'to make atonement for our souls before the Lord' (Nu. 31: 50). Plainly here the verb *kipper* is in the nature of a denominative, meaning 'to offer a *kōpher*'. This meaning is clear also in Genesis 32: 20, where Jacob thinks that his present to Esau will have the effect of 'ransoming' him from his brother's wrath.[1] Isaiah 47: 11 lends further support, especially if the emendation of *shahrāh* ('dawning thereof') to *shahadhāh* ('to buy it off') be accepted. This would yield an interesting parallelism for the thought of the verse would then run: 'Therefore shall evil come upon thee; and thou shalt not know how to buy it off (*shahadhāh*): and mischief shall fall upon thee; and thou shalt not be able to ransom it away (*kapperâh*).'[2]

In other instances the *kōpher* is not money, but life. Thus Moses says: 'Now I will go up unto the Lord; peradventure I shall make atonement for your sin' (Ex. 32: 30). But when he pleads with the Lord his method of 'making atonement' is by offering his own life

---

[1] With this expression should be compared *hillâ 'eth-penē-* which BDB explain as 'lit. *make the face of* any one *sweet* or *pleasant*', and thus 'mollify, appease, entreat the favour of'. The idea in *kipper* is similar, but carries with it the thought that the making of the face sweet is by specific means, namely, the offering of a gift. It is the turning away of anger by means of a *kōpher*.

In passing we note that the suggestion often put forward that '*akhapperâh phānāyw* here means 'I will cover his face' will not fit the context, for Jacob goes on 'and afterward I will see his face'.

[2] *Cf.* Herrmann: 'In Is. 47, 11 *kpr* means "pay *kōpher*", "provide *kōpher*", "avert through *kōpher*" in parallel to *shhd* ("provide *shōhadh*", "avert through *shōhadh*"), from which *kpr* appears to be a denominative from *kōpher* just as *shhd* from *shōhadh*; thereby it is a question of the averting of a destruction in death' (*op. cit.*, p. 304).

BDB give *shahadhāh* as the probable reading, citing in support a number of Hebraists. But it should be borne in mind that other scholars from the analogy of the Arabic read 'charm it away' with RV mg. (see authorities in BDB *sub shāhadh* and *shāhar* respectively). If this is accepted as the sense of the word there is again an interesting parallelism, and one in which the meaning of *kpr* remains as suggested above.

BDB bring out the connection of the verb with *kōpher* in their section on *kipper* where the meaning of Is. 47: 11 is given as 'and disaster will fall upon thee, thou wilt not be able to propitiate it (by payment of a *kōpher*, see Is. 43: 3).' *shōhadh* occurs in parallelism with *kōpher* in Pr. 6: 35.

for them (verse 32). Here again *kipper* means 'to pay a *kōpher*', but the *kōpher* in question is a life. Most instructive for an understanding of *kipper* is 2 Samuel 21: 1–14, where we read of a famine due to Saul's treatment of the Gibeonites. David called them and asked: 'What shall I do for you? and wherewith shall I make atonement (*'akhappēr*), that ye may bless the inheritance of the Lord?' (verse 3). That the Gibeonites understood by *'akhappēr* 'pay a *kōpher*' is clear by their answer: 'It is no matter of silver or gold between us and Saul, or his house'; and their recognition of the life-for-life principle comes out in the second part of their answer: 'neither is it for us to put any man to death in Israel' (verse 4). Eventually seven descendants of Saul were delivered to the Gibeonites to be hanged and these formed the *kōpher* demanded (though that term is not explicitly used). The whole passage is most instructive.

Numbers 35: 33 is almost a statement of the very principle on which the Gibeonites acted. The two preceding verses have said that for murder no *kōpher* may be paid, and the reasoning goes on: 'So ye shall not pollute the land wherein ye are: for blood, it polluteth the land: and no expiation can be made for the land for the blood that is shed therein, but by the blood of him that shed it.' In its context the last section of the verse must mean 'No *kōpher* is acceptable for murder, other than the blood of the murderer', and once again we have strong evidence of the close connection between the two words. The Song of Moses (Dt. 32) gives us a further example of the same principle at work. Yahweh 'will make expiation (*wekhipper*) for his land, and for his people' (verse 43), and in verses 41, 42 we have the blood of the enemy specifically indicated. The expression, 'For he will avenge the blood of his servants' (verse 43), clearly indicates that a life-for-life transaction is meant.

It is this necessity for paying for blood with blood that is behind Deuteronomy 21: 1–9, where we get the further idea of pro-pitiating the divine wrath by means of a *kōpher*. A murder has been committed, the body being left lying in a field, and the perpetrator of the crime is unknown. Since no *kōpher* has been paid by 'the blood of him that shed' blood (Nu. 35: 33), the wrath of God must be assumed to rest on the community. In order to remove it the elders of the nearest city are to take a heifer to a prescribed place and there to break its neck. It is difficult to see in this anything other than an offering of a propitiatory character,[1] wherein the blood of the beast is the *kōpher* for the blood of the man. On this ground Yahweh is prayed to grant His people atonement, and the passage assures them that the blood will thus be atoned (verse 8).

There are other occurrences of *kipper* where the cultus is not in question, most of which are readily understood in the way we have outlined above. Thus, when we read, 'By mercy and truth iniquity is purged' (Pr. 16: 6), the meaning would seem to be that these qualities are a sort of price paid – the language is figurative – whereby the wrath attendant on iniquity is bought off. A few verses later we have the verb again in the statement that 'The wrath of a king is as messengers of death: but a wise man will atone it',[2] *i.e.* will provide a *kōpher* for it.

The idea that is to be discerned in the last mentioned passage of a gift turning away wrath probably underlies other passages wherein the thought is one of forgiveness. The forgiveness that is in mind when *kipper* is used is one which involves the turning away of wrath, and the imagery of the word implies that it is by the offering of a *kōpher*. Thus in Isaiah 27: 9 we have the thought of forgiveness, but it is a forgiveness that is brought about when Jacob 'maketh all the stones of the altar as chalkstones that are beaten in sunder, so that the Asherim and the sun-images shall rise no more'. The nation is being castigated for idolatry, which is probably the sin above all others that is said in the Old Testament to arouse the wrath of God, and the path of expiation is the beating small of the idolatrous altars and the abolition of the worship served by them. This is regarded as the *kōpher* by which forgiveness is obtained.

[1] S. R. Driver goes rather further than I would think justified when he says, 'the heifer in this rite is manifestly designed as a substitute for the unknown murderer, and bears the penalty which ought properly to be his' (*ICC, Deuteronomy*, pp. 241f.). We see the force of this rite if we imagine that after it has been performed the murderer is discovered. Presumably in this case he would not be allowed to go scot free, which ought to be the case if the penalty has been borne. The real significance of the rite is that it averts the divine wrath from the community; it is the *kōpher* whereby immunity from punishment for the crime is purchased.

The Mishnah says that if the slayer were found after the killing of the heifer, he was to be put to death (*Sot.* 9: 7).

[2] Pr. 16: 14. BDB under *kipper* comment, 'pacify the wrath of a king, Pr. 16: 14 (e.g. by a gift)'.

The particular *kōpher* which is to be offered is not mentioned in
Ezekiel 16: 63, but the explicit mention of the wrath of God
(verses 38, 42) makes it clear that we are still moving in the same
circle of ideas. In Psalm 78: 38 the parallelism makes 'forgave
(atoned) their iniquity' almost equivalent to 'turned he his anger
away', and similarly in Psalm 79: 9, the removal of wrath as the
way of purging sins is clear from the references to the divine anger
in the situation (verses 5, 6, 8). In Psalm 65: 3, 'As for our transgressions, thou shalt purge them away', there is by no means as
clear a reference either to a *kōpher* or to divine anger, though the
magnitude of the sin is stressed in the preceding 'Iniquities prevail
against me', which perhaps points to the arousing of such an anger.
The precise meaning of Daniel 9: 24 is not easy to determine, but
the expression 'Seventy weeks are decreed upon thy people and
upon thy holy city, to finish transgression, and to make an end of
sins, and to make reconciliation for iniquity' seems to indicate,
at any rate, that the 'troublous times' of the period mentioned are
in the nature of a *kōpher* playing its part in making the reconciliation.

There is a similar idea behind Jeremiah's prayer against his
enemies: 'Forgive not their iniquity . . . deal thou with them in the
time of thine anger' (Je. 18: 23). The anger of the Lord and the
refusal to accept a *kōpher* are here in close connection.

The thought of propitiation is very clear when Phinehas slew
Zimri and Cozbi at the time of the sin of Baal-Peor to stay the
plague which followed the kindling of the Lord's anger (Nu. 25:
3–9). Of this action we read: 'Phinehas, the son of Eleazar, the son
of Aaron the priest, hath turned my wrath away from the children
of Israel, in that he was jealous with my jealousy among them, so
that I consumed not the children of Israel in my jealousy . . . he
was jealous for his God, and made atonement for the children of
Israel' (Nu. 25: 11–13). Here the zealous priest by offering up
the lives of the evil-doers is thought of as rendering the *kōpher*
which averts the divine wrath. There can hardly be serious doubt
that here we have propitiation in the fullest sense,[1] or that this
propitiation is the turning away of wrath by the offering of a
kōpher.

[1] *Cf.* Dodd in *JTS*, XXXII, 1931, p. 355, 'the story is one of "propitiation" in
the crudest sense.'

There remain two passages in both of which the reference is to the purging away of uncleanness (2 Ch. 30: 18; Is. 6: 7). In neither case can it be said that the payment of a *kōpher* seems indicated, though neither is inconsistent with a propitiation of the divine wrath, for ritual defilement is thought to provoke the anger of the deity in many religions. But it should be noticed that these passages are both later than 1 Samuel 3: 14 where *kipper* has begun to have a cultic application. It is accordingly not impossible that cultic ideas are behind the use of the word in these passages. If so, the general argument from the secular use of the word would, of course, remain unaffected.

From the foregoing examination of the evidence it appears that, when *kipper* is used in the Old Testament to denote the making of an atonement by means other than the use of the cultus, it usually bears the meaning 'to avert punishment, especially the divine anger, by the payment of a *kōpher*, a ransom', which may be of money or which may be of life. Thus extra-cultic *kipper* denotes a substitutionary process. This is so plain as to need no comment in the cases where life is substituted for life, and the principle is really the same when the sentence is commuted for a money payment. In each case the essence of the transaction is the provision of an acceptable substitute.

The fact that, in practically all of the passages we have examined, *kipper* and *kōpher* are closely connected seems very significant, for when we are seeking to establish the meaning of a word it is the *usage* in Hebrew that is decisive.[1] In examining the meaning of *kipper* scholars often adduce words from other Semitic languages; but while due allowance must be made for the importance of such evidence, in the last resort it is the way the Hebrews actually used the word which really counts. The importance of this is that the usage of the two words *kipper* and *kōpher* indicates, as we have seen, that *kōpher* is probably the more original, and that *kipper* may well be regarded as a denominative from *kōpher*. The seven places where atonement is made through offering a *kōpher* of life, and the

---

[1] *Cf.* G. F. Moore: 'by a fault of method which has been fruitful of error in the study of the OT, the investigation has frequently set out from etymological assumptions instead of from the plain facts of usage' (*Enc. Bib.*, IV, col. 4220). So also E. König: 'the Heb. usage of the word *kipper* is the *only* starting-point from which to determine the original signification of the word' (*ET*, XXII, p. 380).

nine where the *kōpher* is money or goods or a metaphorical price, seem to be conclusive, embracing as they do the majority of the non-cultic occurrences of the term.

(ii) *The cultic use of kipper.* It is not easy to find out exactly how the sacrifices were thought to make atonement, as the verb *kipper* acquired a technical meaning which completely overshadowed any other. In most places it means 'to accomplish reconciliation between God and man' without anything to indicate how that reconciliation is obtained. The word has taken on a conventional meaning. However, indications are not lacking that the above-mentioned relationship between *kōpher* and *kipper* gives us the key to the understanding of the cultic references.

Thus if we take the incident narrated in Numbers 16: 41–50 we have a making of atonement which may be held to be a link between the cultic and the non-cultic usages. Here the congregation has murmured against Moses and Aaron and a plague has broken out as a consequence of the Lord's anger against the people (verse 46). The means of averting the wrath is by Aaron's making an offering of incense (verses 46f.), and such an action by a duly consecrated priest must surely be regarded as within the scope of the cultus. But it was not one of the prescribed offerings, being purely an oblation made in time of grave emergency for the specific purpose of turning away the anger of the Lord, and the affinities of this with a *kōpher*-payment are obvious. If it be objected that there was no great money value in the offering of a small quantity of incense, so that the atonement obtained is out of all proportion to the price paid, the answer must be that the atonement obtained is always out of all proportion to the price paid,[1] even in the case of the non-cultic atonements, as for example the half-shekel, or the payment to secure immunity when one's ox has gored a man. There is always an element of grace in atonement. But just as, notwithstanding this, we can appreciate the place of the *kōpher*-payment in non-cultic practice, so in the processes of the cultus we may recognize both the element of grace and the

---

[1] *Cf.* the Midrash on Numbers: 'Moses pondered: Who is in a position to give ransom for his soul? . . . The Holy One, blessed be He, told him: "I do not ask for ransom in accordance with My means, but in accordance with their means . . ."' *Midrash Rabbah, Numbers* 12: 3 (Soncino trans., pp. 451f.).

necessity for the worshipper to make his offering if he would be forgiven his sin.

We have already noted the incident in Numbers 31 wherein the men of war offered part of the spoil which they called 'the Lord's oblation' and which was 'to make atonement for their souls before the Lord'. There seems no reason to regard this as other than a non-cultic process, for there is no hint of sacrifice being offered. But there is not a great deal of difference between this and the offering of the princes in Numbers 7, for included in their oblation (*qorbān*) were 'one silver charger, the weight thereof was an hundred and thirty shekels, one silver bowl of seventy shekels, after the shekel of the sanctuary . . . one golden spoon of ten shekels', which objects of precious metal seem similar to the offering of the men of war. But we cannot separate the gift of the princes from the cultus, because under the comprehensive term *qorbān* are included not only the precious metal, but also burnt, sin and peace offerings.

The affinity of the cultus with *kōpher* seems clear also in Numbers 15: 25, 'And the priest shall make atonement (*wekhipper*) for all the congregation of the children of Israel, and they shall be forgiven; for it was an error, and they have brought their oblation ('*eth-qorbānām*), an offering made by fire unto the Lord', *etc.* Here the sacrifice that makes atonement is expressly said to be *qorbān*, a word which, as G. Buchanan Gray puts it, 'vividly expressed the sense of gift'.[1] It seems impossible to escape the conclusion that in this passage *kipper* stands for a process of making atonement by the offering of a suitable gift (other passages also have the idea of the gift element in sacrifice, *e.g.* Dt. 16: 16; Jdg. 6: 18, 19; Is. 18: 7; Zp. 3: 10, *etc.*[2]).

It would seem that it is in this circle of ideas that we are to understand the statement that 'the iniquity of Eli's house shall not be atoned with sacrifice nor offering for ever' (1 Sa. 3: 14). The house in question had been guilty of sin against the Lord which

---

[1] *Sacrifice in the Old Testament* (Oxford, 1925), p. 51.

[2] Davidson says: 'whatever older or more primary ideas of sacrifice may have been, in the Old Testament at least sacrifice is of the nature of a gift to God' (*The Theology of the Old Testament*, Edinburgh, 1904, p. 353). He also says: 'The traditional explanation has been that the death of the victim was a *poena vicaria* for the sin of the offerer. And it is probable that this idea did become attached to sacrifice' (*ibid.*), though he questions whether this thought is to be found in the law.

aroused His wrath against them. Perhaps this wrath could be turned away (according to the thought of the day) by payment of a *kōpher* and the lives now forfeit be in this manner redeemed? The words of verse 14 emphatically repudiate this idea. No sacrifice or offering will form a *kōpher* under these circumstances. In this undeniably early passage the cultus is regarded as a means of offering a *kōpher*, and this is probably significant for an understanding of the cultus.

This was apparently the way the cultus was regarded by the Jews at Yeb, in Egypt. When the priests wrote to Bigvai, the governor of Judea, urging him to give command concerning the rebuilding of their temple, they said that, if he acceded to their request, they would offer sacrifices on his behalf and pray for him, 'and it shall be a merit to you before Ya'u the God of Heaven more than a man who offers to him sacrifice and burnt-offerings worth as much as the sum of a thousand talents'.[1] The mention of the money equivalent indicates clearly that the thought of a gift availing before God is for the writers the rationale of sacrifice.

Possibly the provision in the case of the guilt offering for an extra one fifth to be added to full restitution in certain cases points in the same general direction. Thus, in the matter of an unwitting trespass 'in the holy things of the Lord', it is provided that 'he shall make restitution for that which he hath done amiss in the holy thing, and shall add the fifth part thereto, and give it unto the priest: and the priest shall make atonement for him with the ram of the guilt offering, and he shall be forgiven' (Lv. 5: 16). Here the extra fifth looks uncommonly like a sort of *kōpher*, and the same may be said for other examples of the guilt offering.

It is especially interesting to note that when restitution was owed to a man, but could not be paid because the man was dead, and there was no kinsman, it was still necessary for the restitution (the full amount owed plus one fifth) to be paid, but to the Lord (Nu. 5: 8). It would seem that there was a principle involved, namely that a *kōpher* must be paid if atonement was to be effected.

To adduce further examples would entail a long discussion which would be out of place here. If there is anything in the thesis which is being maintained then the use outside the cultus coupled with these few examples of the continuity of the cultic with the

---

[1] A. Cowley, *Aramaic Papyri of the Fifth Century B.C.* (Oxford, 1923), p. 114, no. 30, lines 27f.

non-cultic use should suffice to demonstrate the point. The general impression produced by the sacrificial system, that an offering of a propitiatory character is being made, is perhaps worthy of notice also. It is not so much from consideration of details as from the general sweep of the whole that conviction is obtained.[1]

It is also worth noticing that the prophets witness to a belief that sacrifice was the offering of a gift to Yahweh which would incline Him to be favourable. Passages like Isaiah 1: 11ff.; Micah 6: 6ff., show clearly that such a theory of sacrifice was present to the minds of the worshippers. The prophets denounce much in the attitude of the people, in particular pointing out the prime importance of ethical considerations; but it may be significant that they nowhere suggest a different theory of sacrifice. It seems reasonable to expect that had they held this theory to be wrong they would have both said so, and also have indicated the better theory.

Thus it would seem that the verb *kipper* carries with it the implication of a turning away of the divine wrath by an appropriate offering. This meaning accords well with the general usage of ἐξιλάσκομαι, and it seems clear that this verb is used so often to translate *kipper* precisely for this reason.

It remains to be considered whether the conclusions we have reached regarding the ἐξιλάσκομαι = *kipper* equation are affected by the evidence afforded by those passages in the LXX where ἐξιλάσκομαι renders Hebrew words other than *kipper*. We have already noted that this Greek verb is the translation of *kipper* eighty-three times; for the rest it translates *ḥṭ'* five times, *ḥllh* three times, *plll* and *'shm* once each (also *yd'* once, but this seems to rest on a misunderstanding of the Hebrew),[2] and eleven times there is no Hebrew equivalent.

So far as *ḥṭ'* 'to un-sin, to make a sin offering' is concerned, very little needs be said. Its use is practically indistinguishable from that of *kipper* in the places where ἐξιλάσκομαι translates it. Thus in 2 Chronicles 29: 24 the verb signifies 'they made their blood a sin offering', which is close to the usage we have already noted, especially to that non-cultic use of *kipper* wherein there is a life-for-life conception. In Ezekiel, where all the remaining examples are

---

[1] Cf. the statement quoted from the Jewish Encyclopedia on p. 174 below.

[2] Or perhaps a different (and now lost) reading. Either way it sheds no light on our problem.

found, it is very difficult to find any difference between this use of ἐξιλάσκομαι and that where *kipper* is the underlying Hebrew. This is especially plain in Ezekiel 43: 20 where it is impossible to say which of the two Hebrew verbs the Greek word translates.

hilláh means 'to appease, mollify', and three times it occurs as the Hebrew for which ἐξιλάσκομαι is the translation (Zc. 7: 2; 8: 22; Mal. 1: 9). Each time the thought of propitiation is quite clear, as Dodd notes when he calls these three occurrences 'unmistakeable examples of the ordinary classical and Hellenistic sense of ἐξιλάσκεσθαι = "to propitiate" '.[1]

The use of ἐξιλάσκομαι to translate *plll* ('to interpose', hence 'to do judgment', or by another line of development, 'to pray') in Psalm 105(106): 30 is very unusual, and despite Dodd's objection is probably to be understood in the light of the story in Numbers. The psalmist is recalling the atonement wrought by Phinehas at the time of the sin of Baal-Peor and the translator substitutes 'and he made propitiation' for 'and he interposed', or 'wrought judgment'.

The one occurrence of ἐξιλάσκομαι as the translation of '*shm* presents us with a difficulty, as the Hebrew verb means 'to be guilty' and it is hard to fit ἐξιλάσκομαι into this circle of ideas. Probably, as Dodd suggests, the translators were influenced by the close kinship between '*shm* and *ht'* in which case we must think of the passage for our present purpose as coming close to the group already considered.

Thus there is nothing in the use of ἐξιλάσκομαι to translate other Hebrew roots which conflicts with the conclusions we have already reached from our study of its translation of *kipper*. The thought of the offering of a ransom which turns away the divine wrath from the sinner is still seen to be the basic meaning of the verb.

We conclude this section by noticing the constructions used with ἐξιλάσκομαι. Since it is sometimes said that the verb is often used in the sense 'to expiate' it is worth noting that it is never followed by an accusative of sin in the canonical Scriptures of the Old Testament (unless we include Theodotion's Daniel under the heading 'canonical'). One is in Theodotion's Daniel, where the 'seventy weeks' decreed upon the people look like a manifestation of divine wrath (9: 24). The remaining six are in Sirach, three of them

[1] *JTS*, XXXII, 1931, p. 355.

certainly referring to removal of wrath (Sir. 3: 30; 5: 6; 28: 5), and probably two more also (Sir. 20: 28; 31: 33). This evidence cannot be said to afford strong support for views which reject propitiation. It can be supported by only two passives with sin as subject (Dt. 21: 8; 1 Sa. 3: 14), in both of which it is possible to think of propitiation. The grouping of the nine accusatives of a cultic object (altar, sanctuary, *etc.*) with this class is not warranted, for the meaning is not the same (Lv. 16: 16, 20, 33 (twice); Ezk. 43: 20, 22, 26; 45: 18, 20; *cf.* also the curious accusative of 'blood' in 2 Ch. 29: 24). If one expiates a sin it is clean gone, but if one cleanses an altar it is still there. It seems best to recognize that the verb has a complex meaning, but to see the removal of wrath as the basic idea. Wrath could be removed with reference to a sin, or with reference to an (unclean) altar, *etc.*

Again, God is the subject of the verb three times, followed by dative of person (Ezk. 16: 63), by περί (Sir. 16: 7), and by ὑπέρ (2 Ch. 30: 18). Not much can be made of this, however, because in the first and last of these the verb is in the passive, and the sense is 'be propitiated'. With these two passives which have God as the subject should be classed three passages with God as the object and where the meaning clearly is 'propitiate' (Zc. 7: 2; 8: 22; Mal. 1: 9). The idea of propitiation is found also with a human object (Gn. 32: 20), while the one accusative of 'wrath' (Pr. 16: 14) has much the same meaning. The verb is most often used in a personal sense, the commonest construction being περί with genitive of person, 'to make propitiation concerning a person' (58 times, *e.g.* Ex. 30: 15, 16; Lv. 1: 4). Sometimes περί of sin is added (Lv. 4: 35), or ἀπό of sin (Lv. 4: 26) or of uncleanness (Lv. 15: 15, 30). Once we find ὑπέρ of person (Ezk. 45: 17), and once ἐπί with animal (Lv. 16: 10).

For the rest, the verb is used absolutely ten times (as Lv. 6: 30), with περί of sin twice (Ex. 32: 30; Lv. 5: 10), with περί or ἐπί of things four times (Ex. 30: 10; Lv. 8: 15; 14: 53; 16: 18), and there are two passives, one with the land as subject, and one where the verb is impersonal with dative of person (Nu. 35: 33; 1 Sa. 6: 3).

These constructions reveal that the word is used in a variety of ways, but there is no preponderance of expressions which could be construed of expiation of sin. Rather the emphasis seems to be on the relation between persons, a fact which accords better with a meaning like 'propitiate' than 'expiate'. It is clear that ἐξιλάσκομαι in the LXX is a complex word, but the averting of anger seems to represent a stubborn substratum of meaning from which all the usages can be naturally explained. This is so even in the case when God is subject, for, while the Old Testament is emphatic about the reality and seriousness of the wrath of God, the removal of that wrath is due in the last resort to God Himself. 'He will many times turn away his anger' (Ps. 77(78): 38 (LXX); cf. also Jb. 14: 13; Ps. 85: 4–6; Pr. 24: 18; Is. 48: 9; 57: 16; 60: 10).

To sum up: I accept the verdict of such scholars as Westcott and Dodd that in the Old Testament there is not the usual pagan sense of a crude propitiation of an angry deity, and that this is shown in the use of ἱλάσκομαι, etc. in the LXX. The one example with God as the subject of the verb (other than in the passive), the paucity of examples of its use with Him as the object, and the study of the Hebrew words translated by ἱλάσκομαι and its cognates all alike draw us to this conclusion. In the foregoing treatment we have not been greatly concerned to defend this point of view, but this should not be understood as minimizing its significance. It is of the utmost importance that we should understand that propitiation in the crude sense is not possible with the God of Israel, and that the Greek words used reflect this view of the deity. We cannot be too grateful to Dodd and others for their convincing demonstration of this truth.

However, in their anxiety to do justice to this great truth, these scholars seem to go too far. When we reach the stage where we must say, 'When the LXX translators used "propitiation" they did not mean "propitiation"', it is surely time to call a halt. No sensible man uses one word when he means another, and in view of the otherwise invariable Greek use it would seem impossible for anyone in the first century to have used one of the ἱλάσκομαι group without conveying to his readers some idea of propitiation.

It is contended that while care is taken to avoid the crude use natural to pagans, yet the words of the ἱλάσκομαι group as used in the LXX were not eviscerated of their meaning, nor were they given an entirely new meaning. Rather there is a definite continuity, and in particular the removal of wrath seems to be definitely in view when this word-group is used. We have noticed that in many passages where one or other of these words is used there is a plain statement that Yahweh is angry, and in others there is a clear implication that this is so, and these passages (taken in conjunction with the essential meaning of ἱλάσκομαι, etc.) must be held to set the tone for the rest.

Examination of this word-group brought us inevitably into the circle of ideas associated with *kipper*, where we have seen reason for postulating a close connection between *kipper* and *kōpher*. This further strengthens the conclusion that ἱλάσκομαι, etc., retain the idea of putting away the divine anger, since it means that in the cultus itself there is the thought of a ransom being paid, a ransom which we may not unjustly regard as a propitiation. As the Jewish Encyclopedia puts it: 'Every sacrifice may be considered thus as a kofer, in the original sense a propitiatory gift.'[1]

Thus we conclude that the sense of propitiation seems to be established from the passages in which ἱλάσκομαι and its cognates occur.

V. CONCLUSION

The preceding sections have shown that the wrath of God is a conception which cannot be eradicated from the Old Testament without irreparable loss. It is not the monopoly of one or two writers, but pervades the entire corpus so that there is no important section of which it can be said, 'Here the wrath of God is unknown!' The ubiquity of the concept must be stressed, because of the tendency in some circles today to overlook it or to explain it away. The concept may need to be understood carefully, but it is so much part and parcel of the Old Testament that, if we ignore it, we cannot possibly enter into a proper appreciation of the Hebrew view of God or of man.

Above everything else, the concept of the wrath of God stresses the seriousness of sin. On the Old Testament view sin is not just a mere peccadillo which a kindly, benevolent God will regard as of

[1] II, p. 275. S. R. Driver makes a thorough examination of *kipper* in his article on 'Propitiation' in *HDB* and concludes that, when the verb is used in a ritual sense, it means 'to make propitiation', and in other places it signifies 'deal propitiously with', or 'be propitious to'. See also his commentary on Deuteronomy (*ICC*), pp. 425f.

no great consequence. On the contrary, the God of the Old Testament is One who loves righteousness (Pss. 33: 5; 48: 10; *etc.*), and whose attitude to unrighteousness can be described as hatred. 'These are the things that ye shall do; Speak ye every man the truth with his neighbour; execute the judgment of truth and peace in your gates: and let none of you imagine evil in your hearts against his neighbour; and love no false oath; for all these are things that I hate, saith the Lord' (Zc. 8: 16f.) is a typical statement. And not only does God hate sin, He hates sinners also: 'The Lord trieth the righteous; but the wicked and him that loveth violence his soul hateth. Upon the wicked he shall rain snares; fire and brimstone and burning wind shall be the portion of their cup. For the Lord is righteous; he loveth righteousness', *etc.* (Ps. 11: 5–7). Such passages reveal the strongest possible repulsion in the face of everything that is evil. It is from the very heart of a God who not only loves His people but also hates evil that there proceeds such pleading as, 'I sent unto you all my servants the prophets, rising up early and sending them, saying, Oh do not this abominable thing that I hate' (Je. 44: 4). Not surprisingly, we find passages in which those who love God are called upon to exercise the same attitude, 'O ye that love the Lord, hate evil' (Ps. 97: 10).

Modern men find a difficulty with this aspect of the Old Testament teaching, in part at least because they have so well learned that God is love. But it is important to notice that this was a truth known and valued by men of Old Testament times. They apparently did not find it insuperably difficult to combine the ideas that God loved them and that He hated all evil and would punish it severely. Both thoughts are emphasized, for example, in Hosea's prophecy. On the one hand we have the beautiful picture of Yahweh wooing the nation (2: 14f.), statements such as, 'I drew them with cords of a man, with bands of love' (11: 4), or 'How shall I give thee up, Ephraim? how shall I deliver thee, Israel? how shall I make thee as Admah? how shall I set thee as Zeboim? mine heart is turned within me, my compassions are kindled together. I will not execute the fierceness of mine anger, I will not return to destroy Ephraim' (11: 8f.), and the unforgettable picture of a father teaching a baby son to walk in 11: 1–3. On the other hand we have the most categorical statements of God's loathing of the evil that was in the nation coupled with the certainty of divine visitation and punishment: 'All their wickedness is in Gilgal; for there I hated them: because of the wickedness of their doings I will drive them out of mine house: I will love them no more; all their princes are revolters. Ephraim is smitten, their root is dried up, they shall bear no fruit: yea, though they bring forth, yet will I slay the beloved fruit of their womb. My God will cast them away, because they did not hearken unto him: and they shall be wanderers among the nations' (9: 15–17); 'He hath cast off thy calf, O Samaria; mine anger is kindled against them' (8: 5); 'For Israel hath forgotten his Maker, and builded palaces; and Judah hath multiplied fenced cities: but I will send a fire upon his cities, and it shall devour the castles thereof' (8: 14).

Such examples could be multiplied from many parts of the Old Testament, and they demand some explanation. It is open to us to say that there are divergent ideas which have not been harmonized; but if we are to be true to the records we cannnot simply say that half the evidence does not exist. But in view of the fact that we have both truths expressed, and expressed very strongly, by one man as we have just seen (and what is true of Hosea is also true of other Old Testament figures), it seems better to say that divine love and the divine wrath are compatible aspects of the divine nature. There is a divine wrath, but if we may put it this way, it is always exercised with a certain tenderness. Even when He is angry with man's sin God loves man and is concerned for his well-being in the fullest sense. There is a divine love, but it is not a careless sentimentality indifferent to the moral integrity of the loved ones. Rather it is a love which is a purifying fire, blazing against everything that hinders the loved ones from being the very best that they can be.

Indeed wrath may be thought of as especially wrath against the loved ones for, as J. Fichtner points out,[1] wrath is connected much more often with the covenant name 'Jehovah' than with any other of the divine names. There are times when the wrath of God is spoken of as directed against the heathen, and the importance of these passages should not be minimized (wrath is directed against *all* evil). But more often wrath is God's reaction against sin in His chosen people, in those whom He loves.

Much, it would seem, depends on what we understand by wrath. If we think of an uncontrollable outburst of passion, then we have a

[1] *TWNT*, V, p. 396.

pagan conception, completely inapplicable to the God of the Old Testament.[1] But if we think rather of a wrath which is the reverse side of a holy love, a flame which sears but purifies, then we have a conception which is valuable not only for an understanding of the ancient Scriptures, but also for any right conception of the nature of God. 'Neither doth he abhor anything that is evil' (Ps. 36: 4, Prayer Book version) is a terrible condemnation of a man's character. The Hebrews did not ascribe such moral flabbiness to the God they worshipped.

It is against such a background that the Old Testament idea of propitiation is to be studied. Where there is sin, the Old Testament teaches, there is wrath. But this does not mean that all men are to be consumed, for that wrath is the wrath of a loving father who yearns for His children to come to Him.[2] There is forgiveness with God, and this forgiveness necessarily involves the laying aside of wrath.[3] But it is important to note that the removal of this wrath is due not to man's securing such an offering that God is impressed and relents, but to God Himself. This alone is sufficient to show that we are not dealing with the pagan idea when we speak of flropitiation. Such a passage as Leviticus 17: 11, 'For the life of the pesh is in the blood: and *I have given it to you upon the altar to make atonement* for your souls', clearly indicates the position.[4] The cultus may well be regarded as a means of turning away the wrath of God from the sinner by the offering of a *kōpher*; but it is so, not because the God of Israel can be bought, but because He has *given* to the people this means of averting wrath. That it is not an un-

---

[1] *Cf.* G. O. Griffith: 'we picture "wrath" as we might think of the fury of a storm. The Hebrew Prophets, when they spoke of the "wrath of God", ethicized the idea of anger so that it meant the absolute implacable hostility of the Divine Holiness to every form of moral evil' (*St. Paul's Gospel to the Romans*, Oxford, 1949, p. 21), or again: 'The wrath is no fitful outburst of personal anger but the implacable antagonism of holiness for evil, an antagonism that burns eternally' (*op. cit.*, pp. 85f.).

[2] *Cf.*, for example, Ho. 11: 1–4 with Ho. 11: 5f.

[3] G. Buchanan Gray says: 'The ideas of expiation of sin and propitiation of God are in Hebrew thought closely related' (*op. cit.*, p. 74).

[4] *Cf.* P. T. Forsyth: 'Given! Did you ever see the force of it? "I have given you the blood to make atonement. This is an institution which I set up for you to comply with, set it up for purposes of My own, on principles of My own, but it is My gift." The Lord Himself provided the lamb for the burnt offering' (*The Work of Christ*, London, 1948, p. 90).

conditional means many passages in the prophets and elsewhere plainly show. The cultus does not work like a bribe, but it is the divinely appointed way of removing wrath, of propitiation. As P. T. Forsyth puts it: 'Atonement in the Old Testament was not the placating of God's anger, but the sacrament of God's grace. It was the expression of God's anger on the one hand and the expression and putting in action of God's grace on the other hand. . . . The sacrifices were in themselves prime acts of obedience to God's means of grace and His expressed will.'[1]

Thus, our conviction that ἱλάσκομαι and its cognates include as an integral part of their meaning the turning away of wrath rests partly on the examination of the occurrences of these words in the Septuagint, and partly on the fact that, quite apart from the words themselves, there is a formidable body of evidence that the wrath of God was a conception to be reckoned with on the Old Testament view. These two lines of thought reinforce one another and lead us to the conclusion that, on the biblical view, an element of wrath inheres in the divine nature, but that, by God's own appointment, this wrath may be averted. This averting we may properly term 'propitiation', if that word is understood as excluding the pagan idea of a process of celestial bribery. It may have to be used with care, but there is no reason for jettisoning it altogether.

---

[1] Ibid., p. 90. It is of interest in connection with the foregoing that H. Wheeler Robinson regards 'propitiatory' as one of the four chief ways of regarding the sacrifices (Redemption and Revelation, London, 1942, pp. 249f.).

CHAPTER VI

PROPITIATION (2)

IN THE PRECEDING CHAPTER we noted that there are four passages in the New Testament which are specially important for an understanding of propitiation, but that is not to say that we have exhausted the concept of propitiation when we have examined them. In the New Testament, as in the Old, a good deal depends upon our conception of the place and nature of the wrath of God. If this wrath is regarded as a very real factor so that the sinner is exposed to its severity, then the removal of the wrath will be an important part of our understanding of salvation; whereas if we diminish the part played by the divine wrath we shall not find it necessary to think seriously of propitiation. Accordingly we begin our discussion of the New Testament teaching on this subject by examining those passages where the wrath of God is mentioned.

I. THE WRATH OF GOD IN THE NEW TESTAMENT

There is neither the same richness of vocabulary nor the same frequency of mention in the New Testament treatment of the wrath of God as in the Old. Nevertheless, the relevant passages show that for the early Christians the divine wrath was just as real as it was for the men of the old covenant.

In our section on wrath in the Old Testament we noted the view held by some that for the prophets wrath signifies nothing more than an impersonal process of retribution. Such views are held, too, with regard to the New Testament. For example, C. H. Dodd says that, in the teaching of Jesus, 'anger as an attitude of God to men disappears, and His love and mercy become all-embracing'.[1] St. Paul, he thinks, agrees with this in substance and retains the concept of the wrath of God 'not to describe the attitude of God to man, but to describe an inevitable process of cause and effect in a moral universe'.[2] In support he appeals to Romans 1: 18f. It is difficult to see how such views can be substantiated.

[1] MNTC, Romans, p. 23.
[2] Ibid.

There are two Greek words particularly used to denote the divine anger, namely θυμός and ὀργή. The two seem at times to be used synonymously: Büchsel, indeed, denies that we can distinguish between them. Etymologically there is a distinction, for θυμός derives from θύω which means to rush on or along, and, as Grimm-Thayer put it: 'to rush along or on, be in a heat, breathe violently; hence Plato correctly says, Cratyl. p. 419e θυμὸς ἀπὸ τῆς θύσεως κ. ζέσεως τῆς ψυχῆς; accordingly it signifies both *the spirit* panting as it were in the body, and the *rage* with which the man pants and swells.'[1] ὀργή on the other hand is from ὀργάω which signifies '*to be getting ready to bear, growing ripe* for something'.[2] It comes to mean the natural disposition or character, any movement of soul, especially strong emotion, and so anger. This leads to a distinction between the two words such that θυμός more readily denotes passionate anger, arising and subsiding quickly, whereas ὀργή is adapted to a more settled emotion,[3] and Grimm-Thayer cite Plato and Gregory Nazianzum to show this.

This original distinction is not always observed, but from it we can see that ὀργή is a more suitable term for the divine wrath than θυμός, and, in point of fact, the latter term is used only once of God's anger outside the Apocalypse, in which book the thought of a passionate wrath is in keeping with the vivid imagery used throughout.[4] The point of all this is that the biblical writers habitually use for the divine wrath a word which denotes not so much a sudden flaring up of passion which is soon over, as a strong and settled opposition to all that is evil arising out of God's very nature.

In the Gospels the actual term 'wrath' is not of frequent

[1] Lexicon *sub* θυμός.

[2] LS, *s.v.* The Eighth edn. says the word means 'Properly *to swell and teem with moisture*'.

[3] Thus G. Stählin says of ὀργή: 'Nevertheless this word includes an element of consciousness, even of deliberation, which is absent from θυμός; in Jas. 1: 19 (βραδὺς εἰς ὀργήν) for example ὀργή could hardly be replaced by θυμός' (*TWNT*, V, p. 419).

[4] To cite Stählin again: 'But one could well say that θυμός, to which there cleaves the idea of outbursting passion, is well suited for the representation of the vision of the seer, but not as a designation for the Pauline conception of the wrath of God' (*op. cit.*, p. 423).

occurrence.[1] But Jesus Himself is once said to have been angry
(Mk. 3: 5), and He spoke of the siege of Jerusalem as 'wrath unto
this people' (Lk. 21: 23), while His forerunner warned men of
'wrath to come' (Mt. 3: 7; Lk. 3: 7). We also read of the disobedient (or unbeliever; ὁ ἀπειθῶν τῷ υἱῷ) that 'the wrath of God
abideth on him' (Jn. 3: 36), where wrath is the portion of the sinner,
corresponding to the believer's reception of eternal life.

But in other places where the term 'wrath' does not occur we
find strong expressions for the divine hostility to all that is evil.
Thus Jesus taught explicitly that men stand in danger of a hell
which may be described as a 'hell of fire' (Mt. 5: 22, *etc.*), or as 'the
eternal fire' (Mt. 18: 8), a place where 'their worm dieth not, and
the fire is not quenched' (Mk. 9: 48). God is to be feared, for He,
'after he hath killed hath power to cast into hell' (Lk. 12: 5). Jesus'
severe strictures on Capernaum and other cities (Mt. 11: 20, 24),
and on the Pharisees (Mt. 23), show an intolerance of evil, which
we see again in 'except ye repent, ye shall all in like manner perish'
(Lk. 13: 3, 5), and in 'whosoever shall blaspheme against the Holy
Spirit hath never forgiveness, but is guilty of an eternal sin' (Mk. 3:
29). It is in keeping with this general attitude that we read of Judas,
'good were it for that man if he had not been born' (Mk. 14: 21),
and that, on the day of judgment, the verdict on some will be,
'Depart from me, ye cursed, into the eternal fire' (Mt. 25: 41 and
cf. verse 46). In the parables judgment is a persistent theme (*e.g.* Mt.
13: 42, 50; 18: 34; 21: 44; 22: 7, 33). So, too, is the idea of the
'outer darkness' where there will be 'weeping and gnashing of
teeth' (Mt. 8: 12; 13: 42, 50; 22: 13; 24: 51; 25: 30; Lk. 13: 28). In
the face of all this it is difficult to maintain that Jesus had discarded
the conception of the wrath of God. For Him the divine reaction
in the face of evil was a solemn and terrible reality.

Nor is the case different when we turn to the rest of the New
Testament. It is sometimes said that there is significance in the fact
that 'the wrath' occurs often without being definitely associated
with God. This is said to point to a semi-personalization, wrath
being conceived of as something different from, and almost

---

[1] Stählin introduces his section on 'The Revelation of the Divine Wrath' by
saying: 'Wrath is an integral trait in the evangelists' portrait of Jesus. To be sure,
the subject is mentioned only seldom in express words . . . but the fact is clearly
more often there' (*op. cit.*, p. 428).

independent of, God.[1] To this there are two answers. The first is that more than one conclusion can be drawn from the occurrence of 'the wrath'. It is quite legitimate for us to hold that the prophets who spoke of the coming day of wrath when God would punish sin had done their work so well that the fact that the wrath that was to be revealed was God's wrath did not require emphasis. The second is that the association of 'the wrath' with God is not so tenuous as some would have us believe. 'The wrath' (ἡ ὀργή) is specifically said to be of God (Jn. 3: 36; Rom. 1: 18; Eph. 5: 6; Col. 3: 6; Rev. 19: 15). In addition ἡ ὀργή σου (Rev. 11: 18) and τῆς ὀργῆς αὐτοῦ (Rev. 14: 10; 16: 19) obviously refer the wrath to God, while most people would agree that Romans 9: 22 is correctly translated by 'What if God, willing to shew his wrath' (with AV, RV, RSV, etc.). Again 'the wrath of the lamb' (Rev. 6: 16) associates wrath personally with a divine Being. θυμός is used to convey the idea of an anger specifically linked with God in Revelation 14: 10, 19; 15: 1, 7; 16: 1; 19: 15, while in Revelation 16: 19 the anger is clearly that of God. Nor have we told the whole story when we have listed the passages where there is an explicit connection of 'wrath' with God, for there are some passages without this where it is quite plain that such a link must be postulated. Thus C. Anderson Scott includes in a list of passages where 'Directly or indirectly St Paul connects God with the idea of anger or wrath' Romans 2: 5; 3: 5; 5: 9; Ephesians 5: 6; Colossians 3: 6; 1 Thessalonians 1: 10, while he thinks 'the same reference is less clearly expressed' in Romans 4: 15; Ephesians 2: 3; 1 Thessalonians 5: 9.[2] He also refers to Romans 1: 18; 1 Thessalonians 2: 16.

Nor have we yet finished. What are we to make of 'the revelation of the Lord Jesus from heaven with the angels of his power in flaming fire, rendering vengeance to them that know not God, and to them that obey not the gospel of our Lord Jesus: who shall

---

[1] So Sydney Cave (to whose writings the present writer owes a debt he can never repay): 'they (i.e. Law and Wrath) are almost personified powers, which, owing to God their origin, act on in partial independence of God, and are hostile to men as He is not' (*The Doctrine of the Work of Christ*, London, 1937, p. 43). The idea is categorically rejected by F. V. Filson: 'it is unwarranted to separate wrath from God, personalize it, and so make it a personal power independent of God ... Paul was not thinking of a separate being called Wrath' (*St. Paul's Conception of Recompense*, Leipzig, 1931, p. 40, n.2). Similarly Stählin (*op. cit.*, p. 425).

[2] *Christianity According to St. Paul* (Cambridge, 1932), p. 78.

suffer punishment, even eternal destruction from the face of the Lord and from the glory of his might' (2 Thes. 1 : 7–9)? This plainly means that the apostle expected a day to come when that which he elsewhere designates as 'the wrath of God' will have full operation. It is impossible to hold that he is referring to an impersonal retribution, for he speaks of the revelation of a person. Similarly, in Romans 2: 5–9, although we do not encounter the phrase 'the wrath of God', we cannot feel that the apostle is thinking of an impersonal retribution which operates while God remains apart, little more than a spectator. Paul's vigorous language gives us rather a picture of a God who is personally active in dealing with sinners. As Hebrews 12: 29 puts it, 'our God is a consuming fire.'[1]

P. T. Forsyth has a valuable Addendum to his *The Work of Christ* in which this question is discussed with great force. He asks: 'When a man piles up his sin and rejoices in iniquity, is God simply a bystander and spectator of the process? Does not God's pressure on the man blind him, urge him, stiffen him, shut him up into sin, if only that he might be shut up to mercy alone? Is it enough to say that this is but the action of a process which God simply watches in a permissive way? Is He but passive and not positive to the situation? Can the Absolute be passive to anything? If so, where is the inner action of the personal God whose immanence in things is one of His great modern revelations?'[2]

---

[1] R. V. G. Tasker speaks of some severe sayings of Jesus and comments: 'These are sayings of terrible severity, but they are just as much part of the revelation of God made known in Christ Jesus as those sayings and deeds of the Master which so conspicuously display the divine love and mercy. To thrust these severe sayings on one side and to concentrate attention solely upon passages of the Gospels where the divine Fatherhood is proclaimed is to preach a debilitated Christianity, which does not and cannot do what Christ came into the world to do, viz. save men from the wrath to come' (*The Biblical Doctrine of the Wrath of God*, London, 1951, p. 36).

[2] *Op. cit.*, p. 242. He also says: 'The love of God is not more real than the wrath of God' (*ibid*). *Cf.* Emil Brunner: 'His Holy Will is unconditionally active: if it is not effective for blessing or salvation, then, in consequence of the human break in the divine order, it works in the opposite direction, and produces disaster. But this will be personal. God is present in this anger, it is actually *His* anger' (*The Mediator*, London, 1942, p. 518). So P. Althaus: 'So long as God is God He cannot deny in Himself His holiness and His wrath' (*Mysterium Christi*, ed. G. K. A. Bell and A. Deissmann, London, 1930, p. 198); or again: 'Sin has not only determined the attitude of men but also the relation between God and men. Man's attitude is only a part of the relationship; the whole relationship is determined by the wrath of God' (*op. cit.*, p. 200).

We saw earlier that Dodd sees in Romans 1: 18f. the concept of 'the wrath of God' used 'to describe an inevitable process of cause and effect in a moral universe'. But in these very verses we find the personal activity of God brought out, for when St. Paul might well say that the sins of the heathen produced inevitable results, or might make use of some similar impersonal expression, he seems to go out of his way to lay stress upon the divine activity. 'God gave them up . . . unto uncleanness' (verse 24); 'God gave them up unto vile passions' (verse 26); 'God gave them up unto a reprobate mind' (verse 28). It is true that sin has its consequences; but for St. Paul this does not take place apart from God, for His activity is to be discerned in those consequences. Indeed the whole of this section might be regarded as an expansion of the opening words, 'For wrath of God is being continually revealed from heaven upon all impiety and unrighteousness of men'. And, as H. Wheeler Robinson says: 'this wrath of God is not the blind and automatic working of abstract law – always a fiction, since "law" is a conception, not an entity, till it finds expression through its instruments. The wrath of God is the wrath of divine *Personality*.'[1]

II. THE ἱλάσκομαι WORD-GROUP IN THE NEW TESTAMENT

We turn now to the actual terminology of the word-group which has generally been understood to convey the thought of propitiation. There are four passages to be discussed, the remainder being concerned with matters other than the interpretation of the work of Christ. Logically, perhaps, we should first examine the occurrence of the verb ἱλάσκομαι; but in view of the importance and difficulty of the passage in which ἱλαστήριον occurs we shall begin with this word.

a. ἱλαστήριον

Most recent writers have seen in ἱλαστήριον a reference to the mercy-seat, and, since this was in normal use only on the Day of Atonement,[2] have concluded that Romans 3: 25 must be inter-

---

[1] *Redemption and Revelation* (London, 1942), p. 269.

[2] There are numerous references to the ark of the covenant (of which the mercy-seat was the lid), as being used outside the holy of holies, *e.g.* Jos. 3: 3; 4: 5, *etc.*, and the well-known incident in 1 Sa. 4 when the Philistines captured it. That it was the

preted in terms of the ceremonies of that day. The term clearly refers to the mercy-seat in Hebrews 9: 5. But this does not decide the meaning of the word in the Romans passage (the only other occurrence of the word in the New Testament). It seems to me that there is much to be said for the idea which was vigorously upheld in earlier days, and still has some protagonists, that the word is not so specific, and is to be understood as something like 'means of propitiation'.

The form of the word does not help us much, for the meaning of the -τηριον termination is not completely clear. There are examples of its use for place, as ἀκροατήριον, and also for means as σωτήριον, and there are not wanting advocates for either meaning as the correct one for ἱλαστήριον.[1] It is plain that the usage and not the form must decide the question.

There is some doubt whether ἱλαστήριον in Romans 3 is an adjective or a noun. The adjectival form does occur, and for example, we find it qualifying θυσία in a papyrus from the Fayûm,[2] θάνατος in one reading of 4 Maccabees 17: 22, and μνῆμα in

---

practice to carry the ark with the armies in time of war seems clear, cf. Uriah's remark to David, 'The ark, and Israel, and Judah, abide in booths' (2 Sa. 11: 11). Many recent writers are of opinion that the ark was in regular use in connection with cultic practices such as an enthronement festival or sacred marriage. The last mention of the ark in 2 Ch. 35: 3, an instruction to put it into the temple, shows that it was still used in some manner not now known. But as our primary concern is with the later usage, that with which the men of the New Testament were concerned, we may set aside these practices. All the more is this so since the *kappōreth* is not mentioned in any such passage, and it may well have been the case that it was not carried round with the ark. That it was more than merely a lid to the ark seems implied by the reference to the holy of holies in 1 Ch. 28: 11 as 'the house of the *kappōreth*' and the designation of Yahweh as 'thou that sittest upon the cherubim' (Ps. 80: 1). The *kappōreth* clearly had existence in its own right, and was very closely associated with the presence of Yahweh.

[1] See F. Blass and A. Debrunner, *A Greek Grammar of the New Testament*, trans. R. W. Funk (Cambridge, 1961), p. 59, for the view that the termination signifies place. J. H. Moulton and W. F. Howard, however, amply document both 'place' and 'instrument or means' (*A Grammar of New Testament Greek*, II, Edinburgh, 1919, p. 342). They class ἱλαστήριον under the latter heading. A. T. Robertson thinks that the termination usually signifies place, but for ἱλαστήριον in Romans he takes the meaning to be 'propitiatory gift' or 'means of propitiation' (*A Grammar of the Greek New Testament*, London, n.d., p. 154).

[2] B. P. Grenfell and A. S. Hunt, *Fayûm Towns and their Papyri* (London, 1900), p. 313 (no. 337).

Josephus.[1] But not a great number of examples of this use of the word can be cited, and none where a substantive such as θῦμα is understood. Rather than understanding some such noun[2] it would seem better to take it as being predicate to the relative ὅν.[3] Grammatically there seems nothing against this, and when all is said and done it must remain as a possible understanding of the term, the only important objection, it would seem, being the statistical one, that ἱλαστήριον occurs quite often as a neuter noun and only rarely as an adjective. This consideration, it seems to me, must guide us in the Romans passage. We cannot assume that Paul used the rarer rather than the more usual form without some good evidence, and such does not seem to be adduced. We conclude therefore that ἱλαστήριον in this passage is probably the noun.

By the same criterion we take it to be the neuter noun rather than the masculine, although this latter seems to be understood by some of the Latin versions with their *propitiatorem*[4] (according to Sanday and Headlam the Syriac is ambiguous, but may be meant to support this reading). This understanding of the term has had some distinguished supporters, James Morison for example citing Wyclif 'an helpere', Purvey 'forgiver', Cranmer 'the obtainer of mercy', Erasmus 'reconciler' (though he also gives the more usual 'propitiatory'), Melanchthon 'propitiator', and others,[5] while to these E. H. Gifford adds Aquinas, Estius and van Hengel.[6] Despite these great names this understanding of our term is to be rejected,

---

[1] *Ant.* xvi. 7. 1.

[2] Yet G. F. Moore says 'the interpretation "atoning *sacrifice*" (after the analogy of σωτήριον, χαριστήριον, τελεστήριον, etc.) is not entirely certain, though highly probable', *Enc. Bib.*, col. 4229. Similarly Charles Hodge (*in loc.*) favours 'propitiatory sacrifice', and J. Denney uses the same expression in his paraphrase of the passage in *Studies in Theology* (London, 1895), pp. 115f. F. Platt says: 'Its interpretation as "a propitiatory offering" – a means of rendering God consistently favourable towards sinful men and the means of reconciliation between God and man – is the most natural, and is indeed the only meaning suitable to the context of Ro 3; other Pauline passages harmonize with it better than with any other meaning' (*HDAC*, II, p. 283).

[3] So W. Sanday and A. C. Headlam, *ICC, in loc.*; J. Denney, *Expositor's Greek Testament*, II (London, 1900), p. 611; Vincent Taylor, *ET*, L, 1938–39, p. 296; *et al.*

[4] See Sanday and Headlam, *in loc.*

[5] *A Critical Exposition of the Third Chapter of Paul's Epistle to the Romans* (London, 1866), p. 284.

[6] *The Epistle of St. Paul to the Romans* (London, 1886), p. 98.

for in the first place, such a use of ἱλαστήριον does not seem to be attested from antiquity, and in the second, if this is what Paul wished to say there seems no reason why he should not have used ἱλαστής.

The word is used in a variety of ways, and it may be convenient to reproduce Deissmann's summary:

'1. Votive offerings to deities or to the deity are most frequently of all so designated (Cos inscriptions, Josephus, Dio Chrysostom, Johannes Kameniates).

'2. The golden plate above the ark . . . (the LXX and quotations from or references to it in Philo and the Epistle to the Hebrews).

'3. The ledge of the altar (₲).

'4. The place of the altar (Sabas).

'5. The altar (Hesychius, Cyril).

'6. Noah's ark (Symmachus).

'7. A monastery (Menander, Joseph Genesios).

'8. A Church (Theophanes Continuatus).'[1]

The word was obviously used in a wide variety of ways. It is, however, said by some that Paul thought in terms of the *kappōreth* only.

1. The main reason for thinking this is that, in the LXX, ἱλαστήριον is usually the translation for *kappōreth*. Hatch and Redpath list twenty passages (out of twenty-seven where ἱλαστήριον is found) where it renders this Hebrew word. LXX usage, it is argued, would be decisive for St. Paul, and thus we must think that in Romans 3 he means by ἱλαστήριον what the LXX translators characteristically meant by it.

But what is this LXX usage? In the first place the almost invariable habit of the translators of the Old Testament into Greek was to use the article, the only exception being in the first place where the word occurs, and there it is not alone, but in company with ἐπίθεμα. This unusual translation of *kappōreth* has been the cause of much speculation, but for our present purpose we note that ἐπίθεμα may well have served much the same purpose as the article. The article indicates that it is not 'a propitiating thing' but 'the propitiating thing' which is meant, and ἐπίθεμα likewise has the effect of removing ἱλαστήριον from the realm of the general. In view of the fact that Exodus 25: 16(17) seems to mean, 'thou shalt

[1] *Enc. Bib.*, col. 3033.

make a *kappōreth* of pure gold', it may well have seemed gratuitous to introduce an article in the Greek. On the other hand, to make ἱλαστήριον anarthrous would have been to leave it very general, perhaps even unintelligible, in view of the wide range of meaning covered by the term, and thus something different was required. Once the idea had been introduced there was no difficulty in pointing back to '*the* propitiating thing', and thus the need for such a rendering did not arise again.

T. W. Manson suggests that ἐπίθεμα may be a gloss.[1] In many ways this is attractive, and it would certainly solve some problems, but the evidence adduced is not really strong, and there remains the suspicion that not sufficient weight has been attached to the maxim *difficilior lectio potior*. In view of the absence of ἐπίθεμα everywhere else it is difficult to see how the great majority of the MSS should support the longer text unless it be original.

Other explanations than the one put forward above have been offered and, for example, Deissmann thinks that ἱλαστήριον means 'propitiatory thing', ἐπίθεμα being added at its first occurrence to show just exactly what it is that is meant. Büchsel thinks that ἱλαστήριον here is an adjective qualifying ἐπίθεμα: 'From this it is evident that τὸ ἱλαστήριον of itself does not mean a spatial object, but the atoning thing in general (*das Sühnende ganz allgemein*).'[2]

It may be that there is some such significance in the fact that this translation occurs in the first place where the expression is met, but one wonders whether we are not asking for rather more in the way of consistency from the LXX translators than they always supply to us. ἱλαστήριον ἐπίθεμα, 'propitiatory cover', is a not unintelligible rendering of *kappōreth*, and it is not beyond the bounds of possibility that, after using this once, the translators slipped later on into the simpler ἱλαστήριον without there being any profound significance in the process.[3]

Then we must notice that when they use ἱλαστήριον to translate

---

[1] *JTS*, XLVI, 1945, p. 3.

[2] *TWNT*, III, p. 320.

[3] James Morison thinks that *kappōreth* combines the ideas of 'propitiation' and 'cover', but translators into Greek, if using only one term, must choose between these ideas. Thus ἱλαστήριον retains propitiation and loses cover, while ἐπίθεμα (Josephus) retains cover and loses propitiation. This passage manages to express both ideas (*op. cit.*, pp. 290–91).

kappōreth the LXX translators always have something in the context to make clear which propitiating thing ἱλαστήριον is to denote. There is never a passage where this word denotes the *kappōreth* without some clear indication of what is meant, *e.g.* the mention of the ark of the covenant, or of the cherubim, or both. As a matter of fact there is something similar where it denotes other things. Thus in Ezekiel, though the meaning of 'settle' or 'ledge' is not perfectly clear, the context clearly connects the term with the altar (Ezk. 43: 14, 17, 20), and when Symmachus uses the term of the ark (Gn. 6: 16(15), Heb. *tēbhāh*), the context makes plain what is meant. The same might be said of Philo, who speaks of the cover or lid of the ark and goes on to explain that it is called the ἱλαστήριον. What makes Amos 9: 1 so difficult to interpret as it stands, and strengthens our conviction that the LXX rests on a misreading of the Hebrew, is precisely this, that the context gives no indication of what is meant. In the one place where *kappōreth* occurs without mention of the ark, *etc.*, namely 1 Chronicles 28: 11, the LXX renders with ἐξιλασμός. This reading raises difficulties of its own, but the point is that ἱλαστήριον by itself was evidently not regarded as definite enough to point us to the *kappōreth*.

We must also bear in mind the significance of the Ezekiel and Amos passages, where ἱλαστήριον is used of objects other than the *kappōreth*. Amos 9: 1 (unless based on a lost Hebrew variant) is the result of misreading the Massoretic text or mistranslation, but the point is that the reader of the LXX would come across ἱλαστήριον at this point where he would hardly understand it to refer to the *kappōreth*. So with the five references in Ezekiel. They very clearly have no connection with the *kappōreth*, but they must be included as part of the LXX usage.

I do not see how the conclusion is to be avoided that, even on LXX premises, anarthrous ἱλαστήριον does not necessarily denote the mercy-seat. The word itself means 'propitiatory', and if the mercy-seat could be so designated, so also could one of the ledges on Ezekiel's altar (or even Noah's ark, according to Symmachus). ἱλαστήριον might denote the *kappōreth*, but that was because it referred to its function, and not because it formed an exact translation of the Hebrew term. If the *kappōreth* was 'propitiatory', so too were other things.

2. T. W. Manson contends that, in Christian literature outside

the New Testament, ἱλαστήριον denotes a place. He goes on to reason that in Romans 3 it will conformably denote 'the place where the mercy of God was supremely manifested'.[1] The passages to which he draws attention are those where ἱλαστήριον denotes the sanctuary, the whole church, and a monastery. But if we ask why churches might be termed ἱλαστήρια we are answered in the words of Johannes Kameniates, that they are 'as it were propitiatory gifts dedicated by the community to the deity (ὥσπερ τινὰ κοινὰ πρὸς τὸ θεῖον ἱλαστήρια)'.[2] And if this is so for churches, it probably explains the use of the same term for monasteries and sanctuaries.

Manson also sees the sense of place in references to the ἱλαστήριον in Ezekiel. 'They mark the place where the altar stands and the sacrificial ritual is performed.'[3] There may be a hint at location here, but in such an expression as 'place of atonement' it is atonement rather than place to which this word directs our attention. It is along these lines that we must understand the references in the lexicographers Hesychius and Cyril. Manson's statement that the two treat ἱλαστήριον and θυσιαστήριον 'as practically interchangeable terms' seems a little too definite. Hesychius defines ἱλαστήριον as 'καθάρσιον. θυσιαστήριον'. This appears to mean that the explanation he prefers is καθάρσιον, though, on occasion, the word may signify θυσιαστήριον. In his footnote to Hesychius, Joannes Alberti cites Cyril's explanation 'θυσιαστήριον, ἐν ᾧ προσφέρει (legend. videtur προσφέρε) περὶ ἁμαρτιῶν'. It is not that ἱλαστήριον and θυσιαστήριον in themselves are of similar meaning, but that that aspect of the latter in which it appears as cleansing from sin brings it into the circle of meaning of the former. It is the altar in its propitiatory aspect which may be denoted by ἱλαστήριον.

So is it with the sanctuary. It is there that rites take place directed towards the averting of punishment due to sin and the inclining of the Deity to be favourable, and accordingly from one aspect the sanctuary may be regarded as ἱλαστήριον.

[1] Op. cit., p. 4. H. P. Liddon cites Levy (Chald. Dict.) as assigning to kappōreth the meaning 'a place of expiation', Explanatory Analysis of St. Paul's Epistle to the Romans (London, 1893), p. 75.

[2] Cited in Enc. Bib., col. 3031.

[3] Op. cit., p. 3. This is supported by Schleusner's understanding of 'azārāh as 'atrium, crepido altaris, sive: spatium, in quo sacerdotes circa altare obambulare poterant' (Novus Thesaurus Philologico-Criticus: sive Lexicon in LXX, London, 1829, sub ἱλαστήριον).

Thus in none of these passages is there any stress on the notion of place, and it seems better to regard ἱλαστήριον as denoting 'means of propitiation' than a place. This is much more applicable also in the case of the references to Noah's ark (which Manson adduces), for the ark would not naturally be interpreted as a place.

3. The concept of Christ as a ἱλαστήριον is connected in Romans 3 with the law and the prophets (Rom. 3: 21f.), and Büchsel[1] and others urge that we must see accordingly a reference to the central point in the expiation of sin according to the Torah, namely the Day of Atonement ceremonies.

This is hardly a convincing argument. If on other grounds we could establish the connection of ἱλαστήριον as applied to Christ with the Day of Atonement ceremonies, this would be an interesting confirmation, but of itself it carries little weight. The reference to law is in verse 21, that to ἱλαστήριον in verse 25, and there is nothing to show that the two are thought of as being in close connection. Again, it does not appear why we should link ἱλαστήριον with the law rather than with the prophets. Further, it is not the ἱλαστήριον which is witnessed by the law and the prophets, but the righteousness of God, and however closely we think of these as being connected, they are not the same thing.

4. T. W. Manson suggests that Romans 1–3 'is really an elaborate confession of sin for all mankind, with its climax at iii. 23', and that it 'is followed immediately by a description of the death of Christ which can be properly understood only by being brought into relation to the ritual acts of the High Priest on the Day of Atonement',[2] this being apparently a reference to the 'in his blood'.

This, too, is difficult to accept. As a confession of sin Romans 1–3 must surely be unique with its 'the wrath of God is revealed from heaven against all ungodliness and unrighteousness of men' (1: 18), the threefold 'God gave them up' (1: 24, 26, 28), 'thou art without excuse, O man' (2: 1), 'reckonest thou this, O man' (2: 3), 'we before laid to the charge both of Jews and Greeks, that they are all under sin' (3: 9). This is not penitence, but polemic. The gist of Paul's argument is not 'Let us confess sin that an atonement may

---

[1] *TWNT*, III, p. 322.
[2] *Op. cit.*, p. 7.

be found for us',[1] but, 'All are sinners whether they acknowledge it or not, and are in need of the atonement which God, on His own initiative, provided'.

5. The emphatic αὐτοῦ in the expression ἐν τῷ αὐτοῦ αἵματι is strongly urged by Gifford, who, indeed, makes it his prime consideration in urging a reference to the mercy-seat, his idea being that the *kapporeth* was sprinkled with the blood of sacrifices, but Christ was propitiatory in His *own* blood.

But in the first place the αὐτοῦ does not seem to be so emphatic that it will carry all this,[2] and in the second, even allowing it to be emphatic, it might well be understood otherwise. For, apart from Christ's sacrifice, however propitiation be thought to be effected, be it by sacrifice, offering of votive gifts, Noah's ark, a church or sanctuary or what you will, it is always by something external. But Christ obtained propitiation by His *own* blood.

6. The Greek Fathers from Origen onwards seem usually to take ἱλαστήριον in the sense of the mercy-seat.[3] This is impressive, but while paying due respect to this weight of opinion, we must remember that the Fathers who mention the term were separated by centuries from the apostle, and their understanding of the term cannot be held to be decisive.

7. The appropriateness of the idea appeals to many, and Sanday and Headlam put it thus, 'on Christ rests the fulness of the Divine glory, "the true Shekinah," and it is natural to connect with His Death the culminating rite in the culminating service of Atonement'.[4]

Nothing much need be said about this. That such an idea is appropriate need not be doubted. But then other ideas are also appropriate, and we find ourselves in the morass of subjectivity.

---

[1] *Cf.* W. D. Davies, 'The tones of confession may be audible in Rom. 3. 10f. but in the rather philosophical explanation of the origin and growth of human sinfulness, Rabbinic in thought but Stoic in expression, which we find in Rom. 1. 18f.; in the argumentative indictment of Rom. 2. 1f. and in the tortuous thought of Rom. 3. 1f. it is impossible to overhear them' (*Paul and Rabbinic Judaism*, London, 1948, p. 242).

[2] W. D. Davies thinks it 'doubtful . . . whether the αὐτοῦ is to be emphasized' (*ibid.*).

[3] See the evidence collected in Gifford, Addit. Note on Rom. 3: 25 (*op. cit.*, p. 97).

[4] *Op. cit.*, p. 87.

Nygren gives a touch of objectivity to this argument by referring to the context. He lists a number of concepts associated with the mercy-seat, and proceeds: 'These are the thoughts that Paul has in mind. He presents the same concepts – the manifestation of God, God's wrath, His glory, the blood, the mercy seat.'[1] But none of these things necessarily directs attention to the *kappōreth*. God might manifest Himself in a burning bush; His wrath might be put away by means other than the ceremonies associated with the *kappōreth* (as in Ex. 22: 10–14); His glory is everywhere to be seen in the Old Testament, and does not seem to be at all closely linked with the *kappōreth*; the blood was far more often sprinkled elsewhere than on the *kappōreth*. None of these ideas leads us naturally and inevitably to the *kappōreth*, and even their conjunction seems perfectly explicable in terms of the great general idea which Paul was unfolding, and without reference to the mercy-seat.

Thus, while the evidence for seeing in ἱλαστήριον a reference to the Day of Atonement ceremonies cannot be said to be inconsiderable or lacking in variety, it is not by any means irrefutable. Let us turn now to considerations which may be urged on the other side.[2]

1. There is first and foremost the fact that ἱλαστήριον is in use to denote a wide variety of objects, as we have already noted, and that it has no necessary connection with the Day of Atonement. Outside the Old Testament its usual meaning was 'votive gift',[3] and it is clear that the word in itself is connected with the removal of the divine wrath without being specially linked with any one means of accomplishing this.[4] Of course, it is quite possible that within a

---

[1] *Commentary on Romans* (London, 1952), p. 157.

[2] I have not specially noted the view of C. Anderson Scott who holds that 'We may then translate or paraphrase' Rom. 3 : 25 thus: 'Whom God set forth a victim unto blood as one able to effect reconciliation through faith' (Abingdon Commentary *in loc.*; he has similar statements elsewhere). His view involves many improbabilities as Vincent Taylor has shown, *ET*, L, 1938–39, pp. 295ff.

[3] *Cf.* Büchsel, 'Outside biblical and Jewish Greek the neuter substantive ἱλαστήριον has been shown to mean "votive gift" ' (*TWNT*, III, p. 321).

[4] Vincent Taylor interprets the word broadly, and while regarding it as adjectival, gives 'means of expiation' or 'atonement' as the best translation of the term, rejecting a reference to the Day of Atonement, *op. cit.* p. 296 (see also *Forgiveness and Reconciliation*, London, 1946, p. 39). H. Moule took 'the native meaning' to be 'price of expiation' (*The Epistle of St. Paul to the Romans*, London, 1896, p. 93n.). K. Barth, with a glance at the etymology of *kappōreth*, renders 'covering of propitiation' (*in loc.*).

particular group of people, say the Jews or the Christians, it may have acquired a technical meaning, but for this we require evidence. We have already noted that, while the LXX often uses ἱλαστήριον of the *kappōreth*, this is not invariable, and even where it is found, the article is prefixed, and there is some reference in the context to the ark or the cherubim. We find this usage in the only other place in the New Testament where ἱλαστήριον occurs, namely Hebrews 9: 4, 5, 'the ark of the covenant overlaid round about with gold . . . and above it cherubim of glory overshadowing the mercy-seat'. Here the writer mentions both the ark and the cherubim, and he uses the article with ἱλαστήριον. But all three are absent from Romans 3, and we must recognize that what Paul says is that Christ was set forth to be '*a* propitiation' not '*the* propitiation', while the context is barren of any reference to surrounding objects of furniture. It is very difficult to see in this general term, used in a general way, an allusion to a specific article of the Temple furniture. Contrast the way in which Paul refers to the Passover in 1 Corinthians 5: 7, τὸ πάσχα ἡμῶν, where the article and the pronoun reinforce the natural meaning of the term πάσχα to make the meaning clear.[1] There is no equivalent in Romans 3.

2. The usage of authors of the period like Josephus and Philo is against a connection with the Day of Atonement. Josephus uses the word, not with reference to the *kappōreth*, but as an attributive adjective, referring to a white stone as a 'propitiatory monument (ἱλαστήριον μνῆμα)',[2] while when he refers to the *kappōreth* he calls it ἐπίθεμα.[3]

It is sometimes said that Philo uses the term to denote the *kappōreth* but this does not quite meet the situation. Several times he calls the *kappōreth* by some such name as ἐπίθεμα or πῶμα and proceeds to explain that it is called ἱλαστήριον in the Scripture.[4]

---

[1] James Denney made this point, saying of the reference of ἱλαστήριον to the mercy-seat, 'there are grammatical reasons against this rendering. Paul must have written, to be clear, τὸ ἱλαστήριον ἡμῶν, or some equivalent phrase. Cf. 1 Cor. v. 8 (Christ *our* passover). A "mercy-seat" is not such a self-evident, self-interpreting idea, that the Apostle could lay it at the heart of his gospel without a word of explanation' (*op. cit.*, p. 611).

[2] *Ant.* xvi. 7. 1.

[3] *Ant.* iii. 6. 5.

[4] See, for example, *De Vit. Mos.* ii, 95, 97; *De Profug.* 19. In *De Cherub.* 8 there is

While he could hardly expect the Greek public for which he wrote to have a detailed knowledge of the Hebrew Scriptures, and thus his explanations should not be held to prove too much, yet they show that the general public of his day had a clear idea of what ἱλαστήριον meant, and this idea was not the *kappōreth*.

It may not be without interest that a modern Jewish writer like J. Klausner does not recognize a reference to the *kappōreth* in Paul's use of ἱλαστήριον. In fact he explicitly contrasts the two, preferring in Paul the sense of 'propitiatory death' as with the Maccabean martyrs. He says, 'Paul made use of the word *hilastērion* of IV Macc. 17: 22 in the very same sense (Rom. 3: 25), while in the LXX this word is the translation of *kapporet* ("mercy-seat" or "ark-cover").'[1]

3. The Epistle to the Romans does not move in the sphere of Levitical symbolism, and a reference to the *kappōreth* here would be out of character. It is not so much that there is objection to an idea appearing once only, for we have such phenomena elsewhere in the New Testament (*e.g.*, the Rock in 1 Cor. 10: 4, and the Brazen Serpent in Jn. 3: 14). It is rather that a reference to the *kappōreth* here would be like a geological erratic – something for which the context gives us no preparation, and which is not followed up in any way. It is difficult to imagine that Paul would take one solitary Levitical concept, and use it once with no explanation or hint that he was referring to an object of Temple furniture. Such a procedure might be intelligible in Hebrews, but seems quite out of place in Romans.

There is also the thought that the Day of Atonement would lend itself so well to illustrating various aspects of the atonement, that if Paul really had it in mind here we would expect him to develop the thought further, and perhaps to have referred to other parts of the ritual.[2]

4. Sanday and Headlam point out that it is harsh to make Christ at one and the same time Priest, Victim, and place of sprinkling,

---

no such explanation, but here we have the cherubim associated with the ἱλαστήριον to make the allusion clear.

[1] *From Jesus to Paul* (London, 1946), p. 140, n. 13.

[2] 'Gess justly observes that if this type had been familiar to St. Paul, it would have been found elsewhere in his letters; and if it were not so, the term would have been unintelligible to his readers', F. Godet, *in loc.*

even though there is warrant for thinking of Him as both Priest and Victim. To think of Him as Priest and Victim is a striking paradox, but to bring in the third term, 'place of sprinkling', makes the imagery intolerably complicated, the mercy-seat (or the place of atonement) being sprinkled with its own blood. There is also the point that the Christian place of sprinkling is rather the cross than the Christ.

5. It is also to be taken into consideration that the *kappōreth* belonged to past history, and had not been sprinkled with blood for centuries, so that we are not dealing with some contemporary practice. The rite of sprinkling the blood was carried out, as we see from the Mishnah,[1] but there was no *kappōreth* to sprinkle. Instead the sprinkling was done on the traditional site of the ark, namely a stone three finger-breadths high called *'ebhen sheˑthiyyâh*.[2] The sprinkling then was regularly carried out on a known site, with a name of its own, and this name neither *kappōreth* nor ἱλαστήριον. Nor can it be argued that this sprinkling would be little known, for it is mentioned in the Mishnah, in Josephus[3] and other places.[4] It would have been known to any who took an interest in the Jewish Day of Atonement ceremonies, because of the importance of the blood manipulation, and one who took no such interest would not detect an allusion to the Day of Atonement ceremonies in Paul's words.

This difficulty is met in part by the consideration that the synagogue and not the Temple had become the focus of Judaism. Men were more used to hearing the Torah read than to seeing the sacrificial ritual performed, and the argument runs that they would accordingly be familiar with the *kappōreth* from its being mentioned in the Scriptures. But while there is some force in this, it does not seem decisive. In the first place the *kappōreth* is not mentioned with great frequency in the Scriptures (outside Exodus-Leviticus it occurs only once in Numbers and once in 1 Chronicles). And in the second place it is not the kind of thing that forces itself on the attention. Deissmann could say, 'the out-of-the-way passages referring to the ἱλαστήριον may very well have remained

---

[1] *Yom.* 5: 3, 4.
[2] SB, III, pp. 179ff.
[3] *Ant.* iii. 10. 3.
[4] See SB for details.

unknown even to a Christian who was conversant with the LXX: how many Bible readers of to-day, nay, how many theologians of to-day – who, at least, should be Bible readers, – if their readings have been unforced . . . are acquainted with the *kappōreth*?'[1]

There is also the point that those who heard the word read would almost certainly interpret it in the light of the familiar use of the term, the sense 'propitiatory'. Deissmann illustrates this by pointing out that modern readers who come across *Gnadenstuhl* or 'mercy-seat' in the Bible would never interpret either in terms of 'cover'.

6. The verb προέθετο is congruous with the idea of a general means of propitiation, but not so much so with that of the *kappōreth* if, as most scholars hold, it is to be understood in the sense of 'publicly set forth'. This is not absolutely certain, for in the only two other places where this verb occurs in the New Testament (Rom. 1: 13 and Eph. 1: 9), it means 'to set before the mind', 'to purpose',[2] a meaning which would give good sense here. The use of the middle would favour it too, but we would anticipate that it would be followed by the infinitive. For grammatical reasons such as this, and because of the excellent sense 'set forth publicly' gives in this context (which contains a number of expressions indicative of publicity), most accept this as the true meaning.[3] This is rather against the idea 'mercy-seat' for ἱλαστήριον for the *kappōreth* was hidden away and not in the public view. Indeed what went on at the *kappōreth* was the very part of the Day of Atonement cere-monies that was not at all public. It does not quite meet this to say that there is a contrast between the secret *kappōreth* and the public setting forth of Christ, for, for this to be the case, ἱλαστήριον must be recognized immediately as pointing to the *kappōreth*. Such a contrast can be effective only if the term used is sufficiently un-ambiguous for the allusion to be detected. But this is not the case with ἱλαστήριον.

7. The similarity of Romans 3 and 4 Maccabees 17: 22 may be

---

[1] *Bible Studies* (Edinburgh, 1901), p. 132.

[2] The cognate noun πρόθεσις habitually signifies purpose in the New Testament, but not too much can be made of this, for it is also used of the shewbread.

[3] MM favour the idea 'offered', 'provided', citing an inscription, 'offering money for the ransom etc.' and a prescription for fever, 'Apply a warm bottle to the feet'. This would give excellent sense in the Romans passage, but it has received strangely little attention.

of significance. There we read of the death of the seven brothers, and the passage proceeds 'they having as it were become a ransom for the nation's sin; and through the blood of these righteous men and τοῦ ἱλαστηρίου θανάτου αὐτῶν (or τοῦ ἱλαστηρίου τοῦ θανάτου αὐτῶν) the divine Providence delivered Israel that before was evil entreated'. The wrath of God was conceived of as resting on the people (see 2 Macc. 7: 32–8), and the death of the brothers is viewed as a propitiatory offering which would avail to turn away this wrath. Thus we have several similarities with the Romans passage – both view the wrath of God as being active, both refer to blood being shed, 4 Maccabees thinks of the death as a ransom (ἀντίψυχον) and Romans 3 as redemption (ἀπολύτρωσις), both regard the death as vicarious, and both see the hand of God in it. All this creates a strong presumption that the term ἱλαστήριον is used with similar meaning in the two passages. It is not necessary to assume dependence: it is simply that the ideas being expressed in the two passages are similar.[1]

While this examination of the evidence shows that it is difficult to give a final proof either way, yet it is contended that the balance of probability is strongly in the direction of seeing in ἱλαστήριον in Romans 3 a general reference to the removal of the wrath of God, rather than a specific reference either to the mercy-seat, or to the Day of Atonement ceremonies.

The other point of controversy about ἱλαστήριον in Romans 3 is whether we should understand it in terms of propitiation or of expiation. A considerable number of recent writers profess the latter. There is nothing in the immediate context which decides the point. But we may obtain help from the wider context. The first three chapters of Romans (after the opening remarks) form a

[1] Cf. Büchsel: 'In 4 Macc. 17 also it is God who provides the means of atonement and thus saves; only through substitutionary dying, through personal self-offering not through the Temple cultus with its offering of beasts is the community atoned' (TWNT, III, p. 323). He draws attention also to 1: 11; 6: 28f., and he renders the important part of the latter: 'Make my blood a means of atonement for them and take my soul substitutionarily for their souls' (ibid., n. 23).

4 Maccabees is generally regarded as more Greek than Hebrew in its outlook, but its community of thought in respect of this incident with the earlier books of Maccabees makes the expression cited important. Hastings Rashdall regards it as 'highly probable' that this passage was the source of St. Paul's 'thought and expression' (The Idea of Atonement in Christian Theology, London, 1919, p. 132).

closely-knit piece of reasoning in which the apostle unfolds his conception of the way in which a man comes to be accepted with God. In 1 : 15 he mentions preaching the gospel, and this leads him to consider the essential nature of the gospel, which he sees in the thought of 'a righteousness of God' being at work, and of the just living by faith (Rom. 1: 16, 17).

It is not always realized that this first mention of justification by faith leads immediately in logical sequence to the thought of God's wrath. 'For (γάρ) wrath of God is being continually revealed from heaven upon all impiety and unrighteousness of men,' etc. (Rom. 1: 18). Agar Beet is not overemphasizing the importance of this point when he says: 'the entire weight of *vv.* 16, 17, which contain a summary of the Epistle, rests upon the assumption that all men are, apart from the Gospel, under the anger of God.'[1] Salvation for Paul is essentially a salvation *from* as well as a salvation unto.

Having introduced the thought of the divine wrath, the apostle proceeds to enlarge upon the theme by showing more fully that this wrath is to be discerned in its outworkings consequent upon man's sin. The thought of God's wrath is never out of sight throughout the remainder of this section of the Epistle as Paul builds up his case that Gentiles and Jews are alike sinners and alike come under the wrath and judgment of God, which in this situation he regards as being much the same thing, as we see from 2 : 5 and 3 : 5, 6, where judgment and wrath are inseparable.

In the remainder of chapter 1 Paul shows how the wrath of God rests upon the pagan world. And just as the present aspect of this wrath comes out in this chapter, so the future aspect[2] of wrath is

[1] *A Commentary on St. Paul's Epistle to the Romans* (London, 1881), pp. 50f. *Cf.* F. Godet: 'The transition from ver. 17 to ver. 18, indicated by *for*, can only be this: There is a *revelation of righteousness* by the gospel, because there is a revelation of *wrath* on the whole world' (*Commentary on St. Paul's Epistle to the Romans*, I, Edinburgh, n.d., p. 164). It is one of the curiosities of modern scholarship that Moffatt renders γάρ here by 'but', and that Dodd bases his comment on the mistranslation. Dodd says, 'The adversative conjunction "but" in i. 18 shows that the revelation of God's "anger" is contrasted, and not identified, with the revelation of His righteousness' (*op. cit.*, p. 18). But the conjunction γάρ is not adversative. If, as we must, we substitute 'illative' for 'adversative' in the first part of Dodd's statement should we not reverse the positions of 'contrasted' and 'identified' in his conclusion?

[2] 'But the future wrath is certain. A religious man like Paul never doubts this. On the contrary, he is convinced that this delay is a storing up of wrath for the

developed in chapter 2 with its 'thou condemnest thyself' (verse
1); 'We know that the judgment of God is in accordance with
truth upon them that practise such things' (verse 2); 'And dost thou
reckon . . . that thou wilt flee away from the judgment of God?'
(verse 3); 'Thou storest up for thyself wrath in a day of wrath and
revelation of God's righteous judgment' (verse 5); 'To them that
are factious . . . wrath and anger, affliction and anguish' (verses
8f.); 'For them that without law have sinned, without law also
shall perish: and them that in law have sinned, through law shall
be judged' (verse 12); 'God will judge the secrets of men' (verse
16). Such words as these leave no doubt as to the apostle's burning
conviction that the wrath of God is a terrible reality, and that the
evil-doer has a frightful prospect before him. The remainder of the
chapter shows the Jew to be guilty before God, just as the Gentile
is, and chapter 3 carries on to show that this does not conflict with
the fact that the Jews are the chosen people. Then he is able to sum
up his argument so far in the words 'we have already accused both
Jews and Greeks of being all under sin' (3: 9). He emphasizes this
with a catena of quotations from the Old Testament, and reinforces
it with a statement that the purpose of the law was 'that every
mouth might be sealed, and all the world be brought to trial before
God' (3: 19).

It is in this context that the critical passage 3: 21–26 must be
studied. The whole force of the preceding portion of the Epistle
has been to demonstrate that all men, Jews and Gentiles alike, lie
under the condemnation and the wrath of God. The two conceptions we have seen to be intertwined, and neither can be
separated out from the argument. But now, Paul says, a new factor
enters the situation. The whole effect of the law had been to show
that men are blameworthy before God, that they are sinners (Rom.
3: 20). But now, quite apart from the law, there is a righteousness
of God revealed, a righteousness leading to the sinner's justification
through the work of Christ 'whom God set forth ἱλαστήριον'. The
context demands for this term a meaning which includes the idea
of propitiation, for Paul has brought heavy artillery to bear in

great last day of wrath and those who do not receive punishment for sin now will
certainly receive it in full measure then. The contentious, disobedient and unrighteous will receive full retribution from the wrath and anger of God' (F. V.
Filson, *op. cit.*, p. 48).

demonstrating that God's wrath and judgment are against the sinner.[1] And, while other expressions in verses 21–26 may be held to deal with the judgment aspect, there is nothing other than this word to express the turning away of the wrath. Wrath has occupied such an important place in the argument leading up to this section that we are justified in looking for some expression indicative of its cancellation in the process which brings about salvation. More than expiation is required, for to speak of expiation is to deal in sub-personal categories, as Horace Bushnell long ago pointed out,[2] whereas the relationship between God and man must be thought of as personal in the fullest sense.

It remains to be noticed that there is a substitutionary thought in the passage. We have already drawn attention to the similarity between this passage and 4 Maccabees 17: 22, and in this latter passage the offering is definitely said to be ἀντίψυχον, a term which cannot be emptied of the thought of substitution. This does not prove that substitution is involved in the passage in Romans, but it does show that substitution represents a natural way of understanding that passage.

Substitution, too, is implied in the context. As we have seen, our verse comes as the climax of an argument in which Paul has developed the thesis that all men are under the wrath of God with all that that means, but that now a new way appears. By the blood of Christ a propitiation is effected so that those who are of faith no longer need fear the wrath. Thus we see that, whereas originally sinners were liable to suffer from the outpouring of the wrath of God, Christ has suffered instead of them, and now they may go free. But to say this is to say substitution.

This does not conflict with that other main thought of this passage that the righteousness of God is revealed in the means whereby men are justified. It is true that there is a certain stress on this revelation (cf. verses 21, 25, 26), but mere revelation as such has no power to free men from sin. What has the power to do this is the

[1] Cf. R. W. Dale: 'St. Paul's intention was to demonstrate that the whole world is exposed to the Divine wrath, and that if men are to be saved, that wrath must be somehow averted. That this was his intention, becomes clearer the more rigorous the examination to which the whole argument is subjected' (The Atonement, London, 1902, p. 232).

[2] '. . . we propitiate only a person, and expiate only a fact, or act, or thing' (Forgiveness and Law, London, 1874, p. 83).

particular action which is revealed, a propitiatory action whereby the wrath of God is averted and men are brought into a new relationship with God, and this action is essentially substitutionary. As Büchsel puts it: 'But revelation and substitution form here no contradiction, but the revelation among men only takes place when simultaneously a substitution for men finds place . . . A revelation without substitution would not surpass the law in legal efficacy, and thus would not bring men effectual ἀπολύτρωσις.'[1] Or again, he says in a note that that which is only a declaration 'would bring no more than a condemnation of sin, not an overcoming of sin, which comes about through this that He who reveals God, dying for the sinner, stands in his place'.[2]

b. ἱλάσκομαι

Since the verb is used on but two occasions in the whole New Testament, and one of these does not refer to the work of Christ for men (Lk. 18: 13), this section reduces to an examination of Hebrews 2: 17. There the true humanity of Christ is said to be necessary so that He might become a merciful and faithful high priest in the things of God εἰς τὸ ἱλάσκεσθαι τὰς ἁμαρτίας τοῦ λαοῦ. This verse presents us with some difficulties and we will examine them in order.

First of all, whereas in many of the Old Testament passages in which this and cognate words are used we have seen a reference implicit or explicit to the wrath of God, this is lacking here. This, however, is not conclusive, if only for the reason that there is nothing in the context to compel us to give up the idea of wrath. Accordingly, in the last resort, we must be guided by the plain meaning of the term in contexts where the wrath is unmistakable. But there are some indications that wrath may be in mind here. One of them is the fact that Christ is said to be a 'merciful' high priest in His atoning action. This word indicates that sinners were in no good case. They could look only for severe punishment as a recompense for their evil deeds, a thought which reminds us of what is called 'the wrath of God' in other passages. Another is that Christ is said to be a high priest 'in things pertaining to God', thus directing our minds to the Godward rather than the manward

[1] *TWNT*, III, p. 323.
[2] *Op. cit.*, p. 323, n. 24.

aspect of atonement.[1] A Godward aspect expressed by ἱλάσκομαι is likely to include propitiation, to put it mildly.

Then the accusative after the verb attracts our attention, for, despite much that is written these days, it is a very unusual construction. We have already examined the one example in profane Greek[2] and have seen that it may well be held to involve the idea of propitiation. Much is made by some scholars of the fact that it is to be found in the Greek Old Testament. There is, however, only one accusative of sin after ἱλάσκομαι, while after ἐξιλάσκομαι there are none in the canonical Scriptures (though one occurs in the Theodotianic text of Dn. 9: 24 and there are six in Sirach). In one or possibly two places the verb is in the passive with sin as its subject. This cannot be said to be a very impressive list when we remember that the two verbs occur 116 times between them, and that there are four or five places where the construction is accusative of person with the plain meaning 'appease, propitiate'.

The six examples of the accusative of sin in Sirach are of interest, more especially in view of the fact that it is sometimes said that with this construction these verbs have the meaning 'expiate'. But these passages say things like, 'And say not, His compassion is great; he will be pacified for the multitude of my sins: for mercy and wrath are with him, and his indignation will rest upon sinners' (Sir. 5: 6). The meaning here is obviously that the man who complacently trusts that God's mercy will be his salvation will find that God's wrath is extended towards him. Even though there is an accusative of sin the context shows that the verb includes an element of propitiation, and the same is true in probably five out of the six examples.[3] Since it is at least arguable that the examples in Psalm 64(65): 4 and Daniel 9: 24 (Th.) are also best understood if the thought of propitiation is included, it would seem that there is not much ground for thinking that this construction does away with the thought of averting wrath. Rather the contrary would seem to

---

[1] Cf. G. Milligan: 'it was in the performance of that which was necessary towards God, and not in priestly privileges towards man, that the essence of Christ's Priesthood lay' (*The Theology of the Epistle to the Hebrews*, Edinburgh, 1899, p. 105, n. 3).

[2] See above, pp. 147f.

[3] Cf. also Sir. 16: 11 where the comment of F. Delitzsch seems to give the sense, 'The atonement, ἐξιλασμός, is the removal of the ὀργή' (*Commentary on the Epistle to the Hebrews*, II, Edinburgh, 1887, p. 456).

be true, that the accusative of sin after ἱλάσκομαι or ἐξιλάσκομαι, in the few places where it occurs, seems generally to imply propitiation.

It should further be borne in mind that in the New Testament period the accusative often replaces a prepositional construction with little if any change of meaning. Thus ἀπορέω 'to be perplexed' is followed by περί (Lk. 24: 4 and Jn. 13: 22); but in Acts 25: 20 we have the accusative, although the meaning appears to be much the same. Similarly εὐδοκέω is usually followed by ἐν (Mt. 3: 17; 1 Cor. 10: 5, etc.), but the direct object is found (Mt. 12: 18[1]). Compare also πενθέω ἐπί (Rev. 18: 11), accusative (2 Cor. 12: 21); κλαίω ἐπί (Lk. 19:41; 23: 28), accusative (Mt. 2: 18); θαυμάζω ἐπί (Lk. 2: 33), or περί (Lk. 2: 18), accusative (Lk. 7: 9; 24: 12); ὑπομιμνήσκω περί (2 Pet. 1: 12), accusative (Jn. 14: 26); διαμαρτύρομαι ἐνώπιον (2 Tim. 4: 1), accusative (2 Tim. 4: 1);[2] κόπτομαι ἐπί (Rev. 1: 7; 18: 9), accusative (Lk. 8: 52); φοβέομαι ἀπό (Lk. 12: 4), accusative (Mt. 10: 28); ὀμνύω ἐν (Mt. 23: 16) or κατά (Heb. 6: 13), accusative (Jas. 5: 12); φεύγω ἀπό (1 Cor. 10: 14), accusative (1 Cor. 6: 18); φυλάσσω ἀπό (Lk. 12: 15), accusative (Acts 21: 25).

The point of such examples as these is not that they form exact parallels to ἱλάσκομαι, for this might well be disputed at least in some of the cases, but that they demonstrate that among the New Testament writers there was great freedom in the use of constructions. In particular the accusative was often used in places where we would hardly have anticipated it, and where satisfactory prepositional constructions were available and in use. Under these circumstances it does not seem wise to lay great stress upon the occurrence of the accusative in Hebrews 2: 17. In the case of none of the verbs above can it be said that its meaning has been seriously modified by using the accusative instead of the prepositional construction, and accordingly it may fairly be asked, Why should we believe that it is otherwise with ἱλάσκομαι?

Thus it seems best to take the accusative in Hebrews 2: 17 as an accusative of general respect and to understand the meaning of the expression as 'to make propitiation with regard to the sins of the people'. This is better than ignoring the usual meaning of the verb

---

[1] The accusative is read by ℵ*, B, 115, 244, 892, etc., though εἰς ὅν is also found.

[2] Cf. F. Blass-A. Debrunner, Grammatik des neutestamentlichen Griechisch (Göttingen, 1943), pp. 72f.

and making it signify here nothing more than 'expiate'. To take this line is to give the verb its sense from its object, a procedure to which John Owen raised his objection long ago.[1] Though I would not be prepared to endorse every detail of his treatment of this passage, his observation on the verb under discussion is surely valid: 'In the use of this word, then, there is always understood – (1st) An *offence*, crime, guilt, or debt, to be taken away; (2dly.) A *person offended*, to be pacified, atoned, reconciled; (3dly.) A *person offending*, to be pardoned, accepted; (4thly.) A *sacrifice* or other means of making the atonement. Sometimes one is expressed, sometimes another, but the use of the word hath respect unto them all.' It is a valuable point that the verb often implies more than is explicitly expressed.

A further point is that there are some manuscripts which read ταῖς ἁμαρτίαις instead of τὰς ἁμαρτίας in this verse; Moffatt cites 'A 5. 33. 623. 913, Athan. Chrys. Bentley, etc.' This is a surprisingly impressive list, although we need not take the reading very seriously if we are endeavouring to arrive at the true text. There seems no doubt that some scribe or scribes altered the accusative to the dative, a case which occurs much more often in this connection. But the fact that this variant has arisen shows that the accusative was felt to be a difficult construction after ἱλάσκομαι. This seems to indicate that the alleged meaning of 'expiate' was not one which was accepted in the circles in which this variant arose.

Thus there is no really good reason for denying to ἱλάσκομαι in this verse its usual significance. The objections usually alleged are seen on examination to be of little weight, whereas there are not wanting some indications that the word is used in its normal sense. As we saw in our section on the Old Testament usage, the normal use of the verb with regard to the sacrifices is one which includes an element of propitiation, and this element seems clearly to be implied in this verse also in the priestly activity of Christ.

c. ἱλασμός

This word occurs twice, both times in the First Epistle of St. John, and on both occasions it occurs in an expression referring to Christ

---

[1] *An Exposition of the Epistle to the Hebrews*, ed. W. H. Goold, III (Edinburgh, 1862), pp. 474ff.

as 'the propitiation for our sins'. The first passage assures us that 'if any man sin, we have an Advocate with the Father, Jesus Christ the righteous: and he is the propitiation for our sins' (1 Jn. 2: 2). The second is concerned with the love of God, 'Herein is love, not that we loved God, but that he loved us, and sent his Son to be the propitiation for our sins' (1 Jn. 4: 10). Here again objections have been raised to the traditional rendering, as by Dodd who says: 'The common rendering "propitiation" is illegitimate here as elsewhere.'[1]

The reasons alleged are those we have already noticed, namely that ἱλάσκομαι, etc., are thought to have evolved in the LXX a meaning strange to non-biblical Greek, and no new consideration is brought forward in connection with the Johannine passages. Indeed it is noticeable that there is a certain caution in Dodd's approach for he says: 'Here we have less confidence in appealing to LXX usage than in the case of Paul and Hebrews, for the Johannine Epistles are probably less influenced by the LXX than any other New Testament writings.'[2] However, he notes that ḥaṭṭā'th is variously rendered ἱλασμός and τὸ περὶ ἁμαρτίας and he thinks that 'The Johannine expression looks like a combination of these alternative translations'.[3] On these grounds he groups the Johannine usage with those previously considered and thinks the term means simply a cancelling of guilt and purification of the sinner. But Dodd has shown only that the Johannine passages link up with the LXX, and if our conclusion that in the LXX this word-group conveys the thought of propitiation is sound, then a similar meaning will be required here.

In support of this there are one or two considerations. The first of these is the context. Of the first of these sayings even Dodd can say, 'in the immediate context it might seem possible that the sense of "propitiation" is in place'.[4] The point is that Christ is said to be 'an Advocate with the Father', and if we sinners need an advocate with God, then obviously we are in no good case, our misdeeds prevail against us, we are about to feel the hostility of God to all that is sinful. Under these circumstances we may well speak of

[1] *The Bible and the Greeks* (London, 1935), p. 95.
[2] Op. cit., p. 94.
[3] Op. cit., p. 95.
[4] MNTC, *The Johannine Epistles*, p. 26.

Christ turning away the wrath of God, and thus ἱλασμός is a natural word in the context.

Again, in addition to the word from the ἱλάσκομαι group we have a reference to Christ as 'the righteous', and a few verses earlier there is a mention of His blood (1 Jn. 1: 7). In these things we may discern a striking coincidence with Romans 3: 25, where the propitiation occurs in a passage which several times refers to God's righteousness, and which says the propitiation is in Christ's blood. As our examination of the Romans passage demonstrated, as we believe, that the thought of propitiation is to be discerned there, the coincidences of language suggest that this idea is to be found also in 1 John.

In 1 John 4: 10 if ἱλασμός be given its usual meaning we have one of those resounding paradoxes which mean so much for the understanding of the Christian view of sacrifice. It is to God Himself that we owe the removal of God's wrath (cf. Col. 1: 21f. for a similar statement with regard to the removal of enmity), whereas, if the more colourless 'expiation' is understood, the verse is much less striking.

A further point is that the nature of the allusion is such as to stress the fact that Christ is the offering which turns away the wrath, rather than to draw attention to any activity in thus averting the wrath. This is well put by B. F. Westcott: 'Christ is said to be the "propitiation" and not simply the "propitiator" (as He is called the "Saviour" iv. 14), in order to emphasise the thought that He is Himself the propitiatory offering as well as the priest (comp. Rom. iii. 25). A propitiator might make use of means of propitiation, outside himself. But Christ is our propitiation.'[1]

In all this there is nothing to make us alter our previous conclusions with regard to the meaning of this word-group. There is no crude process of celestial bribery, but a word is chosen which reminds us of the very real wrath of God[2] manifested against all unrighteousness, a wrath which we need no longer fear, for Christ is 'the propitiation for our sins'.

A not unimportant consideration is that the ἱλάσκομαι words were not understood by the early Christians as signifying ex-

[1] *The Epistles of St John* (London, 1892), p. 44.
[2] *Cf.* E. Brunner: 'This revelation of the divine mystery of love in the midst of the reality of wrath is the "propitiation" (ἱλασμός)' (*op. cit.*, p. 520).

piation. Both 1 Clement and Hermas, for example, use the verb ἐξιλάσκομαι with the accusative of the Deity in the sense 'propitiate'[1] so that if the LXX translators and the New Testament writers evolved a new sense for the word-group it perished with them. But in view of the universal usage among pagan writers, early and late, in Philo and Josephus, and in such Christian writers as those mentioned, it is much better to understand the New Testament writers in the normal fashion as referring to propitiation and not expiation.

III. CONCLUSION

What are we to say of all this? Some theologians unhesitatingly reject the whole idea of the wrath of God and of propitiation as being unworthy of the Christian view of God. Thus N. Berdyaev can say: 'The wrath of God described in the Bible is simply an exoteric *motif* reflecting the wrath of the Jewish people.'[2] Or again: 'Anger in every shape and form is foreign to God, Whose mercy is infinite.'[3] Such citations could be multiplied almost indefinitely, for there are many modern writers to whom the concept of the wrath of God is anathema.

One must have a certain sympathy with such positions, for nothing can be more certain than that the Christian view of God is that He is love, and nothing can be held for one moment which interferes with the clear perception of this basic truth. Without it Christianity becomes meaningless. Nevertheless the fact must be faced that the Bible in both Old and New Testaments speaks often of God's wrath.

Perhaps the difficulty arises because we are making a false antithesis between the divine wrath and the divine love. We are handicapped by the fact that we must necessarily use terms properly applicable to human affairs, and for us it is very difficult to be simultaneously wrathful and loving. But, upon analysis, this seems to be largely because our anger is such a selfish passion, usually involving a large element of irrationality together with a lack of

---

[1] 1 Cl. vii. 7, Herm. v. I, 2, I. The passages are quoted in *TWNT*, III, p. 315, n.67.

[2] *Freedom and the Spirit* (London, 1944), p. 92.

[3] *Op. cit.*, p. 175.

self-control. Nevertheless, even in human affairs, such a thing as 'righteous anger' is not unknown when some, at least, of the more unworthy elements are absent, and we catch a glimpse of a fiery zeal for the right which may be perfectly compatible with pure love.

Those who object to the conception of the wrath of God should realize that what is meant is not some irrational passion bursting forth uncontrollably, but a burning zeal for the right coupled with a perfect hatred for everything that is evil. It may be that wrath is not a perfect word to describe such an attitude, but no better has been suggested, and we must refuse to accept alternatives which do not give expression to the truth in question. Perhaps there is a certain anthropomorphism involved in the use of the term wrath, but it must not be forgotten that, 'A false anthropomorphism is to be laid to the charge not of those who maintain that there is, in the Biblical sense of the word, such a thing as the wrath of God. It is rather to be laid to the charge of those who encourage the idea that God is like an easy, good-natured, benevolent man.'[1] We sometimes find among men an affection which is untempered by a sterner side, and this we call not love but sentimentality. It is not such that the Bible thinks of when it speaks of the love of God, but rather of a love which is so jealous for the good of the loved one that it blazes out in fiery wrath against everything that is evil. D. M. Baillie gives expression to this when he speaks of God's wrath as being 'identical with the consuming fire of inexorable divine love in relation to our sins'.[2]

[1] L. Pullan, *The Atonement* (London, 1907), p. 194. *Cf.* Emil Brunner: 'If we understand it properly it has nothing whatever to do with primitiveness, with naïve anthropomorphism. On the contrary, it is the necessary expression of God, taking himself and us seriously. He takes us so seriously that our changed attitude with regard to him produces a change in his attitude towards us. . . . The term "God's wrath" therefore means that the breach of communion, which has been made from our side, means also a breach for God. It means that our guilt is guilt in his sight too, that our separation from him is a reality for him too, that his holy will, encountering resistance, becomes in itself resistance: "God resisteth the haughty." God's law must not be broken; if we do break it, it will break us' (*The Scandal of Christianity*, London, 1951, pp. 77f.).

[2] *God Was In Christ* (London, 1948), p. 189. Similarly T. H. Hughes speaks of 'the urge or chafing of love' (*The Atonement*, London, 1949, p. xxv), and Dr. Maldwyn Hughes refers to the divine anger as 'nothing else than unquenched and quenchless holy love' (*What is the Atonement?* London, n.d., p. 56).

Now if there is such a divine hostility to evil it is obvious that something must be done about it if man, sinner as he is, is ever to be accepted before God. Sometimes Scripture directs attention to the cause of the hostility and speaks of sin as remitted or purged. But sometimes also it points us to the hostility itself, and speaks of its removal in terms of propitiation. The evidence that the Bible means what it says when it uses this term is so strong that, as we saw earlier, S. R. Driver can speak of propitiation as one of the three main categories used in the New Testament to interpret the death of Christ.[1] From a slightly different point of view Denney says: 'If the propitiatory death of Jesus is eliminated from the love of God, it might be unfair to say that the love of God is robbed of all meaning, but it is certainly robbed of its apostolic meaning.'[2] The writers of the New Testament know nothing of a love which does not react in the very strongest fashion against every form of sin.

It is the combination of God's deep love for the sinner with His uncompromising reaction against sin which brings about what the Bible calls propitiation. Since God would not leave man to suffer all the consequences of his sin, Christ suffered, and as J. C. Lambert puts it, 'while springing from the Divine love, the death of Christ is represented in the Epp. not less clearly as *a propitiation for sin* . . . any interpretation of the mass of NT evidence seems difficult and forced which does not recognize that, in the view of these writers, Christ's death was really our death in a vicarious and propitiatory sense'.[3] This statement stresses once more the fact that propitiation is understood as springing from the love of God. Among the heathen, propitiation was thought of as an activity whereby the worshipper was able himself to provide that which

---

[1] See above, p. 144.

[2] *The Death of Christ* (London, 1951), p. 152; and similarly Heinrich Vogel says: 'whoever thinks he can smile at God's wrath will never praise him eternally for his grace' (*The Iron Ration of a Christian*, London, 1941, p. 102). P. T. Forsyth often gives expression to such a thought, as when he says of the love of God: 'It has been detached from the idea of propitiation with which the Apostles identify it (1 John iv. 10), and regarded as an infinite dilation of human affection (where the real revelation is held to be). Judgment is viewed but as a device of the Father instead of a constituent of His Fatherhood as holy. Little wonder then that love has gone thin in the expansion and lost power. It has ceased in the process to be understood as Holy Love' (*The Justification of God*, London, 1948, pp. 85f.).

[3] *HDCG*, I, p. 433.

would induce a change of mind in the deity. In plain language he bribed his god to be favourable to him. When the term was taken over into the Bible these unworthy and crude ideas were abandoned, and only the central truth expressed by the term was retained, namely that propitiation signifies the averting of wrath by the offering of a gift. But in both Testaments the thought is plain that the gift which secures the propitiation is from God Himself.[1] He provides the way whereby men may come to Him. Thus the use of the concept of propitiation witnesses to two great realities, the one, the reality and the seriousness of the divine reaction against sin, and the other, the reality and the greatness of the divine love which provided the gift which should avert the wrath from men.

Those who seek to reduce the concept of propitiation to a mere expiation do not, in general, face the questions which expiation raises, such as 'Why should sin be expiated?' 'What would be the consequences to man if there were no expiation?' 'Would the hand of God be in those consequences?' It seems evident on the scriptural view that if sin is not expiated, if men 'die in their sins', then they have the divine displeasure to face, and this is but another way of saying that the wrath of God abides upon them. It seems that expiation is necessary in order to avert the wrath of God, so that nothing seems to be gained by abandoning the concept of propitiation.

Then there is the question of the meaning to be given to expiation. As commonly used the term seems to signify the removal of sin or guilt, but neither of these is a *thing* which can be objectively removed. Expiation can be given an intelligible meaning only when we move into the realm of personal relations. Sin has altered the relations between God and man, and expiation cannot be understood apart from the effects of the expiatory act on these relations. Unless we are prepared to say that in expiation all that happens is a subjective change in man, it would seem that we are committed to the view that expiation has a Godward aspect so that God now treats the sinner differently from before. Instead of God's

[1] See, for example, Lv. 17: 11; Rom. 3: 25. For the implication *cf.* J. G. Simpson: 'All that we can now say is that, when it is the Eternal Son who offers Himself without spot to the Eternal Father, the ethical objection to a propitiatory sacrifice vanishes' (*What is the Gospel?* London, 1914, p. 192).

severity the sinner experiences God's grace, which is only another way of saying that propitiation has taken place. If we give expiation a fully personal meaning it seems then that we are brought back to propitiation; if we do not it is difficult to see how we are to understand the term. Certainly propitiation, when carefully safeguarded, is a more intelligible concept than an impersonal expiation.

If we are to retain the Christian conception of God with its insistence on the divine activity in the affairs of men, and the divine abhorrence of sin, it seems necessary to retain some such conception as propitiation. Certainly we must retain the idea of the wrath of God, for, as Edwyn Bevan has pointed out, the idea that God cannot be angry is neither Hebrew nor Christian, but something borrowed from Greek philosophy.[1] But not only is the Hebrew and Christian idea of a God who can be wrathful different from the Greek philosophic view. It is a superior idea. Granted that it contains an element of anthropomorphic imagery, it yet points to a reality within the divine being which gives point and force to moral sanctions.[2]

Then, too, unless we give a real content to the wrath of God, unless we hold that men really deserve to have God visit upon them the painful consequences of their wrongdoing, we empty God's

[1] 'Greek philosophy had long ago repudiated emphatically the conception common to primitive and popular Greek religion and to the Old Testament. Anger was a weak and discreditable emotion, it taught, in men, and to attribute such an emotion to a divine being was absurd and blasphemous. Deity, every novice in Greek philosophy knew as an axiom, must be *apathēs*, without disturbing emotions of any kind. The idea of the Divine anger was not something which penetrated into Christianity from its pagan environment: it was something which the Church maintained in the face of adverse pagan criticism' (*Symbolism and Belief*, London, 1938, p. 210).

[2] From a somewhat different angle Hodgson says: 'We cannot draw a breath or lift a finger except by our use of that share of His power which He has entrusted to us for our earthly life. How can we be sure, when we use it to sin with, that He continues holy, that He is still there in unsullied perfection, able, when we come to a better frame of mind and repent of our sin, to welcome us back to share in His life of goodness? . . . The wrath of God and divine punishment are essential elements in a doctrine which is to face the facts of evil and retain a fundamental optimism. The belief that God has sworn in His wrath that men who do certain things shall not enter into His rest enables the Church to open its worship each day with the words, "Come, let us sing unto the Lord, let us heartily rejoice in the strength of our salvation" ' (*The Doctrine of the Atonement*, London, 1951, p. 60).

forgiveness of its meaning.[1] For if there is no ill desert, God ought to overlook sin. We can think of forgiveness as something real only when we hold that sin has betrayed us into a situation where we deserve to have God inflict upon us the most serious consequences. When the logic of the situation demands that He should take action against the sinner, and He yet takes action for him, then and then alone can we speak of grace. But there is no room for grace if there is no suggestion of dire consequences merited by sin.

One final point is that the process of propitiation envisaged in the Bible is one which involves an element of substitution. In both Old and New Testaments the means of propitiation is the offering up of a gift, the gift of a life yielded up to death by God's own appointment. The Scripture is clear that the wrath of God is visited upon sinners or else that the Son of God dies for them. Either sinners are punished for their misdoings or else there takes place what Hodgson calls 'that self-punishment which combines the activities of punishing and forgiving'.[2] Either we die or He dies. But 'God commendeth his own love toward us, in that, while we were yet sinners, Christ died for us' (Rom. 5: 8).

---

[1] Cf. Bevan, op. cit., p. 246.
[2] Op. cit., p. 79.

CHAPTER VII

RECONCILIATION

I. INTRODUCTION

T. H. HUGHES LAYS IT DOWN 'that in the New Testament the basic idea of the Atonement is that of reconciliation'.[1] This idea must be based upon the general climate of New Testament thinking rather than upon specific references, for when we consult a concordance we find that passages dealing specifically with reconciliation are few, though important. The conception is explicit in two notable Pauline passages (Rom. 5: 10f. and 2 Cor. 5: 18–20), in both of which we find the verb καταλλάσσω and the noun καταλλαγή. The verb is found nowhere else in the New Testament and the noun only in Romans 11: 15 where the rejection of the Jews is 'the reconciliation of the world'. The compound verb ἀποκαταλλάσσω refers to the death of Christ twice (Eph. 2: 16; Col. 1: 20f.). Other words from this word-group occur in the New Testament, but they are not applied to the atonement.

However, it is clear that the concept of reconciliation is sometimes present when the actual word itself does not occur, for example when 'making peace' is spoken of. This opens up for us the whole New Testament conception of peace with God. Other conceptions may also be linked with that of reconciliation. Thus Vincent Taylor treats of freedom, sonship, fellowship with God and sanctification under the heading of reconciliation.[2] But it scarcely seems as though all these conceptions are to be considered as properly part of the idea of reconciliation, and we shall confine ourselves in this treatment to those passages which speak of reconciliation and of peace.

We examine first of all καταλλάσσω and its cognates. This word-group derives ultimately from ἄλλος. The basic significance of

---

[1] *The Atonement* (London, 1949), p. 312. Similarly, Vincent Taylor: 'The best New Testament word to describe the purpose of the Atonement is *Reconciliation*' (*The Atonement in New Testament Teaching*, London, 1946, p. 191).

[2] See *Forgiveness and Reconciliation* (London, 1946), pp. 7of.

ἀλλάσσω is accordingly either to change (make other) or to exchange (provide an other). A good example of the first meaning is found in Acts 6: 14, while in Romans 1: 23 we have the second use.[1] This basic meaning is modified and confirmed in the various compounds. For example, ἀντάλλαγμα is used of the price for which a thing is purchased, or more generally for an equivalent or substitute, as in Mark 8: 37, 'for what shall a man give ἀντάλλαγμα (in exchange for) his life?' ἀπαλλάσσω signifies 'to make other through removal' (as in Acts 19: 12).[2]

The exact significance of the preposition in καταλλάσσω is not easy to determine (though *cf.* Moulton and Howard quoted below), but the basic idea of changing remains. The word was in use for the process of money-changing where one set of coins was exchanged for an equivalent set. Other uses of a more metaphorical sort also arose, and the one which is of particular interest to us is that the word came to signify 'to make other a state of enmity', 'to exchange enmity for friendship'. The noun καταλλαγή has a meaning corresponding to that of the verb, 'exchange', 're-conciliation', the latter being its New Testament significance.

For the rest διαλλάσσω is very similar in meaning to καταλλάσσω, but as it is not used in the New Testament of the atonement it scarcely concerns us. ἀποκαταλλάσσω is not found before the New Testament where it occurs in Ephesians and Colossians,[3] Epistles in which καταλλάσσω is not found. The meaning is much the same as that of the last-mentioned verb, but probably with an intensi-fication. Thus J. H. Moulton and W. F. Howard say it means '*to effect a thorough change* (perfective κατά) *back, reconcile*'.[4]

II. THE καταλλάσσω WORD-GROUP IN THE SEPTUAGINT

καταλλάσσω is found but once in the canonical Scriptures of the Old Testament, namely Jeremiah 31(48): 39, where MT reads *'êkh*

---

[1] *Cf.* also Ps. 105: 20, καὶ ἠλλάξαντο τὴν δόξαν αὐτῶν ἐν ὁμοιώματι μόσχου κ.τ.λ.

[2] Other uses, of course, arise from this, a common one being 'to free' as in Heb. 2: 15.

[3] Büchsel thinks Paul may have coined the word (*TWNT*, I, p. 259).

[4] *A Grammar of New Testament Greek*, II (Edinburgh, 1919), p. 298.

ḥattâh, but where the LXX appears to mean, 'How is it changed!'
The passage does not help us much.

The noun καταλλαγή occurs in Isaiah 9: 5 where it is doubtful
whether the LXX can be derived from MT. The former seems to
mean 'For they will recompense for every robe obtained by deceit,
and (every) garment with compensation (μετὰ καταλλαγῆς)'.
Although the passage is difficult it seems clear that καταλλαγή is
used in its older sense of something given in exchange, an equivalent
or substitute.

ἀποκαταλλάσσω does not occur in the LXX. The use of the other
words in this word-group does not help us greatly, with one
exception, namely the use of διαλλάσσω when the Philistine lords
say of David, 'wherewith will this man be reconciled to his
master?' (1 Sa. 29: 4). The point here is that David is spoken of as
being reconciled, although the enmity to be removed is not his,
but Saul's. This has its importance for an understanding of passages
wherein man is said to be reconciled to God.

III. RECONCILIATION IN JUDAISM

According to Strack-Billerbeck, 'In Rabbinic writings the two
verbs *ritstsâh* and *piyyēs* are especially used for καταλλάσσειν'.[1] Both
these verbs speak of the removal of enmity, the first having the
idea of causing to be pleasant, and the second of calming. Thus
both imply a previous enmity, and sometimes there is an explicit
reference to 'wrath', or similar evidence of ill-feeling in the
context.

Reconciliation is sometimes between men, but often this is part
of the process of reconciliation with God. Thus R. Jose used a
parable: 'A man lent his neighbour a *maneh* and fixed a time for
payment in the presence of the king, while the other swore to pay
him by the life of the king. When the time arrived he did not pay
him, and he went to excuse himself to the king. The king, however,
said to him: The wrong done to me I excuse you, but go and
obtain forgiveness from your neighbour.'[2] The application of the

[1] III, p. 519.
[2] b *R.H.* 17b (Soncino trans., p. 70). So also *Ber.* 31b: 'R. Eleazar said: From this
we learn that one who suspects his neighbour of a fault which he has not committed must beg his pardon; nay more, he must bless him' (Soncino trans., p. 192).

parable is not far to seek, and it is typical of the teaching of the Rabbis that a man must be reconciled with his fellow if he would expect to be reconciled with his God. The responsibility for reconciliation is, of course, with the person doing the wrong. Sometimes, however, we hear of the wronged one taking the initiative in an attempt to heal the breach.[1]

God is thought of as angry with men because of sin, and reconciliation accordingly becomes necessary. A number of midrashes speak of reconciliation after the episode of the Golden Calf. For example, a saying of R. Isaac is recorded: 'Moses reconciled God with Israel through the second Tables.' It goes on to put forward the curious explanation that Moses pretended to be angry with the people, causing God to say that they both could not be angry with them, and thus He became reconciled to them.[2] In another place we are told that, when he found that God's wrath was towards the people because of the calf, 'Moses instantly rose and sought mercy from Him, begging Him to be reconciled with them'. But God put away only part of His wrath, and when the tabernacle was built Moses wondered whether this would do away with the remainder of the wrath: 'is He reconciled with them and will He display towards them the Attribute of Mercy?' The answer is that He is reconciled. A little later in the same section this is given in the words of R. Berekiah, the priest, speaking in the name of R. Judah son of R. Simon: 'The Holy One, blessed be He, said to Moses: "Formerly there was hostility between Me and My children, there was enmity between Me and My children, there was contention between Me and My children. Now, however, that this Tabernacle has been made there will be love between Me and My children, there will be peace between Me and My children." This explains the text, "*For He will speak peace unto His people*," namely to Israel, because they have made the Tabernacle.'[3]

Such passages as the ones we have so far quoted would perhaps

---

[1] *Yoma* 87a has much to say about the duty of being reconciled and praises R. Zera for giving opportunities to any who had wronged him to effect reconciliation: 'When R. Zera had any complaint against any man, he would repeatedly pass by him, showing himself to him, so that he may come forth to (pacify) him' (Soncino trans., p. 435). The passage then goes on to speak of Abba taking the initiative in seeking reconciliation with a man who had wronged him.

[2] *Dt. R.* 3: 15 (Soncino trans., p. 84).

[3] All these citations are from *Nu. R.* 12: 1 (Soncino trans., pp. 448f.).

leave the impression that the Rabbis dwelt on the wrath of God in a very anthropomorphic fashion, and it is true that they sometimes did. But there are many passages reflecting a nobler view of God. Thus on the verse, 'She (*i.e.* Jerusalem) is become as a widow', Rab Judah says: '(The verse implies) blessing; "*as a widow*"; not a real widow, but a woman whose husband has gone to a country beyond the sea (fully) intending to return to her.'[1] Here the disciplines of suffering imposed upon the nation are seen as temporary. God will shortly cause them to cease. So also we read: 'Come and see how different from the character of one of flesh and blood is the action of the Holy One, blessed be He. As to the character of one of flesh and blood, if one angers his fellow, it is doubtful whether he (the latter) will be pacified or not by him. And even if you would say, he can be pacified, it is doubtful whether he will be pacified by mere words. But with the Holy One, blessed be He, if a man commits a sin in secret, He is pacified by mere words.'[2] This must not, of course, be interpreted as meaning that right inward dispositions are not necessary, but the saying is a strong affirmation that God is merciful.

Sometimes the thought of reconciliation takes on a cosmic aspect (as in Col. 1: 20). Thus, 'R. Safra on concluding his prayer added the following: May it be Thy will, O Lord our God, to establish peace among the celestial family, and among the earthly family, and among the disciples who occupy themselves with Thy Torah.'[3] This may be given a different twist, as when we read that God 'made peace (*hishlîm*) between His works and His creatures. How so? He caused the fire to be at peace with Abraham our father; He caused the sword to be at peace with Isaac; He caused the angel to be at peace with Jacob.'[4] Here it is God who makes peace. Sometimes also Israel is held to have done this, as when the nation's acceptance of the Law is regarded as the means of making peace with God and thus preventing the destruction of the world (*Gn. R.* 66: 2; *Cant. R.* 7: 1).

We may notice here that Josephus makes use of the verb καταλλάσσω on three occasions. Twice he uses it of human re-

---

[1] b *Taan.* 20a (Soncino trans., p. 99).
[2] b *Yoma* 86b (Soncino trans., p. 429).
[3] b *Ber.* 16b–17a (Soncino trans., p. 99).
[4] *Cant. R.* 3: 11. 1 (Soncino trans., p. 171).

conciliations, namely when the woman says to David: 'be first reconciled to your own son and let your anger toward him cease',[1] and when the Levite who went after his concubine (Jdg. 19) 'redressed her grievances and was reconciled to her'.[2] The third occasion tells of Samuel who 'all night long set himself to entreat God to be reconciled to Saul and not wroth with him'.[3] This verb also occurs three times in 2 Maccabees (1: 5; 7: 33; 8: 29). In all three cases the verb is in the passive with God as subject, e.g. 'and if for rebuke and chastening our living Lord hath been angered a little while, yet shall he again be reconciled with his own servants'. There may be discussion as to whether in the New Testament references God can be said to be reconciled to men, but there can be no doubt as to the position in Maccabees.

The noun καταλλαγή is found with reference to the restoration of the temple worship, 'and (the place) which was forsaken in the wrath of the Almighty was, at the reconciliation of the great Sovereign, restored again with all glory' (2 Macc. 5: 20). Here again the noun is used to signify reconciliation, and the mention of the divine wrath makes it clear that it is God who is reconciled, and not simply men.

Thus the Jews certainly held that God was angry when men sinned, and that this demanded an act of reconciliation. They do not hesitate to speak of God as being reconciled to men, by which they mean that His just wrath is removed. There is divergence of opinion about the method of effecting reconciliation, but the best Rabbinic thought had risen to the idea that God Himself brings about the reconciliation. On the human side the Rabbis looked for repentance and a readiness to be reconciled to other men.

IV. THE RECONCILIATION TERMINOLOGY IN THE NEW TESTAMENT

The chief difficulty to be solved in the New Testament use of reconcile, reconciliation, etc., is whether, in the process of reconciliation, God can be said to be reconciled to man, or whether

[1] *Ant.* 7: 184 (Loeb edn. V, p. 459).
[2] *Ant.* 5: 137 (Loeb edn. V, p. 65).
[3] *Ant.* 6: 143 (Loeb edn. V, p. 239). *Cf.* Büchsel: 'When God allows it to come about that He gives up His wrath and is gracious again, then one calls this a καταλλαγῆναι of God' (*TWNT*, I, p. 254).

the process is one in which man only is reconciled. As we have seen the Old Testament says little in set terms about the matter (though it often speaks of the wrath of God and of its removal, and this is nothing else than the reconciliation of God). The idea that God is reconciled to man is seen in the Rabbinic writings, in the apocrypha and in authors like Josephus. Yet all this amounts to no more than that it was quite usual in early times to think of God as being reconciled to man, and that καταλλάσσω and its cognates (or their equivalents) were used of this reconciliation of God.

The New Testament must be allowed to speak for itself, and when it does so we are immediately struck by the fact that God is never said in so many words to be reconciled to man. Almost always He is the subject of the verb and is said to reconcile man to Himself. This manner of speaking puts emphasis on the truth that the process of reconciliation originates with God. It is only by the outworking of His love that man can be brought into right relationships with his Maker. This is not, however, conclusive of itself. The argument from silence is always precarious, and doubly so when, as here, there are few passages in question.

Under the general heading of reconciliation there are various sections to consider, for the New Testament speaks of ideas such as those of making peace, fellowship, *etc.*, which may well be held to be parts of the same conception as that denoted by καταλλάσσω (we have already noted that Vincent Taylor discusses a wide range of topics under the heading of 'reconciliation'). But for our purpose it will suffice to consider the thoughts of enmity, of making peace, and those denoted by such words as καταλλάσσω.

a. ἐχθρός *and* ἔχθρα

The New Testament undoubtedly teaches that men are enemies of God: 'While we were enemies, we were reconciled to God' (Rom. 5: 10); 'And you, being in time past alienated and enemies in your mind in your evil works' (Col. 1: 21); 'Whosoever therefore would be a friend of the world maketh himself an enemy of God' (Jas. 4: 4). There is no disputing the fact that Scripture regards man as constituting himself God's enemy by the fact of his sin. But in view of the fact that the New Testament strongly insists on the all-pervading love of God it seems to many today that God cannot be thought of as regarding man with hostility. In other words, in view of the love of God, it is said that when man is spoken of as God's enemy that must be understood as meaning that man is hostile to God with a one-sided hostility, a hostility which meets with nothing but love in return.

The usage of ἐχθρός and ἔχθρα in the New Testament does not furnish a completely final argument, although there are some points which should carry weight. Thus there is the repeated injunction to 'love your enemies' (Mt. 5: 44; Lk. 6: 27, 35), or, again, Paul's 'if thine enemy hunger, feed him; if he thirst, give him to drink' (Rom. 12: 20), which indicate that the attitude of the Christian in the face of hostility is to be one characterized by love; he may not respond with vindictiveness. It is impossible to think that the attitude of God will be less worthy than that He requires from His people. Indeed we are assured that God loves men, even while they are sinners and enemies (Rom. 5: 8-10).

But that does not mean that God will remain inactive in the face of sin. After all it is possible for a Christian to be righteously angry and still retain an attitude of love. We cannot think that this is impossible with God. This being so, we cannot overlook the fact that ἐχθρός commonly denotes a mutual hostility (although it can also be used when the hostility is on one side only). We see something of this in such a passage as Galatians 4: 16, 'So then am I become your enemy, because I tell you the truth?' where Paul speaks of himself as the enemy, although the hostility immediately in mind is on the side of the Galatians.[1] This usage prepares us for Romans 11: 28, where the Jews are said to be 'enemies for your sake', an expression which most scholars hold to indicate that they are being treated by God as enemies. The general context seems to demand such a meaning, especially the 'for your sake (δι' ὑμᾶς)' and the parallelism with ἀγαπητοί which must be taken in the sense of 'beloved of God'. C. Anderson Scott thinks that too much weight should not be attached to 'grammatical symmetry' and understands the passage to mean, 'Seen in the light of the Gospel, still hostile to God for your sakes: but in the light of election still beloved for the fathers' sakes'.[2] But this does not seem to do justice to the apostle's thought. Throughout the chapter he is arguing that salvation came to the Gentiles only because Israel fell away from her vocation as

---

[1] A similar conclusion might perhaps be drawn from 2 Thes. 3: 15.
[2] *Christianity According to St. Paul* (Cambridge, 1932), pp. 77f.

God's people (see verses 11, 12, 15, 19, *etc.*). He does not mince his words when he speaks of God's attitude to Israel, for he thinks of the nation as being cast away (verse 15), he likens them to branches broken off (verses 17, 19, *etc.*), he says, 'God spared not the natural branches' (verse 21), and he directs attention to God's action toward Israel as a striking example of 'severity' (verse 22). Moreover, if there were only a hostility of the nation without a corresponding reaction on God's part, it is difficult to see how this could avail to bring salvation to the Gentiles. The whole tenor of the chapter, as well as the specific points of language noted above, indicates that the nation is thought of as the object of God's hostility in verse 28, and most scholars accept this point of view.

Again, 'he must reign till he hath put all his enemies under his feet' (1 Cor. 15: 25f.), shows that God is not regarded as passive in opposition to His enemies. The same conclusion may perhaps be drawn from Luke 19: 27, though this verse must be used with caution as it occurs in a parable. In Acts 13: 10, Elymas is called the 'enemy of all righteousness'. But God is not passive, for it is due to 'the hand of the Lord' that the sorcerer is struck blind. Similarly Paul speaks of 'perdition' as the end of certain 'enemies of the cross of Christ' (Phil. 3: 18f.), and James says that God 'resisteth the proud' (Jas. 4: 6).

Thus a consideration of the passages in which the term 'enemy' occurs indicates that God takes action against those who are His enemies. Admittedly this is not a complete and final proof that God is rightly said to be hostile to His enemies. But the evidence certainly points in that direction.

With regard to ἔχθρα, a state of enmity usually denotes a reciprocal hostility, as when Herod and Pilate are said to have been 'at enmity between themselves' (Lk. 23: 12). On the other hand, when we read that 'the mind of the flesh is enmity against God; for it is not subject to the law of God, neither can it be' (Rom. 8: 7), it seems that a hostility from the side of man only is meant, although the following 'they that are in the flesh cannot please God' indicates that even here the divine reaction is not being overlooked. For the rest 'enmities' is one item in a list of 'the works of the flesh' (Gal. 5: 20). This does not help us much, unless we assume that what can be referred to as a 'work of the flesh' cannot under any circumstances be referred to God, a proposition which is negatived by the fact that in the same verse 'wraths' (θυμοί) also occurs, and the thought of 'the wrath of God' is quite scriptural. ἔχθρα also occurs in James 4: 4, 'Ye adulteresses, know ye not that the friendship of the world is enmity with God?' in a context which implies the divine re-action against those who are His enemies (*cf.* verses 6, 9–10). It is found also in Ephesians 2: 15f., in the first of which verses it refers to the mutual enmity between Jew and Gentile, while in the second the same enmity may be in view, though the thought seems to be extended so as to include the enmity between man and God. Whichever way it be understood the enmity is slain through the cross. W. Foerster's comment on this verse, 'Enmity with one another and enmity against God (not enmity from the side of God as Gal. 3: 10, but against God as Rom. 8: 7)'[1] sums up much in this discussion. The passages in which ἔχθρα occurs may not prove a divine enmity against men but other passages in the Bible do.

For the fact seems to be that the question of whether, prior to the effecting of reconciliation, God is to be conceived of as in some sense hostile to man must be determined from the general scriptural position, and not from those passages in which ἐχθρός or ἔχθρα are found. And it is surely not without significance that it is only in the Scriptures that we find this thought of an enmity caused by sin. It is not always taken into account that sinful man is not hostile to God. He is quite content to get alone amiably with his Maker, and does not, in point of fact, regard his sin as a just cause for enmity. He himself is not greatly concerned about the trifle of wrongdoing that is in him, and he cannot see why God should be. Now if Jones says that Smith is his enemy, but Smith says, 'No, I am peaceable!' then we must decide that there is enmity from the side of Jones, even though the term 'enemy' is fastened on Smith. So when sinful man is content to let bygones be bygones, but nevertheless God (through the mouth of His servants) speaks of an enmity, it is hard to see how it can be maintained that there is no enmity from the side of God. The point is that it is God's demand for holiness which causes the enmity, and not a conscious hostility on the part of man towards God.

It is important to be clear that there is, on the scriptural view, a definite hostility on the part of God to everything that is evil. Throughout both Old and New Testaments we come across a

[1] *TWNT*, II, p. 815.

multiplicity of passages speaking of 'the wrath of God', of the divine activity in punishing evil, of the demand for the follower of God to 'hate evil', and many similar things. Thus, quite apart from details of interpretation of particular passages, there is strong and consistent teaching that God is active in His opposition to all that is evil. Nor will it do (as some seem inclined) to differentiate between God and the punishment of wrong. They see in 'the wrath' a semi-personalized entity separate from God, and not truly expressive of Him. Others, again, think of wrath as the working out of an impersonal law of retribution, and there are other ways of avoiding the scriptural position.

But all such shifts seem incompatible with a genuine belief in the sovereignty and immanence of God. If God really made the universe a moral universe in which punishment follows sin, then He cannot be exempted from responsibility when it does so. We may choose to call the result the outworking of the wrath of God as the scriptural writers do, or we may prefer some other way of putting it, but the important thing is that we do not overlook the *fact*. Scripture is insistent that God reacts in the strongest possible way to men's sin.[1]

This does not compromise the conception of the love of God. We are not forced to choose between a God of wrath and a God who loves; rather, the wrath is the obverse side of the love. E. H. Gifford has an apposite remark, 'Human love here offers a true analogy: the more a father loves his son, the more he hates *in him* the drunkard, the liar, or the traitor'.[2] If this be quite possible in a

---

[1] *Cf.* C. Ryder Smith: 'The concept of wrath, even when it is regarded as the sequel of justice, seems to revolt the mind of to-day, but it is doubtful whether any theist can escape it. When a theist looks at the world, is he not bound at least to say: "God has made the world in such a way that if men and nations sin, misery befalls them"?... Where a modern theist says that God has so made the world that if men sin, they suffer, the Biblical writers speak of "the wrath of God". It is true that, at first sight, there is the difference that the former attributes indirect action to God and the latter direct action, but it is very doubtful whether such a distinction exists for omnipotence, and, in any case, is there any ultimate difference between the two? Both ascribe a certain responsibility to God' (*The Bible Doctrine of Salvation*, London, 1946, p. 128).

[2] *The Epistle of St. Paul to the Romans* (London, 1886), p. 114. He understands 'enemies' in Rom. 5: 10 of God's enemies, and says: 'By God's enemies are here meant those who lie under His wrath, and they are reconciled to Him, when that wrath is removed in the remission of sins' (*ibid.*).

human father with all his failings we cannot account it incredible in God from whose wrath are absent all those imperfections which mar the human emotion of righteous anger even at its purest.

Nor must it be overlooked that the very fact that Christ had to die to reconcile men to God is a witness in itself to the hostility from the divine side, especially since His death is a death which avails for us. 'One died for all', says St. Paul, 'therefore all died' (2 Cor. 5: 14). But why should all die? Surely this points to a divine hostility, a divine hostility made manifest in the sentence of death. A. Schlatter puts it this way, 'As Paul saw in the death of Christ the death prepared for him he recognized that he had God against him. The God who condemns to death treats man as His adversary whom He withstands'.[1]

We conclude then that the biblical teaching on ἐχθρός and ἔχθρα taken in conjunction with the wider biblical teaching on the wrath of God indicates that there is a very real hostility on the part of God to all that is evil, and that this hostility is not incompatible with a deep love of God for sinners.

b. καταλλάσσω and καταλλαγή

One of the most important passages under this heading is Romans 5: 8-11, where we are reminded of the love of God shown in the cross, of our being justified in Christ's blood and saved from the wrath through Him, and then: 'For if, while we were enemies, we were reconciled to God through the death of his Son, much more being reconciled, shall we be saved by his life; and not only so, but we also rejoice in God through our Lord Jesus Christ, through whom we have now received the reconciliation.'

Here let us notice first of all that there is an aspect of reconciliation which is outside man, an objective element. We are said to have received the reconciliation, which, therefore, is in some sense independent of us. Obviously reconciliation must be personal to be effective, and we must enter into a state of being reconciled; but, nevertheless, there is a sense in which a reconciliation can be said to be proffered to us. In other words the New Testament view is that reconciliation was wrought on the cross before there was anything in man's heart to correspond.[2] There is an objective aspect to re-

---

[1] *Paulus der Bote Jesu* (Stuttgart, 1934), p. 565.
[2] *Cf.* Denney: 'unless we can preach a finished work of Christ in relation to sin, a

conciliation, and this may well be held to imply that there is a sense in which God can be said to be reconciled to man. As James Denney puts it: 'Reduced to its simplest expression, what an objective atonement means is that but for Christ and His Passion God would not *be* to us what He is.' He goes on to indicate the seriousness of rejecting this position by saying, 'The alternative is to say that quite independent of any value which Christ and His Passion have for God, God would still be to us what He is. But this is really to put Christ out of Christianity altogether'.[1]

Then there is the term ἐχθρός which St. Paul applies to men in their state prior to reconciliation (Rom. 5: 10). It may be granted that in this context the major idea conveyed by ἐχθρός is that men were hostile to God, for the apostle is trying to show us the greatness of the love of God and he insists that even when men were hostile to God He effected reconciliation. But this does not mean that we have exhausted the meaning of the term ἐχθρός. As we saw in the previous section, it is a word which may well imply a severe reaction on the part of God to man's sin. While it is, of course, true that the usage in other passages does not determine the meaning in this, it does show us that there is scriptural warrant for thinking of an opposition of God to sin and sinners which can be referred to by the use of ἐχθρός. As Vincent Taylor says, 'We must conclude that in Rom. v. 10 ἐχθροί describes, not only the hostile attitude of men, but also their character in the eyes of God. He sees them as enemies; and yet He reconciles them to Himself.'[2]

Seen, then, in the wider context of New Testament thought, Romans 5: 8–11 indicates a reconciliation in which there is a Godward as well as a manward aspect. The immediate context also favours this idea, for the words about reconciliation are immediately preceded by a reference to 'the wrath' from which

---

καταλλαγή or reconciliation or peace which has been achieved independently of us at an infinite cost . . . we have no real gospel for sinful men at all' (*The Death of Christ*, London, 1951, p. 86). Similarly P. T. Forsyth: 'Reconciliation was finished in Christ's death. Paul did not preach a gradual reconciliation. He preached what the old divines used to call the finished work. . . . He preached something done once for all – a reconciliation which is the base of every soul's reconcilement, not an invitation only' (*The Work of Christ*, London, 1948, p. 86).

[1] *The Christian Doctrine of Reconciliation* (London, 1918), p. 239.
[2] *Forgiveness and Reconciliation* (London, 1946), p. 75.

men are saved through Christ,[1] a thought which is typically Pauline, and which we saw in Chapter Five is developed in the first three chapters of the Epistle.

In addition to the context, the meaning of the verses in question points in the same direction. Thus we are said to be reconciled by the death of Christ, and this seems to indicate a Godward rather than a manward aspect of the atonement. As H. P. Liddon says, 'Christ's death removed God's enmity against man, and man's enmity against God only ceased, as a moral consequence of faith. καταλλαγέντες and καταλλάγημεν must, therefore, be understood to express, not merely the reconciliation of the moral nature of the Christian with God, but the new relation of God to man in Christ which made this possible.'[2]

It is quite true that when a man comes to a position of faith in Jesus there is a change of heart and outlook, such that his enmity to God is done away. It is also true that the display of divine love which we see on the cross is a powerful force in bringing him to this position of faith. But it is more than difficult to think that Paul is trying to express either of these truths in this passage. If he had wished to say something like that he had a splendid opening when he spoke of God as commending His own love to us (verse 8). But his point in making this statement is not to lead on to the thought that this love induces men to lay aside their enmity. Rather it is to stress that it was 'while we were yet sinners' that 'Christ died for us'. From there he goes on to speak of justification, of being saved from wrath, of being reconciled while still enemies. The apostle is not indifferent to the new life, for he goes on to mention it as a consequence of reconciliation – 'much more, being reconciled, shall we be saved by his life'. Being saved by or in His life is surely another way of putting what Paul says in 2 Corinthians 4: 10f., 'that the life also of Jesus may be manifested in our body. For we which live are alway delivered unto death for Jesus' sake, that the life also of Jesus may be manifested in our mortal flesh'. Thus there

---

[1] *Cf.* Godet on Romans: 'The enmity must above all belong to Him to whom *wrath* is attributed; and the blood of Christ . . . did not flow in the first place to work a change in our dispositions Godward, but to bring about a change in God's conduct toward us' (*Commentary on St. Paul's Epistle to the Romans*, I, Edinburgh, n.d., p. 330).

[2] *Explanatory Analysis of St. Paul's Epistle to the Romans* (London, 1899), pp. 100f.

is a change in man such that, instead of living his own fleshly life, he now shows Christ living in him. But this seems to be the consequence of reconciliation and not reconciliation itself.

We are not helped here by the fact that the English terms for reconciliation, *etc.*, do not denote exactly the same things as their Greek counterparts. If, in English, we speak of God and man as reconciled, we think of a reconciliation in which right relationships now exist on both sides. Perhaps the same is true with the Greek terms when reconciliation is thought of as being fully consummated. But it is also possible to use the Greek terms to mean that God has dealt with the obstacle to fellowship, and that He now proffers reconciliation to man. Thus Paul can speak of men 'receiving the reconciliation'.[1] It is a gift which God gives. Now if it is a gift which God gives it must exist in order to be given. There is thus a sense in which reconciliation exists before men receive it. It is not denied that it is also possible to think of reconciliation as something which calls for man's co-operation, for 'Be ye reconciled' is also a word of St. Paul. All that is being insisted is that the usages of the Greek and the English words are not quite the same. The Greek can be used of a more one-sided process than the English, and there is more than a hint at a largely one-sided process in Romans 5: 9–11.

The other great passage on reconciliation is 2 Corinthians 5: 17ff.: 'Wherefore if any man is in Christ, he is a new creature: the old things are passed away; behold, they are become new. But all things are of God, who reconciled us to himself through Christ, and gave unto us the ministry of reconciliation; to wit, that God was in Christ reconciling the world unto himself, not reckoning

---

[1] *Cf.* Denney: 'It is very unfortunate that the English word reconcile (and also the German *versöhnen*, which is usually taken as its equivalent) diverge seriously, though in a way of which it is easy to be unconscious, from the Greek καταλλάσσειν. We cannot say in English, God reconciled us to Himself, without conceiving the persons referred to as being actually at peace with God, as having laid aside all fear, distrust, and love of evil, and entered, in point of fact, into relations of peace and friendship with God. But καταλλάσσειν, as describing the work of God, or καταλλαγή, as describing its immediate result, do not necessarily carry us so far. The work of reconciliation, in the sense of the New Testament, is a work which is *finished*, and which we must conceive to be finished, *before the gospel is preached*' (*The Death of Christ*, London, 1911, p. 103).

unto them their trespasses, and having committed unto us the word of reconciliation. We are ambassadors therefore on behalf of Christ, as though God were intreating by us: we beseech you on behalf of Christ, be ye reconciled to God. Him who knew no sin he made to be sin on our behalf; that we might become the righteousness of God in him. And working together with him we intreat also that ye receive not the grace of God in vain.'

Here we have no mention of wrath in the context as we have in the Romans passage,[1] and the context has much to say about the new life in Christ, which indicates the close connection between reconciliation and the resultant Christian victorious living. It is thought by some to point to reconciliation as essentially an activity within man, but this seems to be going too far, and to be neglecting some of the points that Paul is making.

First let us notice that the process the apostle has in mind is one which is wrought by God. 'All things', he tells us, 'are of God, who reconciled us'; 'God was in Christ reconciling the world unto himself', 'him . . . he made to be sin on our behalf'. Though it is true that there is an aspect in which men may be exhorted to be reconciled to God, yet there is no question but that Paul is thinking of something God has done for men, and not of some merely human activity.

In verse 19, moreover, reconciliation is explained as 'not reckoning unto them their trespasses'. This is in keeping with much in the Scriptures which assures us that the obstacle to fellowship between God and man is sin, so that if there is to be peace between the two something must be done about that sin. It can be alleged, of course, that it is necessary for man to forsake his sin and that, when he does this, there is reconciliation with God. Thus C. Anderson Scott equates reconciliation with 'the flooding of human hearts with the love of God, the disappearance of hostility, the joyful acceptance of forgiveness',[2] and similarly C. Ryder Smith, in discussing the idea of the wrath of God, says, 'but here (*i.e.* Rom. iii. 23–26), as always, it is taken for granted that, if man repents, the

[1] Yet R. H. Strachan can say this wrath 'must be in the background if we are to see, in these verses, as I think we must, Paul's expression of what he regarded as the essential meaning of the Cross of Christ' (*MNTC*, 2 *Corinthians*, p. 116).

[2] *Christianity According to St. Paul* (Cambridge, 1932), p. 84. He adds: 'This is not all that Paul has to say about the "Atonement," but it is the heart of it.'

"wrath" of God dies'.[1] There is of course truth in these statements, for if a man truly repents, has his heart filled with the love of God, finds his hostility to God disappear and accepts forgiveness gladly, then he is certainly reconciled to God.

But it is difficult to believe either that this is the whole story or that this is St. Paul's meaning in the passage which we are considering. Such statements come perilously close to leaving Christ out of reconciliation,[2] and it is the activity of Christ that Paul is especially concerned to stress, and in particular the necessity of His death. For although in these verses the apostle does not specifically mention the death of the Lord, there is not the slightest doubt but that he has it in mind. On Paul's view it is only through this death that man's trespasses are put away, and thus the cross is vividly present to his mind in verses 19, 21. He is not thinking of reconciliation as basically subjective to man, as though Christ's activity were simply to make a display of the divine love such as would arouse in men feelings of love and gratitude and would cause them to repent and be reconciled. When he says that God made Christ 'sin' for us it seems clear, at least, that he conceived of the death of the Lord as availing in an objective manner to put away man's sin.[3]

It is common in these days to assert that Paul here means nothing more than that Christ entered into a perfect sympathy with sinners, much in the same manner as a loving mother feels deeply for her erring son. Such analogies are often drawn out to show that

---

[1] *The Bible Doctrine of Salvation* (London, 1946), p. 218.

[2] R. Travers Herford, speaking not of reconciliation in particular, but of Christianity in general, says: 'Paul grasped the fact that the Christian religion was founded on a Person, not an Idea' (*Judaism in the New Testament Period*, London, 1928, p. 227). The comment has relevance to the point we are discussing, for the Christian view of reconciliation is not simply an Idea, such that if a man repents all will be well; it concerns a *Person*. And the characteristic Christian thought is that reconciliation is wrought by Christ, and is to be found only in Him. 'God's reconciliation rested upon this, that on His Eternal Son, who knew no sin in His experience ... sin's judgment fell' (P. T. Forsyth, *op. cit.*, pp. 82f.).

[3] *Cf.* Forsyth: 'The greatest passage which says that God was in Christ reconciling says in the same breath that it was by Christ being made sin for us. The reconciliation is attached to Christ's death, and to that as an expiation' (*The Cruciality of the Cross*, London, 1948, p. 68). J. Scott Lidgett says: 'Christ enters into our sin, takes it upon Himself, is wrapt in it. He stands for us and with us, as though a sinner, and in that capacity He dies on our behalf' (*The Spiritual Principle of the Atonement*, London, 1914, p. 42).

the mother may have a more intense suffering than the son, that she may loathe the sin more than he does in his imperfect penitence, and so on. But, true as all this is, it does not seem that this is what Paul is saying. Rather the verse is to be understood along with Galatians 3 : 13, which speaks of Christ becoming 'a curse' for us, as indicating that He bore to the full the consequences of sin.[1] When God made Him sin that we might become 'the righteousness of God', then in some way He took upon Him our sin and we bear it no more. As Denney puts it, 'Christ died for us, died that death of ours which is the wages of sin. In His death, all sinless as He was, God's condemnation of our sin came upon Him; a divine sentence was executed upon the sin of the world.'[2] Or to quote a more recent writer, the verse means that 'He made Him die that death which is the wages of sin, as our substitute'.[3] Such also is the interpretation of G. Schrenk: 'Because the Christ is substitutionarily ἁμαρτία for us, may we be δικαιοσύνη ἐν αὐτῷ.'[4] Such interpretations are much nearer to the thought of Paul than those which minimize the force of the passage.

Arising out of all this is what Paul calls 'the word of reconciliation', the message to men that they must 'be reconciled to God'. This stresses the need for men to respond to the divine grace. Reconciliation is not something which is carried through independently of men's reaction. While it is true that, in some sense, reconciliation can be thought of as offered to men on the basis of Christ's work, yet it cannot be thought of as availing in the case of any individual man until he himself has become reconciled to God. But if there is anything in what we have been saying, the need for this action on the part of the sinner should not blind us to the fact that the really important part of reconciliation is in the action of

[1] H. Wheeler Robinson also takes these two verses together saying of the idea of Christ becoming a curse for us in Gal. 3 : 13: 'This is one of the clearest indications that St. Paul conceived the death of Christ as both substitutionary and penal, its parallel being that of 2 Cor. v. 21, where the Sinless is said to be made sin in our behalf, that we might obtain acquittal and become actually righteous' (*Redemption and Revelation*, London, 1942, p. 231).

[2] *Studies in Theology* (London, 1895), p. 112.

[3] A. B. Macaulay, *The Death of Jesus* (London, 1938), p. 174.

[4] *TWNT*, II, p. 212. Similarly L. S. Thornton says of this verse and Gal. 3 : 13: 'Whatever these mysterious phrases may mean, they certainly put our Lord in the place of sinners' (*The Common Life in the Body of Christ*, London, 1950, p. 445).

God and not in the sinner's response. Because God has made Christ sin for us, because God is not reckoning to men their trespasses, therefore there is a word of reconciliation, a message of good news that can and must be proclaimed to men. Well may Paul exhort his readers to 'receive not the grace of God in vain'. But it is 'the grace of God' and not merely some subjective change in their own hearts of which he is speaking.[1]

Apart from these two passages καταλλάσσω occurs only in 1 Corinthians 7: 11, where St. Paul charges those married 'That the wife depart not from her husband (but and if she depart, let her remain unmarried or else be reconciled to her husband)'. It is surely of significance that while the wife is envisaged as the party actively seeking the reconciliation she is exhorted to 'be reconciled', indicating a change from her side as well as his.[2]

The noun καταλλαγή is found also in Romans 11: 15, 'For if the casting away of them (i.e. the Jews) is the reconciling of the world', but this does not help us greatly. Paul is here developing an argument that it is because the Jews were temporarily rejected that reconciliation came to the Gentiles, but he does not indicate in what manner this reconciliation was effected. So for our understanding of the term, we are dependent upon the passages already considered.

c. ἀποκαταλλάσσω

Under this heading two passages fail to be considered, namely Ephesians 2: 11ff. and Colossians 1: 19ff. The former begins with the enmity between Jew and Gentile, when the Gentiles were 'separate from Christ, alienated from the commonwealth of Israel, and strangers from the covenants of the promise, having no hope and without God in the world'. But the coming of Christ has altered all that. He 'made both one, and brake down the middle wall of partition, having abolished in his flesh the enmity, even the

---

[1] Cf. the passages quoted on p. 230, n.3. From verses 19, 21 Büchsel thinks that 'the reconciliation includes also justification within itself' (TWNT, I, p. 258).

[2] Büchsel comments: 'Were the woman in such a case to remain completely passive, there would arise no new union, no reconciliation between her and her husband' (TWNT, I, p. 256). J. Pearson understands 'be reconciled' here as 'appease and get the favour of her husband' (An Exposition of the Creed, Oxford, 1890, 365, p. 644).

law of commandments contained in ordinances; that he might create in himself of the twain one new man, so making peace'. From this point the apostle goes straight on to consider the change wrought by Christ in the relationship of men to God, and says that He 'might reconcile them both in one body unto God through the cross, having slain the enmity thereby'. The upshot of it all is that the Gentiles 'are no more strangers and sojourners, but . . . fellow-citizens with the saints, and of the household of God'.

This passage strongly insists on the divine initiative in the process of reconciliation. Indeed the whole process is described from the point of view of Christ, and men are not said to do any-thing in the matter. They were 'far off', they are 'made nigh' and all is the work of Christ. There is nothing here like the 'Be ye reconciled' of 2 Corinthians 5, although it may fairly be said that such an aspect of the subject is implied. But the point is that it is the divine initiative and the divine effort that is in view; the human response is not so much as mentioned.

This might accord well with the contention that, in recon-ciliation, God does not need to be reconciled. But in fact the passage does not indicate this. That all is of God is freely admitted, but that does not carry with it the thought that there is no divine reaction against sin to be dealt with. The fact that it is to God that the reconciliation is due does not determine what the process of reconciliation is.

Everything depends on what we are to understand by 'the enmity'. If it is only man's enmity against God, then there is no Godward aspect of reconciliation in mind, but if it includes the thought that God reacts severely against sinners, then such an aspect cannot be dismissed. There is nothing in the immediate context which decides the point. The argument flows on evenly whatever interpretation of 'the enmity' we adopt. But if we pay attention to the wider thought of the Epistle (confining ourselves to this one writing since there are some who do not think it Pauline), we cannot overlook the strenuous divine reaction against evil. All men are thought of as 'by nature children of wrath' (Eph. 2: 3). Again, the writer says, 'Let no man deceive you with empty words: for because of these things cometh the wrath of God upon the sons of disobedience' (5: 6). Masters are urged to forbear threatening on the grounds that they themselves have a Master in heaven, 'and there is no respect of persons with him' (6: 9). Certain persons, namely, fornicators, the unclean and the covetous, are expressly said to be excluded from the kingdom of God (5: 5). Even the enthusiasm with which the writer speaks of salvation seems to be partly because he has in mind what men are saved from, as well as the new state into which they are saved. Taking the Epistle as a whole it seems clear that the author thinks of God as hostile to evil. Therefore we can believe that an element in his thought of reconciliation is that this hostility is removed for them that are 'in Christ Jesus'.

This is supported by the statement in 2: 17f. that Christ 'came and preached peace (εὐηγγελίσατο εἰρήνην) . . . for through him we both have our access in one Spirit unto the Father'. The good tidings is that God has removed the barrier which separated sinners from Himself. The idea that all that men have to do is to realize that He has always loved them and will receive them is inadequate to explain the passage. The writer is referring to a new situation called into being by Christ's death on the cross. Because of that death, there is good news. Men now need not fear to draw near to God for the enmity has been 'slain'.

Again, it may not be without significance that the writer is led into his discussion of reconciliation by a consideration of the enmity between Jew and Gentile, and this was an enmity on both sides. This is not conclusive, but as far as it goes it points to a reconciliation affecting both parties.

Thus, surveying all the evidence, it would seem that in this passage the writer is thinking of the removal of the divine wrath against sin as the effect of the death on the cross, and of peace being made between God and man accordingly. Admittedly a final proof of this is lacking, but it is contended that this is the most natural way of reading the available evidence.

The other passage in which ἀποκαταλλάσσω is used tells us that it was the Father's good pleasure through Him 'to reconcile all things unto himself, having made peace through the blood of his cross' (Col. 1: 19f.). The argument goes on: 'And you, being in time past alienated and enemies in your mind in your evil works, yet now hath he reconciled (or as P46, B and Hil. read, "you have been reconciled") in the body of his flesh through death, etc.'

Once more the stress is on the activity of God. It was His good pleasure that reconciliation should be effected, and the emphasis throughout the passage is on what He has done, and not on any puny effort of man.

Each time reconciliation is mentioned we have a reference to the means. The first time 'having made peace through the blood of his cross' is added; the second time reconciliation is said to be 'in the body of his flesh through death'. Thus it is clear that reconciliation is closely tied up with the death of the Lord, and the implication is that this death really did something by way of removing barriers. Once more it is clear that such explanations as that the death is an indication that God loves men and that if they turn to Him all will be well are inadequate as summaries of the thought of the writer. It is difficult to escape the impression that what Paul is teaching us is that the death of Christ did something quite apart from the stimulus it has on the feelings and actions of man.

It is sometimes argued that the statement of the nature of the enmity shows that reconciliation takes place only from the manward side. Men are said to have been 'alienated and enemies in their mind in their evil works'. This, it is said, shows that reconciliation means the alteration of this state of affairs and the substitution of a better state of mind and of better works. But this goes beyond the evidence. It is not disputed that the hostility in men's minds and actions is real and serious, nor that it must be removed before there can be completely harmonious relations between God and men. But it can be maintained that this exhausts the concept of reconciliation only by holding that God's reaction to all this is not serious. That this is not the thought of the writer of the Epistle is shown by his mention of 'the wrath of God' as coming 'upon the sons of disobedience' (Col. 3 : 6), his statement, 'For he that doeth wrong shall receive again for the wrong that he hath done; and there is no respect of persons' (Col. 3 : 25), and the possibility of failing to attain 'the prize' (Col. 2 : 18). These general considerations and the fact that the passage under discussion seems to imply that sinners are in no good case because of the attitude of a holy God to their sin show that St. Paul thought of the cross as the veritable means whereby sin was put away and reconciliation effected.

That man's response to this is important is undoubted, and that that response leads to a thoroughgoing reformation of man is clear.

But the point is that it is man's response to something that God has done for him; it is not in itself the process of reconciliation.

Thus it is clear that certain ideas run through the passages where the reconciliation words are used in the New Testament. Common to all are the thoughts that it is the sin of man which represents the barrier to communion with God, and that this must be dealt with if reconciliation is to take place. It is this which gives point to the idea that God can be said to be reconciled to man, for it is manifestly impossible for God to regard man in quite the same way before the barrier is removed as He does after that takes place. At the same time the reconciliation is always God's work, and in several ways we have the truth stressed that it is the love of God that is the dominant factor in bringing reconciliation about.

There is support for the idea that the reconciliation includes an aspect of reconciliation of God in the usage of διαλλάσσω, a word closely allied in meaning to καταλλάσσω. We have noted that this word was used in the LXX of David being reconciled, though it was Saul's enmity which was to be removed, and therefore we would have expected the text to say that Saul rather than David was to be reconciled. We have exactly the same usage in Matthew 5:23f., 'If therefore thou art offering thy gift at the altar, and there rememberest that thy brother hath aught against thee, leave there thy gift before the altar, and go thy way, first be reconciled to thy brother . . .' Here again it is the one taking the initiative who is said to be reconciled, and this usage seems to be established for καταλλάσσω by 1 Corinthians 7:11. Thus the linguistic usage gives us ground for thinking that when reconciliation is applied to the relations between God and men it will signify, in part, that God is reconciled as well as man. Moreover, as Handley Moule says, καταλλαγή and its cognates 'habitually point to the winning rather the pardon of an offended King than the consent of the rebel to yield to His kindness'.[1] Similarly T. J. Crawford long ago pointed out that καταλλάσσω and διαλλάσσω are used in the biblical writings 'to signify the removal of enmity, not from the *offending*, but from the *offended* party'; and again he says 'when one party is said "to be reconciled to another" or "to reconcile himself to another," the *latter*, and not the former, according to the Hellenistic idiom, is the

[1] *Outlines of Christian Doctrine* (London, 1892), p. 79.

party whose friendship and favour are conciliated'.[1] Too often this is overlooked. Men argue as though the familiar English usage were decisive, whereas, of course, it is the meaning of the Greek that is important. And that points to what, for want of a better term, we can speak of only as a change from the divine side as well as the human.

d. Making peace

The actual expression 'making peace' does not occur very often in the New Testament, but it is a common idea that believers have peace with God. Since this is not thought of as applying to natural man (cf. Eph. 2: 3, 'by nature children of wrath'), it may fairly be held to imply the thought of making peace.

It will be worth our while to notice a little of the content of the term εἰρήνη (peace). Among the Greeks it was used primarily to denote that state of rest which results from cessation of hostilities, peace in opposition to war. But in the LXX the term receives an extension of meaning. This is due to its being used as the regular translation of the Hebrew *shālôm*,[2] a word of wider meaning than εἰρήνη in profane Greek writings. *shālôm* can be used to denote the state of rest when there is no war, and it is used in this way in about thirty-eight of its 236 occurrences in the Old Testament. But this cannot be regarded as the word's essential meaning. It is better regarded as part of a wider conception of general well-being. Because such well-being is promoted in times when there is no war, and because indeed such times may be regarded as an integral part of the general well-being, the term *shālôm* was felt to be not inappropriately used to describe the condition of absence of strife. But that should not blind us to the fact that the essential meaning of the word is to be sought elsewhere. BDB find it in the thought of 'completeness, soundness, welfare' and so 'peace'. G. von Rad

[1] *The Doctrine of Holy Scripture respecting the Atonement* (Edinburgh, 1871), p. 67. *Cf.* also Pearson: 'in the language of the Scripture to reconcile a man to God, is in our vulgar language to reconcile God to man' (*op. cit.*, 364, p. 643).

[2] εἰρήνη is found 282 times in LXX, the Hebrew being *shālôm* 192 times (including three verses marked with a query in HR), while 76 times either there is no Hebrew or it is doubtful whether εἰρήνη is based on the present text. For the rest it translates *beṭaḥ* nine times (two queries), *shqṭ* and *shlwh* once each, while HR include one passage each (queried each time) under *hlq*, *lqḥ* and *tsḥ*. From these figures it is plain that *shālôm* is the Old Testament equivalent of εἰρήνη.

thinks that 'The groundmeaning of the word is "well-being" and indeed with a manifest emphasis on the material side'.[1] E. de W. Burton says *shālôm* 'has as its fundamental idea "soundness," "prosperity," "well-being" '.[2] There can be no doubt that the word conveyed to the Hebrews the thought of well-being in the widest of senses.

A full examination of such a rich and many-sided concept would take up more space than we have at our disposal, and we content ourselves with noticing one or two of the more important points. *shālôm* is often used in connection with material prosperity (*e.g.* Lv. 26: 5ff.). But sometimes we detect a more spiritual note, as when the psalmist says, 'Mercy and truth are met together; righteousness and peace have kissed each other' (Ps. 85: 10). So too the prophet writes, 'the work of righteousness shall be peace; and the effect of righteousness quietness and confidence for ever' (Is. 32: 17).[3] In such passages we must feel that more than material prosperity is in mind, and that *shālôm* has an ethical content. This we might also deduce from the fact that sometimes *shālôm* is ascribed to the Lord, as in Job 25: 2, 'He maketh peace in his high places', or in 1 Kings 2: 33 where it is said that unto David and his house 'shall there be peace for ever from the Lord'. In line with this is the name 'Jehovah-shalom', 'the Lord is peace' (Jdg. 6: 24). There are implications also in the expression 'covenant of peace' which we meet in a number of passages and where it is clear that the peace in question comes from the Lord (Nu. 25: 12; Is. 54: 10; Ezk. 34: 25; 37: 26; Mal. 2: 5). Thus, while we may not say that the New Testament conception of peace with God is already to be discerned in the Old Testament, yet we can say that the way was being prepared especially in the concept of a peace which includes an ethical content, and which takes its origin from God.

As εἰρήνη was used so regularly to translate *shālôm*, it was inevitable that it should pick up some of the wide meaning associated with the Hebrew term. The reader of the LXX must have come to see, from the variety of contexts in which the word was used, that εἰρήνη denoted more than a cessation of hostility. In particular he

---

[1] *TWNT*, II, p. 400.
[2] *ICC, Galatians*, p. 425.
[3] For similar thoughts see Is. 26: 2, 3; Ps. 119: 165; Pr. 12: 20; Je. 33: 6; Zc. 8: 19; Mal. 2: 6; *etc.*

was bound to see that the word often denotes a blessing which comes from God (Nu. 6: 26; Is. 45: 7; Zc. 8: 12), and that it frequently has an ethical content (Ps. 33: 14; Is. 32: 17; Zc. 8: 12; Mal. 2: 6; *etc.*).

During the period between the two Testaments this usage continues, and other elements are imported into it. We have already noted that the Rabbis think of an enmity between God and man and of various ways in which reconciliation is effected.[1] The Zadokite fragment speaks of the Lord as striving with all flesh (1: 2), but not much can be made of this, for the words are 'Based almost verbally on Jer. xxv. 31'.[2] The Old Testament often speaks of the Lord as having a controversy with men, and of reconciliation, inasmuch as punishment does not always come upon them. But the point is that this reconciliation is not indicated by the use of *shālôm* (or εἰρήνη), and in this respect the Zadokite fragment continues the Old Testament usage. In the *Testaments of the Twelve Patriarchs* εἰρήνη is used in connection with the judgment of God, as when judgment is executed for a period (*Test. Lev.* 18: 2), but later 'there shall be peace in all the earth' (verse 4). Peace comes from God, and there is an interesting passage where 'the angel of peace' makes his appearance. The patriarch Dan says, 'Draw near unto God and unto the angel that intercedeth for you, for he is a mediator between God and man, and for the peace of Israel he shall stand up against the kingdom of the enemy' (*Test. Dan* 6: 2). Here there is a conflict between God and man, or at any rate between God and Satan, with evil in man very much the point at issue. But, although peace is used of the successful outcome, it seems rather in the sense of 'well-being, prosperity' than of a state of peace between God and man.

Somewhat similar, though closer to the thought of a state of peace between God and man, is the usage in the Ethiopic Enoch. Here we find the thoughts of peace and judgment connected: 'And the earth shall be wholly rent in sunder, and all that is upon the earth shall perish, and there shall be a judgment upon all (men). But with the righteous He will make peace, and will protect the

---

[1] See pp. 216ff.
[2] Charles, *Apocrypha and Pseudepigrapha*, II (Oxford, 1963), p. 799. The citations following are from this translation.

elect, and mercy shall be upon them' (En. 17: 8). Similarly peace seems closely allied to forgiveness: 'And ye shall have no peace nor forgiveness of sin' (En. 12: 5), 'And there shall be forgiveness of sins, and every mercy and peace and forbearance' (En. 5: 6 and cf. En. 5: 4; 16: 4).

In Josephus there seems little to help us. He uses εἰρήνη of Abraham's returning in peace after recapturing Lot and the Sodomites,[1] which is quite a common usage. There is probably an ethical content when he refers to the Essenes as 'ministers of peace'.[2] There is also an interesting passage in which he refers to Saul's having peace of soul,[3] but as this peace is rest from demons probably not much can be made of the reference. Philo once says that God is peace: 'Know then, good friend, that God alone is the real veritable peace',[4] and again, he thinks of God as the only source of peace, speaking of God, 'Whose voice granted to Phinehas the highest of blessings, peace – a gift which no human being can bestow'.[5] When he says that 'the results of continence are stability and peace'[6] he seems to be giving εἰρήνη an ethical content.

Thus in these various Jewish writings there seems to be a tendency to retain something of the wider meaning given to εἰρήνη in the LXX. In particular peace is often regarded as coming from God, and the ethical note is not seldom struck. Those writers who use it in connection with the judgment of God upon sin are getting near to the New Testament idea of peace following upon God's dealing with sin.

A striking feature of the New Testament use of εἰρήνη is the frequency with which it is associated, directly or indirectly, with God. It is a difficult word to classify, as one group of meanings shades off into another, and there must always be a large subjective element in any classification adopted. But it may be said that of the ninety-two times the word occurs, fifteen refer to peace as opposed to war, personal strife, or confusion, while in all the others it is possible to see implied the thought that God is the giver. Peace is

[1] *Ant.* i. 179.
[2] *Bell.* ii. 135.
[3] *Ant.* vi. 211.
[4] *De Som.* ii. 253.
[5] *Vit. Mos.* i. 304.
[6] *De Jos.* 57.

specifically connected with the Father or the Son about forty times, including the salutations in the Epistles.

Particularly important from our present point of view are those passages which directly associate peace with God. First there are those which indicate a tranquillity in the believer. This is not the possession of all men; it is a specifically Christian peace. As Burton says, it is a 'Tranquillity of mind, which comes from the assurance of being reconciled with God and under his loving care'.[1] A good example of this usage is John 14:27 where Jesus says, 'Peace I leave with you; my peace I give unto you: not as the world giveth, give I unto you'. Here peace is expressly associated with the speaker – it is 'His' peace – and it is also expressly differentiated from the peace which the world gives. Similar is the Lord's statement a little later, 'These things have I spoken unto you, that in me ye may have peace. In the world ye have tribulation: but be of good cheer; I have overcome the world' (Jn. 16:33). Here again peace is associated with Christ, and it is contrasted with the tribulation that is the world's gift. The peace in question seems to rest on the fact that Christ has overcome the world. So again St. Paul says: 'For the mind of the flesh is death; but the mind of the spirit is life and peace' (Rom. 8:6). His subsequent reference to the mind of the flesh as enmity with God enables us to say with confidence that the peace he is thinking of is one in which that enmity has been overcome. It is a peace which results from the work of Christ for man.[2]

So completely is the idea accepted that peace comes from God that He can be referred to as 'the God of peace', an expression which implies that the bringing about of peace is a characteristic feature of His activity. A particularly instructive example is Romans 16:20, 'And the God of peace shall bruise Satan under your feet shortly'. In the very sentence in which He is designated 'God of peace' that same God is pictured in the warlike activity of bruising Satan. Nothing could more graphically illustrate the fact that peace in the New Testament is not simply the absence of war. It is a much more positive concept, and one which, as here, may be

---

[1] Op. cit., p. 426.

[2] Other passages in which peace signifies a tranquillity of mind or soul, and which we should understand as a result of the work of Christ for man in accordance with the accepted Christian position, include Rom. 14:17; 15:13; Gal. 5:22; Eph. 6:23; 2 Thes. 3:16; 2 Pet. 3:14.

compatible with struggle. It stands for spiritual well-being at the highest level, a prosperity of soul resulting from being in right relationship with God.[1] God brings about this relationship by His victory over Satan. The thought that God is the God of peace and the connection with the atoning work of Christ are to be discerned also in the great benediction at the end of the Epistle to the Hebrews: 'the God of peace, who brought again from the dead the great shepherd of the sheep with the blood of the eternal covenant, even our Lord Jesus' (Heb. 13: 20). From such passages it is clear that the giving of peace is a distinctive divine activity, and that it is associated with the atoning death of Christ. The passages in question do not say in so many words that we have peace because Christ died, but it is hard to see how this inference can be avoided. (*Cf.* the references to 'the God of peace' in Rom. 15:33; 2 Cor. 13: 11; Phil. 4:9; 1 Thes. 5:23; and 'the Lord of peace' in 2 Thes. 3: 16.)

There are a few passages wherein peace seems to be nearly identical with salvation. Thus in his speech in the house of Cornelius Peter refers to 'the word which he sent unto the children of Israel, preaching good tidings of peace by Jesus Christ (εὐαγγελιζόμενος εἰρήνην διὰ 'Ιησοῦ Χριστοῦ)' (Acts 10: 36). It is very difficult to distinguish here between εἰρήνη and εὐαγγέλιον, and the content of the εἰρήνη in question must be that the enmity caused by sin has been done away with in Christ. It is not otherwise with Romans 5: 1, where 'peace with God through our Lord Jesus Christ' is mentioned in the closest of connections with justification by faith, and where εἰρήνη seems to include more than simply tranquillity of mind. So also we find a reference to 'the gospel of peace' (Eph. 6: 15), where the meaning seems to be that the tidings are to be proclaimed that peace in the fullest sense is the result of God's activity in Christ. But in this connection the most important passage is Ephesians 2: 14f. in which Christ is designated as 'our peace', He is referred to as 'making peace', and as preaching 'peace to you that were far off, and peace to them that were nigh'. The passage is not without its difficulties, for the writer begins with the enmity between Jew and Gentile, and this does not drop entirely out of his thought. But at

---

[1] P. T. Forsyth speaks of 'peace – by which he (*i.e.* Paul) meant not calm but the life-confidence of reconciliation and co-operation with God' (*Positive Preaching and the Modern Mind*, London, 1949, p. 111).

the same time the thought of the deeper enmity between sinful man and God comes in.[1] Christ, by His atoning death, has done away with the enmity. He has brought about a comprehensive peace, one which includes complete wholeness spiritually, and right relations with God issuing in right relations with man. So completely is Christ identified with this process of making peace that He can be said to be 'our peace'. Nothing could convey more definitely the thought that peace is not of man's devising, but a divine gift (cf. also Gal. 6: 16; Phil. 4: 7; Col. 3: 15).

This thought of a broadly-conceived peace coming from God is important. The New Testament does not regard man in his natural condition as at peace with God. Rather, so long as he is outside Christ, he is at enmity with God 'because the mind of the flesh is enmity against God; for it is not subject to the law of God, neither indeed can it be: and they that are in the flesh cannot please God' (Rom. 8: 7f.). It is unnecessary to labour the point, for it is the common New Testament view of man untouched by the gospel. But it is also the characteristic New Testament teaching that God did not allow matters to rest there. In the Person of Jesus Christ He intervened and brought about a new state of affairs and it is this which is called 'peace'. It includes a great deal more than a cessation of hostility, as we have seen; but it does include this. Indeed, this is the basis of the other blessings included in the conception. It is because a state of peace exists between God and His creation that His will to bless operates unhindered.

We have seen that there are some passages in which this thought of peace is connected explicitly with the atonement wrought by Christ, and such a connection must be postulated of the passages where it is not expressed. For, on the one hand, nothing that man can do can effect this result. And, on the other, something must be done if a state of peace is to come about. Scripture insists upon the

---

[1] Cf. Foerster: 'One will not rightly evaluate the passage if one does not see that the law plays a double role, it divides the heathen from the commonwealth of Israel, and Israel from God. Through the law enmity between Jew and heathen stands opposed, and enmity of man and God. Therefore verse 14, αὐτὸς γάρ ἐστιν ἡ εἰρήνη ἡμῶν, is to be taken in a comprehensive sense: when Christ abolished the law He did away with the double disorder in mankind, that with one another and that against God. εἰρήνη denotes peace with God and peace among mankind, and therewith a comprehensive "order"; a salvation of all relationships' (TWNT, II, pp. 413f.).

seriousness of sin as separating man from God, and never gives countenance to any such thought as that man will one day simply drift into the kingdom of God, forgiven because God is like that. It is only because God in Christ took the initiative that peace could possibly come into existence.

V. THE NEW TESTAMENT CONCEPT OF RECONCILIATION

Such is the evidence upon which we must base our doctrine, and the conclusions which have in fact been drawn from it are diverse. On the one hand many insist that the Scriptures which speak of God as reconciling man to Himself are the significant ones, and that reconciliation takes place when man recognizes his sinfulness and the greatness of God's love. On the other hand there are those who insist upon the objective nature of the atonement, and stress the demands of the holiness of God, of the righteousness of God, and who refuse to dismiss from the consideration of this subject the passages which speak, for example, of the wrath of God.

Perhaps none have argued more fervently for the former position than Dr. J. Oman. He is insistent that God does not need to be reconciled to us. 'To be reconciled is to be forgiven, and to be forgiven is to be reconciled, yet Christ's whole manifestation of the Father depends on putting reconciliation first in our thoughts. We are not reconciled when, upon conditions, God has forgiven us, but we are forgiven when we know that He is waiting to be gracious. No word of religious insight says we need to beseech God to be reconciled to us.'[1] The same writer puts emphasis upon reconciliation as a factor in life here and now, as reconciliation to one's lot. 'As enmity against God is primarily enmity against the lives He has appointed for us, because we insist on using them for other ends than His, so reconciliation to God is primarily reconciliation to our lives by seeking in them only His ends. Its immediate significance is *reconciliation to the discipline He appoints and the duty He demands*. It is thus, in the first place at least, concerned with this life, not another, being the promise of sitting in the heavenly places amid the tumult of the present hour and not of sitting in a remote heaven in a passionless eternity.'[2] He defines

[1] *Grace and Personality* (Cambridge, 1919), p. 217.
[2] *Op. cit.*, pp. 118f. (Oman's italics).

reconciliation: 'Reconciliation to God may be defined as a recognition of God's gracious relation to us through blessedness in our use of the world, our dealings with our fellow-men and our loyalty to His Kingdom.'[1]

We admire the learning and sincerity with which Dr. Oman argues his case, and agree that his contention that God's grace is primary in the manner of reconciliation is essentially right. But when full allowance has been made for all this we must beg leave to doubt whether justice is being done to all the scriptural teaching on the subject, and in particular to that aspect of reconciliation which connects it with the death of the Son of God. On Dr. Oman's view it is hard to see why Christ need have died at all, for all that is necessary is 'a recognition of God's gracious relation to us'. But the Scripture seems insistent that on Calvary something was done which has effects quite outside man. In other words all those passages which indicate an objective atonement cry out for explanation, and on the view we are considering they find none.[2] In the last resort everything depends upon the situation we conceive to result as a consequence of man's sin. If all that sin means is that man has wandered away from God, but that he may one day wander back again with nothing to consider other than his own situation and desires, then such views as the one we have been considering are adequate. But if man has come under condemnation so that the sentence of God is against him, then more is required than repentance if man's rightful relationship to God is to be restored. If God's attitude to sin is expressed in condemnation then God's attitude is involved in reconciliation, for reconciliation cannot come about independently of that condemnation.[3]

Our next point might be introduced by a quotation from James

[1] Op. cit., p. 121.

[2] Vincent Taylor objects to 'the view that reconciliation depends upon man's humble acceptance of the revelation of God made in Christ', saying: 'The real gravamen of the charge is that the attempt to say what the love of Christ does, as distinct from what it reveals, is largely abandoned. Attention is concentrated upon the psychology of man's response to that which, happily he has observed, rather than upon a work of God in Christ which is wrought on his behalf' (Forgiveness and Reconciliation, London, 1946, pp. 107f.).

[3] 'The thing that has to be dealt with, that has to be overcome, in the work of reconciliation, is not man's distrust of God, but God's condemnation of man' (J. Denney, Studies in Theology, London, 1895, p. 103).

Denney, who makes it clear that reconciliation of the type we have been advocating does not carry with it the rider that it was won in the face of God's opposition. Rather, it comes from Him and is entirely due to His desire to bless us. Denney says: 'He is not reconciled in the sense that something is won from Him for us against His will, but in the sense that His will to bless us is realised, as it was not before, on the basis of what Christ has done, and of our appropriation of it.'[1] James S. Stewart notices this statement and comments: 'But is this not using the language of reconciliation in two distinct meanings? Surely what happens on God's side is so essentially different from what happens on man's side that to apply the one term to both can only cause confusion.'[2] To me it seems that, paradoxically, there is truth in both these statements. Denney's statement seems to be correct, for as we have endeavoured to make clear in the foregoing sections, reconciliation in the Scripture depends on more than man's response to God's gracious invitation. Reconciliation matters to God as well as to man, and, as Denney says, 'His will to bless us is realised, as it was not before'.

Nevertheless one must sympathize with Stewart's difficulty, and it is possible that it brings to a head much of the objection to such a view of reconciliation as that advocated by Denney. Denney does not say that reconciliation means the same thing to God as it does to man, and this would probably be admitted to be the truth by most who hold views similar to his. Certainly I am of the opinion that the change which takes place in man is not the same as the change in God. There are unworthy elements in man's most perfect action which are absent from anything that God does; and in any case the situations are different. Man has departed from God by his sin, and erected the barrier which separates the two. The fault for the estrangement lies wholly on man's side. Thus, if reconciliation is to take place, there must be a complete change of attitude on man's past. He must repent of his sin and turn away from it. This has no parallel from God's side.

Moreover, reconciliation as man sees it comes about from outside. But this is not the case with God. God was reconciling the world to Himself. We cannot say that God was reconciled by any third party. Rather He must be thought of as reconciling Himself.

---

[1] The Christian Doctrine of Reconciliation, London, 1918, p. 238.
[2] A Man in Christ (London, 1947), pp. 221f.

Even to say that Christ reconciled God does not give us the true picture, for it suggests a disharmony in the Godhead and also raises a doubt as to the constancy of God's love. But we must insist that God's love for us remained unchanged throughout the process of reconciliation. P. T. Forsyth draws a distinction between 'a change of feeling and a change of treatment', and he goes on to say, 'God's feeling toward us never needed to be changed. But God's treatment of us, God's practical relation to us – that had to change'.[1] The distinction is important. God's love never varied. But the atonement wrought by Christ means that men are no longer treated as enemies (as their sin deserves), but as friends. God has reconciled Himself.

Thus we may speak of God as being reconciled. It may be necessary, indeed it is necessary, to use the term carefully, when we apply it to God. But then does not this happen with all our language? We must face the position that whenever we talk about God we must do so in language devised to describe man, and accordingly there must always be a certain reserve. This applies to reconciliation as well as to other terms. When we say that God is reconciled to man, this does not mean that, with various imperfections, He completely alters His attitude to man. Rather it is our groping way of expressing the conviction that, though He reacts in the strongest possible way against sin in every shape and form so that man comes under His condemnation, yet when reconciliation is effected, when peace is made between man and God, then that condemnation is removed. God now looks on man no longer as the object of His holy and righteous wrath, but as the object of His love and His blessing.

We must not overlook the fact that the relationship between God and man is a mutual affair. Some write as though man were the only factor affecting the position. After they have said 'God is love' there is no longer need to pay attention to the Deity, and all their attention is focused upon what man does.[2] Reconciliation

---

[1] *The Work of Christ* (London, 1948), p. 105. In another place he says: 'The Cross meant more change in God than in man . . . Real and thorough religion is theocentric more than anthropocentric' (*The Justification of God*, London, 1948, p. 37).

[2] *Cf.* W. Milligan's comment on sacrifice and reconciliation: 'The leading or central idea of Sacrifice was not mere pardon of sin, or atonement, or the procuring

becomes then the change in man's attitude to God and that is all. But as A. E. Garvie says: 'When it is said that man is reconciled to God, and not God to man, what is ignored is that the relation of God and man is mutual, and involves a moral reciprocity. We may once for all dismiss as contemptible the current caricatures of evangelical theology that it represents God as implacable and vindictive, when it simply insists that moral perfection cannot be indifferent to moral differences in man, and must condemn sin even as it approves righteousness. This condemnation must be conveyed to and approved by the conscience of the forgiven in the very act of forgiveness.'[1] It is impossible to bow God out of His universe, and to maintain that He is indifferent to the moral condition of His people. His love is consistent and does not alter; but we cannot reason from that that the expression of that love is always the same. Love may be likened to a flame. Without changing its essential nature it may give warmth and light, or it may sear and burn. All that sinful men can see of a holy God is that aspect that we call the wrath of God. But when the Son of God Himself has dealt with that wrath, then men may know the warmth of His love. We do not impugn the consistency of God, but we insist that the relation between God and man is a mutual one, and that this must be borne in mind in understanding the biblical doctrine of reconciliation.[2]

---

of the Divine favour, by which the relation of only one of the two parties to the other – that of God to His creature – was affected; while the love of God, contemplated by faith, was simply left to work as a motive of gratitude upon the heart. The relation of both parties to one another was involved in the Sacrifice itself. That act expressed all that was implied, alike for God and Israel, in the restoration of the covenant. It brought both back into a state of mutual reconciliation and fellowship' (*The Resurrection of Our Lord*, London, 1884, p. 276).

[1] *A Handbook of Christian Apologetics* (London, 1913), p. 121.

[2] *Cf.* P. T. Forsyth: 'Our reconciliation is between person and person. It is not between an order or a process on the one hand and a person on the other. Therefore a real and deep change of the relation between the two means a change on both sides. That is surely clear if we are dealing with living persons.... Any reconciliation which only means change on one side is not a real reconciliation at all' (*The Work of Christ*, London, 1948, p. 75). Or H. Maldwyn Hughes: 'What the Atonement achieves is a change in the relation of persons, and no such change can be brought to pass without both parties being affected. Reconciliation is necessarily twofold ... when God reconciles us to Himself, our relation to Him, and His relation to us are both set on a new basis' (*What is the Atonement?* London, n.d., pp. 20f.).

A further point is that no true reconciliation can take place unless the cause of the estrangement is truly faced and dealt with. If it is ignored or glossed over, then a species of uneasy truce may result, but there can be no real restoration of fellowship, no true reconciliation. As Dr. H. Maldwyn Hughes says: 'there can be no reconciliation between persons by ignoring the deep-seated ground of offence. This must be eradicated and destroyed if the reconciliation is to be complete and lasting. If God and man are to be reconciled, it cannot be by the simple expedient of ignoring sin, but only by overcoming it.'[1] It is the consistent teaching of Scripture that man could not overcome the cause of the enmity. The barrier which the sin of man had erected the wit of man could not find means to remove. But in the death of Him whom God 'made sin' for man the cause of the enmity was squarely faced and removed. Therefore a complete reconciliation results, so that man turns to God in repentance and trust, and God looks on man with favour and not in wrath.

We maintain, therefore, that there is no good reason for rejecting the conclusion to which the biblical evidence points, namely, that reconciliation includes what we must call a change on the part of God as well as on the part of man, since the wrath of God is no longer directed towards man. We may well sum up the position in the words of D. W. Simon: 'Taking the Pauline language in its natural sense, there is no evading the recognition of three points – *first*, that a change – call it by any name that may be liked – was brought about in the relation of God to man as well as in that of man to God; *secondly*, that this change was due to the intervention of Christ; and, *thirdly*, that God Himself was the originator of what may be anthropomorphically termed the plan or method, by which the change in Himself and in man was brought about and justified.'[2]

VI. RECONCILIATION AND SUBSTITUTION

Throughout this discussion substitution has been very much in the background, for the very good reason that reconciliation has in itself no very close connection with substitution. Reconciliation

---

[1] *Op. cit.*, p. 146.
[2] *The Redemption of Man* (London, 1906), pp. 271f.

has to do with the bringing about of harmonious relations where these did not exist before, and the metaphor directs attention to an estrangement and to the overcoming of that estrangement. The metaphor in itself is concerned only with these things.

But in the particular manner in which the estrangement is overcome it is possible that substitution may occur. In the particular case of the atonement the root cause of the estrangement is man's sin; so long as that sin is there, harmony with God is impossible. Accordingly reconciliation proceeds by doing away with sin, and the method of doing this was by the atoning death of Christ. Whatever may be the case with other acts of reconciliation, Scripture is clear that the reconciliation between God and man could be brought about only by the death of the Son of God. Accordingly we may discern a substitutionary element, for as Büchsel says, 'The reconciliation comes into existence through the death of Jesus (Rom. 5: 10), which here obviously not only benefits us, (being) a revelation of the love of God (Rom. 5: 8), but is a substitution for us (2 Cor. 5: 20, 14f.).'[1]

---

[1] *TWNT*, I, p. 258.

CHAPTER VIII

JUSTIFICATION (1)

I. INTRODUCTION

THE FIRST IMPRESSION ONE RECEIVES on turning to the subject of justification after dealing with the concepts examined in the earlier chapters of this book is that the material to be considered is very abundant. We have noted that propitiation, although an important conception, is used with reference to the atonement only four times in all in the New Testament. Similarly reconciliation, in which some modern scholars are inclined to see the essential New Testament teaching with regard to the atonement, occurs in only five passages, all of them Pauline. By contrast, he who would expound justification is confronted with eighty-one occurrences of the adjective δίκαιος, ninety-two of the noun δικαιοσύνη, two of the noun δικαίωσις, thirty-nine of the verb δικαιόω, ten of the noun δικαίωμα, and five of the adverb δικαίως. On examination much of this may prove to have little relevance to the atonement, but it remains that the bare enumeration of the number of passages to be considered indicates that we are here dealing with a conception of great importance for the evaluation of the atonement. The tendency in some quarters to disparage the importance of justification in comparison with one or other of the alternative ways of looking at God's great work for men is not one which is reflected in our sources. Particularly is this true of St. Paul who uses the conception so frequently that we are compelled to think that for him it was a dominant idea.

The derivation of the root from which these words are derived is shrouded in obscurity. What emerges from the discussion is that the two meanings of 'custom' and 'right' seem to go back as far as we can trace the words. Accordingly, if our endeavour is simply to find out what the word-group meant in New Testament times, the search for the original root meaning is largely academic. For centuries these two ideas had been conveyed by the words in question. At least this is clear for δίκη,[1] which is possibly the basic word of the group, though it is not possible to authenticate it for all the members. But as used in the first century there does seem to be a flavour of 'rightness', of 'justness' about these words. They do not indicate something arbitrary, but something in conformity with some standard of right. The righteous man is one who is adjudged right by such a standard, and righteousness indicates a state of having attained to the standard in question.

It is necessary to say a word or two more about the verb δικαιόω which in the New Testament is translated 'to justify' but which has been understood in more ways than one. Since verbs in -όω commonly express a causative idea it is urged by some that δικαιόω must mean 'to make righteous'. But in the first place verbs of this class denoting moral qualities do not have the causative meaning (*e.g.* ἀξιόω means 'to deem worthy' not 'to make worthy' and similarly with ὁμοιόω, ὁσιόω, *etc.*). And in any case the meaning of a word is to be determined in the last resort by the way people used it. We cannot say that, since a verb is formed in such and such a fashion, therefore the Greeks must have understood it to mean so and so. All that we can do is to note how they did in fact use it, and deduce from that what it meant to them. By this test δικαιόω certainly does not mean 'to make righteous'. In Greek literature generally it seems to mean 'to hold as right', 'to deem right', and thence 'to claim or demand as a right', and 'to do a man right or justice'. This latter was commonly taken to mean 'to punish for wickedness' so that, interestingly enough, in many profane contexts the thought is that of chastisement, in striking contrast with the use in the Bible. Neither the word structure nor the use of the verb outside the Bible, then, gives countenance to the idea that 'to make righteous' is the meaning we are to understand.[2]

---

[1] See, for example, the evidence cited by W. K. C. Guthrie, *The Greeks and their Gods* (Boston, 1956), pp. 123–7.

[2] F. Godet goes so far as to say: 'As to δικαιόω, there is not an example in the whole of classic literature where it signifies: *to make just*' (*Commentary on St. Paul's Epistle to the Romans*, I, Edinburgh, n.d., p. 157). J. Morison (*Critical Exposition of the Third Chapter of Paul's Epistle to the Romans*, London, 1866, pp. 179, 183) and A. Plummer (*ICC, St. Luke*, p. 208) have similar statements.

II. LAW AND JUDGMENT IN THE OLD TESTAMENT

There is in the LXX a wealth of material for the student of justification. The words for 'righteous', 'righteousness', *etc.* occur
hundreds of times and even this is not the whole story. The
thoughts of righteousness, justification and the rest are inextricably
bound up with other concepts like those of judgment, pleading in
the law court, and, especially, law itself. Even in a short treatment
it is necessary to take some notice of this, for it has the effect of
putting justification in its context. Justification is not an isolated
concept. It is part of a whole way of viewing God and the world
which sees in law a means of understanding the divine ordering of
things. To the men of the Old Testament God was a God of law,[1]
and a very great deal in their religion cannot be understood if this is
lost sight of.

The importance of law as a category for understanding the ways
of God is seen in Abraham's question, 'Shall not the Judge of all the
earth do right?' (Gn. 18: 25). God is designated by the legal term,
'Judge'. His relationship to the whole earth may be expressed in
legal categories. And the question gives expression to the certainty
that He will act in accordance with moral law. The gods of the
heathen could not be depended on in this way. They might be
expected to react in the most capricious fashion. Not so Jehovah.
This difference in understanding the connection of the deity with
law may well be the basic reason for the superiority of the religion
of Israel to those of the nations round about. Yahweh's actions
were always in accordance with law. He could be depended upon
to act righteously. And because He was righteous He demanded of
His people that they should also act righteously, act in accordance
with ethical law. If they did not, then this same ethical nature of
Yahweh demanded that He should punish them. It was inevitable
that the wrath of God should be the divine reaction to all sin. The
Hebrew could depend on it. It was God's nature to act in this way.
Jeremiah can say, 'Yea, the stork in the heaven knoweth her

---

[1] H. G. G. Herklots even goes as far as to say, 'He was *law*' (*A Fresh Approach to
the New Testament*, London, 1950, p. 18; Herklots' italics). *Cf.* P. T. Forsyth, 'The
holy law is not the creation of God but His nature' (*The Atonement in Modern
Religious Thought: A Theological Symposium*, London, 1903, p. 79).

appointed times; and the turtle and the swallow and the crane observe the time of their coming; but my people know not the judgement of the Lord' (Je. 8: 7, mg.). Judgment is as natural to the Lord as the movements of the birds are to them.

Judgment[1] and justification are often connected. The Psalmist can pray, 'Enter not into judgement with thy servant; for in thy sight shall no man living be justified' (Ps. 143: 2), which shows quite plainly that the two ideas are linked. But perhaps the most decisive passage occurs in Deuteronomy: 'If there be a controversy between men, and they come unto judgement, and the judges judge them; then they shall justify the righteous, and condemn the wicked' (Dt. 25: 1). Justification is clearly part of the whole process of judgment. When men have a controversy they come to the judges. The process whereby their dispute is resolved is called 'judgment'. And in the judgment when the verdict is given in favour of one party he is said to be 'justified'. Justification is clearly the declaration in favour of a party to a law-suit. Many passages could be cited linking justification with some aspect or other of judgment.[2] They make it very plain that righteousness is in the Old Testament bound up with legal conceptions. Some study of the latter must accordingly be attempted.

The word which leaps to the mind when one speaks of law in the Old Testament is tôrâh, which may be defined as 'direction, instruction, law' (BDB). Whether we take the basic idea to be 'law' or, as probably most modern scholars would prefer, as 'instruction', it is not in dispute that it is closely associated with Yahweh. In more than eighty of its 220 occurrences it is explicitly said to be His ('the law of Yahweh', 'my law', 'thy law', etc.). A further sixteen times it is ascribed to Moses which, in view of the fact that the Old Testament uniformly regards the patriarch as having received the law from God, amounts to much the same thing. In most other places it seems to be implied that the tôrâh is from the Lord. In fact I have been able to find no more than seventeen places where it

---

[1] For the concept of judgment see further my *The Biblical Doctrine of Judgment* (London, 1960).

[2] *E.g.* Pss. 51: 4; 143: 2; Is. 43: 9, 26; 50: 8. So also 'the thoughts of the righteous are judgement' (Pr. 12: 5). Even a full list of such passages would not tell the whole story, for judgment may be regarded as an integral part of righteousness without any of the righteousness words actually being used (*e.g.* Zc. 8: 16f.).

seems clear that the word is used of anything other than a law from God.[1]

If anything, this is even more striking with other words for law. Thus from the root *ḥqq* we derive the description of Yahweh as 'our lawgiver' (Is. 33: 22), and two words for 'statute', *ḥōq* and *ḥuqqāh*. The former is directly connected with Yahweh in 87 of its 127 occurrences and the latter in no less than 96 out of 104. The bare statistics are enough to show that Yahweh was thought of as One who has a deep interest in law. And the statistics are reinforced by the way in which the words are used. Thus the phenomena of nature are governed by law. God makes 'a statute for the rain' (Jb. 28: 26), and an 'everlasting statute' which governs the limits of the sea (Je. 5: 22). It is from such ordinances as these that Jeremiah can reason to the continuing mercy of the Lord (Je. 31: 36). Law is thus not simply a demand that God makes on His people: it is the way in which He administers His universe. He can be relied to act according to law.

We might draw similar conclusions from other legal terms. The noun *mishpāṭ* is connected with Yahweh about 180 times, often in the sense of 'laws' (when it differs but little from the words we have already considered).[2] It may also be used more generally, sometimes linked with the righteousness words, *e.g.* 'Thy righteousness is like the mountains of God; thy judgements are a great deep' (Ps. 36: 6); 'I am the Lord which exercise lovingkindness, judgement, and righteousness, in the earth: for in these things I delight, saith the Lord' (Je. 9: 24). Here judgment and righteousness seem to be part of the essential nature of the Lord, and it agrees with this that the verb *shāphāṭ*, which is used of the divine activity over sixty times, may be used in the participial form to denote the Lord as Judge (Ps. 50: 6; Jdg. 11: 27).

---

[1] It is often pointed out that *tôrâh* is used of priestly instruction (as in Je. 2: 8; 18: 18; Ezk. 7: 26; Ho. 4: 6; Hg. 2: 11; Mal. 2: 6, 7, 8, 9, *etc.*). But, though a priestly *tôrâh* be recognized, it was clearly held to be due not to the priests themselves, but to the Lord (Ho. 4: 6; Mal. 2: 6ff.).

[2] N. H. Snaith distinguishes between *tôrâh* and *mishpāṭ*: 'They are different in that *torah*, at this early stage, meant an original pronouncement, whilst *mishpaṭ* meant a decision according to precedent. But both equally are the word of God' (*The Distinctive Ideas of the Old Testament*, London, 1944, p. 75). On the other hand J. Pedersen maintains that *mishpāṭ* is 'the same as *ḥōḳ* (the established), *tōrā* (instruction), *miṣwā* (tradition)' (*Israel*, I–II, London, 1926, p. 351).

The list could be continued. The root *ykh* is employed to tell us that 'he shall judge between many peoples, and shall reprove strong nations afar off' (Mi. 4: 3; *cf.* Is. 11: 4 and the 'daysman' of Jb. 9: 33). Similarly *dyn* may be used in a beautifully trustful appeal to the Lord as Judge, an appeal moreover based on the fact that the Judge is 'the righteous God' (Ps. 7: 8f.). *ríbh* may be used of Yahweh's interventions on behalf of His people ('Blessed be the Lord, that hath pleaded the cause of my reproach from the hand of Nabal', 1 Sa. 25: 39; *cf.* also Je. 50: 34; Is. 50: 8, the last-mentioned being notable for its connection of justification with legal processes). Or it may refer to the Lord's accusations against His people (Is. 45: 9; 57: 16; Je. 2: 9, 29, *etc.*).

Nor would the story be complete if we went through all the technical legal terms. There are verbs like *shlm* which have no necessary legal significance, but which yet are relevant. When, for example, Adoni-bezek says, 'as I have done, so God hath requited me' (Jdg. 1: 7), he is clearly implying that he has been judged by God and dealt with on the basis of that judgment. The thought is carried further by Jeremiah, who says that 'the Lord is a God of recompences (*'ēl gemūlôth*), he shall surely requite' (Je. 51: 56; *cf.* 2 Sa. 3: 39). 'Thou renderest to every man according to his work' (Ps. 62: 12) is the general principle, and many passages could be cited to show its operation. Words like *pqd* are often used to convey the thought of the Lord's righteous activity in judging men.

We should not overlook the significance of the use of *shephāṭîm* to denote God's mighty acts. To take an example, the Lord says, 'I will lay my hand upon Egypt, and bring forth my hosts, my people the children of Israel, out of the land of Egypt by great judgements' (Ex. 7: 4; so also Ex. 6: 6; 12: 12; Nu. 33: 4; Ezk. 5: 10, *etc.*). The series of events leading up to the deliverance of Israel might well be regarded as a signal display of the divine power. Instead they are viewed as an exercise in judgment. They are viewed in terms not merely of might, but of justice. All is in accordance with law.

Significant also is the fact that the men of the Old Testament sometimes seem to go out of their way to use legal illustrations when they have the divine activity in mind. Today we are inclined to be suspicious of 'legalism'. Indeed, if we can convict an opponent of too great an interest in law we are half-way to confuting him. No-one today is interested in a legalist. But we should not read this attitude back into antiquity. Legal categories were used not by way of compulsion, because the legal facts were plain and must be stated. They were used from choice. They were eagerly seized on and used with delight. The men of the Old Testament loved a good legal scene, and they never tire of depicting their God as taking part in one. 'The Lord standeth up to plead, and standeth to judge the peoples. The Lord will enter into judgement with the elders of his people' (Is. 3: 13); 'the Lord sitteth for ever: he hath prepared his throne for judgement. And he shall judge the world in righteousness, he shall minister judgement to the peoples in up-rightness' (Ps. 9: 7f.). Or consider the very majestic legal scene depicted by Micah, 'Hear ye now what the Lord saith: Arise, contend thou before the mountains, and let the hills hear thy voice. Hear, O ye mountains, the Lord's controversy, and ye enduring foundations of the earth: for the Lord hath a controversy with his people, and he will plead with Israel' (Mi. 6: 1f.; cf. Is. 41: 1, 21; 50: 8; Je. 25: 31). The list could be prolonged. Yahweh and law went well together.

It is in accordance with this outlook that men can wish to plead, as in a law-court, before the Lord (Jb. 23: 3f.; Je. 12: 1). We some-times come across statements like 'he is not a man, as I am, that I should answer him, that we should come together in judgement' (Jb. 9: 32). Such passages make plain the immense gulf between God and man. They do not modify the principle that God delights in law and judgment.

The interest in law is to be discerned also from the fact that God requires men to exercise judgment (Ps. 33: 5; Pr. 21: 3; Is. 5: 7; 56: 1, etc.). The repeated prediction of an eschatological judgment (Is. 32: 1; Je. 23: 5; 33: 15, etc.) is also significant. Judgment is not a temporary accommodation to man's present position. It endures to the end of time.

We cannot leave this section of our subject without noticing that covenant is a legal conception. As we noted in the chapter on that subject, covenant is the characteristic way of viewing the relation-ship between God and His people. It was the covenant which gave Israel its standing in the eyes of God. Now a legal basis is inherent in the very nature of covenant (cf. Jos. 24: 25), and often this comes

to the surface, for example in 1 Chronicles 16: 17 (= Ps. 105: 10),
'And confirmed the same unto Jacob for a statute, to Israel for an
everlasting covenant'. Here the parallelism makes 'statute' very
nearly the same thing as 'covenant'. Or, again, Jeremiah applies the
concept of law in nature to illustrate covenant: 'Thus saith the
Lord: If my covenant of day and night stand not, if I have not
appointed the ordinances of heaven and earth; then will I also cast
away the seed of Jacob,' etc. (Je. 33: 25f.). The orderly movement of
day and night is spoken of as itself due to a covenant with the Lord,
thus equating covenant and law; then this is applied to show the
permanence of the covenant with the nation.

From this brief examination it seems quite clear that the Old
Testament consistently thinks of a God who works by the method
of law. This is not the conception of one or two writers but is
found everywhere. It is attested by a variety of conceptions, many
of them taken straight from forensic practices. Among the heathen
the deity was thought of as above all law, with nothing but his
own desires to limit him. Accordingly his behaviour was completely unpredictable, and while he made demands on his worshippers for obedience and service, there were few if any ethical
implications of this service and none of a logically necessary kind.
Far otherwise was it with the God of the Hebrews. The Old
Testament never conceives of anything outside Him which can
direct His actions, and we must be on our guard against the
thought of a law which is over Him. But Yahweh was thought of
as essentially righteous in His nature, as incorporating the law of
righteousness within His essential Being. Accordingly He works
by a method which may be called law – He inevitably punishes
evil-doing and rewards righteousness. He himself acts righteously,
and He demands that His people do the same. This is the consistent
teaching of the Old Testament. As G. Quell says, 'That God lays
down the right and as a righteous God is bound to right means for
Old Testament piety with all its variation, a proposition which
may not be surrendered'.[1] Thus, as we approach the question of
the use of justification in the Old Testament, we are dealing not
with an isolated conception which appears briefly now and then,
but with an idea of law which runs through and through the
ancient Scriptures.

[1] TWNT, II, p. 178.

III. THE δίκαιος WORD-GROUP IN THE SEPTUAGINT

In both Hebrew and Greek 'justification' and words like 'righteous-ness', *etc.*, come from the same root (which fact in itself shows the essentially forensic meaning of the word-group). Our net must therefore be widely cast. So frequent are these words that it will not be possible in a brief examination to do more than glance at a few passages. But we trust that these are representative.

a. Justification

The basic significance of the Hebrew root *tsdq*, from which the righteousness and justification words take their origin, has been the cause of much discussion, the derivations receiving most support being those which see the essential idea in the notions of hardness and straightness. We cannot here enter into a discussion of the merits of the various suggestions put forward, and can only lay it down that such considerations as those adduced by Snaith[1] seem to indicate that the latter is the idea to be preferred, and that the word-group points us to the thought of a standard. '*Tsedeq*, with its kindred words, signifies that standard which God maintains in this world. It is the norm by which all must be judged. What this norm is, depends entirely upon the Nature of God.'[2] If this is so, then the idea of righteousness is conformity to God's standard, and justification will be a process in which this conformity is either attained, or declared to be attained.

When we turn to those passages where the verb 'to justify' occurs, there can be no doubt that the meaning is to declare righteous rather than to make righteous. Thus we find a direction that the judges 'shall justify the righteous, and condemn the wicked' (Dt. 25: 1). The forensic background is unmistakable and the verb can mean only 'to declare righteous' or 'to acquit'. The same usage is seen in 'I will not justify the wicked' (Ex. 23: 7), and in the woe to them that 'justify the wicked for reward' (Is. 5: 23). The legal content of the term is brought out from another angle when we read, 'let them bring forth their witnesses that they may be justified' (Is. 43: 9), where legal proof based on the testimony of witnesses is the ground for justification.

---

[1] *Op. cit.*, pp. 72ff.
[2] *Op. cit.*, p. 77.

These are typical passages, and although there are places where the forensic note is not so strong they do not invalidate our conviction that the basic idea is one of acquittal. Both in Hebrew and Greek the verb in question is capable of being used in a variety of non-legal contexts, quite like our verb 'to judge'. But again, like this verb, the Hebrew and Greek verbs in question remind us of processes of law, and take their essential meaning from those processes of law. That a declaratory process rather than a making righteous is meant is clear from the fact that the verb is applied to Jehovah (Ps. 51: 4), for it is an impossible thought that He should be 'made righteous' in any sense other than 'made righteous before men' or 'declared righteous'.

Finally, let us notice the important words of the psalmist: 'enter not into judgement with thy servant: for in thy sight shall no man living be justified' (Ps. 143: 2). Here we are face to face with the ultimate question in religion, and the conclusion is that it is impossible for any man to have confidence in his standing before God on the ground of his deeds.

b. *The righteousness of men*

The noun and the adjective from this root reveal the same essentially forensic significance. The righteous are those acquitted at the bar of God's justice, and righteousness is the standing of those so acquitted. Thus J. Skinner explains his view that in the Old Testament 'the forensic element preponderates' in the idea of righteousness by saying: 'what is meant is that questions of right and wrong were habitually regarded from a legal point of view as matters to be settled by a judge, and that this point of view is emphasized in the words derived from *tsdq*. This, indeed, is characteristic of the Heb. conception of righteousness in all its developments: whether it be a moral quality or a religious status, it is apt to be looked on as in itself controvertible and incomplete until it has been confirmed by what is equivalent to a judicial sentence.'[1] The Hebrew concept is not grasped by making a facile equation with the Greek δικαιοσύνη or the English 'righteousness';

---

[1] *HDB*, IV, p. 273. *Cf.* L. Köhler the righteous man 'means primarily the one who, when accused of a crime, is in a position to prove his innocence,' *Hebrew Man* (London, 1956), p. 174.

it is not an ethical term, but a religious. It takes its origin in the forensic sphere and makes its home in the law of God.

The forensic background to the concept is seen clearly in such a passage as Isaiah 5: 23, which pronounces a woe upon them that 'take away the righteousness of the righteous from him', for obviously a moral quality cannot be taken away from a man. What is meant is that wicked judges will, for the sake of gain, give the verdict to the wrong party, thus depriving the innocent of the status of acquittal which is his due. This is the sin which is described as 'condemning the just (or righteous)' (Pr. 17: 15), while in Proverbs 24: 23f. to say to the wicked 'Thou art righteous' is apparently an illustration of the saying 'It is not good to have respect to persons in judgment'. An instructive passage along similar lines is Deuteronomy 16: 18–20, where words from the *tsdq* root ('just', 'righteous') are freely intermingled with legal terms ('judges', 'judgement', *etc.*).

Such intermingling is far from being rare, and indeed 'to do judgement and justice' is a stock Old Testament phrase. There are also references to 'violent perverting of judgement and justice' (Ec. 5: 8) and the like. In the same category we must place Amos's impassioned plea, 'Let judgement run down as waters, and righteousness as a mighty stream' (Am. 5: 24).

The forensic use of words from this root is often found in the book of Job, as when the patriarch says: 'Behold now, I have ordered my cause; I know that I shall be justified' (Jb. 13: 18). Here he can mean only that he will be declared righteous, as by a judge giving sentence in a lawsuit. So also, when the Lord says to Job, 'Wilt thou also disannul my judgement? wilt thou condemn me, that thou mayest be righteous?' (Jb. 40: 8), the forensic note of the passage and the opposition of condemning to being righteous show that 'righteous' here means something very like 'declared righteous legally'. It is this which gives us the background against which we must understand the question thrice repeated with slight changes: 'How should man be just with God?' (Jb. 9: 2, and see 15: 14; 25: 4). In each case it is standing with the Lord that is in question, and the implication is that man is completely unable of himself to attain such right standing.

It is, of course, true that 'righteous' comes to have an ethical meaning and in many passages this is to be stressed. But this meaning develops naturally out of the forensic idea and we need not doubt that the legal idea is the basic one.

c. The righteousness of God

The Old Testament consistently thinks of Jehovah as a just (or righteous) God. He is often depicted as a Judge, for example, 'the heavens shall declare his righteousness: for God is judge himself' (Ps. 50: 6); 'he cometh to judge the earth: he shall judge the world with righteousness' (Ps. 96: 13); 'the Lord of hosts shall be exalted in judgement' (Is. 5: 16). It is clear that the men of the Old Testament delighted to view God in His capacity as Judge.

An interesting insight into the stress placed on this aspect of the divine nature is to be found in an expression in the Song of Deborah. With reference to recalling the great deliverance wrought by the Lord the singer says: 'there shall they rehearse the righteous acts (mg. righteousnesses) of the Lord' (Jdg. 5: 11). The actions in question were, of course, displays of power. But the thing which appealed to the Hebrew was that they were not simply displays of power, they were evidence of the righteous nature of their God. 'The righteous Lord loveth righteousness' (Ps. 11: 7). Nor is this regarded as temporary, but as a permanent element in God, for He can say, 'my righteousness shall not be abolished . . . my righteousness shall be for ever' (Is. 51: 6, 8).

It is implied in the thought that God is the righteous Judge that He demands right living on the part of men. This is expressed so often in the Old Testament that it is superfluous to make quotations to prove it. It is fundamental that the Lord has set His law before men and that He expects them to walk therein.

A very interesting feature of Old Testament teaching on the righteousness of God is that it is often linked with salvation, as when the psalmist says: 'The Lord hath made known his salvation: his righteousness hath he openly showed' (Ps. 98: 2), or when the prophet gives the words of the Lord; 'my salvation shall be for ever, and my righteousness shall not be abolished' (Is. 51: 6). This connection is met with sufficiently often for us to think that it is not accidental; righteousness includes a salvation aspect. But it is always a salvation in accordance with ethical laws, a salvation which accords with righteousness. It is a deliverance of the people of God, who are proper objects of such deliverance just because they are the people of God. In passing we note that this is not the same as the New Testament teaching on the righteousness of God. There we have the different thought that 'the righteousness of God' brings salvation (and salvation in a fuller sense) to sinners.[1]

d. Imputed righteousness

In view of the importance of the concept of imputed righteousness for New Testament doctrine we must notice its occurrence in the Old Testament, although it cannot be thought of as a leading Old Testament idea. It is recorded that Abram 'believed in the Lord; and he counted it to him for righteousness' (Gn. 15: 6). Again, Phinehas stood up, 'and executed judgement: and so the plague was stayed. And that was counted unto him for righteousness unto all generations for evermore' (Ps. 106: 30f.). Both men are brought into right relationship with God: they are given the status of being 'right' with Him. In the case of Phinehas there is an action that is applauded, but the motive is important, as we see from Numbers 25: 11: 'he was zealous for my sake among them.' These two examples, and especially that of Abram, are important as showing that men might be reckoned as righteous before God on grounds other than that of having lived meritorious lives.

IV. THE PLACE OF FAITH

Since we can scarcely think of the New Testament doctrine of justification without adding 'by faith', it is worth our while to inquire whether this has roots in the Old Testament, or whether it was a completely new thought in New Testament times. Certainly Paul did not think he was enunciating an entirely novel doctrine, for he speaks of Abraham as being justified in the same way as Christians of his own day, namely by faith. Indeed, he uses the example of that patriarch as a means of showing to the men of his day that God has always worked on the principle that men are justified by faith.

There is no formal statement of the doctrine in the Old Testament, and if we look for a complete enunciation of this truth we shall be disappointed. For that we must wait until New Testament days. But the essence of the doctrine is there nevertheless. If we

[1] See below, pp. 277ff.

understand justification by faith to include this at least, that man is accepted in the sight of God, not on the grounds of what he himself has accomplished, but on account of the divine mercy shown in forgiving love, there are many passages which may be cited. So, too, if we are seeking an indication that the proper attitude on the part of man is trust in God and not in his own deeds we shall not have far to look.

Thus, as regards acceptance on the grounds of the divine mercy, God's gift is completely unearned: 'Ho every one that thirsteth, come ye to the waters, and he that hath no money; come ye, buy, and eat; yea, come, buy wine and milk without money and without price' (Is. 55: 1). The ground on which men are accepted is clearly God's mercy and not their own deeds: 'Seek ye the Lord while he may be found: call ye upon him while he is near: let the wicked forsake his way, and the unrighteous man his thoughts: and let him return unto the Lord, and he will have mercy upon him; and to our God, for he will abundantly pardon' (Is. 55: 6f.). Again, Micah can say: 'Who is a God like unto thee, that pardoneth iniquity, and passeth by the transgression of the remnant of his heritage? he retaineth not his anger for ever, because he delighteth in mercy. He will turn again, he will have compassion upon us; he will subdue our iniquities; and thou wilt cast all their sins into the depths of the sea' (Mi. 7: 18f.), while his next verse, 'Thou wilt perform the truth to Jacob, and the mercy to Abraham, which thou hast sworn unto our fathers from the days of old', takes us back to the patriarchal age quite in the manner of St. Paul. It is as though he would say: 'God deals with men in mercy and has always dealt with them so.'

These are great passages and express great thoughts. We might continue for long without exhausting the supply, for the mercy of God is one of the leading conceptions of the Old Testament. It is integral to Israel's faith that the Lord is a God of mercy – 'his compassions fail not; they are new every morning' (La. 3: 22f.). Accordingly, wherever men have a profound sense of sin God is recognized as man's only hope: 'If thou, Lord, shouldest mark iniquities, O Lord, who shall stand? But there is forgiveness with thee . . . I wait for the Lord, my soul doth wait, and in his word do I hope' (Ps. 130: 3–5). So in the prayer of Daniel 9 the sin of the people is stressed (verses 5ff.), but there is nevertheless an atmos-

phere of hope, for 'to the Lord our God belong mercies and forgivenesses' (verse 9), and 'we do not present our supplications
before thee for our righteousnesses, but for thy great mercies'
(verse 18).

This conception almost carries with it the other point that man's
right attitude to God is one of trust, for if acceptance is due to God's
mercy then man obviously cannot rely on what he himself does.
He must rest his faith elsewhere. It is this which underlies Habakkuk
2: 4, 'the just shall live by his faith'. The Hebrew word '*emûnâh*, as
E. H. Gifford notes,[1] usually conveys the thought of fidelity rather
than of trust, of 'the faith which may be relied on, rather than the
faith which relies'. But, for a Hebrew, faithfulness under difficult
circumstances could arise only from reliance on Jehovah, so that
the two thoughts are not really so far apart. We may well feel that
the Greek versions are justified when they render the word by
πίστις, and the English versions when they translate 'faith'. But,
however we translate, the thought of the verse is that the righteous
will live by his constant reliance on God.

Be that as it may, there is no lack of passages indicating the importance of trust in the Lord. Thus the psalmist sings: 'I have
trusted in thy mercy; my heart shall rejoice in thy salvation' (Ps.
13: 5), while nothing could more fully express the attitude of
humble dependence upon God than the words of another psalm:
'Our soul waiteth for the Lord: he is our help and our shield. For
our heart shall rejoice in him; because we have trusted in his holy
name. Let thy mercy, O Lord, be upon us, according as we hope
in thee' (Ps. 33: 20–22). There are many similar passages in the
Psalms, but the conception is by no means confined to them. Thus
Nehemiah thinks of Abraham's acceptance with God and says:
'Thou . . . foundest his heart faithful before thee' (Ne. 9: 8), while
the prophet expresses his confidence in the words: 'Behold, God is
my salvation; I will trust, and not be afraid: for the Lord Jehovah
is my strength and my song; he also is become my salvation' (Is.
12: 2). Again we find passages like, 'Thou wilt keep him in perfect
peace, whose mind is stayed on thee; because he trusteth in thee.
Trust ye in the Lord for ever: for in the Lord Jehovah is everlasting
strength' (Is. 26: 3f.). This too is a list which might be continued
almost indefinitely, for trust in the Lord is evident throughout the

[1] *The Epistle of St. Paul to the Romans* (London, 1886), p. 62.

Old Testament. But enough has been said to indicate the position, and we close this section by drawing attention to the fact that this attitude of trust is connected now and then with one or other of the words from the *tsdq* group, as in Psalm 64: 10: 'The righteous shall be glad in the Lord, and shall trust in him,' or Psalm 31: 1: 'In thee, O Lord, do I put my trust; let me never be ashamed: deliver me in thy righteousness.'

V. JUSTIFICATION AND FAITH IN JUDAISM

The forensic meaning which we have seen to lie at the basis of justification in the Old Testament is, if anything, intensified in the Rabbinic writings. There is a lively interest in the whole subject, and it is everywhere assumed that being righteous means being accepted with God because acquitted by His judgment.

The judgment of God is thought of in several ways. There is the conception of a judgment being worked out now, and thus 'At four times in the year is the world judged'.[1] The thought is quite common that every year on New Year's Day God weighs the merits and demerits of men, assigning rewards and punishments, but that He then gives them until the Day of Atonement to repent of their misdoings before His decree becomes unalterable.[2] But upon them who do not repent He visits His wrath, and thus we get the conception of temporal punishments.

But the judgment in the world to come is more important, and there are many references to it. 1 Enoch 1–5 is taken up with a description of this judgment, and there is a well-known passage in Wisdom which describes how the righteous only 'seemed to have died . . . For even if in the sight of men they be punished, their hope is full of immortality; and having borne a little chastening, they shall receive great good. . . . But the ungodly shall be requited,' *etc.* (Wisdom 3: 2–10, RV), and again: 'They shall come, when their sins are reckoned up, with coward fear' (4: 20, RV). This final judgment will be with complete justice: 'Thou hast judged well, Thou hast condemned well, and well provided Gehenna for the wicked and Paradise for the righteous.'[3]

---

[1] Mishnah, *R.H.* i. 2. The times are Passover, Pentecost, New Year, and Tabernacles.

[2] See for example b *R.H.* 17a, b.

[3] b *Erub.* 19a (Soncino trans., p. 129).

The very nature of this judgment presupposes that man is able to acquire merit in the sight of God by his own efforts, and we find this assumed throughout the Rabbinic literature. If we may take a typical statement: 'When R. Eliezer fell ill, his disciples went in to visit him. They said to him: Master, teach us the paths of life so that we may through them win the life of the future world. He said to them: Be solicitous for the honour of your colleagues, and keep your children from meditation, and set them between the knees of scholars, and when you pray know before whom you are standing and in this way you will win the future world.'[1]

As R. Eliezer is dated *c*. AD 90 we have a statement of the Jewish view not far removed from New Testament times, and it shows us clearly that the Judaism of that time took it as an axiom that man is able to acquire merit in God's eyes, the only question being how it was to be done. Many answers are given to this question, and in general we may say that good deeds rest on some law of God, merit being acquired by keeping His commandments. The study of the Torah and the doing of almsdeeds are mentioned especially often.

Every good deed was thought to have a certain quantum of merit attached to its performance, while similarly every evil deed incurred a corresponding portion of demerit. The final judgment represented a weighing up of the merits and demerits acquired by a man during the course of his lifetime, and this is often represented as a weighing in the scales. If the good deeds outweighed the bad, then the man was adjudged righteous, and entered into blessedness, whereas, if the bad deeds predominated, Gehenna was his portion. This is very important for our study, because the writers of the various books of the New Testament were for the most part pious Jews, and we should be clear that first-century Judaism thought of the righteous not so much as those possessed of certain moral qualities, as of those who obtained the verdict at the tribunal of God. 'Righteous' was a forensic term.[2] Of course it is possible that the Christian writers repudiated this as they did much of the Jewish system, but we shall require evidence for this. We cannot merely assume it.

Certain consequences follow from the Jewish system. One of

[1] b *Ber.* 28b (Soncino trans., p. 173).
[2] On this point see SB, IV, pp. 3–19.

them is that there is no place for assurance. No matter how well a man may have lived, it is always possible for him to slip into some bad sin which will outweigh all his merits. Hence the dictum of Hillel: 'trust not in thyself until the day of thy death.'[1] Also man does not know the precise amount of merit attached to each good deed, and so cannot know where he stands. *Berakhoth* 28b gives us a moving picture of an aged Rabbi who, although a good man, was facing death with alarm, not knowing whether he was bound for Paradise or Gehenna. Such uncertainty seems inevitable if the Rabbinic presuppositions are taken seriously, and it forms a striking contrast with the Christian's assurance of salvation.

Also it leaves little place for the mercy of God. It is true that the Rabbinic writings delight to dwell on the mercy of the Lord, but in practice they leave little room for this mercy to operate. It has some scope, as for example when a man's merits and demerits are equal. Then God presses down the merit side of the scales. But in general man ultimately decides his own eternal destiny by his own deeds, and the function of God is that of a just Judge.

Finally we must mention briefly that Judaism attached importance to faith. But the faith meant was rather a species of intellectual belief than what Christianity knows as faith. It was regarded as itself one of the many meritorious works, so that he who exercised it acquired merit before God. There is nothing in Judaism to match the enthusiastic allegiance to, and committal of oneself to, a person, which means so much for the Christian idea of faith.

---

[1] *Ab.* ii. 5.

270

CHAPTER IX

JUSTIFICATION (2)

I. NEW TESTAMENT TEACHING

IT IS IMPORTANT TO APPROACH the subject of justification in the New Testament by way of the Old Testament and later Jewish writings. Many have fallen into serious error by taking it for granted that everyone knows what 'righteous' and 'righteousness' mean, even if there may be room for a little discussion on 'justification'. In the Scriptures 'righteousness' does not have exactly the same meaning as it has come to have in western civilization of the twentieth century, or that it had in profane Greek of the first. The words of this group were associated in non-biblical Greek with ethical conduct. Thus δικαιοσύνη was one of the four cardinal virtues, and the adjective δίκαιος denoted the sort of conduct associated with this virtue.

But, while it is true to say both that the New Testament inculcates the very highest ethical standards, and that these standards may sometimes be indicated by words from the righteousness word-group, yet the characteristic meaning of the word-group is to be derived from Hebrew rather than Greek roots. We have seen that in the Old Testament the righteous man is the one who is accepted before God, the one who secures the verdict of acquittal. This sort of thinking was developed and elaborated by the Rabbis. They pictured a great assize when all men would be tried before God. Some would be accepted as righteous, while others would be condemned as wicked. It is from minds accustomed to this way of regarding righteousness that the New Testament terminology is derived. Basically the righteous man is the one who is accepted before God, the one who conforms to His way.

Now if a man is accepted, is truly accepted before God, he finds himself in such a relationship to the heavenly Father, the fount of all love and holiness and purity, that he can never be the same man again. In scriptural language, he is born again, and the new life he now lives is one in which ethical qualities have a prominent place.

This being so there is room for confusion between the qualities denoted respectively by the Hebrew and the Greek ways of looking at the terms in question. It may be true that, ultimately, the Christian comes to practise what is involved in the Greek understanding of δικαιοσύνη, but his starting-point is the Hebrew idea. The New Testament can scarcely be understood until that is realized.

a. δίκαιος

G. Schrenk begins his treatment of δίκαιος in the New Testament by underlining the distinction from the usual Greek usage upon which we have been insisting. 'The New Testament δίκαιος is separated by a deep gulf from the Greek ethical ideal, from the contemplative method which isolates man in his deeds as self-sufficient.' Later he says: 'In substance the New Testament δίκαιος is broadly determined by the Old Testament.'[1] This is borne out by an examination of the passages in which the term occurs.

It is possible to get a wrong impression if we make our beginning with the statements of Pilate's wife, of Pilate himself, or of the centurion at the cross, all of whom refer to Jesus as 'righteous' (Mt. 27: 19, 24; Lk. 23: 47). In such passages we discern something akin to the Greek conception of righteousness. But these are not the typical New Testament statements, and we go astray if we take our standard from them, and then proceed to force other passages into this mould.

Rather must we begin with passages like Matthew 25: 31f., which pictures a great assize in the typical Jewish fashion and refers to those who are acquitted as 'the righteous' (see particularly the culmination of the scene, 'these shall go away into eternal punishment: but the righteous into eternal life'). Again, the story of the Pharisee and the Publican is introduced with: 'And he spake also this parable unto certain which trusted in themselves that they were righteous' (Lk. 18: 9). Similarly the Jewish spies, sent forth to trap Jesus into an unwary statement, 'feigned themselves to be righteous', and in this character commended the Lord for teaching the way of God truly (Lk. 20: 20f.). In both these incidents the Jewish colouring is unmistakable, and it would be a violence of

[1] *TWNT*, II, pp. 189, 190.

exegesis to interpret 'righteous' in other than the usual Jewish sense. (*Cf.* also Mk. 2: 17; Lk. 14: 14; 15: 7, *etc.*)

It is clear that the Hebraic idea of the righteous as those accepted by God is to be found in the New Testament. But that is not to say that there is no advance on the Old Testament conception. In the New Testament the requirements for adjudging a man as righteous are different from those accepted in Judaism. Whereas, for the ordinary first-century Jew, the righteous man was the one who had performed many meritorious deeds, for the Christian he was one with faith in Christ Jesus. Thus St. Paul can quote from Habakkuk, 'the righteous shall live by faith', but he is not merely repeating a generally accepted idea. He has transformed the conception of faith, and conceives of it as a warm personal trust in Jesus as a living Saviour. A man becomes righteous, acceptable with God, when he has such a faith. We find similar citations of the passage from Habakkuk in Galatians 3: 11; Hebrews 10: 38, and in each case faith is understood in a Christian sense. The same thought is expressed in a different form in Romans 5: 19, 'through the obedience of the one shall the many be made righteous'. Here again 'righteous' is a term signifying those accepted by God, and the ground of this acceptance is the work of Christ. It scarcely needs to be pointed out that faith on the part of the recipient of the divine gift is implied here, just as the activity of Christ is implied in the passages we have just been considering where salvation is linked with faith.

It may be freely admitted that we do not find this expressed uniformly throughout the New Testament. St. Matthew's Gospel, for example, is more closely identified with the Jewish conception than are the Epistles of St. Paul. But it is no part of our purpose to trace the growth of Christian doctrine. We are concerned, rather, to show what this conception means in its definitive Christian form. When we approach the New Testament with this in view we find, in the first place, that δίκαιος is characteristically used to denote those accepted with God, and in the second, that men are accepted with Him, *i.e.* are righteous, only on the grounds of their faith and of the work of Christ.

When we have grasped the fact that the righteous are those accepted by God, some of the controversy concerning imputed and imparted righteousness seems beside the point. What difference does it make whether we impute or impart a *status*? Denney has well said on this matter: 'the distinction of imputed and infused righteousness is unreal. The man who believes in Christ the propitiation – who stakes his whole being on sin-bearing love as the last reality in the universe – is not fictitiously regarded as right with God; he actually is right with God, and God treats him as such. He is in the right attitude to God the Redeemer, the attitude which has the promise and potency of all rightness or righteousness in it, and it only introduces intellectual and moral confusion to make artificial distinctions at this point.'[1] Those who come relying trustfully on the work of Christ for their acceptance with God are accepted as righteous, and if we bear in mind the essentially forensic nature of the term 'righteous' there seems little need to dwell unduly on imparted or imputed righteousness. By the same token it may be possible to cavil at Denney's inclusion of a reference to 'the promise and potency of all rightness or righteousness', for men are justified on Paul's view not on account of any merit of their own, potential or actual, but only on account of Christ's work and of their faith.

The adjective δίκαιος is applied to God in five passages (Jn. 17: 25; Rom. 3: 26; 2 Tim. 4: 8; 1 Jn. 1: 9; Rev. 16: 5). In the first of these the reference is quite general, 'O righteous Father, the world knew thee not'; but in the last of them the meaning clearly has to do with the process of judging, 'Righteous art thou, which art and which wast, thou Holy One, because thou didst thus judge'. Here there can be no doubt but that God is shown to be righteous by the process of just judgment, and this accords with the expression 'the Lord, the righteous judge' (2 Tim. 4: 8). In 1 John God is spoken of as 'faithful and righteous to forgive us our sins', which we may well understand as indicating that God's forgiveness is in accordance with the laws of His holy nature. The remaining passage is that in which St. Paul says that the propitiatory death of Jesus was 'for the shewing of (God's) righteousness at this present season: that he might himself be just, and the justifier of him that hath faith in

---

[1] *The Christian Doctrine of Reconciliation* (London, 1918), pp. 164f. Again he says: 'When He pronounces the sinner δίκαιος, he *is* δίκαιος. Before he saw Christ and believed in Him he was all wrong with God: God could do nothing but condemn him. Now, in virtue of his faith, he is all right with God, and there is henceforth no condemnation for him. Nor in all this is there anything unreal, anything akin to legal fiction' (*op. cit.*, p. 292).

Jesus'. This is a critical passage for St. Paul's view of justification, and it is clear that we must understand that God is δίκαιος in the very act whereby He justifies sinners, namely in the atonement wrought on Calvary. We have seen that in the Old Testament God is thought of as acting in accordance with the eternal law of righteousness which is part of His very being, and it would seem that it is this which Paul is here affirming. The act of forgiveness is not one in which God treats the moral obligation as of comparatively little account. It is not the triumph of His love over His righteousness. God acts righteously and this in the very act of forgiveness. Nor is this an isolated thought. Throughout the New Testament there is the underlying thought that God is not capricious, but that He always acts in accordance with His holy nature. Sometimes this comes to the surface, as, for example, when Paul writes to the Thessalonians: 'it is a righteous thing with God to recompense affliction to them that afflict you, and to you that are afflicted rest with us' (2 Thes. 1: 6f.). It is much more congenial to the modern mind to dwell on the love of God than to think of His righteousness, but we must bear both aspects in mind if we are to be true to the Scriptures. The New Testament regards the righteousness of God as something far too important to be ignored or glossed over. Even the act of forgiveness which might be thought of as an act of mercy is seen to be also an act of righteousness.

b. δικαιοσύνη

There are many passages in the New Testament where the use of δικαιοσύνη is akin to that in Judaism. Thus, when our Lord says, 'except your righteousness shall exceed that of the scribes and Pharisees, ye shall in no wise enter into the kingdom of heaven' (Mt. 5: 20),[1] it is quite clear that righteousness is a concept common to Judaism and the new religion. But at the same time it must be recognized that there is a radical novelty. Granted the premises of the Pharisees, it is difficult to see how their righteousness could be

---

[1] The connection of righteousness with law, quite in the manner of Judaism, might be inferred from statements about sin such as: 'Where there is no law, neither is there transgression' (Rom. 4: 15) or 'sin is lawlessness' (1 Jn. 3: 4). On the latter E. A. Knox remarks: 'S. John does not define sin as transgression of a definite command, issuing from authority and revocable by authority, but as lawlessness, antagonism to that principle of law which is of the very essence of the nature of God' (*The Glad Tidings of Reconciliation*, London, 1916, p. 127n.).

exceeded. But Jesus did not grant their premises. He was not thinking as they were of the accumulation of merit by the performance of law-works, of punctilious conformity with the letter of the law. For Jesus, with His emphasis on the spirit rather than the letter, righteousness took on a new meaning. While there is undoubted continuity with Judaism, there is also a new departure. This is typical of the New Testament conception of righteousness. It cannot be completely understood apart from its Hebraic ancestry, and it cannot be completely explained by that Hebraic ancestry.

Some suggest that the essence of the New Testament idea of righteousness is to be found in kinship with mercy. It is pointed out, for example, that in Matthew 6: 1 some texts read δικαιοσύνην and others ἐλεημοσύνην, and it is inferred that in New Testament times righteousness was held to be nearly identical with mercy, the forensic idea being merely incidental. But this is an illegitimate use of textual criticism. Textual variants are not always, or even usually, synonyms. No more impressive is the appeal to the association of salvation with righteousness in Isaiah 40–66, and to such facts as the use of both δικαιοσύνη and ἔλεος to translate ḥeṣed in the LXX. As we have seen, in the Old Testament the forensic idea is basic and the association with mercy incidental, and nobody who has taken the trouble to examine closely the ninety-two examples of the use of δικαιοσύνη in the New Testament will doubt that the forensic use is primary there also. It is true that δικαιοσύνη, especially as applied to the dealings of God with man, includes an element of mercy. But the primary conception is undoubtedly forensic. When, for example, St. Paul speaks of the righteousness which is by faith, he is not thinking in terms of mercy in men, but of their legal standing before God. Righteousness seems to stand occasionally in opposition to mercy, as in Titus 3: 5, 'not by works done in righteousness, which we did ourselves, but according to his mercy he saved us', although it is true that it is human righteousness that is being contrasted with the divine mercy.

The whole idea of righteousness has been modified for New Testament writers because Jesus Christ has come into the world. 'He that doeth righteousness is righteous, even as he is righteous' (1 Jn. 3: 7) brings the very conception of righteousness into the closest of relationships to the life of the incarnate Lord. This again is a thought which recurs, and it underlies many passages where it is not explicit. For the early Christians all things were made new, their standards of righteousness included, because the Son of God had come into the world. Accordingly, there are many passages which exhort believers to lives of righteousness. Indeed, it is just as characteristic of the New Testament that righteousness in the ethical sense should be a distinguishing mark of those who are Christ's, as it is that it is not their own righteousness that brings them salvation, but the righteousness of God. (Compare the aim of an upright life in Phil. 3: 10ff. with the express disclaimer of the value of any 'righteousness of mine own' in verse 9.)

But although there is this clamant demand for right living, and although the righteousness terminology is used in part to express it, yet it remains true that this is not the characteristic nor distinctive use of this terminology. As in the Old Testament and in Judaism generally, the forensic basis of this word-group is the really important thing.

We see this in such a passage as Romans 9: 30-32: 'What shall we say then? That the Gentiles, which followed not after righteousness, attained to righteousness, even the righteousness which is of faith: but Israel, following after a law of righteousness, did not arrive at that law. Wherefore? Because they sought it not by faith, but as it were by works. They stumbled at the stone of stumbling.' The forensic idea is very strong here. The Gentiles did not seek before God that righteous standing which the Jews sought by the way of works of merit. Nevertheless they attained to righteousness, namely the righteousness that is of faith. The Jews who were very anxious to establish themselves as righteous before God failed to do so because they came by the way of law works instead of by that of faith, which is the way God has appointed. It is quite clear that righteousness is being used to denote a standing, a status, a verdict of acquittal, and not an ethical quality. In that righteousness plainly means here acceptance with God, 'rightness' before Him, we can see the Hebraic background; but in that this acceptance is to be found not in any works of merit, but only by the way of faith, we see the distinctively Christian contribution. The further reference to the 'stone of stumbling' is also integral to the Christian idea, for faith is not something grounded on mere subjectivism. It is something which operates on the basis of what Christ did on

Calvary. The divine activity mediated to believers by their faith is essential to the Pauline conception of righteousness.

The point which is stressed over and over again is that this righteousness is not a matter of human merit, not a work of law. Paul was no stranger to the righteousness of the law, and he tells us that he had been 'blameless' regarding it. But his contact with Jesus Christ had changed his ideas. His aim now was 'that I may gain Christ, and be found in him, not having a righteousness of mine own, even that which is of the law, but that which is through faith in Christ, the righteousness which is of God by faith' (Phil. 3: 6–9). Here he expressly disclaims the righteousness which is of the law, and elsewhere his words are, if possible, even stronger, as, 'if righteousness is through the law, then Christ died for nought' (Gal. 2: 21; this seems to imply that righteousness not only is not, but cannot be, through the law).[1] Or take Romans 4: 14f., 'For if they which are of the law be heirs, faith is made void, and the promise is made of none effect; for the law worketh wrath' (which again means that if men may attain righteousness by law works then the revelation in Christ is useless); or Romans 10: 4, 'For Christ is the end of the law unto righteousness to every one that believeth' (which makes it clear that there can be no way of law for the believer). It is hardly necessary to pursue the point further. It can scarcely be disputed that for St. Paul it was absolutely basic that no righteousness of human origin could avail in the sight of God.

We have already noticed that he speaks of righteousness as something which comes from God, and this is another point which means much to him. It is not peculiar to him, and we find it, for example, underlying the beatitude, 'Blessed are they that hunger and thirst after righteousness: for they shall be filled' (Mt. 5: 6). Here it is plain that the people in mind have realized that their own efforts do not, and cannot, produce righteousness before God, and it is He Himself who will fulfil their longing.[2] So again when men are exhorted, 'Seek ye first his kingdom and his righteousness' (Mt. 6: 33), righteousness just as much as the kingdom must be

---

[1] As Burton says, 'The argument of the sentence is from a Christian point of view a *reductio ad absurdum*' (*ICC, Galatians*, p. 141).

[2] On this verse Schrenk says: '. . . in opposition to the Jewish conception of merit the δικαιοσύνη is seen as a gift which God bestows on him who longs after Him' (*op. cit.*, p. 200).

regarded as a gift to be sought from God. Similarly, when Noah 'became heir of the righteousness which is according to faith' (Heb. 11 : 7), it seems that righteousness is regarded as a gift from God.

But it is in the writings of St. Paul that this thought receives its fullest expression. He speaks of grace reigning 'through righteousness unto eternal life through Jesus Christ our Lord' (Rom. 5 : 21), where righteousness means very nearly the gift of eternal life. The thought of our dependence on God is implied also in the Pauline expression, 'the righteousness of God'. Much has been written about this expression, and in particular controversy has raged about whether it should be understood as referring to a quality of God's own nature, or whether it is a way of referring to the gift of righteousness bestowed upon believers. The considerations adduced by W. Sanday and A. C. Headlam[1] seem sufficient for concluding that both aspects are involved. On the one hand, passages like Philippians 3 : 9 leave us in no doubt that it is a righteousness of God which is the apostle's possession and whereby he is saved. On the other hand, we cannot overlook the fact that the New Testament consistently thinks of God as righteous, and there are not wanting passages where the expression ἡ δικαιοσύνη τοῦ θεοῦ must be held to indicate a divine quality (e.g. Rom. 3 : 5, 25f.). It would be true to say, with F. Delitzsch, that this is 'the harmony of God's actions with His law',[2] but this should not be understood in any static way. δικαιοσύνη is a dynamic term bringing home to us that salvation owes its origin to God. We can be accounted as righteous only because of His activity. In the gospel, Paul says, there 'is revealed a righteousness of God' (Rom. 1 : 17). The essential content of the gospel is closely related to the righteousness of God. This comes out again in Romans 3 : 21f.: 'But now apart from the law a righteousness of God hath been manifested . . . even the righteousness of God through faith in Jesus Christ unto all them that believe.'

This righteousness is further defined by being brought into relationship with the death of Christ. The Lord's death was for the showing forth of God's righteousness (Rom. 3 : 25f.). We are reminded of the conjunction of righteousness with salvation in the

---

[1] ICC, Romans, pp. 24f.

[2] Commentary on the Epistle to the Hebrews, II (Edinburgh, 1887), p. 433.

Old Testament (especially in Is. 40–66), but the thought here goes further, and that in more directions than one. Thus, whereas salvation in the Old Testament is concerned largely, if not exclusively, with deliverance from temporal ills, here it is concerned with expiation of sin.[1] St. Paul is dealing with a more fundamental issue than were the men of the old covenant when they used this terminology. Then, too, as we saw when we were dealing with δικαιοσύνη in the LXX, there is a difference with regard to the people being saved. In the Old Testament we have a picture of God delivering the downtrodden and oppressed, but it is always 'the righteous', οἱ δίκαιοι, who are thus delivered. St. Paul's thought here is in marked contrast. He is thinking of men who were utterly unable to achieve the status of 'righteous'. A little later he speaks of God 'that justifieth the ungodly' (Rom. 4: 5), and that is his thought here too. The righteousness of God with which he is concerned is a righteousness which takes men in their sins, alienated from the mind of God, subject to the wrath of God, and justifies them.

Not only is it a righteous thing that God intervenes to save His people. He saves in a manner which accords with right. The very act wherein He delivers men is one in which He shows Himself to be righteous. Paul says that God set forth Christ 'to be a propitiation . . to shew his righteousness, because of the passing over of the sins done aforetime in the forbearance of God; for the shewing, I say, of his righteousness at this present season: that he might himself be just and the justifier of him that hath faith in Jesus'. The fact that God had not always punished sin with full severity in the past, but had 'passed over' such sin, gave rise to the danger that He might not appear to men to be completely righteous. But now, in the cross, He has for ever removed that danger. He has shown Himself completely righteous.

This is not always recognized and, for example, C. Ryder Smith writes: 'To put Paul's meaning in modern terms, he is saying:

---

[1] *Cf.* L. S. Thornton: 'The biblical doctrine of justification as exemplified in deutero-Isaiah acquired in St. Paul's teaching a more specific meaning. Through his act of expiation our Lord made it possible for God to declare us "not guilty", thus releasing us from Law, Sin and ultimately Death' (*The Common Life in the Body of Christ*, London, 1950, p. 56 n. 2); and he adds that this 'includes a vindication of God's righteousness'.

"God pleased to make man so that it was possible for him to sin; He also made man so that every sin should spread its evil infection through the mass of mankind; we have just seen the hideous result (Romans i: 18 – iii: 18); God, who must have foreseen this, would not even be righteous if He did not find a way to save men from this; He has found such a way by sending His Son." [1] But while there is truth in this, one cannot feel that it expresses Paul's essential meaning. 'How could God be righteous if He did not forgive?' is the question before Ryder Smith. But the question that worried Paul was rather, 'How could God be righteous if He did forgive?' Ryder Smith's paraphrase suggests that the end is all-important – it is the fact that men are saved that shows God to be righteous and the means are relatively unimportant. But Paul at this point of his argument is more concerned with the means than the end. It is not salvation in general, but salvation by the way of the cross that shows God to be righteous.

Classical Protestantism has understood this to mean that Christ bore the penalty of our sin, and that God in this way showed that the eternal law of righteousness cannot be allowed to suffer dis-repute.[2] Calvin puts it thus: 'As the law allowed no remission, and God did remit sins, there appeared to be a stain on divine justice. The exhibition of Christ as an atonement is what alone removes it.'[3] Or, to quote a later divine: 'the plan of salvation which the Bible reveals supposes that the justice of God which renders the punishment of sin necessary has been satisfied . . . the Scriptures recognize the truth that God is just, in the sense that He is deter-mined by His moral excellence to punish all sin, and therefore that the satisfaction of Christ which secures the pardon of sinners is rendered to the justice of God. Its primary and principal design is . . . to satisfy the demands of justice; so that God can be just in

---

[1] *The Bible Doctrine of Salvation* (London, 1946), p. 218.

[2] *Cf.* J. Scott Lidgett: 'Thus, for the apostle, the solemnity of the dealing with the Jewish law involved in the death of Christ lay in this, that though its form was Jewish, even governed by the text, "Cursed is every one that hangeth on a tree," yet that Jewish form was the special and peculiar expression of universal principles, and represented a demand and a satisfaction so divine that they are the revelation of the means by which the righteousness of God wrought for the salvation not only of the Jew, but of the world' (*The Spiritual Principle of the Atonement*, London, 1914, p. 46).

[3] *In loc.* (Owen's translation).

justifying the ungodly.'[1] This kind of interpretation has been vigorously assailed, but it does appear to give the gist of the apostle's argument at this point. It may well be true to say that there is more to the atonement than this. But, in view of the undoubtedly forensic colouring of the passage, and the general drift of Paul's argument, we can scarcely deny that he is here giving expression to the view that Christ bore the penalty for man's sin, and so showed the divine concern for law. This is admitted by such a theologian as Hastings Rashdall, although his own view of the atonement is so very different. He says: 'St. Paul does not quite say why God could not remit the penalty of sin without the death of His Son. But it cannot be denied that those theologians who declare that this would be incompatible with God's justice – the justice which requires that somehow sin should be punished – or with the consistency which demands the infliction of the particular punishment which God had threatened, namely death – are only bringing out the latent presuppositions of St. Paul's thought.'[2]

It is objected to this interpretation that the bearing of penalty by one in the place of another is not really just, so that when Christ suffers for us it is not a matter of fulfilling legal requirements. There is some force in this objection, and there would be more if we were dealing with a human law. But the fact is that we are not. The law in question is the law of God's holy nature, and that nature is merciful as well as just. Thus God's justice, while it is not capricious but works by the method of law, is a justice which finds a large place for mercy and is not hard, bare, and legalistic. At any rate, whether our legal categories can find a place for mercy or not, those of the Bible can and do. In the very passage we are considering there is a mention of the forbearance (ἀνοχή) of God which leads to the passing over of sins. Neither justice nor mercy must be whittled down; but neither must they be separated.

The forensic thought seems to underlie passages where righteous-

---

[1] Charles Hodge, *Systematic Theology*, II (London and Edinburgh, 1878), pp. 492f.
[2] *The Idea of Atonement in Christian Theology* (London, 1919), pp. 91f. The idea of bearing penalty is present in some passages where none of the δίκαιος words occurs, for example in Rom. 8: 3, on which Rashdall comments: 'What can this mean but that in the death of Christ the judgement pronounced against the sin of Adam and his posterity was satisfied?' (*op. cit.*, p. 93).

ness is spoken of as a gift, *e.g.*, 'much more shall they that receive the abundance of grace and of the gift of righteousness reign in life' (Rom. 5: 17). If righteousness is a gift, obviously it cannot be a quality of living. A standing before God seems the only interpretation adequate to the context. As G. O. Griffith says: 'Certainly, if righteousness means "good works" it cannot be bestowed; but Paul's point is that this is not what it does mean: fundamentally it means *right relationship*, and it is this that God provides.'[1] So, too, when it is said that 'him who knew no sin he made to be sin on our behalf; that we might become the righteousness of God in him' (2 Cor. 5: 21), there is clearly a forensic thought, although it is probably true that more than that is intended to be conveyed by the expression.[2] So is it in 1 Corinthians 1: 30, where Christ is said to be 'made unto us wisdom from God, and righteousness and sanctification and redemption'.

We come now to the question of imputation which has seemed to very many to be a necessary corollary of the forensic view. Traditional Protestantism has made much of the doctrine of imputed righteousness and has given it precision by saying that the merits of Christ are imputed to believers. Thus Calvin can say 'the Son of God, though spotlessly pure, took upon him the disgrace and ignominy of our iniquities, and in return clothed us with his purity'.[3] But in modern times this position has been strenuously opposed, and for example N. H. Snaith maintains that, if we hold to imputed righteousness, 'we have not emancipated ourselves from that very doctrine which Paul spent most of his life in combatting – namely, that salvation is by righteousness'; and he goes on to say: 'The fact of the matter is that God does not require

[1] *St. Paul's Gospel to the Romans* (Oxford, 1949), p. 108.
[2] Thus A. Schlatter: 'He makes His righteousness manifest in us; it forms us within and without, gives us a will and a destiny, makes us one with God's will and gives us a portion in His life' (*Paulus der Bote Jesu*, Stuttgart, 1934, pp. 568f.). The forensic meaning of the verse is well brought out by Rashdall when he says: 'This can hardly mean anything but that God treated the sinless Christ as if He were guilty, and inflicted upon Him the punishment which our sins had deserved; and that this infliction made it possible to treat the sinful as if they were actually righteous.' He regards this as one of 'a few passages which necessarily suggest the idea of substituted punishment or substituted sacrifice. But there they are, and St. Paul's argument is unintelligible without them' (*op. cit.*, p. 94).
[3] *Institutes*, II, 16. 6 (trans. Beveridge, I, p. 439).

righteousness at all, in any shape or shadow, as a condition of salvation. He requires faith.'[1]

It is very difficult to substantiate either extreme from Scripture. Against Snaith, righteousness is definitely said to be imputed to Abraham on the grounds of his faith (Rom. 4: 3), and the general principle is laid down that 'to him that worketh not, but believeth on him that justifieth the ungodly, his faith is reckoned for righteousness' (Rom. 4: 5). The chapter then goes on to deal further with the subject, culminating in the statement that 'it was not written for his sake alone, that it was reckoned unto him; but for our sake also, unto whom it shall be reckoned' (verses 23f.). In view of plain statements like these it seems impossible to hold that Paul found no place for the imputation of righteousness to believers. On the other hand he never says in so many words that the righteousness *of Christ* was imputed to believers, and it may fairly be doubted whether he had this in mind in his treatment of justification, although it may be held to be a corollary from his doctrine of identification of the believer with Christ.[2]

But, if our primary idea is correct, then the basic thought in righteousness is of a standing with God,[3] and we should think of a status conferred on men by God on the grounds of the atoning work of Christ. There is a sense in which it can be said to be imputed, for it is in no sense an ethical righteousness attained by the believer by the performance of good works, but rather a gift from without, from God. But it seems preferable to regard the idea of conferred status as primary, rather than to look at the whole subject through the comparatively few passages which speak of imputation.

Next we must notice that, while on the one hand St. Paul stresses the fact that righteousness is a forensic affair, on the other he insists

---

[1] *The Distinctive Ideas of the Old Testament* (London, 1944), p. 164.

[2] *Cf.* E. A. Knox: 'Why should he not speak of an imputed righteousness, or of Christ's righteousness reckoned to him? If Christ lives in him, what should God see in him, of what should God take account in him, but of the living indwelling Christ in all His perfect righteousness?' (*op. cit.*, p. 74).

[3] 'The righteousness which is the content of justification is, according to Paul, neither imputed nor imparted; it is a status conferred, not as had previously been believed, on the ground of merit, but on the ground of faith; and that faith was faith in God particularly as He was revealed in the sacrifice of Christ' (C. Anderson Scott, *Christianity According to St. Paul*, Cambridge, 1932, p. 97).

strongly that it is attained only by faith, thus linking up the conception with the inner spiritual life of the believer. Both this inner experience and the outward status must be kept in mind (*cf.* Rom. 4: 11, 13; 9: 30; 10: 6; Phil. 3: 9, *etc.*).

Among the Jews there could be no justification until the day of judgment (for as long as ever a man lived it was always possible for him to sin and fall away from his momentary right standing). That justification has such a future aspect is recognized (*cf.* Gal. 5: 5). But while this is not overlooked, it does not receive the emphasis in the Christian view. Rather the glorious truth insisted upon by St. Paul is that justification is a present experience. This comes out sometimes in specific expressions like the 'now' of Romans 3: 21, or the frequent use of the present tense in alluding to justification. But it is not so much from isolated passages as from the general tenor of his teaching that we gather the importance of this truth. Because justification is an act of God rather than of man there is an assurance about it which means that it is not presumptuous to speak of being justified now. Justification is both present and future, but it is the present aspect which receives emphasis in the New Testament.

c. δικαιόω

We have seen that there is good ground for thinking that both δίκαιος and δικαιοσύνη are understood in the New Testament in terms of their forensic background. When we come to consider δικαιόω the forensic nature of the term is even clearer, and in point of fact it is difficult to explain any of the occurrences of the verb without recourse to the forensic.

The continuity with the Jewish usage is to be discerned in a number of passages. Thus Jesus said 'every idle word that men shall speak, they shall give account thereof in the day of judgment. For by thy words thou shalt be justified, and by thy words thou shalt be condemned' (Mt. 12: 36f.). The idea is clearly that of an assize such as the Jews conceived of at the day of judgment, and the opposition of καταδικασθήσῃ to δικαιωθήσῃ seems to put the matter beyond doubt. So is it in Acts 13: 39 and Romans 3: 4.

This last passage refers to God as justified, which is enough to show that the meaning of the word must be something like 'declare righteous', for it is impossible to think that the apostle (or, for that matter, the psalmist Paul is quoting) meant that God was to be 'made righteous'. He is affirming that in the process of judgment God's words would show that He is righteous. We have another reference to God's being justified (Lk. 7: 29), and one to Christ's (1 Tim. 3: 16). This little group of passages is very important, for it shows, at the very least, that the New Testament writers could understand δικαιόω as signifying 'to declare righteous' or 'to show as righteous'.

Equally conclusive are the passages wherein men are said to justify themselves, as in the case of the lawyer of Luke 10: 29, or the Pharisees of whom Jesus said: 'Ye are they that justify yourselves in the sight of men; but God knoweth your hearts: for that which is exalted among men is an abomination in the sight of God' (Lk. 16: 15). In this latter passage particularly it is quite plain that the justification in question is a declaring, or showing, to be just: the second half of the verse shows that there cannot be the thought of making righteous.

Not every one of the passages we have so far noted is forensic in the sense that it describes a court-room scene. It is obvious that a metaphorical element is quite common. But that should not blind us to the fact that, in each case, there is the implication of a judgment given and of a favourable verdict. The case is not unlike those of English verbs like 'to judge' and 'to acquit'. These can be used in connection with matters far remote from law-courts. Nevertheless they are undeniably derived from legal practice and they retain the essential part of their legal significance. So is it with δικαιόω. It may be used, it is used, in connection with matters where there is no formal giving of sentence in a law-court. But that does not alter the facts that the verb is essentially a forensic one, in the Bible as elsewhere, and that it denotes basically a sentence of acquittal. Thus it is that R. S. Franks can say: 'What St. Paul means by justification is simply the forgiveness of sins, expressed in legal terminology. Justification signifies the pronouncing of the sinner righteous before God.'[1]

This comes out clearly in such a passage as Romans 2: 13, 'for not the hearers of a law are just before God, but the doers of a law shall be justified'. Paul goes on to speak of 'the day when God shall

[1] *The Atonement* (London, 1934), p. 62. He goes on to say that justification 'proceeds upon no legal principle: it is purely an act of grace'.

judge'. He is evidently arguing in terms of current Jewish ideas, and we have already seen that that meant that the justified were those acquitted at the bar of God's justice. But quite apart from the fact that the words irresistibly recall Rabbinic conceptions, their plain meaning is that a certain class are reckoned as righteous, as acquitted.[1] There is an ineluctable forensic element here. And this seems to be true whenever St. Paul uses the term. He has in his mind the thought that all men are tried before God, and by God. The verb denotes the giving of the verdict whereby they are adjudged righteous or acceptable with God.

There are several places where St. Paul makes it quite clear that this status is not achieved by human effort, by works of law. 'We reckon therefore that a man is justified by faith apart from works of law' (Rom. 3: 28) comes as the climax of his argument in the early part of Romans. His statements elsewhere are, if anything, even more emphatic. 'Knowing that a man is not justified by works of law, but only through faith in Jesus Christ, even we believed on Christ Jesus, that we might be justified by faith in Christ, and not by works of law: because by works of law shall no flesh be justified' (Gal. 2: 16, RV mg.). 'Now that no man is justified by law in the sight of God is evident' (Gal. 3: 11). Such statements rule out the remotest possibility of justification being wrought by merely human effort. St. Paul does not even speak of 'the works of the law', the Jewish law, but uses the anarthrous term 'law', law in general. No works of law can avail in the sight of God.

St. James takes up rather a different position when he expressly says that 'by works a man is justified, and not only by faith' (Jas. 2: 24), and when he uses the examples of Abraham and Rahab to reinforce his position. But it should be noted that he recognizes implicitly the place of faith. His polemic is directed not against faith as such, but against faith without works. He reiterates that that sort of faith is dead, 'faith, if it have not works, is dead in itself. . . . For as the body apart from the spirit is dead, even so faith apart from works is dead' (Jas. 2: 17, 26). Moreover the Epistle does not inculcate a demand for law-works in the accepted sense; there is no

---

[1] The apostle is, of course, dealing with a hypothetical case, and not laying down the way in which men in point of fact are justified. Elsewhere (Gal. 2: 21; 3: 11, *etc.*) he makes it quite clear that men cannot attain justification by their own efforts in keeping the law.

thought of an accumulation of merit by the performance of deeds in accordance with the letter of the law. Rather there is a stress on love (2 : 8f.), humility (4 : 6f.) and kindred qualities. The 'works' of James are very like 'the fruit of the Spirit' of Paul. While we must recognize that James has expressed his point of view in very un-Pauline language, yet the fact remains that he does not replace Paul's scheme of justification by another based on law-works. He does not mean by works what Paul means, and he does not mean by faith what Paul means. His demand is for a 'faith that worketh by love' (Gal. 5 : 6), if we may borrow a Pauline phrase, and his polemic is directed against those whose faith is revealed to be a hollow sham, by the absence of lives of service.

When St. James speaks of 'the implanted word, which is able to save your souls' (Jas. 1 : 21), he appears to be thinking of a divine activity operative in salvation, and this thought is brought out by St. Paul over and over again. This was part of the divine plan, for the Scripture foresaw 'that God would justify the Gentiles by faith', and so 'whom he called, them he also justified' (Gal. 3 : 8; Rom. 8 : 30). Again Paul can give a triumphant question and answer: 'Who shall lay anything to the charge of God's elect? It is God that justifieth' (Rom. 8 : 33). Not only is justification impossible by any works of law, by anything done in merely human strength. It is of the very marrow of Paul's thought that it can be effected only by an act of God, and gloriously, it *is* so effected. This justification is, of course, associated with the cross, for we are 'justified by his blood' (Rom. 5 : 9).

This thought of justification by divine action is not unlike that suggested by Jesus in the parable of the Pharisee and the publican. The publican confesses his sinfulness and throws himself on the mercy of God. He relies wholly on God and produces no law-works whatever. Jesus says, 'This man went down to his house justified' (Lk. 18 : 14).

It remains only for us to notice that, though justification is effected only by a divine action, it does not become operative in the lives of individuals until they exercise faith. This is to be found in many passages, the principle being: 'to him that worketh not, but believeth on him that justifieth the ungodly, his faith is reckoned for righteousness' (Rom. 4 : 5). Faith, of course, is not merely an intellectual adherence to a set of propositions, but the response of the whole man to the divine act on Calvary, as he trustfully commits himself to his Creator, and rests in Him for time and for eternity. This doctrine represented a radical novelty in St. Paul's day, as G. O. Griffith reminds us: 'It is often said that to speak of "justification by faith" is to use language which, to the modern man, is meaningless. What is as often forgotten is that such language was as meaningless to ancient man also, apart from the Gospel which gave it significance.'[1] It is hardly fair to speak of the doctrine as one which was acceptable enough in the first century, but which cannot be accepted today because our thought-world is different. The thought-world of the first century was different also! But St. Paul made so much of this aspect of the gospel, even though the language was unfamiliar to his hearers, because it seemed an aspect which was vital. We may or may not like imagery with forensic associations. But the heart of the Christian gospel is that, while no works of our hands will avail to make us acceptable before God, we are acceptable if we come in faith on the grounds of God's own action in Christ. And this great truth St. Paul delighted to express in the forensic language of justification.

d. Other words of the δίκαιος group

Of the other words in this word-group δικαίωμα is used most often in the New Testament. Mostly it has the sense 'ordinance' as in LXX, and we see, for example, almost the LXX usage in Luke 1: 6 where we read that Zacharias and Elizabeth were both 'walking in all the commandments and ordinances (ἐντολαῖς καὶ δικαιώμασι) of the Lord' (cf. also Rom. 2: 26; Heb. 9: 1, 10). The connection with legal concepts is plain, and the forensic sense of the term clear.

But the word has many shades of meaning, and we find it used, for example, in a prayer that 'all the nations shall come and worship before thee; for thy δικαιώματα have been made manifest' (Rev. 15: 4). RV renders, 'thy righteous acts', but there is doubt whether δικαιώματα can really bear this meaning (though some commentators accept it here or in Rev. 19: 8 or Rom. 5: 18). Such a meaning is certainly not demanded by the context, and Charles' explanation seems preferable: 'δικαιώματα here means the judicial sentences of God in relation to the nations either in the way of

[1] Op. cit., p. 106.

mercy or condemnation.'[1] This is in accordance with the inherent meaning of the word itself, and also with the evidence adduced by Charles.

Of the other passages containing δικαίωμα, Romans 5: 16 reads, 'for the judgment came of one unto condemnation, but the free gift came of many offences unto justification'. The opposition to κατάκριμα and the reference to judgment fix the sense of δικαίωμα as 'sentence of justification', or 'acquittal'. This probably settles the meaning of the word also in verse 18, although the structure of this latter verse with δικαιώματος answering to παραπτώματος leads some commentators to prefer the meaning 'righteous act' or the like. If the former be the correct way of understanding the term, then St. Paul is referring to the Father's sentence of acquittal; if the latter, he has in mind the Son's act of expiation. While it would not be beyond the apostle to use the word in two such different senses within such a short compass it does not seem necessary to understand the passage in this way. The reasons adduced by such commentators as Gifford, Godet, Sanday and Headlam and by Schrenk in the *Wörterbuch* seem sufficient for holding that 'sentence of justification' is the meaning here.

This leaves us only with Revelation 19: 8: 'And it was given unto her that she should array herself in fine linen, bright and pure: for the fine linen is the righteous acts of the saints.' Here, again, there are many who accept the meaning given to the word by the revisers. But in view of the fact that this is a meaning we have not been able to find elsewhere, it is probably better to understand the word of the sentence of justification which gives the saints their standing in the sight of God.

The noun δικαίωσις differs from δικαίωμα in being the act of justifying of which δικαίωμα is the concrete expression. It occurs twice only in the New Testament (Rom. 4: 25; 5: 18). The former passage tells us that Jesus our Lord 'was delivered up for (διά) our trespasses, and was raised for (διά) our justification'. A good deal of ingenuity has been expended upon the two διά's, and some divergent results have been attained. But the position seems to be, as Gifford says, that διά with the accusative 'simply traces an effect to a cause, it marks the *existence* of a causal relation between them,

---

[1] *In loc.*

without defining its *particular character*.[1] Thus 'for our trespasses' may grammatically mean 'because we had trespassed', or 'to atone for our trespasses'. Similarly, 'for our justification' might signify 'because our justification had been accomplished', or 'with a view to our justification'. There seems no conclusive reason that can be urged in favour of either way of taking justification, but possibly the former view is more in harmony with St. Paul's usual way of stating the fact of justification. But in any case if we adopt the latter view it must be in the sense that the resurrection is the completion of God's mighty act of justification, and not as though the resurrection were a justifying act quite apart from the death.[2]

The other passage containing the word reads: 'So then as through one trespass the judgment came unto all men to condemnation; even so through one sentence of justification the free gift came unto all men to justification of life' (Rom. 5: 18). The expression used here, εἰς δικαίωσιν ζωῆς, is unusual. It is probably to be understood of justification with a view to life. As Gifford says, 'The genitive expresses the effect or purpose: *"justification"* is unto, or in order to, *"life"*.'[3] The context (cf. verses 17, 21) shows that life is to be understood in an eschatological sense, and the passage thus indicates that justification issues in eternal life. Justification here is opposed to κατάκριμα, and thus there can be no doubt that it is a forensic term, meaning 'the act of acquitting'.

None of the other words from this root has great importance for our present inquiry. δικαίως occurs with the meaning 'justly' (Lk. 23: 41; 1 Pet. 2: 23; the forensic sense is plain in the latter case), and

[1] *The Epistle of St. Paul to the Romans* (London, 1886), p. 109.
[2] See Godet *in loc.* for a fuller statement of the view adopted here, and in addition to Gifford, Schrenk in *TWNT*, II, p. 228, for the alternative view. *Inter alia* the latter says: 'Because death and resurrection continually occur in the closest connection, because the Crucified is that which He is only since He is at the same time the Risen One, Paul can say both: we are justified through the death of Jesus, and also: He is risen on account of our justification.'
  L. S. Thornton comments on this passage: 'justifying faith is the faith of those "who believe on him that raised Jesus our Lord from the dead" in accordance with Scripture. . . . Once again our salvation depends, not only upon the substance of what is believed, but also upon the form in which it is believed. Unless our faith with regard to the resurrection of the Christ implies a miraculous work of God like that which is carefully stated in Romans 4[17-22] our justification is in jeopardy' (*op. cit.*, p. 278).
[3] *Op. cit.*, p. 120.

also with the meaning 'righteously' (1 Cor. 15: 34; 1 Thes. 2: 10; Tit. 2: 12). δίκη is personified justice in Acts 28: 4, and it signifies 'punishment' in both its other occurrences (2 Thes. 1: 9; Jude 7). δικάστης means 'judge' in Acts 7: 27, 35 (being cited from Ex. 2: 14 both times). δικαιοκρισία is found only in the expression 'the day of wrath and revelation of the righteous judgement of God' (Rom. 2: 5). Here the wrath of God visited upon sinners is recognized as showing God's judgment to be righteous.

Thus in all this word-group we may discern a close connection with the law-court and with judgment generally. The forensic sense is sometimes very strong, and sometimes scarcely perceptible, which is what we would expect when we are dealing with so many occurrences of the words. But almost throughout we are able to detect the forensic undertone, and it is quite clear that many important passages will yield up their meaning only when we recognize that the imagery is taken from processes of law. In particular we have reached the important conclusion that justification is in essence a matter of right status or standing in the sight of God, the status which shows that we are accepted with Him.

II. THE SIGNIFICANCE OF JUSTIFICATION

Some theologians make little of the forensic element in justification, and some exclude it altogether. Thus John Oman objects to the category of law and says: 'We are justified because by faith we enter the world of a gracious God, out of which the old hard legal requirements, with the old hard boundaries of our personality and the old self-regarding claim of rights, have disappeared, a world which is the household of our Father where order and power and ultimate reality are of love and not of law.'[1] This is finely said, and nobody, surely, would dispute the description of the new life we enter by faith. But whether this is a description of what the New Testament understands by justification is another matter. The consequences of the atonement are many, and the blessed state of the believer may be indicated in many ways, of which Oman's words point us to one, and that a very important one. But it is only by ignoring much scriptural evidence that this can be called justification, for, as the preceding examination should have made

[1] *Grace and Personality* (Cambridge, 1919), p. 206.

clear, justification is essentially a *legal* concept. It may well be that there are other spheres more important to Christianity than that of law, but that does not give us grounds for using the legal terminology to describe those other spheres. Justification is essentially concerned with the legal status of the believer, and we must leave descriptions of the new life for other categories.

We might urge a similar objection against the position which says, 'To be justified, then, is not to have the consequences of sin condoned or even obliterated, but so to be reconciled to God in spite of sin, that we can face all evil with confident assurance of final victory over it, and by God's succour transform all its consequences, whether the evil be natural or moral, the outcome of our own sin, or from necessary fellowship with others in His family'.[1] Again we may say that there is truth in what is being said, and that it is a very real part of the Christian faith that believers are reconciled to God, and that they rely on Him to give them victory over evil. But this is not what the Bible means when it speaks of justification. There seems little point in transferring the name 'justification' from its proper sphere to some other which pleases the theologian better.

Similarly we protest against those views which see the essence of justification in the changed nature of the believer. W. Fearon Halliday comes near to this when he says: 'it has not always been seen that no man can be justified before God unless his nature is so changed that the assent of God is the assent to a reality.'[2] It is quite true that sanctification and justification should not be sundered, but rather kept in the closest of relations to one another. But this does not mean that we are to confuse the one with the other. If a man is truly justified by faith, then that faith will surely lead him in the power of God to a new life, and the one experience may well be held to imply the other. But that is not the same as saying that the two experiences are in essence the same. Though in practice they may go together, yet for purposes of discussion they may be considered separately, and justification is the name given in the Bible to the changed status, not the changed nature.

[1] Oman, *op. cit.*, p. 221. *Cf.* also E. Wolf, 'Justification means deliverance from sin' (*Biblical Authority for Today*, ed. A. Richardson and W. Schweitzer, London, 1951, p. 282).

[2] *Reconciliation and Reality* (London, 1919), p. 154.

If we do not like the doctrine of justification it is more straight-forward to abandon it altogether, rather than to retain the name while applying it to something other than the scriptural doctrine. This is what N. Berdyaev has done, asserting that justification is both impossible and unnecessary. 'In reality grace can change man but not justify him, because it is the free action of divine power working upon human nature. For the rest, we may well ask is the justification of man necessary so far as God is concerned? It seems as if we are faced here with a juridical notion created by the limitations of human thought, which were incapable of accepting the divine truth of Christianity.'[1] Again he can say: 'The meaning of the coming of Christ into the world lies in a real transfiguration of human nature, in the formation of a new type of spiritual man. . . . In Christianity the central idea is that of transfiguration, not justification.'[2]

But we can hold such views only if we give up altogether the attempt to ground our views on Scripture. There can be not the slightest doubt to anyone who has worked much with a con-cordance that justification is one of the very central truths of the New Testament. It is employed far more often than reconciliation and most other ways of interpreting Calvary. We may very fairly doubt, in view of the central place assigned by the New Testament to the death of Christ, whether even the change in man is thought of as often as justification. And even where the new life is thought of it is the consequence of the new standing before God which is justification. While we may welcome Berdyaev's reminder that the power of the divine love operative within man is an integral part of the Christian way, we must decline it as a substitute for justification.

---

[1] *Freedom and the Spirit* (London, 1944), p. 351. He goes on to say: 'Even in Orthodoxy the theology of the schools is infected with this idea of justification, although to a lesser degree than in Catholicism. Theological doctrine holds that man is saved by Christ and that he is reconciled to God by the sacrifice of Christ.

'But if we go into the matter more deeply we shall see that many are not saved *by* Christ but *in* Christ, in the new spiritual race which Christ began, in the new nature, and in the new spiritual life. Christ is above all the revelation of this new life, and of the kingdom of God. Justification and salvation are only secondary moments in the path of spiritual progress – a truth which Orthodoxy grasps more easily than Catholicism.'

[2] *Op. cit.*, p. 176.

Justification, then, is a conception which is deeply rooted in the Scriptures, and it witnesses to the importance of law in the divine economy. This witness cannot be set aside by a facile appeal to the antithesis between law and love, because it is the very Scriptures which tell us that God is love that stress the place of law. But indeed it may be doubted whether the antithesis is a valid one. While it is true that there is a legalism which is far removed from love, and at times in the history of Christian doctrine it is some such legalism which has been posited of God, yet there is no inherent contradiction in affirming that God works by law and by love.[1] Indeed we cannot affirm that God is love in any meaningful sense unless we also say that God is law; for unless an element of law inheres in the divine nature we can have no guarantee that the love we see today will not be replaced by wrath tomorrow. It is perhaps a recognition of this truth, coupled with a realization of the legal significance of justification, which causes one so far removed from being a legalist as R. S. Franks to say: 'God's righteousness is His love considered as a law of conduct.'[2] So too, Denney says emphatically: 'It cannot be too often repeated that if the universal element, or law, be eliminated from personal relations, there is nothing intelligible left: no reason, no morality, no religion, no sin or righteousness or forgiveness, nothing to appeal to mind or conscience.'[3]

Now, if God is thus a God of law, this has two consequences of importance to our present inquiry. The first is that He will require men to live in accordance with His law; the second that His forgiveness can be only such as is consonant with the law of His holy nature.

Concerning the first, Scripture insists over and over that God

[1] *Cf.* Gustaf Aulén: 'The will of God, thus revealed in His Law, is nothing but the will of His Love. The Law no less than the Gospel is an expression of His Love' (*Church, Law and Society*, New York, 1948, p. 66). 'Law and Gospel belong together . . . they are only different sides of one and the same message' (*op. cit.*, p. 100).

[2] *Op. cit.*, p. 152. H. Bushnell says: 'Consider and make due account then, of the fact, that the eternal law of right, which we cannot well deny is the basis of God's perfections, and of all law human and divine, is only another conception of the law of love' (*The Vicarious Sacrifice*, London, 1866, p. 252: and *cf.* pp. 187, 254).

[3] *The Death of Christ*, London, 1911, p. 277. So, too, H. Wheeler Robinson: 'The law of righteousness itself belongs to the divine nature' (*Redemption and Revelation*, London, 1942, p. 273).

294 THE APOSTOLIC PREACHING OF THE CROSS

demands that men should live in accordance with the law which He sets before them. Moreover, it is part of the very nature of law as we know it that it attaches penalties to the breaking of the law, and in this respect the scriptural law is no exception. Again and again we are told that God views the breaking of the law with the gravest displeasure, that His wrath is extended towards the sinner, and that none can expect immunity, for there is no respect of persons with Him. It is quite in accordance with Romans 6: 23 (and much other Scripture besides) when W. Milligan speaks of death as 'the first demand of the Divine law upon the sinner',[1] or when B. F. Westcott says, 'The particular act (*i.e.* of sin) calls for a proportionate reparation, the moral discipline of the debtor coinciding with the satisfaction due to the broken law'.[2] Modern man may have largely lost sight of it, but the Bible insists that sin is followed by punishment, and that that punishment is more than the temporal consequences of sin.

So we come to our second point, that God's forgiveness can be only such as is in accordance with the law of His own holy nature. We cannot expect God to make light of the moral demand when He deals with the situation posed by man's sin. It would be no answer to the needs of the situation for the Creator to say, 'It does not matter. I freely forgive'. P. T. Forsyth puts it strongly when he says that God 'could not trifle with His own holiness. He could will nothing against His holy nature, and He could not abolish the judgment bound up with it. Nothing in the compass of the divine nature could enable Him to abolish a moral law, the law of holiness. That would be tampering with His own soul. It had to be dealt with. Is the law of God more loose than the law of society? Can it be taken liberties with, played with, and put aside at the impulse even of love? How little we should come to think of God's love if that were possible. . . . God's holy law is His own holy nature. His love is under the condition of eternal respect. It is quite unchangeable.'[3] While we may be convinced from our knowledge

---

[1] *The Resurrection of Our Lord* (London, 1894), pp. 140f.

[2] *The Epistles of St John* (London, 1892), p. 39.

[3] *The Work of Christ* (London, 1948), pp. 112f. He also says: 'The moral law differs from every other law in having a demand, and a universal demand, a claim upon us for ever. And that has to be made good as well as the rents and bruises in us from our own collision with it. It is not a gap that has to be made good and sound.

of God as love that He will not leave man to be punished with the full rigour of the penalty prescribed, yet we must hold that His forgiveness will be such as to uphold and not such as to set at nought the moral law.

It is in this context that we must understand the biblical teaching on justification. Justification in itself, as we have seen, is a legal term indicating the process of declaring righteous, but in itself it does not say how this is to be done. There is an element of the paradoxical in the New Testament idea of the way in which, in fact, men's justification is accomplished. For St. Paul can speak in Romans 4: 5 of 'him that justifieth the ungodly' (that acquitteth the guilty!). Nevertheless we are not to think of God as relaxing the moral law in order to accomplish this paradox, for it is categorically stated that He is δίκαιος in the very act of justification (Rom. 3: 26). This truth is repeated over and over again by P. T. Forsyth who insists that justification is the justification of God as well as that of man, and indeed the justification of God before it can be the justification of man. 'We are bidden to recognise that God's demand on man takes the lead of man's demand on God. And both are overruled by God's demand on God, God's meeting His own demand. And we learn unwillingly that only God's justification of man gives the secret of man's justification of God.'[1] 'We can only understand any justification of man as it is grounded in this justification – this self-justification – of God. The sinner could only be saved by something that thus damned the sin.'[2]

This, then, is the significance of justification. It is not the only way of viewing the atoning work of Christ, and we must certainly give due consideration to other aspects if we are to have an adequate and balanced view of Christ's great work for us. But we cannot do without justification with its insistence that part of what was done on Calvary concerned the inflexible law which is at the very basis

---

it is a claim, because we are here in a moral and not a natural world. It is one thing to make good a gap and another thing to make good a claim. The claim must be met' (op. cit., p. 124). Cf. also Hodgson's remarks about punishment quoted on p. 212 above.

[1] The Justification of God (London, 1948), p. 40.

[2] The Cruciality of the Cross (London, 1948), pp. 102f., and cf.: 'God could only justify man before Him by justifying Himself and His holy law before men' (The Work of Christ, London, 1948, p. 136).

of the being of God. That law was honoured in the process whereby forgiveness was wrought.[1]

III. JUSTIFICATION AND SUBSTITUTION

There is no inherent connection between justification and sub-stitution, and there have been systems which included the one without the other. Thus Rabbinic Judaism, to name no other, was insistent that it is possible for a man to be justified before God because of his accumulation of merit, a form of justification in which there is no thought of substitution. But in the particular way in which Christ accomplished our justification it may well be held that there is a definitely substitutionary emphasis.

Among the older Protestant theologians this was almost taken for granted. Thus Calvin can say: 'Our acquittal is in this – that the guilt which made us liable to punishment was transferred to the head of the Son of God (Is. liii: 12). We must specially remember this substitution in order that we may not be all our lives in trepidation and anxiety, as if the just vengeance, which the Son of God transferred to himself, were still impending over us.'[2] From a slightly different point of view James Morison speaks of δικαιόω as referring to 'a judicial declaration of the reality of the sub-stitutionary righteousness judicially found in the possession of believers'.[3] The very fact of man's justification was held by such theologians to imply a process of substitution.

In later times this emphasis was lost, especially as men came to think of the essence of the atonement as consisting in salvation from the power rather than the penalty of sin. It became almost axio-

---

[1] The importance of the place of law in God's manner of working is not obscured by remembering that the New Testament emphasizes that God is Father, for, as J. Scott Lidgett reminds us: 'Fatherhood is, by necessity, legislative and judicial. The very intensity of its desire to foster the true life of its children forces it to watch them with sleepless vigilance, to lay upon them those laws which promote that life, and to visit their departures from truth and goodness with stern fidelity. So far from true fatherhood being easy-going in these respects, its eye is more searching and its judgment more inflexibly righteous, than those of any judge less nearly concerned in the conduct of those who appear before him' (*op. cit.*, p. 230).

[2] *Institutes*, II, 16. 5 (trans. Beveridge, I, p. 439).

[3] *A Critical Exposition of the Third Chapter of Paul's Epistle to the Romans* (London, 1866), p. 198.

matic that substitution could have no part in a right understanding of atonement, and the real meaning of the cross was sought elsewhere.[1] But more recently there are some writers who realize that this reaction is too extreme. Thus F. W. Camfield says that in the work of Christ 'we are met by the reality of substitution', and he goes on to affirm roundly 'Justification and substitution stand or fall together'.[2] Again, no less a person than Karl Barth suggests that we need to learn again what the Scriptures say about and mean by substitution,[3] and he can say: 'Yes, exactly in the depths of our misery He intercedes for us, and substitutes Himself for us, warding off the wages justly due us and suffering and making restitution what we could not suffer and where we could not make restitution.'[4]

These words last quoted look very much like an affirmation that there is a substitutionary process at work in the method of justification – the wages of our sin are averted by the substitution of the Christ, and He suffered what we could not suffer. This thought is to be found also in other writers. Thus H. Maurice Relton repeats over and over again that there is a substitutionary aspect to the atonement, and sums up much of his argument when he says: 'We have seen that there is a real element of substitution in the Calvary Sacrifice. . . . We have suggested that it consists in His paying the debt of sin in a final agony of dereliction; a spiritual death, which is sin's wages.'[5] But this is only another way of saying that the Christian method of justification is one which is substitutionary. This is affirmed also by H. Wheeler Robinson when

---

[1] Sometimes it was admitted that the biblical conception of justification was substitutionary, and this aspect of it was rejected. Rashdall says: 'it is clearly St. Paul's conception that Christ has paid that penalty in order that man may not have to pay it. It is impossible to get rid of this idea of substitution, or vicarious punishment, from any faithful representation of St. Paul's doctrine' (*op. cit.*, p. 92).

[2] *SJT*, I, p. 289. The full quotation is: 'Christ was crucified because man, confronted by the last things strove to push them out of his way. But here also we are met by the reality of substitution. Man in faith ceases to justify himself. He now looks to Christ as his justification. And his justification is no mere human experience, but an objective reality to which man's whole existence is related. Justification and substitution stand or fall together.'

[3] *God in Action* (Edinburgh, 1936), p. 123.

[4] *Op. cit.*, pp. 16f.

[5] *Cross and Altar* (London, n.d.), p. 110.

he equates justification with 'the acquittal of the sinner through the (forensically) substituted bloodshedding of Christ'.[1] We conclude this list of citations with one from A. Schlatter who comments on 2 Corinthians 5: 21: 'he suffers what God does to sin, and makes visible what happens when man has God against him.'[2]

This brief list of citations makes it clear that, while a substitutionary view of justification may not be widely popular today, at least it may not be dismissed as obscurantist. It still makes its appeal to minds both devout and profound. Admittedly when we have said 'substitution' we have not described justification, much less the atonement; for a full understanding of either much more is necessary. But what we maintain is that we cannot enter into such an understanding unless we lay hold on that aspect of the truth which is expressed by the word 'substitution'. There is no condemnation now for them that are in Christ Jesus, and the reason for this may be stated, at least in one aspect, by saying that Christ bore our condemnation so that we bear it no more. But this is nothing less than to say that we are justified by a substitutionary process.

---

[1] *Redemption and Revelation* (London, 1942), p. 235.
[2] *Op. cit.*, p. 568.

CHAPTER X

CONCLUSION

IN THE FOREGOING PAGES we have surveyed some of the more important words used in the New Testament to describe the atoning work of the Son of God. We have seen that modern research has much light to shed on the meaning of these terms, enabling us to see more clearly what they conveyed to the first Christian writers and readers. We have made no attempt to deal systematically with the bulk of the New Testament evidence, and there are other categories of considerable importance which we have not even noticed. But these studies are in the nature of a preliminary approach wherein we have cleared some of the ground, and begun to appreciate some of the metaphors which the men of New Testament days found helpful when they wished to draw attention to one aspect or another of a divine action they found it impossible to describe fully.

This examination of the evidence has, I think, demonstrated that there is much support for objective as opposed to subjective views of the atonement. None of the concepts we have considered fits naturally into a subjective view. Something happened on Calvary quite objective to man, and it is because of this that we can have the completest assurance of our salvation. In the last resort it depends on what God has done, and not upon some effect of that action upon the human heart (which is not to deny that there is such an effect, and that it is important). Thus redemption points us to a price paid, and we saw that the contention that it means no more than deliverance will not stand examination. It points us to the evil plight in which man finds himself as a result of his sin: he is in a state of slavery from which he cannot break free, and he is also under the condemnation of God (for it was in connection with disasters like these that the ancient world made use of the redemption terminology). But no less is our attention drawn to the price paid, for price was of the very essence of redemption, and was in point of fact that which distinguished redemption from other methods of deliverance. Even though the process might be used metaphorically (*e.g.*

to describe God's action in saving His people from Egypt, or from exile), yet even here there is the thought of cost.

So it is also in the New Testament. The salvation which Christ effects is not thought of as brought about with effortless ease. On the contrary, it is purchased at great cost, at the price of His blood. There cannot be the slightest doubt but that the New Testament writers thought of redemption as an objective thing, as a process whereby Christ paid the price which brought them salvation. The idea that this means no more than that His example inspired them to be better men is hopelessly inadequate. Whatever redemption is, it is something purchased by Christ. In the first place it is outside of man (though the application of redemption to the individual, of course, calls for the exercise of faith, and hence to something subjective).

The people of God on the scriptural view are those who have entered into covenant with Him, and this might well be viewed as an activity of man as well as of God. But the initiative is always thought of as resting with God, and man's part is no more than the accepting of a covenant whose terms have been laid down by God. Thus the very idea of covenant, as the Bible understands it, puts the stress on the divine activity, and this is reinforced by the fact that the covenant in the New Testament is established only because the Son of God died for man and thus put away his sin. There is very little place for human activity in this way of viewing Calvary, and once again we see that atonement is essentially something wrought for, rather than in, man.

It is not otherwise with the use of the term 'the blood', which is often used by modern writers as indicating that in some sense it is the life of Christ that saves men. This is an idea which may be stated in various ways, some of which may demand some sort of subjective view of the atonement, although there are others which find a bigger place for the objective. But our examination of the evidence leads us to think that the view that 'the blood' directs our attention primarily to 'the life' is erroneous, and that, in point of fact, the Scriptures of both Old and New Testaments stress the death when they make use of this expression. While it is not impossible to understand the death in the Abelardian fashion, yet the impression left by those biblical passages which refer to the blood of Christ is that they are pointing us to the death of the Lord considered as the means whereby sin is dealt with, not merely the means whereby man may be inspired to deal with it.

We found it necessary to make a rather full examination of the passages speaking of propitiation, because there is a tendency to think that those scholars who have equated the Greek term with expiation have said the last word. We saw that the Bible has a great deal to say about the wrath of God, and that it leaves us in no doubt as to the fact that, although God is a God of love, yet He does not regard sin complacently, as something which does not matter greatly. On the contrary, sin calls forth the implacable hostility of His holy nature, and until something is done about it this puts the sinner in an unenviable position. If, then, we are correct in thinking that propitiation signifies the removal of the divine wrath by the offering of the Son, then this is strong evidence that the essential process of atonement is something which is done on behalf of man by his Saviour. We get something of the same idea from the concept of reconciliation which implies a state of enmity between God and man, and the removal of this state of enmity by the death of the Christ. The New Testament indicates that the reconciliation was effected by the removal of the cause of the enmity, namely, sin, and this was done in some way by the death of the Lord. These two conceptions, then, alike indicate that the essential process of atonement took place on Calvary, and that it was more than simply man's acquiescence in God's judgment on sin and his turning away from evil to serve God.

When we came to deal with justification we saw that this is essentially a legal term signifying a verdict of acquittal. This has been understood to come about in various ways, many of them congruous with a process of salvation by works as, for example, it was understood among the Jews. But the particular New Testament understanding of justification is that it is brought about by the cross. Man is justified because Christ died, and this seems to include the thought that He bore man's penalty. At the very least it is a further indication that something took place exterior to man in the process whereby his salvation was effected.

Thus each of the concepts we have examined bears its testimony to the fact that subjective views of atonement are inadequate. Again we repeat that this is not to deny that they do draw attention to important truths, or that there is a subjective aspect to the atonement no matter how objective the theory we prefer. But we affirm that the essential process took place once for all on the cross, and such evidence as the concepts we have been investigating points strongly to something which was done quite outside of man, but in some way for his benefit.

The majority of scholars would agree today on some such statement, but there remains the further question of how we are to understand this objective factor, and in particular of whether we are to say that Christ's death was representative only, or that it was also substitutionary. That Christ died as our representative is widely recognized, but most scholars would affirm that there is no need of the substitutionary idea, all that is valuable in it being preserved in the concept of representation. That is to say, it is accepted that He died on our behalf, but not that He took our place.

In the preceding pages we have drawn attention to certain aspects of our subject which bear on this problem. In the light of what has already been adduced it is difficult to resist the conclusion that the idea of substitution must be included in our understanding of the atonement. The concepts of propitiation and justification in particular seem almost to demand that we understand them in a substitutionary manner and, to say the least of it, the other concepts are congruous with this interpretation. We have also seen that there are able scholars who feel that some such way of viewing the atonement is necessary. While it would be out of place to undertake a full examination of the concept of substitution in this place yet a few observations may be in order.

First may we go back to a statement of James Denney: 'God condones nothing: His mercy itself is of an absolute integrity. He is a righteous God, even in justifying the ungodly; and the propitiation which He sets forth in Christ Jesus, dying in His sinlessness the death of the sinful, is the key to the mystery. Once more, is not the word which spontaneously rises to our lips to express this the word substitution?'[1] In these words Denney reminds us of a fact which we must always bear in mind in dealing with the atonement, namely that the forgiveness sinners receive is not at the expense of ignoring sin's consequences. 'God condones nothing', and we must not theorize as though He has become indifferent to the wages of sin. While admittedly it raises problems, substitution

[1] *The Expositor*, Sixth Series, III, p. 449.

does emphasize this aspect of atonement. Alternative concepts do not always do so.

Then let us notice that there is more than one way of understanding substitution, and some ways are more worthy than others. Thus R. C. Moberly says: 'A stranger, hired for money to undergo a loss of limb or liberty, would always be an insult to true equity. But one who was very closely identified with the wrong-doer in condition, or blood, or affection; a tribesman dedicating himself for a tribal wrong; the willing representative of a conquered nation, or army; the father, on behalf of his own child; the husband, for the sake of his wife; is it impossible to conceive circumstances under which a willing acceptance of penalty on the part of some one of these, would as truly be the deepest hope of the transformation of the guilty, as it would be the crown of his own nobleness?'[1] He goes on to develop the thought that we never do see such a close substitution here on earth; but the question remains whether we do not see the circumstances he speaks of perfectly fulfilled in Jesus Christ. At any rate when we speak of substitution in connection with His death, we should bear in mind that He made Himself one with those for whom He suffered, so that the substitution which results is not the substitution of a casual stranger, but of one who stands in the closest possible relationship with those for whom He died.

A very suggestive treatment of the subject is given by P. Althaus in his essay in *Mysterium Christi*, where he distinguishes between what he terms 'exclusive' and 'inclusive' substitution. As an example of the former he cites the miners who work underground in substitution for the rest of the community. Others are excluded from the necessity of going underground. He sees the latter in such activities as that of the mother who suffers for the sin of her lost son and longs to lead him to repentance. 'The substitute watching over the danger and distress of his people desires to lead them to a share in that watch. The significance of substitution here is clearly not that of gain through the relief resulting from the stronger undertaking an act for the weaker, but rather giving those thus represented the active fruitful power which characterises the representative.'[2] Without committing ourselves to believing that

[1] *Atonement and Personality* (London, 1924), p. 78.
[2] *Op. cit.*, p. 214.

Althaus has solved all the problems of substitution we may yet feel that there is something very valuable in the thought that substitution, as we see it in the atonement, is not some purely external thing, which stops when it sees the wages of sin borne by the Substitute. Rather it reaches its consummation only when the sinner has become one with his Substitute, and therefore has come to view sin with the same mind as his Substitute.

'God condones nothing'; 'one . . . very closely identified with the wrong-doer'; 'inclusive substitution'. These three expressions do not represent an 'Open Sesame' to the problems of atonement, but at least they do indicate, when taken together, that a rightly understood substitution is a very fruitful concept, and one we can ill afford to overlook when estimating what Christ did for us on Calvary.

INDEX OF GREEK WORDS

INDEX OF SCRIPTURE PASSAGES

I. THE OLD TESTAMENT

2. THE APOCRYPHA

3. THE NEW TESTAMENT

GENERAL INDEX